Emile Durkheim
on the Family

Understanding Families

Series Editors: *Bert N. Adams, University of Wisconsin*
David M. Klein, University of Notre Dame

This book series examines a wide range of subjects relevant to studying families. Topics include, but are not limited to, theory and conceptual design, research methods on the family, racial/ethnic families, mate selection, marriage, family power dynamics, parenthood, divorce and re-marriage, custody issues, and aging families.

The series is aimed primarily at scholars working in family studies, sociology, psychology, social work, ethnic studies, gender studies, cultural studies, and related fields as they focus on the family. Volumes will also be useful for graduate and undergraduate courses in sociology of the family, family relations, family and consumer sciences, social work and the family, family psychology, family history, cultural perspectives on the family, and others.

Books appearing in **Understanding Families** are either single- or multiple-authored volumes or concisely edited books of original chapters on focused topics within the broad interdisciplinary field of marriage and family.

The books are reports of significant research, innovations in methodology, treatises on fam-ily theory, syntheses of current knowledge in a family subfield, or advanced textbooks. Each volume meets the highest academic standards and makes a substantial contribution to our un-derstanding of marriages and families.

Mary Ann Lamanna
University of Nebraska at Omaha

Emile Durkheim on the Family

UNDERSTANDING
F**A**MILIES

 Sage Publications
International Educational and Professional Publisher
Thousand Oaks ▪ London ▪ New Delhi

For information:

Sage Publications, Inc.
2455 Teller Road
Thousand Oaks, California 91320
E-mail: order@sagepub.com

Sage Publications Ltd.
6 Bonhill Street
London EC2A 4PU
United Kingdom

Sage Publications India Pvt. Ltd.
M-32 Market
Greater Kailash I
New Delhi 110 048 India

Printed in the United States of America

Library of Congress Cataloging-in-Publication Data

Lamanna, Mary Ann.
  Emile Durkheim on the family / by Mary Ann Lamanna.
    p.   cm. — (Understanding families; v. 20)
  Includes bibliographical references and index.
  ISBN 0-7619-1206-1 (c) — ISBN 0-7619-1207-X (p)
  1. Durkheim, Emile, 1858-1917. 2. Family. I. Title. II. Series.
HQ518.L35 2001
306.85—dc21   2001002980

01 02 03 10 9 8 7 6 5 4 3 2 1

Acquiring Editor: Jim Brace-Thompson
Editorial Assistant: Karen Ehrmann
Production Editor: Diana E. Axelsen
Editorial Assistant: Kathryn Journey
Copy Editor: Marilyn Power Scott
Typesetter/Designer: Doreen Barnes
Indexer: Mary Mortensen
Cover Designer: Michelle Lee

Contents

M. and Mme. Durkheim and their grandson, Claude Halphen, 1916. Photo courtesy of Etienne Halphen.

Preface

Emile Durkheim on the Family is intended to make visible this classical sociologist's work on the family. Durkheim's writings on the family are little known, but in fact the family was one of his primary interests. Intended subject of a book that was never written, Durkheim's ideas on the family appeared only in scattered sources, and a number of those sources have not been translated into English. His sociology of the family has not yet been presented and analyzed holistically. The goal of this book is to do that.

The purpose of the book is to bring together Durkheim's ideas on the family from diverse sources and to present his family sociology systematically and comprehensively. I have combed bibliographies of works on Durkheim, searched his journal *Année sociologique* and other journals of the period, followed leads in the many books and articles on Durkheim, scanned compendia of his work and pursued the original sources, read his major books and those less prominent, all in search of material on the family broadly defined. Some things are quite visible to Durkheim scholars and others (e.g., his views on women expressed in *Suicide,* 1897). Much is not. And because the material is so fragmented, getting a clear picture of Durkheim's work on the family requires a book that presents and integrates his writings.

In *Emile Durkheim on the Family,* I have organized Durkheim's ideas topically, described his sociological perspective on the family, and provided analytical commentary. His theories are situated in their historical context, and comparisons are also drawn to present-day sociology of the family and family issues. Chapter topics include Durkheim's life and times; his evolutionary theory of the family; methodologies for studying the family; the changing relationship of kin, conjugal family, and the state; the interior of the family; family policy; gender; and sexuality. Although the presentation of Durkheim's theory is in my own words, quotations from Durkheim's writings are selected to enrich the presentation of his ideas.

An examination of Durkheim's work on the family reveals its close connections to his well-known books and theories and enables us to get a fuller understanding and appreciation of Durkheim as social theorist. For the family studies scholar, this book reveals that Durkheim's work was an invisible forerunner of later themes in sociology of the family. The issues he addressed are still of interest in the field today. *Emile Durkheim on the Family* should interest audiences in sociology of the family, social theory, family science, social philosophy, European intellectual history, women's studies, legal history, and those generally interested in family studies and/or nineteenth- and early twentieth-century Europe. It should be useful to scholars in these areas because it provides a comprehensive view of Durkheim's work on the family and a roster of sources that can be pursued further. For those with a more limited interest, the book offers a broad overview of Durkheim on the family.

There are some technical points regarding the many quotations from Durkheim's work that appear in the book that I would like to explain to the reader. I selected quotations primarily according to two opposite principles. First of all, I chose quotations that were representative of Durkheim's thought. Substantially similar versions of a point might have appeared in more than one publication or debate, sometimes repeated a number of times. I chose these. At the same time, I selected quotes that I was surprised to find in Durkheim's work. To present a quote one would not have thought typical of Durkheim is to expand our understanding of him. Last, I wanted the quotations to give something of the flavor and style of Durkheim's writing, and I chose with that goal in mind.

I myself have done all the translation of Durkheim material included in the book, save for a very few where I could not locate the original source in French. Translation philosophies and styles vary. My preference is to render a natural-sounding expression of what the author has said in the original language rather than a literal word-for-word translation that may sound forced and awkward. Most often, my translation choices do not depart that far from the literal.

I have sometimes eliminated words that do not carry substantive meaning, such as "in effect." I have broken up sentences with many clauses to avoid what in English is considered a "run-on" sentence. That has involved changing punctuation accordingly. Certain French words, such as "morale," have multiple meanings or different meanings from the English; I have tried to explain these in footnotes.

I have used terms that are avoided today, such as "illegitimate," because they capture the tone of the discourse of the times. The same is true regarding gender-neutral pronouns. Nineteenth-century writing used a firm "he" for the human. Also, categories referenced by male pronouns often were in fact uniformly male in composition. To convert these to suit present-day sensibilities would be essentially inaccurate as a characterization of the times.

In the bibliography and in citations in the text, I have used the French system of capitalization for works written in French. The fact that Durkheim is French is not coincidental to my deciding to write this book. When Professor Fabio DaSilva of Notre Dame suggested Durkheim as a paper topic in his theory class, I was not excited. Emile Durkheim was not even my classical theorist of choice; I preferred Simmel. But Durkheim did have the advantage of being French. So what did that have to do with anything? A lot. Professor DaSilva knew that I read French and also that my chosen area of specialization was sociology of the family. He called my attention to an article by Georges Davy, Durkheim's student and later colleague, that summarized the notes Davy had taken on Durkheim's family course. I had not known of Durkheim's interest in the family and was intrigued. A class paper did not seem to be that much of a commitment.

Some years later, I was at work on a book on Durkheim's sociology of the family, which is now completed. Forced (so to speak) to take a broader—and ultimately deeper—look at Durkheim's work, I developed an appreciation for his complex reasoning, his wide interests, his elucidation of so many ideas I had thought to be original with my contemporaries. I got to know a Durkheim who was not so apparent from secondary sources. I see limitations both to Durkheim's interests in the family and his theoretical approach. But he is always interesting, and I have enjoyed the time spent in putting this book together and trying to make it better.

I also began to think of it as a mission. I was surprised to learn there was a Durkheim on the family; who wouldn't have been? I wanted to let others know. That is what I have tried to do in this book—to make varied audiences aware of Durkheim's writing (and speaking) on the family. I wanted not only to make its existence known but also to expand on that so that those who will not necessarily pursue original sources to find

Durkheim's sociology of the family can nevertheless be somewhat informed on the subject.

There is a personal satisfaction for me in a project that depends on working with French. That comes from personal history, the chance factor of growing up next door to a French professor, his wife, and their French-speaking children. I picked up some French by learning the lingo I needed for my baby-sitting job. Younger brothers of the professor came from Quebec for the summer. The visiting brothers, with time on their hands, taught me French vocabulary and grammar a little more systematically. Soon, I was off to college as a French major (for a time) and then to France to study political science and the European community. The Durkheim book project has meant that I could combine my two intellectual interests: sociology and the French language.

I need to begin my acknowledgments with an appreciation for these former St. Louis neighbors, Henri Robitaille and Nancy (Robitaille) Moberly. It is a thanks that goes beyond the language opportunity to a recognition that it is they who prodded me to think of myself as an intellectual. I want to let Professor Emeritus Fabio DaSilva of the University of Notre Dame know that I have never forgotten his initiative in giving me the idea for what has now become a book. He could do that because of his amazing knowledge of the field of sociology and his skill at inspiring his students.

Ideas need a venue for their expression, and it is through Bert Adams and Dave Klein and the *Understanding Families* series that I have been able to write about Durkheim's sociology of the family with the prospect of an audience. They took an interest in *Emile Durkheim on the Family* when it was still somewhat unformed, far from complete. They have been totally encouraging and very patient during the process of writing the book. Their critical feedback and that of an anonymous reviewer have contributed to great improvement of the manuscript over its starting point. (Though they are, of course, not responsible for remaining faults or inadequacies.) I am honored to be included in the quality series that they have put together as *Understanding Families*. They have been a pleasure to work with as series editors, very thoughtful and quite stimulating intellectually.

I also want to thank the editorial and production people at Sage Publications for their work in bringing my book to publication. Jim Brace-Thompson, Sociology Editor, who took over a project in progress, has been very good to work with—very supportive in the final stages of book completion. Karen Ehrmann, Editorial Assistant, handled the transition from manuscript submission to production process smoothly, all the while fielding my numerous questions. Diana Axelsen, Senior Production Editor, and Kathryn Journey, Editorial Assistant, have managed the production process competently and well. I am most directly aware of the work of Marilyn Power Scott, copy editor, because we have had frequent and detailed communication. Her questions and suggestions have contributed greatly to the substance of the book, improving clarity and smoothing wording to enhance the presentation of my ideas. Her adeptness in handling the French language references and the numerous quotations were but one aspect of a professional competence evident to me in every detail of our correspondence. Doreen Barnes, typesetter, did a beautiful—and accurate—job of putting the manuscript into print. Thanks to you all and to unknown others at Sage who have worked on *Emile Durkheim on the Family.*

There are other persons who have contributed to the book in important ways. I am enormously grateful to M. Etienne Halphen, Emile Durkheim's grandson, who sent family photos and gave permission for their use on the cover and in the interior of the book. I am very happy to be able to include these informal photos of M. Durkheim with his wife, daughter (M. Halphen's mother), a grandson, and other family members in a book that has Durkheim's work on the family as its theme. I thank M. Halphen for making this possible and for responding to my request so quickly. I am also very indebted to Geoff Alpert (whose father was Durkheim's biographer) without whom I would not even have known of the existence of these photos. And I thank Stjepan Meštrović (author of three books on Durkheim), who took considerable time and trouble to tell me about Durkheim family photos, to mail me photos several times over, and, in general, to express enthusiasm for the book and offer practical support for its aesthetics.

Thanks to Stephen Turner and to Rebecca Emigh for sending me papers useful in reflecting on Durkheim's work. Every now and then, I mentioned my book project to Bob Antonio of the University of Kansas, and he was always affirming. I owe a huge debt to the University of Nebraska at Omaha (UNO) Interlibrary Loan Department, and I would like to list by name those who did work related to my book: Ben Blackwell, Diane Davis, Molly Fairchild, Jason Gaines, Steve Hunt, Mary Mick, Matt Rohde, John Schneiderman, Catherine Walker, Madaline Williams, and Richard Wyatt. A book whose sources are primarily French and from earlier in the century is a challenge in terms of library resources. The UNO library has some surprising things, including a facsimile edition of *Année sociologique.* But I was very dependent on interlibrary loan resources, and this group filled hundreds of requests, many for obscure French titles, and some of them several times over as I thought of one more thing that needed checking. The UNO Sociology and Anthropology Department has provided me with resources, and more important, with good colleagues.

Numerous friends encouraged me throughout this project, and to attempt to name them one by one would be to risk not including all who should be. At UNO, I would mention especially Lourdes Gouveia, my sociology colleague and friend, and Elvira Garcia and Patrice Proulx, who keep me in touch with the French language. Margaret Porter, Diane and Joe Wood, Diane and Mike Gillespie, Mary Tourek, Jenny White, Catharine Krull, Mary and Pat Sweaney, Susan Poser, and Steve di Magno have helped me finish this book by their friendship, which has kept me going through a long project. My children, Valerie Lamanna and Larry Lamanna, and Janice, his wife, have always helped me to see the world beyond the office.

And finally, to my companion and friend of twenty years, Sam Walker, to whom this book is dedicated, thanks for finding this book an admirable project, for encouraging and supporting my work on it in so many ways, and for being a model as a scholar.

Dedicated

to Sam

1

Introduction

P. Dejardins: But one of the causes which makes the creation of new schools necessary is the inability of the current French family to raise its children.

E. Durkheim: Isn't it an exaggeration to speak so of the family of today? I agree, and I am the first to deplore, that the idea of authority has eroded in family and school. But let us not forget that among our forebears discipline was excessively harsh. Our immediate predecessors struggled to soften it. They went too far, I am convinced, but let us not forget what they accomplished and what we owe them. In sum, it has not been demonstrated that the family is appreciably worse than it was; it is different.

—Libres entretiens (1912:322)[1]

"The family is not declining, it is just changing" is a position attributed to present-day liberals in the "family wars."[2] That many sociologists would be surprised by Durkheim's similar statement signals the degree to which he is both known and unknown. Durkheim, along with Max Weber, can be said to be the founder of the modern[3] discipline of sociology. He continues to be a powerful influence on the field; in fact, recent years have seen a "renaissance of Durkheim studies" (Lukes 1985:v). Yet despite Durkheim's towering presence, some of his work remains obscure. Few sociologists would recognize the foregoing sentences as Durkheim's. His nuanced view of the relationship between the individual and society has been overshadowed by countervailing interpretations of his ideas on social cohesion and social control. And his interest in certain topics is little known.

One such topic is the family. Durkheim's protégé, Georges Davy, re-marked that the topic Durkheim most enjoyed studying and lecturing on was the family (Davy 1919). His nephew, anthropologist Marcel Mauss, wrote about Durkheim's notes for an unrealized book: "Durkheim him-self treated those pages with respect and for several years did not part from them, even while traveling" (Mauss 1925:13). Durkheim's plans for a book on the family are mentioned in his obituary ("Nécrologie" 1918:95-96).

Durkheim's interests in the family are broad. One has only to scan the table of contents of this book to see the range of topics that attracted Durkheim's attention. His analyses are thorough and complex. Over the many years that Durkheim wrote and spoke on the family, he put a cor-nucopia of ideas on the table, for us to think about and use. The sense one has while reading Durkheim is of being part of a collective and ongo-ing enterprise of scholarship on the family. Whether one is of like mind or in sharp disagreement, his work stimulates thought. But to be inspired, to reflect on Durkheim's ideas and make use of them—or to dispute them—it is first necessary to know Durkheim's sociology of the family. His point of view has had an influence on family studies that continues, whether or not he is recognized as the source of it.

The Invisibility of Durkheim's Sociology of the Family

Students of social thought are aware of Durkheim's inclusion of mar-riage and family in his analysis of suicide (Durkheim [1897a] 1930). Recent commentaries explore his concepts of social solidarity and social differentiation with regard to their implications for women (Kandal 1988; Lamanna 1990; Lehmann 1990; Meštrović 1991; Roth 1989-90; Sydie 1987). In examining Durkheim on gender, Sydie does include a discus-sion of family per se, while Lehmann (1995a) comments that "Durkheim's . . . sociology of the family has been relatively neglected" (p. 913). Books situate Durkheim relative to contemporary interest in cultural studies (Alexander 1988) and postmodernism (Meštrović 1991). Still, his sociol-ogy of the family is not well known, despite the expansion of our portrait of Durkheim well beyond his four best-known books (Durkheim [1893] 1978; [1895a]1956; [1897a] 1930; [1912] 1979). Little of Durkheim's work on the family was translated into English before the mid-1970s. Goode observed in 1959 that "of Weber, Pareto, and Durkheim . . . , only Durkheim made enough observations on the family . . . to permit a compilation of his ideas on this institution—and no one has bothered to make such a compilation" (p. 179). This statement is as true today as it was when he made it. Durkheim's writings on the family have not been brought together in an integrated way to form a comprehensive picture of his perspective on the family.

To demonstrate the point about the neglect of Durkheim's interest in the family, we have only to examine biographies and critical reviews of Durkheim's work, surveys of sociology, and compendia of family sociology. The important biographies by LaCapra ([1972] 1985) and Lukes (1972, 1985) have indeed noted his work on the family, and Lukes devoted a short chapter to it (pp. 179-90). Yet Lukes's (1972) brief summary of Durkheim on "Marriage and Sex" is given a minor place in a section called "Practical Concerns" (pp. 530-34). LaCapra's ([1972] 1985) two pages on family and kinship indicate their "importance to Durkheim" (p. 213), but the only real attention is given to inheritance. The *International Encyclopedia of the Social Sciences* entry on Durkheim does not mention family (Parsons 1968) and the "family" entries do not cover Durkheim's work (Kirkpatrick 1968; Smith 1968). Surveys of sociology take no notice of Durkheim's work on the family. There is no mention of Durkheim in the family section of the *Handbook of Sociology* (Huber and Spitze 1988), despite Smelser's (1988) insistence on Durkheim's centrality to sociology.[4] Family review volumes also largely ignore Durkheim.[5] Only Bert Adams, with his converging interests in both classical theory and family, produced substantial development of Durkheim's ideas on the family in his texts (Adams 1971, 1995) and in his essay on the classics (Adams and Steinmetz 1993).[6]

There are glancing references to Durkheim and family here and there over the years.[7] An examination of review volumes in general sociology and sociology of the family contain many casual references to Durkheim and Durkheimian concepts. On the one hand, these illustrate the continuing power of his ideas. On the other, the tangential references to Durkheim, even the allusions to family phenomena, do not provide a firm fix on Durkheim's sociology of the family. Where selections about the family are included in compendia of translations of Durkheim's short pieces, they receive no special attention (Nandan 1980a; Traugott 1978). Some important pieces remain untranslated (Davy 1925, [1931] 1950).

Durkheim's sociology of the family has not been given the significant and focused attention it deserves. Our professional awareness of Durkheim does not, for the most part, acknowledge his keen interest in the family. Thus, most contemporary sociologists are unaware that it was Durkheim, not Talcott Parsons, who gave us much of the structure-functional paradigm of the family. Bellah (1959) did see the significance of Durkheim's family sociology: "Parsons and Bales [1955] in seeing the modern type of the family as the result of specialization and its main functions as those of 'pattern maintenance' and 'tension management' are very close to the Durkheimian view" (noted only in footnotes to an *American Sociological*

Review article; p. 453, fn 36, and see fn 35). But interest is never sustained in the profession collectively. Like America before Columbus, Durkheim's work on the family has been repeatedly discovered, then lost from sight. Bynder's 1969 statement has not really become outdated: "There remains one significant area of social thought with which Durkheim was particularly interested and which has remained almost totally ignored. I am referring to his work in the sociology of the family" (p. 527).

And why is that? Certainly Durkheim's evolutionary theory of the family has an archaic ring that would prevent many from taking it seriously even though Durkheim specifically rejected unilinear evolution. There is much more to Durkheim on the family. Yet the fragmented character of Durkheim's work has meant little awareness of his deep interest in the family area.

The way in which Durkheim's work was presented to American audiences also influenced perception of his theoretical interests. Talcott Parsons (e.g., [1937] 1949) introduced Durkheim to American scholars, and for many many years, Parsons's interpretation and focus were what social theorists knew of Durkheim. Parsons's (1955a, 1955b) own work on the family was segregated from his theoretical analysis of Durkheim.

Translation (or lack thereof) has been another barrier. For many years, Durkheim was read primarily through his major books. Little by little, more of his other work was translated, including other important books (e.g., *Moral Education*) and scattered essays and book reviews. The checkerboard pattern of translation has not highlighted material of interest to sociologists of the family or theorists interested in the family. Some compilations present miscellaneous or only tenuously related items. Others are thematic, but those themes do not include the family. And the quality of translation in a compilation of Durkheim's important *Année* book reviews (Nandan 1980a) has been seriously criticized by a leading French Durkheim scholar (Besnard 1982).

Durkheim's Interest in the Family

In Durkheim's writings taken as a whole, there is extensive treatment of the family. But because Durkheim died before he could write his planned book, there is no systematic and integrated presentation of these analyses. Instead, Durkheim's ideas on the family are scattered throughout a variety of sources: articles, book reviews, sections of his major works, his courses, and the minutes of debating societies—hence the need for a volume that organizes and structures his perspective.

It would be surprising if a person of his intellectual times did not take an interest in the family. Darwin ([1859] 1964) had published his evolutionary theory, and scholars applied this paradigm to social institutions. The amateur ethnographers who were the forebears of modern anthropologists had begun to analyze the exotic societies brought into contact with Europe through exploration, commerce, missionary work, and colonization. Exciting debates took place about matriarchal and patriarchal family forms, about the historical primacy of monogamy or group marriage, about the origins and meaning of the incest taboo (Stocking 1987). The family was an integral part of the theories of society of such systematic thinkers as Marx ([1848] 1988), Engels ([1884] 1972), and Spencer ([1873] 1961, [1876-96] 1898-99). This was equally true of Durkheim, who incorporated ideas on the family into his courses on social organization and his books on social cohesion. He took for granted that the evolution of society was also the evolution of the family, that the family in its recent history had been shaped by industrialization and modernization.

All the while, and especially after the turn of the twentieth century, Durkheim interested himself in the family-related problems of French society. These included such matters as the liberalization of divorce, the status of women, sex education, the socialization of children, economic support of female-headed households, and law with respect to marital property regimes and inheritance. We can view Durkheim as an applied social scientist and find, surprisingly, that problems we think unique to the late twentieth century were matters of concern in the late nineteenth. Durkheim addressed issues with which we still struggle: What is the impact of modernization on the family? How can families and communities maintain their solidarity in an age of increasing individualism? (Bridenthal 1982:226-27; Glendon 1981, 1987, 1989; Goldscheider and Waite 1991; Hafen 1990; Meštrović 1988:18, Popenoe 1988; Skolnick 1991; Stacey 1990). Durkheim's reflections on these matters are complex and interesting, worth examining for process and content. In reading Durkheim on the family, one can see with some clarity the points at issue in a specific area of family study that can then be brought forward to an analysis of present-day family materials and issues. Durkheim was so prolific that there is hardly an area of family science to which he has not spoken.

In recent decades, sociology of the family as a field of study has changed in a way that makes it receptive to a Durkheimian perspective. In mid-twentieth century, the interior world of the family dominated sociological analysis. Alternatively, Parsons's structure-functional conceptual framework was macrosocial but abstract. After a long period in which sociology of the family seemed relentlessly ahistorical and somewhat atheoretical,[8] we have returned to study the family in a broader social context. With the flowering of social history (Ariès 1962; Laslett 1965), the emergence of interest in family law and policy (Cherlin 1998; McIntyre 1995), and the new theoretical perspectives of feminist legal theory (Fineman 1995) and gender theory (Collier, Rosaldo, and Yanigasako 1982), Durkheim's macrosocial, institutional, and legal perspectives on the family deserve new attention.

Before moving on to examine Durkheim's work on the family, we need to understand the man and the context in which he wrote. Novelist Joyce Carol Oates (1973) describes fiction as being a reflexive enterprise, and the same could be said of Durkheim's sociology of the family; he wrote in dialogue with other scholars of his era. Because Durkheim's work was shaped by the social, political, and intellectual controversies of his times, it is crucial to situate him biographically, in terms of self and life course in macrohistorical context. The next sections discuss Durkheim's life and times.

Durkheim's Life and Career[9]

We take Durkheim's eminence for granted. Yet many of today's academics should be able to appreciate the tenuousness and difficulty of his movement from a small provincial town to an elite university and leadership in his profession.

SOCIAL ORIGINS

David Emile Durkheim was born in 1858 in Epinal, a departmental capital in the province of Lorraine. Epinal is on the Moselle River and has some surviving medieval architecture, but impressions vary as to the appeal of this town. Durkheim scholar Stjepan Meštrović (1988) was struck by the "massive old cathedral" (p. 22), whereas a recent guidebook termed Epinal "a city . . . with little charm" (Schmergel 1990:540).

Youngest of four children (an older brother and two sisters), Durkheim grew up in an orthodox Jewish family, the son of a rabbi. Despite the prestige of his father's rabbinical position, the family was economically marginal and austere in lifestyle. Mme. Durkheim, daughter of a commercial family, supplemented the family income with a home-based embroidery workshop. Despite financial pressures, the family appears to have had a close family life typical of provincial France, characterized as "warm and affectionate" (Meštrović 1988:30 citing Greenberg 1976; also see Lukes 1972:9; Strenski 1997:83).

The marginality of the Alsace-Lorraine region to the rest of France deserves some attention. Alsace and, to a lesser degree, Lorraine have a

Germanic as well as French cultural heritage as part of the "middle kingdom" between France and Germany, formed when Charlemagne partitioned his lands among his three sons. French since the sixteenth and fourteenth centuries, respectively, Alsace and Lorraine were seized by Germany during the Franco-Prussian War. Durkheim was twelve when Epinal was occupied by the German army in 1870.[10] At the end of the war, Germany was ceded most of Alsace and about one-fifth of Lorraine. Epinal fell on the French side of the line and remained a border town until the return of Alsace and the rest of Lorraine following World War I (Bainville 1924; L'Huillier 1955; Putnam 1915).

The possible significance of place in Durkheim's background is not German influence but French loyalty. Regional identity is strongly patriotic, and Alsace-Lorraine has always contributed heavily to the military (L'Huillier 1955; Putnam 1915; Schmergel 1990). Although we know nothing specific of Durkheim as a psychological son of the border, his devotion to the French secular state is compatible with his regional origins.

Being Jewish, Durkheim was a member of a religious as well as provincial minority, one that was well established in Alsace-Lorraine. His father was Grand Rabbi of the departments of Vosges and Haute Marne. His grandfather and great-grandfather were also rabbis, and some Durkheim scholars (Filloux 1976; Giddens 1978:11-12; Lukes 1972:39; but not Meštrović 1988:29) speculate that Durkheim was expected to continue the rabbinical line. To what degree Durkheim's Jewish background might have influenced his life and work is sharply debated (e.g., Filloux 1976; Greenberg 1976; Meštrović 1988:22-38; Pickering 1994; Strenski 1997). Schoenfeld and Meštrović (1989) argue that Durkheim's ideas on justice were derived from the principles of the Torah, but Strenski (1997) points out that these ideas were pervasive in the French secular milieu, including on the part of Durkheim's mentors at the Ecole Normale Supérieure (ENS), the site of his higher education (pp. 85-87).

Durkheim seemed the consummate secular Frenchman. In that, he was typical of the urbane, assimilationist Jews of the Third Republic (Greenberg 1976; LaCapra [1972] 1985:27; Meštrović 1988:31-33; Zeldin 1984:452-563). Even his participation in the Dreyfus case[11] did not seem connected to his Jewish background but was grounded in his commitment to universal citizenship and equality (Lukes 1972:333, fn 49; Meštrović 1988:30, citing Durkheim's nephew, Henri Durkheim). Durkheim was very much a republican, a strong supporter of a secular French state.[12]

Biographers believe that Durkheim's departure from the Jewish faith of his childhood, indeed from any religious commitment, was probably crystallized by the influence of his mentors in higher education. During his years at ENS, Durkheim apparently reached a decision that traditional

religion lacked both truth and a moral ordering relevant to contemporary times (Lukes 1972:44, 358-59). Later, as a professor of education in
a secular state, he faced the challenge of fostering moral commitment in
a secular environment (Durkheim [1925] 1974). His later professional
interest in religion (Durkheim [1912a] 1979) had to do with its social
functions, not its theological power.

Durkheim's intellectual interest in social cohesion could reflect his early
experience in a cohesive traditional Jewish community and his perception of its importance as a support for members of a minority (Burns
1991:329; Lukes 1972:24; but not Strenski 1997). Yet for the most part,
Durkheim seems very much a product of the structured, rational, and
secular French educational system. Strenski argues that Durkheim re-
sisted ascriptions of a Jewish identity and identified himself as a Jew only
late in life, in response to the anti-Semitism that emerged during World
War I. He then served on the Board of Directors of the Society for the Aid
of the Jewish Victims of the War in Russia (pp. 4, 7, 114). However, as
early as 1899, Durkheim contributed to H. Dagan's *Enquête sur
l'antisémitisme* (Durkheim 1899a).

EDUCATION

Having been a bright secondary student at the local Collège d'Epinal
(baccalaureate 1874-75), Durkheim went to Paris at the age of eighteen
for advanced secondary preparation at Lycée Louis-Le-Grand pursuant
to admission to the ENS. The *Ecole* was and still is the most prestigious
French institution of higher education. *Normaliens* not only fill the lycée
teaching posts for which they are ostensibly trained, but they are prime
candidates for university posts and prominent in the ranks of government and in research, educational, and governmental institutes. Despite
his prior academic success, Durkheim failed on his first two attempts to
secure admission to the *Ecole*. On his third try in 1879, he succeeded.

Durkheim at the Ecole

Durkheim was not entirely happy with his education. He found ENS
faculty and students brilliant and the intellectual atmosphere intense and
stimulating, but he did not like what he perceived as the elitism of the
institution. He also complained of its "impressionistic humanism and
dilletantism" as he sought out the more scientifically oriented faculty as
mentors (LaCapra [1972] 1985:30-31; Lukes 1972:52-53).

Durkheim appeared to his fellow students to be austere, humorless,
and always serious-minded—"the Metaphysician," as he was nicknamed

(Davy 1919:184). While not very sociable generally, he had some close friends. According to one friend, they saw a more sensitive and tender-hearted man underneath this rather cold exterior, with a preference for "good, simple people" (Maurice Holleaux, cited in LaCapra [1972] 1985:31).

Intellectual Influences

Durkheim's years at the *Ecole* were a formative intellectual experience. He was influenced not only by the faculty but also by fellow students. The future eminence of some of Durkheim's colleagues rivaled Durkheim's own. Classmates included philosophers Henri Bergson and Maurice Blondel, psychologist Pierre Janet, and Jean Jaurès, leader-to-be of the socialist party in France.

Among his important mentors were Numa Denis Fustel de Coulanges ([1864] 1912), a scholar of Roman history who was appointed Director of the *Ecole* in 1880. Durkheim dedicated his required Latin thesis to Fustel, whose influence can be seen in Durkheim's interest in the Roman family, in his adoption of the comparative method, and in the importance he ascribed to religion in social life (Jones 1993; LaCapra [1972] 1985:30; Lukes 1972:58-63).

Charles Renouvier, a neo-Kantian philosopher, shaped Durkheim's commitment to science, to the scientific study of morality, and to the rational amelioration of social problems. Renouvier posited that free will in moral action was not incompatible with naturalistic determination. He believed that it was the state's responsibility to establish economic justice, but he also argued for the importance of what we would today call "civil society," organizations of citizens constructed independent of the state. Renouvier probably generated Durkheim's recognition of individual autonomy and personhood as a hallmark of modern society, to be balanced by cohesion based on interaction and interdependence on others. (Giddens 1978:13; Jones 1986:13; Lukes 1972:54-57). One can see the abstract philosophical foundation for Durkheim's social science in Renouvier's foundational teachings. Renouvier had enormous influence on the leadership and direction of the Third Republic during its first thirty years. In particular, he was the apostle and "ideologist" of republican secular education. This was to be Durkheim's academic situs (Jones 1986:13).

Durkheim dedicated his doctoral dissertation to Emile Boutroux, a philosopher who emphasized scientific and systemic thinking and different levels of conceptualizing reality (LaCapra [1972] 1985:30-31; Lukes 1972:57-58). Durkheim was also influenced by his reading of Comte and by his post-*Ecole* year spent studying in Germany. Durkheim's mentors Boutroux and Renouvier were cognizant of Comte's work, and Durkheim received from them his basic concept of a science of society and the distinctiveness of social phenomena. However, Durkheim found Comte's "law of the three stages" too general to be truly useful, and he sought more specificity for the new science of sociology (Heilbron 1995:263-66).

Durkheim's post-*agregé* study in Germany was related to Third Republic concerns about education. The French government attributed France's defeat in the Franco-Prussian War to Germany's superior education system, so the French Ministry of Public Education sent young scholars to Germany to study that system. In Germany, Durkheim was influenced by the so-called "socialists of the chair," who insisted on the social context of economic phenomena, and by psychologist Wilhelm Wundt's empirical approach to the study of morality. Wundt's analysis gave weight to the idea that there are social causes of behavior independent of individual motivation (Jones 1986:14-15; Lukes 1972:90-91 and see Chapter 4 generally). As striking an intellectual as Durkheim was in his development of the distinctive field of sociology, one can see the foundations of his thinking in some of the ideas advanced by his teachers and mentors.

ACADEMIC CAREER

Success in the French educational system requires not only intellectual talent but also political skill. On the one hand, Durkheim was something of a maverick, with his insistence on doing an unconventional dissertation.[13] Reactions to Durkheim's intellectual style were not always flattering; Bergson called him an "abstraction mongerer" (Lukes 1972:52). Moreover, "he suffered greatly from the strains of academic competition and the fear of failure" (p. 44). Due to illness, perhaps psychosomatic, Durkheim was next to last in the *agrégation*[14] examination in his year (LaCapra [1972] 1985:30). But "at about the age of thirty, he started to acquire the security and stability that were probably necessary for him to control his feelings of anxiety and begin a period of enormous productivity and creativity" (p. 34). Despite his controversial ideas and personal torment, Durkheim excelled academically, receiving his *licence* with major honors. He stood out among the *normaliens* in his maturity and seriousness of purpose. His academic brilliance was recognized even then.

Durkheim had been impatient with the humanistic and literary curriculum of the *Ecole*, which required him to devote most of his first year to the study of Greek and Latin prose and poetry. Throughout his career, he held a negative view of the dilletantism of traditional French philosophy and was equally suspicious of the mystical milieu represented by Bergson's vitalism, philosophers in the Catholic tradition, and the Symbolic poets: "He was continually conscious of a threat from the forces of irrationalism" (Lukes 1972:75). Classicists, traditional philosophers, and other establishment intellectuals were resistant to his ideas, hence reluctant to award him position and power. Yet the force of his intellect convinced many powerful academics to support his appointment to academic posts and to argue the importance of his ideas. Durkheim's oral defense of his doctoral dissertation on the division of labor must have been a powerful one, as it evoked frequent applause. "The defense was widely reported and acclaimed; it was taken to indicate a victory for the new science of sociology over the traditionalists at the Sorbonne" (Lukes 1972:299, and see his Chapter 16 on the reception of Durkheim's ideas).

Durkheim passed the *agrégation* in philosophy in 1882 and taught at lycées in Puy, Sens, and St. Quentin through 1884. The next academic year (1885-86) he spent studying in Germany under the sponsorship of the French education ministry. Durkheim returned to secondary teaching at Lycée de Troyes but soon left for the position of *chargé de cours* in education and social science at University of Bordeaux. He was appointed to this position in 1887 on the recommendation of Louis Liard, Director of French higher education. It was Liard who had sent Durkheim to Germany, and he now wished to include more material on social science in the teacher training curriculum. The need to develop pedagogy and foster attention to the practical aspects of teaching lent legitimacy to offering social science a foothold in the education curriculum. Durkheim's ideas, that is to say, sociology, came to be central to the reform of education: "The convergence of his sociology and the official ideology of republicanism was so great that some contemporary critics spoke caustically of the pervasive hold of 'state Durkheimianism' in the educational system" (Giddens 1978:19).

Although the University of Bordeaux was a sort of farm club for the University of Paris (Clark 1973), the controversial status of sociology slowed Durkheim's climb (Giddens 1978:16). It was fifteen years (1902) before Durkheim was "called to Paris." He had worked very hard at Bordeaux, and Madame Durkheim was a very much a part of that professorial life.

DURKHEIM'S "BEAU MARIAGE"[15]

Louise Julie Dreyfus,[16] whom Durkheim married in 1887, was a member of a family that had come from humble origins in the provinces (Alsace) to arrive at considerable wealth and social influence in Paris. The family business was a foundry, but her uncle had moved into governmental administrative positions. Childless, he left his considerable fortune to his niece and nephews. She came to the marriage with a very substantial dowry, equivalent to what her husband could earn in twenty years of his university position (Charle 1984).

Charle speculates about how the Durkheim-Dreyfus marriage, which he saw as unlikely given the different social positions of the two families, might have come about. Durkheim's rabbinical family lived in genteel poverty, and he himself earned very little teaching at provincial lycées, although he had just been appointed to the faculty at the University of Bordeaux. Although Durkheim's academic degree and university position were respected, economic and intellectual elites lived in different worlds in France. Durkheim resided in the same general area as the Dreyfus family when he first came to Paris, but Julie would have been only ten at the time. Perhaps they simply became acquainted through Jewish social circles, which were not necessarily deeply religious. Charle concludes that the small size of the Jewish community in Paris may have meant a collapsing of social and economic distinctions that were more important among larger sectors of the population. In any event, the economic resources obtained from Mme. Durkheim's family provided a more comfortable life for the Durkheims than is generally thought to be the case.[17]

Mme. Durkheim was a gracious faculty wife, who did yeoman duty behind the scenes. While Durkheim worked ten hours a day, his wife maintained a supportive home and raised two children. Contemporaries speak of her as a fully committed companion during the thirty years of their marriage, a woman who "joyously consecrated her own life to the austere intellectual life of her husband" (Davy as quoted in Charle 1984:48).

> She removed from him all material care, all frivolity, and took charge for him of the education of Marie and André. . . . Up until the end she knew how to assure her husband of the most favorable conditions of work. (Mauss 1927:8-9)

One can wonder about the degree to which Durkheim's interest in and views on the family were shaped by his own *beau mariage* (Charle 1984:45).

Durkheim's work did dominate the household:

> He worked according to a rigid timetable: he would talk at mealtimes, but not afterwards. . . . M. Davy has told me that Durkheim was weighted down by his lecture preparation. . . . His work schedule was, indeed, truly amazing, both at Bordeaux and subsequently at Paris. His health undoubtedly suffered, and his letters reveal a number of mental breakdowns brought on by overwork. (Lukes 1972:99, fn 4 citing Durkheim's nephew Henri, p. 137, fn 1, p. 100, fn 7)

Mme. Durkheim's role was more than that of wife, mother, and household manager. "Without her the *Année sociologique* would have been a crushing burden" (Mauss 1927:9), for she "copied manuscripts, corrected proofs, and shared the administrative editorial work" of the journal (Lukes 1972:99, fn 4). Mme. Durkheim attended Durkheim's public courses and was his literary executrix after his death. Their marriage was in these respects a "two-person career" (Papanek 1973), facilitated by the fact that she was more educated than the typical woman of her time. She grew up in an intellectual atmosphere, for her mother had had a career as a teacher (Charle 1984:45).

Despite his focus on work, Durkheim spent time with his children when they were young:

> Marcel Mauss, . . . Durkheim's nephew, wrote: "[My aunt] was a saint—and she was cheerful as well. My uncle made her lead a life that was more than austere, but she led it with gaiety. It was only when Marie and André were growing up that they drew my uncle out of his domestic and academic circle. A little gaiety and fresh air then came to refresh him. He only returned to the theatre, which he loved, in order to take André there." (Lukes 1972:99, fn 4)[18]

In later life, Durkheim continued to be drawn away from his work for events or pleasures with his now-grown children. His letters to colleague Georges Davy recount the engagement and marriage of his daughter, related social events, and travels undertaken to provide pleasure to his family. He described a trip to Switzerland, rhapsodizing about the beauty of the snow. While his children engaged in sporting activities, he confined himself to walking. Other trips were taken to visit his or his wife's siblings. These activities did cut into his work, and in his letters, he is apologetic for delays in publication of the *Année*. Although Durkheim describes the trips as undertaken at the behest of the happiness of his wife and daughter, reading between the lines, it appears that perhaps *they* initiated travel as a way of getting Durkheim to rest a bit, pulling him away from his exhausting work and later from his worry about his son André, who served on the Eastern front during World War I (Durkheim 1973:300-308, 311-12, letters of 1/7/1913, 4/27/1913, 9/18/1914, 12/21/1914, 4/4/1915, 7/16/16; Lukes 1972:556). As she had been throughout Durkheim's life, Mme. Durkheim was a consolation at the time of André's death. She died in 1926 at age sixty.

SOCIOLOGY ESTABLISHED

At Bordeaux, Durkheim offered the first sociology course given in France. The designation "sociology" as well as "pedagogy" beside his name in the faculty roster at Bordeaux was not initially offered but was adopted in response to Durkheim's insistence and that of Dean of Faculty, Albert Espinas, who identified himself as a sociologist. In 1895, Durkheim's *chargé de cours* position in education and social science became a professorship, the first chair of social science in France (Lukes 1972:109 and Chapter 16 generally; LaCapra [1972] 1985:34, 72).

Durkheim was "called to Paris" in 1902. His attainment of a position in Paris was delayed many years beyond what one might have expected, given his record of accomplishment. Though assertive intellectually, he was quite modest so far as personal ambition was concerned, and he was initially reluctant to have his name put forward for the vacant position in education (Lukes 1972:365-66). Perhaps even more important factors retarding his promotion were the novelty of his ideas and his confrontive manner of presenting them. Some speculated that Durkheim's advancement was partly a generic recognition of the integrity demonstrated by sociologists during the Dreyfus affair. Sociologists may also have been seen as a useful alternative to ultraconservative and leftist political philosophies.

Convinced of the importance of the new discipline, Durkheim sought to expand sociology institutionally through his teaching, especially by his public lectures on social science. These were presented every Saturday morning during the academic year. Smelser (1988) speaks of "Durkheim's great 'public relations' effort of the late nineteenth century" (p. 13). Durkheim also advanced the discipline by training students and placing them well, through his publication and speaking engagements and extensive conference participation, and most of all, through *Année sociologique* (Lukes 1972, Chapter 18; LaCapra [1972] 1985: 34-35).

Durkheim "was a highly effective entrepreneur of sociology—as a teacher, as editor of a distinguished periodical, and as leader of a highly talented and creative group of research scholars" (Parsons 1968:319). His keen mind, hard work, and what must have been effective political skills and organizational talent brought sociology to acceptance, then prominence. Sociology was definitively established in the French university system with the renaming of Durkheim's Paris chair as "Science of Education and Sociology" in 1913.

THE *ANNÉE* SCHOOL

In collaboration with publisher Felix Alcan, Durkheim founded *Année sociologique* in 1896 while still at Bordeaux. The editorial board and reviewers were Durkheim's colleagues in sociology—for the most part, his former students, who formed the first cadre of sociologists in France (Clark 1973). The first issue appeared in 1898, the last in 1912. *Année sociologique* presented reviews of books, journal articles, and conference papers from France, Germany, Italy, the Netherlands, Belgium, England, the United States,[19] Russia, and the Slavic countries, usually within a year of their publication. Durkheim's ambition for *Année sociologique* was to cover all the serious work being done in Europe and America, and one must concede that he succeeded.

Année sociologique was organized by category. These changed over time to reflect the editors' increased knowledge and changing conceptions of the field. Responsibility for reviews was divided among the *Année* staff. Durkheim took the "Domestic Organization" section as his own; it included subsections on "The Family," "Marriage," and "Sexual Morality." "Criminal Sociology and Statistics on Morals," for which Durkheim (1901a) wrote the introduction, also contained material that we would classify as family/gender sociology, as did sections on "Social Morphology" (demography) and "General Ethnography."[20] Durkheim reviewed the work of such well-known contemporaries as Westermarck, Frazer, Bachofen, W. I. Thomas, Kohler, and Marianne Weber. His reviews typically consisted of an exposition of the author's ideas followed by a critique and exposition of *Durkheim's* ideas. In other words, they were a presentation of Durkheim's own theoretical work. Some reviews were very brief; others were lengthy, not limited to the book under review but ranging over controversies in the field. Occasionally, articles authored by editors were published in *Année sociologique*.[21]

INTELLECTUAL PROTAGONISTS

As colleagues on a collaborative project, *Année* sociologists influenced each other and were especially influenced by Durkheim. They became a French "school" of sociology (LaCapra [1972] 1985:41-42; Nandan 1980b). Moreover, "Durkheimian sociology and the doctrines of the [*Année*] school became, to a great extent, symbolic expressions of the [Third] Republic" (Nandan 1980b:24).

Much of Durkheim's repeated insistence on a science of society and the uniqueness of a sociological perspective was directed at strong resistance from the intellectual establishment. Although sometimes reaching out to such cognate fields as philosophy, history, and law in a spirit of mutual investigation, he more often appeared imperialistic, promoting sociology as the premier synthesizing discipline and the necessary framework for moral and philosophical questions: "Durkheim's aggressive claims for sociology and their implied, and usually explicit, criticisms of existing disciples and scholars were not calculated to endear him to the wider academic establishment" (Lukes 1972:296).

Durkheim's forcefulness in his public lectures and in certain intellectual disputes lent his writing and speaking on the work of his contemporaries an adversarial motif. An attack-counterattack series with Gabriel Tarde, Director of Criminal Statistics at the Ministry of Justice, lasted from 1895 through 1904. Tarde identified himself as a sociologist, along with his other professional hats, and he did not like Durkheim's version of sociology. They differed on level of analysis, with Tarde committed to a methodological individualism that Durkheim saw as denying the distinctiveness of the social level. He challenged Tarde's primary concept of "imitation" as an explanation of suicide. The two also differed as to the social effects of crime (Durkheim 1895c:81-89). Although they primarily confronted each other in their writings, in a sort of grand finale, they presented paired lectures and engaged in direct debate (Durkheim 1904b). Only Tarde's death in 1904 put an end to this intellectual clash. According to Lukes (1972), Durkheim did not enjoy these hostile clashes, which sometimes came across as personal attacks. But he also felt righteously aggrieved at being, as he saw it, misrepresented by Tarde (Jones 1986:34, 61, 87-88, 97, 104; Lukes 1972:302-13; and see Clark 1968b).[22]

Durkheim (1889) had an earlier exchange with Tönnies when he critically reviewed Tönnies's (1887) book, *Gemeinschaft und Gesellschaft*. Durkheim acknowledged the similarity of the two theorists' major types of society. But he criticized Tönnies's characterization of modern society as unnatural, arguing that organic solidarity is just as "natural" as mechanical solidarity. This review is important in its early affirmation of modern society.

Tönnies (1896) waited until *The Division of Labor* (Durkheim [1893] 1978) appeared to respond in kind. For the most part, his criticism of Durkheim's work was somewhat general. But he made the still-viable criticism that Durkheim had omitted the negative side of the division of labor. Aldous (1972), who translated the reciprocal reviews, notes that "intellectual controversy has always accompanied the sociological endeavor. . . . [And] some sociologists are able to use discussion with their own fellows as occasions to demonstrate their creativity as well as their commitment to the discipline" (pp. 1192-193).

Thus, Durkheim wrote in dialogue with other intellectuals. Such exchanges sharpened Durkheim's ideas. With *Année sociologique* as a primary vehicle, he squared off regularly with scholars and functionaries who published on the family. These exchanges were not limited to France. We find him responding to reviews published in the young *American Journal of Sociology* (Durkheim 1906e), including a review of his own *Suicide* (Durkheim 1898d; Tosti 1898). He reviewed the work of many American social scientists, including anthropologist Franz Boas (Durkheim 1900a, 1913b) and sociologists W. I. Thomas (Durkheim 1899i) and Thorstein Veblen (Durkheim 1900k, 1900l). He presented his ideas to an Italian audience (Durkheim 1895c, 1897b) and reviewed the work of scholars from many other countries. Moreover, Durkheim was far from being an ivory tower thinker and often wrote to comment on policy issues.

FATHER AND MENTOR: DEATH FROM A BROKEN HEART[23]

Durkheim maintained an active teaching and writing career through his middle years, but his life and career were cut short by World War I. While universities remained open, many students left for military service. At the *Ecole,* 293 of 342 students were called up, and 104 were killed (Lukes 1972:548). University teaching was halfhearted at best, and Durkheim turned his attention from sociology to wartime propaganda (Durkheim 1915a; Durkheim and Denis 1915). Despite his untypical entry into public affairs in this direct way, Durkheim was vilified by several journalists and politicians because of his Germanic name, and he had reason to feel personally threatened. Government spokesmen vigorously defended him (Lukes 1972:557-58; Strenski 1997:45).

In December 1915, Durkheim's only son, André, promising sociologist of the Année school and his intellectual heir, died in a Bulgarian hospital from wounds suffered while serving in the Balkans. The family did not learn of his death right away. He was reported missing in early January, and his death was confirmed in April 1916 (Lukes 1972:555-56; Mauss 1927). Durkheim himself undertook the "cruel and sweet" duty of writing his obituary (Durkheim 1917:446). Following André's death, Durkheim deteriorated physically, a decline many attributed to his sadness and demoralization ("Nécrologie" 1918; Davy 1919). In late 1916, Durkheim had a stroke, recovered somewhat, but died in 1917 at the age of 59, unable to do much work in his last year of life (Lukes 1972:554-59). His friend and colleague, Georges Davy (1919), characterized Durkheim as a "war victim" (p. 181).

CONCLUSION: A LIFE BOTH MARGINAL AND MAINSTREAM

One of the founding fathers of sociology, Durkheim seems to have always existed, inevitable, as it were. He is a central figure in criminology and anthropology as well as sociology. Durkheim did indeed bring the nascent discipline of sociology to full flower in the French academy and polity. Yet in some respects, both personal and professional, his life was one of marginality. He was from Alsace-Lorraine, a province marginal to France, culturally as well as literally. A Jew of rabbinical descent, he left that belief community at a young age. But he could not escape the anti-Semitism of the Dreyfus case and World War I; these two causes were the only ones in which Durkheim took an active political role. He had to struggle to establish his career and his discipline. His experiences of academic failure included being declined admission twice to the ENS and having ranked next to last in his *agrégation* cohort. Durkheim seemed to some to have had few friends at the ENS, and his scholastic difficulties arose in the context of an illness that could have been psychosomatic. Though his brilliance was acknowledged, even his mentors sometimes found him aggravating and controversial. Durkheim's advancement to a position at the University of Paris came only after years of waiting.

Yet Durkheim rose to a position of profound influence in France, in the quintessential French role of leading intellectual who holds no portfolio or electoral mandate but whose ideas shape public policy. Durkheim not only guided the development of academic sociology through his *Année sociologie* school, but he was also an architect of educational reform. "Indeed, at no other time in the history of sociology has a sociologist exerted this degree of influence in a society" (Turner, Beeghley, and Powers 1998:232). Perhaps, that had to do with the times as well as the special talents of Emile Durkheim.

The Times

"May you live in exciting times" is said to be an ancient Chinese curse. The period from the middle of the nineteenth century through World War I was intense intellectually and both politically stable and turbulent for the nations of Western Europe. Victorian England, the French Third Republic (1870-1940), and the German Empire were in one sense models of political stability. Yet for France, defeat in the Franco-Prussian war and the temporary success of Parisian workers in establishing the revolutionary Paris Commune (1871) left behind a sense of vulnerability (Weber 1986:114).

THE THIRD REPUBLIC AND ITS CHALLENGERS

The political beginning of modern France is marked by the 1789 Revolution and the establishment of the Republic. The radical and bloody Reign of Terror phase was ended by Napoleon's coup and eventual establishment of an Empire. Napoleon was overthrown and exiled, to be followed by a series of quasi-constitutional monarchies and short-lived republican regimes. Germany's victory in the Franco-Prussian War (1870-71) ended the last of these, the Second Empire. The quick defeat of France was a blow to French pride and confidence. Following the withdrawal of Germany from France, monarchists, conservative and "radical" (moderate) republicans, and Marxists continued to struggle over the form of government and governmental power. The Paris Commune (a socialist/Marxist rebellion of 1871) and an attempted restoration of the monarchy and military dictatorship both failed. Almost by default, the Third Republic was established. It lasted from 1870-1940, though as a regime of "endless crisis" (Weber 1986, chap. 5).

Long-lived as it was, the Third Republic's essential instability is indicated by the fact that there were forty-nine parliamentary governments between 1875 and 1914. Bombs were set off in the Chamber of Deputies in 1893 and in the vicinity of the President of the Republic in 1905. Threats to Third Republic stability were perceived to come from left and right. On the left were Marxists, socialists, anarchists, and radical republicans. Those on the right who wished to restore the monarchy had little success but only because the Bourbon claimants to the throne did not want to serve as *constitutional* monarchs. Conservative generals McMahon and Boulanger enjoyed popular acclaim and served as heads of state. The republican government was not definitively stabilized until 1894, when the last would-be military dictator, General Boulanger, the original "man on horseback" (Brogan 1966, vol. 1:186), backed down from his attempt to restore the monarchy.

No sooner had this threat to a democratic government subsided than the Dreyfus Affair plunged the country into a different form of political turmoil. Even afterward, Action Française, a conservative Catholic movement, and other antirepublican groups were strong and active in their opposition to a secular nation and the principles of the French Revolution (Bainville 1924, chap. 11; Bernstein 1990:235; Brogan 1966, vol. 1; LaCapra [1972] 1985:18, 56; Weber 1986, chap. 5).

The ordinary conservatism and traditionalism of many republicans, whose primary concern was social order, were also strong social forces. Their unease was triggered not only by organized political action or the threat of military coup but also by the problems of an industrializing society, the very changes that led to the development of sociology (Nisbet 1966). Conservatives were unhappy with the secularization of the schools. The Dreyfus case became, among other things, a controversy over "atheistic" (i.e., secular) teaching in the schools and colleges (Lukes 1972:334-37).

Perceived threats to social order involved assessment of the state of the family. Perceptions of oppression targeted gender as well as class. In this mix of political forces, Durkheim found it necessary to defend the French Revolution's ideals of universal citizenship and a secular state. The 1871 defeat was attributed by many to the weakness of French institutions, especially the educational system. Postwar goals included the building of loyalty to the republic as well as the modernization of knowledge (LaCapra [1972] 1985). As a professor of education, Durkheim sought to provide a philosophical and scientific foundation for pedagogy in a society committed to equality and individual autonomy (Lukes 1972: 46, 77). The broader political agenda informing his work was the presentation of a perspective on socioeconomic change optimistic enough to foreclose revolutionary movements from the left and retrogression from the right.

From Traditional to Modern Society

Durkheim's work and that of other nineteenth-century sociologists, such as Marx, Weber, and Simmel, can be seen as an intellectual response to industrialization, urbanization, and modernization. Socioeconomic change undercut the traditional social order based on an agrarian economy and fixed social hierarchies (Nisbet 1966). Hope for better lives for many were manifest in political and social programs, but fears of social disintegration and chaos also emerged.

Durkheim's novel solution to the tension between freedom and social order was to posit the evolutionary emergence of new structures of social control in modern society that would permit an ordered liberty. In effect, he argued with those who saw the weakening of family, church, and community bonds and control as leading to social chaos. Instead, he posited that the complex division of labor characteristic of modern society leads to a new organizing principle, an "organic solidarity" based on specialization and interdependence (Glendon 1989:298-99, citing Waline 1945:323). In a dialectic of thesis (traditional social order) and antithesis (socialist revolution), Durkheim offered a synthesis that accepts social change but sees it regulated through the evolution of new structures:

> For . . . groups [on the Right] individualism was seen as a pathology, an expression of the decay of the cultural fabric. . . . Durkheim tried to show the futility of condemnation of this sort: the ideals of individualism express the emergence of a new type of social order, which will increase, transcending the traditional form of society that the conservatives defended. (Giddens 1978:10)

That is Durkheim's theory of social change in general terms. In his work on the family, we will see how "the conjugal family" replaces the larger kinship group as a source of personal regulation and moral force (Durkheim 1921).

LAW REFORM IN FRANCE

Political and social change led to law reform. Systematic modification of French family law took place as part of the French Revolution, during the conservative reaction, and again toward the end of the nineteenth century, as the Third Republic addressed social and family change (Glendon 1987:126-27, 1989). The last burst of legislative activity, involving the restoration of divorce and the establishment of greater rights for married women to their earnings and family property, took place during Durkheim's adult life. As we shall see, Durkheim considered legal codes and legislative action to be data about the family. He took an interest in contemporary law and policy as active social forces.

Private and Public Law

French law gives more attention to private law than Anglo-American law does.[24] While no one expects that law will invariably succeed in compelling behavior that meets the ideal, in France, the law is presumed to have a symbolic educational and norm-creating function in private as well as public matters (Glendon 1987:127, 1989).

French law attempts to spell out appropriate kin, marital, and parent-child relationships (see Glendon 1989, chap. 3). Consequently, the preferred character of family relationships is publicly debated as part of a legislative process. Where Anglo-American law historically focused on the *formation* of family relationships and relied on case law to resolve disputes (McIntyre 1995), French law attempts to codify family behavior in ongoing relationships.

Les Deux Frances

The French Revolution created a state that was secular and rational, the legal and political expression of Enlightenment philosophy. Yet a strong Catholic and conservative social heritage continued to shape social norms and political action. Throughout the Third Republic, these two sets of values, representing "*les deux Frances,*" competed in the political arena (Rheinstein 1972:194-221; Weber 1986:22-23). A reactionary force of

Catholic traditionalists never accepted the overturning of traditional society and its institutions. The moderate republican parties were simply
uneasy about social change:

> The sociopolitical background . . . was that of a successful revolution
> (1789), which, however, was not successful enough. That is to say, the
> ideals of liberal individualism proclaimed in the Revolution seemed at some
> considerable distance from the realities of nineteenth-century French soci-
> ety and continued to be actively resisted by strongly entrenched forces on
> the right. (Giddens 1978:9-10)

Some would argue that these conflicting elements were not only represented in the political process but that competing values often coexisted
in the *mentalité* of a single individual (Rheinstein 1972:195). Even among
strong liberal republicans, values of liberty and equality coexisted with
unreflective acceptance of a traditional French bourgeois family life and
other conservative ways. Divorce law, state control over children's education, and the rights of women are examples of legal areas where the
competing values of *les deux Frances* clashed, as we shall see in more
detail in Chapter 5, with regard to socialization, Chapter 6 on policy,
and Chapter 7 on women.

The French Civil Code

Following the French Revolution, lawmakers had the job of implement-
ing its principles of liberty, equality, and fraternity. Leaders envisioned a
direct relationship between the citizen and the state, a state that respected
individual *liberty*. The principle of *equality* implied that there should be
no social distinctions in the law, including those of gender and age as
well as class. Men and women were declared equal; other social distinctions were leveled, and universal individual rights proclaimed.

Not only were conservative sectors resistant to change, but the revolutionaries themselves were ambivalent about proposed changes in family
law. Most had taken the family for granted despite revolutionary rhetoric that "there are no rights except those of individuals and the State"
(Glendon 1989:298-99, quoting Waline 1945:323; also Rheinstein
1972:207-208). Persistence of traditional norms and ideas about sex
differences and patriarchal family relations were in conflict with revolutionary principles of equality and fraternity. Discomfort with the
revolutionary activism and emerging political power of women at the
time of the Revolution was resolved by endorsing "Republican motherhood:" A woman's contribution to the republic would be the maternal
role of creating good citizens.[25] Women's political clubs were outlawed

and their political participation satirized. The "uterine furies" were met with hostility (Hunt 1992:121). Ideological justifications were developed for continued differentiation of the sexes. Pseudoscientific studies and argumentation were invoked (Hunt 1992:114-24, 158). As the nineteenth century wore on, a private/public dichotomy, essentially the "separate spheres" doctrine, justified limits on women's public activity and the glorification of their traditional reproduction and socialization roles.

Still, the spirit of the Revolution led to wiping away of irrational feudal survivals and their replacement by a rational system of laws and governmental units that reduced the patriarchal thrust of traditional family law. Specific reforms included (a) reduction of the share of family property that could be disposed of by the patriarch on his own authority; (b) restriction of paternal authority over children; (c) establishment of Family Councils, which replaced patriarchal authority in providing guidance to minors or young adults (by granting permission to marry under the age of consent, for example); (d) elimination of the distinction in inheritance between males and females and between illegitimate and legitimate children; (e) divorce by mutual consent, including the equal right of women to sue for divorce and obtain custody of children; and (f) compulsory public education rather than parental choice of schooling (Hunt 1992:40-42).

Family law took a step backward with Napoleon's 1804 promulgation of the *Code Civil*. Some revolutionary changes were retained and the Code generally represented a spirit of rationality that was antitraditional. Yet "the family of the Civil Code" represents a firm return to a patriarchal family system as regards rights of both women and children (Glendon 1987:115, 1989:89-90, 97; Hunt 1992:160-63). The conservatizing trend was uneven; equality of inheritance was maintained in principle, and divorce by mutual consent continued to be available until 1816.[26]

The late nineteenth century saw some modification of patriarchal family law. As industrialization shaped new economic and social relationships, kin and male dominance in law no longer corresponded to family reality. The law slowly changed to take account of a changing family (as is presently the situation in Western Europe and North America; Glendon 1989; Weitzman 1981). From 1881 to 1907, women's economic rights were strengthened. Divorce, abolished in 1816, returned in 1884 on limited grounds.[27] Parental control over adult children was lessened, and the circle of heirs was made more limited (Glendon 1987:115, 1989:41-43, 97-102, 159-60). Parents had less power to constrain marital choice. Kin dominance over family property declined, in favor of the interests of the conjugal couple (Glendon 1989, chap. 2 and p. 88).

Policy Studies

The various questions that arose during modification of the Civil Code were formally studied by commissions and other authorities. France, like other Western European countries, employed state statisticians to develop "moral statistics." These were viewed as indicators of the moral or social health of a society at a time when many families seemed to be disintegrating. Academics also engaged in such studies. Family studies in nineteenth-century Europe were more intensely theoretical and macrosocial than in the U.S. (Goode 1959; van Leeuwen 1981). Yet they were also quite practical and policy oriented. Both strains of family studies were directed toward social change: making sense of it, developing social policy. Divorce, marriage rituals, inheritance, poverty, budgets, women's roles, and work and family were among the areas scrutinized. Those who studied the family were largely liberal, but there were more conservative (Le Play) as well as more radical (Marx and Engels) thinkers at work (Bridenthal 1982; van Leeuwen 1981:110-13). Durkheim was often moved to comment on policy, writing major articles on some problems and minor pieces on others (e.g., Durkheim 1888b, 1902c, 1906a).

Durkheim's Politics

Durkheim has been called "a materialist and an idealist, a positivist and a metaphysician, a rationalist and an irrationalist, a dogmatic atheist and a mystic, as well as a 'scholarly forerunner of Fascism,' an agent of 'bourgeois conservation,' a late nineteenth-century liberal, a conservative, and a socialist [citations deleted]" (Lukes 1972:3); "sympathetic to Socialism, a civil libertarian," and antiracist (Kando 1976:149). One scholar has produced *The Radical Durkheim* (Pearce 1989).

If conventional political labels are used, Durkheim is best described as a liberal. Though often cast as a conservative because of his concern for social order and social cohesion, in fact, Durkheim accepted social change rather than seeking a return to traditional society. His politics of personhood were more liberal than not, accepting in principle respect for individual autonomy, secular education, restrictions on inherited wealth, deemphasis on legitimacy of birth in civil status, public discussion of sexuality and sex education, and the availability of divorce in cases of serious marital discord. Durkheim viewed the state as in some degree a liberating force, regulating the economy so as to ensure equality of opportunity (Giddens 1978:32; and see Hughes, Martin, and Sharrock 1995:151-52). The state would counterbalance the social-control reach of communal groups. In turn, the power of the state would be limited by secondary groups, especially newly created professional groups (Durkheim 1902a). For these reasons, I would consider Durkheim a liberal.[28]

I will argue later that Durkheim's intellectual rigidity led to contradiction of his liberal political instincts in many instances. His intellectual *modus operandi* was "on the one hand . . . but on the other hand." This formulaic moderation ultimately limited his genius and distorted his social analysis. Still, Durkheim took frequent issue with more conservative politicians who were alarmed at the transformation of traditional society. He devoted much effort to combating extreme measures proposed by some politicians as necessary to fend off a perceived Marxist threat. His work on law reform and policy on the family had a centrist thrust.

Of course, as the opening quote of this section indicates, Durkheim's politics can be variously labeled, depending on what aspect of his work or his positions receive most emphasis and whether the background is his time or the present. Commitment to the principles of the French Revolution and support for the secular state of the Third Republic are conceded to Durkheim by most scholars.[29] He also welcomed nuclear family autonomy from the extended kin control that was unchecked in the pre-Revolutionary era and still strong in late nineteenth- and early twentieth-century France. At the same time, Durkheim held to conventional or conservative views in his support of bourgeois social norms: the bourgeois nuclear family and opposition to feminist or other challenges to its hegemony or to gender-differentiated roles (Lukes 1972:77; Roth 1989-90:72). Durkheim also failed to see the role of power in producing apparent consensus.[30]

Emphasizing Durkheim's writings on women and his opposition to further liberalization of divorce would produce a picture of a more conservative Durkheim. Here, it is important to distinguish between "status quo conservatism" and "reactionary conservative" (Adams and Sydie 2001:9). Durkheim was not a reactionary conservative who wished to turn the clock back, but the thrust of his views in certain areas and his manner of arguing them does suggest a profound loyalty to the status quo and an effort to find theoretical justification for it.

Standpoint is everything in sizing up Durkheim's politics. Early analyses of Durkheim's work and politics created what some later scholars have called "the myth of conservatism" (Giddens 1976:710). Giddens, in particular, has worked hard to challenge Nisbet's (1966) and Coser's (1960) definition of the situation. Against the backdrop of Durkheim's alleged conservatism, his more liberal tendencies do stand out. "His affiliation was above all to liberal republicanism (Giddens 1976:710; and see Craib 1997:14, 196; Giddens 1978, 1986:23-24; Hughes et al. 1995:151). And he did espouse (a qualified) individualism (Giddens various; Meštrović 1988:100).

If Durkheim were alive today, he would probably be seen as a "communitarian," one who emphasizes social responsibility over individual rights (Etzioni 1993; Glendon 1991). Lehmann, listing off the labels of "conservative," "liberal," "reformer," "radical," "capitalist," and "socialist" that have been applied to Durkheim concludes that he is a "neo-liberal" (1994:8-9) In her various writings, she presents a nicely complex discussion of Durkheim's various political tendencies and of the contradictory viewpoints of Durkheim scholars (see Lehmann 1995b:566-68). Indeed, Durkheim is politically complex. In this volume, Chapter 6 on family policy and Chapter 7 on women and sexuality are particularly revealing in this regard.

Durkheim's relationship to socialism is a complex one. Durkheim attacked Marxist/socialist theories of class conflict as mistaken theoretically and disruptive politically. Durkheim did speak approvingly of some aspects of "socialism" (by this, he usually meant his *own* views on the moral society!). He was sympathetic to the socialist leader Jaurès, and many of Durkheim's *Année* colleagues, including Mauss, were active socialists. Durkheim's remarks on socialism and his ties to socialists were ambiguous enough for some observers to claim his support (Hughes et al. 1995:151-52; Lukes 1972:320-30), although others disagree (Henri Durkheim in Meštrović 1988:29-30; Zeitlin 1968:235) and may have the right of it.[31]

Durkheim disapproved of intellectuals' direct involvement in partisan politics (LaCapra [1972] 1985:63-65; Giddens 1978:12, 17), which he referred to as "the kitchen" (Charle 1984:48). He himself did not endorse any political action save for the Dreyfus movement and World War I (Giddens 1978:13, 17), which he considered moral, rather than political, issues (Lukes 1972, chap. 17). Durkheim was an early and public supporter of the Dreyfus campaign, serving as secretary of the Bordeaux branch of the Dreyfusard Ligue des Droits des Hommes (Lukes 1972:347-49). This was a not without risk, according to his biographer, Dominick LaCapra ([1972] 1985):

> Durkheim himself was a primary object of attack by the anti-Dreyfusard forces. His classes were disrupted. And his collaborators, in the wake of a series of bombings in cafes surrounding the Sorbonne, were even led to fear for his life. (p. 73)

Despite his limited participation in politics per se, Durkheim's social analysis was at the service of his society. While never considering a government post or participating in electoral politics, Durkheim was a visible spokesman on important policy issues of his nation from the time he participated in vivid debates at the *Ecole* (Lukes 1972:49). His first publicly influential views concerned education. But like other classical sociologists, his interests were broad and concerned the whole of the society, including the family.

Durkheim on the Family

The family was the subject of one of Durkheim's first publications. The "Introduction" to his course on the family appeared in the *Annales of the Faculty of Letters of Bordeaux* in 1888 (Durkheim 1888a). Durkheim taught courses on the family at least twice at Bordeaux and once in Paris:

1888-89 The Family: Origins and Principal Types

1891-92 The Family (beginning with the patriarchal family)

1907-08 The Evolution of Marriage and the Family

Courses on the family may also have been offered in 1890-91 and 1895-96 in Bordeaux and in 1905-06 and 1909-10 in Paris, as well as being included in a course on the morality of society in 1903-04.[32] A course on domestic organization, by which Durkheim meant kinship systems, was probably offered in Paris in 1902-03.[33]

The early appearance of course work and publication on the family suggests that Durkheim saw the family as an important object of study. (Remember that he was at this point a professor of education.) His claim to the family and domestic organization sections of the *Année* further indicates the centrality of the family in his thinking.

The "Introduction" to the course on the family (Durkheim 1888a) contains the broad outlines of the ideas and interests of his lifetime work: the division of labor and societal types; methods of social science; the utility of statistical data; a social, not psychological, perspective on human behavior; and moral education. These ideas did not appear one by one throughout his career; rather, they were present at the beginning.

Inspection of materials on his course on the family suggests that Durkheim intended *The Division of Labor* (Durkheim [1893] 1978) to be a central framework for his life's work, since his analysis of the family follows the same scheme. Some scholars (Alexander 1982:214; Gane 1983:235-36; Jones 1986:16-17) argue that Durkheim abandoned or altered his early perspective, while others point to continuity (Bellah 1973; Giddens 1972:12, 41, 1978:82-83; Münch 1988:25; Simpson 1965:527-28). Examination of Durkheim's sociology of the family suggests a persistent interest in the impact of modernization on social institutions. Even where Durkheim struggled with contradictions between his framework of social differentiation and his politics (as we shall see in Chapter 7 with regard to the status of women), he held to the division of labor as foundational to his thought.

A second vantage point on the family was provided by ethnographic materials and evolutionary theory. Kinship and family were matters of great intellectual as well as political interest throughout the nineteenth century. Brought into contact with exotic primitive cultures through the writings and presentations of explorers, travelers, traders, and eventually a colonial establishment, European thinkers took considerable interest in the "savages." Ethnographic writings began to substitute for deductive thinking about primitive social forms. Discussions were influenced by Darwin's (1859) theory of evolution. Scholarly exchanges occupied many pages in books and journals (Stocking 1987).

Durkheim arrived relatively late to this debate over the origins of the family. That gave him all the more to work with. He read English and American ethnography in 1894-95 and reviewed ethnographers in *Année sociologique* throughout its years of publication, crediting them with a substantial impact on his own thinking (Giddens 1978:18-19). But Durkheim always staked out a distinct, definite, and confrontive position. Much of his work on the family is reactive, but in the process, he generated a formal theory of family evolution.

PURPOSE AND ORGANIZATION OF THE BOOK

The purpose of this book is to bring together Durkheim's scattered writings on the family, of varied size, scope, and topic, and to make sense of them—that is, to read Durkheim through a family lens. To construct a reading of Durkheim that focuses on the family is necessarily selective and perspectival, as we will never know what Durkheim himself would have done in a book on the family. But it is important to take up the task, to make the effort, however imperfect, to present the ensemble of Durkheim's thought. I hope to provide enough raw material to be useful to the reader, whatever his or her point of view. To at least make visible Durkheim's keen interest in the family is the purpose of this book.

Presentation of Durkheim's sociology of the family is a challenge. His work on the family is fragmented, and many individual pieces are limited in scope. Some of the materials for his planned book survived at the time of his death but no longer exist (Lukes 1972:179). Still, Durkheim's writings on the family are extensive and published over a lengthy period—from 1888 to 1913 and posthumously. Sources include his course on the family, journal articles, book reviews, his major works, and participation in the debates of learned societies.[34]

These sources constitute Durkheim's sociology of the family, as I bring them together in this book. This first chapter has introduced Durkheim's sociology of the family and presented background information on his life and times. In his course on the family and related publications and reviews, Durkheim developed an evolutionary theory of the family; it is presented in Chapter 2. Chapter 3 turns to methodology: How did Durkheim go about studying the family? I discuss Durkheim's advocacy of the comparative method, used in the analysis of law, history, ethnography, and statistical data.

Durkheim's evolutionary theory presents the development of the family over time. But Durkheim also looked at the family as a system. Chapter 4 examines his analysis of the relations among kin, couples, and the state, and the nuclear family subsystems of husband and wife, parent and child.

The family figures in Durkheim's consideration of social solidarity in modern society. This is a focus of Chapter 5, which also examines the interior of the family, the more social-psychological family phenomena. Family solidarity is addressed by looking at its historical basis in economic communalism. But economically based solidarity has declined as values of affectivity and individualism come to the fore. Durkheim did not dismiss those values. On the contrary, he could be quite lyrical about them. But he remains concerned about the place of the family in creating and maintaining social solidarity.

State statistics were used to identify family problems in the France of Durkheim's day—"family pathology," in Durkheim's terms; "social problems" in ours. Chapter 6 explores Durkheim's advocacy of law and policy solutions to such family problems as divorce and nonmarital births, as well as declining fertility. The numbers found alarming in that era would be welcome today, but concerns were similar, expressed in similar rhetoric and drawing forth competing policy proposals. Broader challenges to the family order appeared in the form of feminism and sexual liberalization, to be discussed in Chapter 7.

Examining how these theoretical and policy challenges were resolved in Durkheimian family sociology leads to an evaluation of Durkheim's work, in Chapter 8. How was it shaped by its historical setting? How does his sociology of the family expand our understanding of his other work? What impact has it had on subsequent sociology of the family? An assessment of Durkheim as a thinker and some implications for the future conclude this volume.

NEW DURKHEIMIAN THEMES

In examining classical theory, one has to ask, What *is* the point of an exploration of past social theory? Extrapolating from Jones (1974), we find two answers: the author's concerns; our contemporary concerns. We can situate a theorist historically and seek to understand the meaning of his or her work in sociointellectual context. Or we can analyze the work as systematics, for its contemporary value as theory.

Both past and present guide this book; that is, I employ both historicist and systematic approaches. The historical context is so important, with its conservative-liberal-radical political tensions very similar to our own late twentieth-century American milieu.[35] Tension between the individual and the community is also an important contemporary concern (Bellah et al. 1985) as it was in Durkheim's era (Lukes 1972:194-99). Present-day communitarians claim Durkheim (Glendon 1991), while Durkheim scholars make clear his sympathy for the individual (Giddens 1978).

By adding Durkheim to the formal study of the family, our understanding of the development of the field of sociology of the family may be enriched. Durkheim was an important predecessor to Ogburn, Burgess and Locke, Parsons, Goode, and Litwak in his analysis of the transformation of the traditional to modern family.

It is clear that we bring current as well as historical concerns and perspectives to the study of Durkheim. Important recent Durkheim scholarship uses terms such as "equality" (Roth 1989-90) and "justice" (Meštrović 1988; see also Lukes 1972:174-76) as class and gender issues frame theoretical analysis (e.g., Kandal 1988; Lehmann 1990, 1994, 1995b; Meštrović 1991, 1992; Sydie 1987).[36] Postmodern theory and cultural studies can be connected to Durkheim's theoretical interests (Alexander 1988; Meštrović 1992). Such resonances bring out aspects of Durkheim's work that went unnoticed in the past.

Interest in Durkheim, always strong, seems intensified by the reemergence of macrosociological and historical perspectives on the family. Durkheim's reliance on legal formulations for evidence of family structure and function fits well with contemporary scholarship (e.g., Glendon 1977, 1981, 1987, 1989). His other methods of choice—ethnography and the use of statistical and demographic data to show historical and geographical variation—although never ignored, are more compelling now as family scholars return to macrosocial questions concerning the relationship of the family to the larger society.

"Family policy" became a watchword in the 1970s, and similar policy concerns of Durkheim's era merit attention. The tension between liberal and conservative solutions that characterized debates in nineteenth- and early twentieth-century France parallels a similar fault line in contemporary American policy and politics. Questions of Durkheim's day bear a remarkable similarity to contemporary issues: the status and role of women, including equality in employment; declining fertility; the support of single-parent families arising from illegitimate births; and divorce.

That Durkheim continues to inform sociology in numerous ways is apparent and speaks to the richness of the Durkheimian heritage. Although the specifics of Durkheim's evolutionary theory sound quaint today, his analysis is directed to basic issues of the family still of significance. As we move into an era characterized as "postindustrial" and "postmodern,"[37] we can see the underlying similarity of our mid- to late-twentieth-century experience to family issues of Durkheim's era. The connection between then and now, the parallel fins-de-siècle, will be a persistent theme of this book.

At the same time, examination of Durkheim's work over time reveals unresolved logical and ideological conflicts. It points to a cognitive rigidity that limits Durkheim's instinctive humanism and his educated brilliance. We see all this in Durkheim's sociology of the family. By highlighting "family" as an essential part of Durkheim's intellectual repetoire, I hope to enrich our systematic understanding of his mind, milieu, and work. For today, more than eighty years after his death, Durkheim remains important. Still with us is "this continuing fascination that Durkheim . . . commands" (Alpert 1974:200).

Notes

1. Translations throughout are by Mary Ann Lamanna unless otherwise noted.

2. This is Popenoe's characterization (1993:527) of the positions of progressives Coontz (1992), Skolnick (1991), and Stacey (1990), though in truth, their views include some serious concerns. See Janet Z. Giele's (1996) "Decline of the Family: Conservative, Liberal, and Feminist Views" for a thorough and nuanced discussion of political perspectives on the family in the late twentieth century.

3. The term *modern* has a multiplicity of meanings. One dictionary defines it as "related or belonging to the present period of history" (Soukhanov 1999:1162), and that would be its common colloquial meaning.

With regard to France, historians use the term *modern* to reference the post-Revolutionary era, from the 1789 French Revolution onward. Indeed, the dictionary cited defines "modern history" as the "period of European history after 1789" (p. 1162), with the caveat that in England, "modern" references the period from the end of the Middle Ages onward.

Last, sociologists use the term "modern" conceptually, as well as historically, to mean the industrial era and the sociocultural patterns that derive from industrialization and urbanization. These include individualism; secularization; faith in rationality, science, and technology; decline of social control by family and traditional community; separation of work from the family home; the development of specialized institutions; increased egalitarianism; and more (see Macionis 2000:427-31). The emergence of sociology itself is associated with the transition from traditional to modern society.

In this book, "modern" is used in either of the last two senses, while "today," "recent," and present" will point to the late twentieth century or the turn of the twenty-first century. The term "contemporary" will be used to refer to whatever era is under discussion.

4. Nor did earlier volumes take note of Durkheim's family sociology. Parsons's (1961) "An Outline of the Social System" in *Theories of Society* does not reference Durkheim in discussing family and kinship. Zelditch's (1964) family chapter in the *Handbook of Modern Sociology* is equally silent.

5. There is no direct mention of Durkheim on the family in the Christensen (1964b) *Handbook on Marriage and the Family*. The Nye and Berardo ([1966], 1981) family theory compendium does not refer to Durkheim on family or kinship nor does Burr's (1973) book on theory construction and the family. The substantive chapters in the first volume of *Contemporary Theories about the Family* (Burr et al. 1979a) have no reference to Durkheim's family sociology, although there are occasional references to Durkheim on deviance and on knowledge. The second volume, which covers various family theories, has only one reference to Durkheim and family, a general comment about child socialization in the family world (McLain and Weigert 1979:182, citing Durkheim [1912] 1979).

In the *Handbook of Marriage and the Family* (Sussman and Steinmetz 1987), only the chapter on religion (Marciano 1987) refers to Durkheim and not to his family sociology. Nor does the *Journal of Marriage and the Family* decade review (Booth 1991) give voice to Durkheim's heritage of ideas on the family. Durkheim is not included or cited in Klein and White's (1996) *Family Theories*.

Landmark books in functional sociology of the family did not take much note of Durkheim. He goes unmentioned by Ogburn (1933), Ogburn and Nimkoff (1955), Bell and Vogel (1960), Goode (1963, [1964] 1982), and Farber (1973). When Smith (1968:305) and Christensen (1964a:7) list evolutionary theorists, they do not include Durkheim. That the family's progression from institution to companionship was earlier noted by Durkheim is not acknowledged by Burgess and Locke ([1945] 1960). Although they include his "Conjugal Family" (1921) in their list of references for the family unity chapter and *Suicide* ([1897a] 1930) for the family crisis chapter, Durkheim is not mentioned or cited in the text itself.

6. Adams and Steinmetz consider Durkheim's one of four "complete theories" to emerge from the classics. They cite Durkheim's first publication (Durkheim 1885), a review of an organic theory of society, as well as the *Division of Labor* ([Durkheim 1893] 1978), to discuss the historical trajectory of family, individual, and society. Earlier, in the first edition of his text on the American family, Adams (1971, chap. 1) devoted a section to "the family in a differentiating society." Subsequently, he refers to Durkheim on gender as well (Adams 1995, chap. 5, fn 1).

The most extended descriptions of Durkheim's family work in English besides that of Adams include George Simpson's (1965) translation of the conclusion to Durkheim's family course, a summary of Durkheim's family theory in *Journal of Marriage and the Family* (Bynder 1969) and in Wallwork's (1972:88-98) book on Durkheim's moral philosophy, Lukes's (1972, chap. 8 and pp. 530-34) biography, Morgan's (1975:61, 90-91, 207) reference to Durkheim's foundational ideas, van Leeuwen's (1981:108-10) briefer summary, and Meštrović's (1991) discussion of turn-of-the-twentieth-century anxiety about the family. Aldous (1991:660) similarly refers to Durkheim's concern about the family as she frames a review symposium of recent books.

7. An *International Encyclopedia of the Social Sciences* article on the family (Smith 1968) calls attention to the overlap between the family and the traditional pole in such societal typologies as Durkheim's (p. 305). Burr et al. (1979b), in the introduction to their two-volume compendium of family theories, refer to Durkheim as one who, together with Malinowski, studied the family in theoretical perspective rather than in a detached empirical fashion (p. 6, citing Goode 1959).

Bridenthal (1982) refers to Durkheim as a forerunner of Ogburn and Parsons, shaping a positivistic paradigm of the family (p. 526). But Farber (1964), in noting that Parsons drew on Durkheim's ideas about differentiation and solidarity to formulate his own theory of family role differentiation, apparently was not aware that Parsons's writings parallel more of Durkheim's work on the family (p. 74).

Parsons himself makes only two references to Durkheim's work and both in the context of child socialization. He credits Durkheim, as well as Mead (1934) and Freud, with the concept of internalization (Parsons 1955b:55), and referring to child and parent, he states that "It is a well-known principle of differentiation of social structures that competitive pressures can be eased by qualitatively differential roles (this was probably first stated by Durkheim)" (p. 96). Sussman (1965) does refer to Durkheim (without specific cite and along with a number of other early theorists) as theorizing that a nuclear family isolated from kin was a structural necessity in urban society (pp. 64, 66).

Lasch (1977) refers in passing to Durkheim's ([1925] 1974) *Moral Education* in condemning the tendency of modern states to remove children from family to state control in the public schools. Glendon (1989), addressing contemporary problems, quotes Durkheim at length: his views on the limited role the modern family, with its loose bonds, can play in fostering social solidarity. Thomas and Rhogaar (1990), writing on family and religion in Sprey's (1990) review of contemporary family theory, refer to Durkheim on solidarity in touting marriage and parenthood as sources of fulfillment (p. 153). Giele's (1988) discussion of the sociology of gender roles refers to Durkheim's expectation that ascribed characteristics will decline in importance (p. 295).

Bryan Turner's (1999) recent book on *Classical Sociology* acknowledges Durkheim's "lectures on the sociology of the family in 1888," but with only a nonspecific citation of Traugott (1978) and no further discussion (p. 236). The recently published second edition of the *Handbook of Marriage and The Family* has a chapter by Brian Vargus (1999) on "Classical Social Theory and Family Studies," subtitled "The Triumph of Reactionary Thought in Contemporary Family Studies." There is a section on "Durkheim's Blend." There mention is made of Durkheim's family course, that he "cherished" his work on the family, that he saw the family as a social institution, and that it lost functions as society advanced but still retained a role (pp. 187-89). But not only are these pages too few to do justice to Durkheim's work on the family; this also does not seem to be the focus of the section. Rather, it emphasizes social solidarity, collective conscience, and religion in more general terms. There are statements I think are mistaken, such as that Durkheim "built upon" Bachofen, Westermarck, Maine, and others (he opposed some of these) and that Durkheim "rejects any individualism as at best 'pathological'" (p. 187). In one place, Vargus states that the moral functions of the family would be "stripped," while in another, quoting Lukes, that the family "should continue to be an important center of morality" (p. 188). The section is very reliant on Lukes's (1972) biography rather than primary sources of Durkheim on the family. Despite their brevity and lack of primary sourcing, perhaps these recent mentions indicate a useful new awareness of Durkheim's work on the family.

8. This is from notes on a presentation made by John H. Scanzoni to the University of Notre Dame Family Seminar in 1973.

9. Biographical facts in this section not specifically cited to other sources are drawn from Lukes (1972). Their interpretation is my own unless otherwise indicated.

10. This calls to mind Daudet's (1927) poignant story, "La Dernière Classe." As the province becomes part of Germany, schoolchildren are instructed in French for the last time.

11. Captain Alfred Dreyfus, an Alsatian Jew, was accused of treason, convicted, and imprisoned on the basis of what were later revealed to be forged documents. His cause was taken up by French liberal intellectuals; author Emile Zola went to prison as a consequence of his vigorous polemic against the anti-Semitism of the French military. Owing to the persistent efforts of Dreyfus partisans, the plot was eventually exposed, and Dreyfus was freed.

The Dreyfus case dominated civic discourse during the period from 1894 to 1906, serving as a battleground for conservative, liberal, and leftist political forces. It revealed the anti-Semitism latent in supposedly democratic and cosmopolitan France. It polarized French society, dividing families, neighbors, friends, and professional colleagues (Bainville 1924, chap. 16; Bernstein 1990:282-83; Brogan 1966, vol. 1). Jewish consciousness of heritage or threat before the Dreyfus case had been rather minimal (LaCapra [1972] 1985:27; Zeldin 1984:452-56). The impact of the Dreyfus case on the social and psychological situation of Jews is discussed in Edmund White's (1999) biography of Marcel Proust, as well as in sources cited regarding Durkheim.

12. Secularization of the French nation was an important aspect of French revolutionary ideology. Yet post-Revolutionary change was not comprehensive. Some changes that did occur were reversed during the Napoleonic era and after. The process of secularization was ongoing—and still controversial—in Durkheim's time. Religious instruction was eliminated from the public schools in 1881, and formal separation of church and state declared in 1905 (Brogan 1966:122).

13. According to Lukes,

> The reception of his doctoral theses by the Sorbonne philosophers at his oral defence gave some indication of future hostilities. According to Bouglé, Boutroux accepted Durkheim's dedication of *The Division of Labor* to himself with a grimace, and Paul Janet at one point smote the table and invoked the name of God. (Lukes 1972:296)

14. The *agrégation* is an examination that authorizes the successful candidate to teach in secondary schools (lycées) and institutions of higher education (de Gramont 1969:197). The *licence* is a prior degree, usually considered the equivalent of our bachelor's degree (because it requires several years of education beyond the secondary level). But it is sometimes equated with our master's degree (because French secondary school completion is termed baccalaureate).

The French equivalent of our PhD is really two degrees or certificates. Several years of study and course work are required to prepare for the exam leading to the title of *agrégé*. The *doctorat d'etat* (available only to French citizens; another doctorate now exists for noncitizens), marks the highest level of academic accomplishment and is expected of university professors. In Durkheim's time, two doctoral theses were required: a Latin dissertation, which Durkheim wrote on Montesquieu, and the primary dissertation, requiring original scholarship (Clark 1973).

15. This section is based on Lukes's (1972) biography of Durkheim and on Christophe Charle's article, "Le Beau Mariage d'Emile Durkheim" (1984). They contradict each other in some respects.

Charle is critical of the accuracy of Lukes's discussion of M. and Mme. Durkheim's family background. He argues that Durkheim biographers' assumptions about the families' economic status is based too much on averages and stereotypes rather than on the particulars of the Durkheims and Dreyfuses. His account seems well grounded in documents and records of the period and statements of Durkheim's relatives and contemporaries. However, not being familiar with either M. Charle or the journal in which his article is published, I cannot compare Charle's and Lukes's accounts with confidence. Charle's account is more detailed, and one of his points of criticism of Durkheim biographers is their neglect of Mme. Durkheim.

16. Charle (1984) consistently refers to Mme. Durkheim as "Julie," implying that she, as well as her husband, was called by the middle name. I have not seen "Julie" used elsewhere, and Charle did not explain his usage. Given that Charle devoted much attention to Mme. Durkheim's family of origin, perhaps he discovered some usage of "Julie" in that research.

17. Charle speculates that Durkheim's favorable location at the juncture of the industrial bourgeoisie and the socialist-inclined academy shaped his writings about socialism and Marxism. According to this perspective, Durkheim's marital good fortune left him with some mistaken assumptions about meritocracy.

18. André was apparently home schooled until the age of ten, when he entered a lycée:

> With several hours of work a day, he had speedily acquired that elementary knowledge which takes so much time in our classes. I was thus able to set him to learning Latin very early and even to give him some rudiments of algebra and geometry that he assimilated without any trouble. (Durkheim 1917:446)
>
> This description is hard to reconcile with Durkheim's demanding work schedule and the reports of Mme. Durkheim's primary role in supervising the children's education.
>
> Less is known about Marie than André, whose obituaries provide some detail on his childhood.

19. Durkheim's work was known in the United States from very early on, although attention, interpretation, and regard varied tremendously over the more than a century he has been read and studied here (Hinkle 1960; Platt 1995; Rawls 1997; Turner 1995b:10-12).

Durkheim wrote the entry on "La Sociologie" for the "Universal and International Exposition of San Francisco" held in the United States just before World War I (Durkheim 1915b). He was an advisory editor of the *American Journal of Sociology* (AJS) from 1894 until World War I (Lukes 1972:397). And note his letter to the editor of the AJS responding to a review of *Suicide* (Durkheim [1897a] 1930), which he felt did not do it justice (Durkheim 1898d).

20. A typical volume (V) contained the following sections of reviews written by Durkheim:

Section on "Sociologie Juridique et Morale"

Organisation Domestique

La Famille

Le Mariage, La Société Conjugale, La Condition de la Femme

Section on "Sociologique Criminelle et Statistique"

Statistique de La Vie Domestique

Statisque de La Moralité Sexuelle

21. For more detail on *Année sociologique,* see Kando (1976) as well as Clark (1973) and biographies of Durkheim (LaCapra[1972] 1985; Lukes 1972).

22. For more detail and citations to original sources, see these references.

23. LaCapra ([1972] 1985) uses this phrase (p. 78), as have others in speaking about the end of Durkheim's life.

24. Private law is the "legal ordering of the relations of citizens with each other in the contexts of tort, contract, property, succession, and family law" (Glendon 1987:127, see also p. 3).

25. Parallel reactions followed the American Revolution. The Enlightenment principle of equality was not successfully implemented so far as women's political participation was concerned. Tension between political equality and traditional gender roles was resolved by invoking a concept of "Republican motherhood" (Kerber 1980, chap. 9).

26. Napoleon himself insisted that divorce be included in the new code (Glendon 1977:202). Some say this was because he anticipated seeking a divorce from Josephine, while others believe he had a broader concern for universal access of the French people to a mode of ending marriage with minimal embarrassment. He himself never used the Civil

Code provision, obtaining his divorce by means of a special legislative bill (Glendon 1977:182, fn 7, 1989:160, fn 54; Rheinstein 1972:209).

The more truly personal touch was Napoleon's insistence on inclusion in the Civil Code of the duty of wives to obey their husbands. It appeared he was having some difficulty with Josephine (Glendon 1977:182, fn 7).

27. In the law, the grounds for divorce were limited and procedures cumbersome, but liberal interpretation of the law by judges made divorce readily available by mutual consent or unilaterally, through the equivalent of "mental cruelty" (see Rheinstein 1972, chap. 8, for a detailed discussion).

28. The term *liberal* is used not in its nineteenth-century and earlier sense of laissez-faire government and market determination of social conditions but in its present-day sense of support for individual rights, equality, and state action on behalf of the disadvantaged or less powerful members of society.

29. Meštrović (1988) does "suspect that Durkheim abhorred the French Revolution" (p. 100).

30. As biographers have noted (LaCapra [1972] 1985:21-23, 63-64; Lukes 1972:132-35). Durkheim took for granted the essential unity of "society," positing a spurious consensus that rhetorically masked competing interests of classes and other groups (Lukes 1972:132-34). To deny class conflict and ideology is to lend support to the status quo (Huber 1973), and in this sense, Durkheim is a conservative (see also LaCapra [1972] 1985:9-21, 57).

31. In disputing socialist views, Durkheim's argument was that social malaise penetrated all sectors of society, not just the working class. He feared and disapproved the latent appeal to violence in revolutionary rhetoric. Durkheim also thought Marx too narrow in his focus on the economy. (While Durkheim avoided acknowledging Marx by name, he presented a series of lectures on the history of socialism that clearly referenced Marx in criticizing the intrusion of class consciousness and violence into the social fabric [LaCapra [1972] 1985:22-23; Lukes 1972:247.) Elsewhere, he refers to "the well-known thesis of Engels" [Durkheim 1910i:365] and "the famous precept: to each according to his work" [Durkheim 1898a:13]).

For a more extended discussion of Durkheim and socialism, and citations to original sources, see Filloux (1977) and Lukes (1972:245-54 and chap. 17).

32. At Bordeaux, his domestic organization course was initially separated from that on "la Morale," but later, the two were joined (Mauss 1969:502-503).

33. There are three sources for the roster of Durkheim's courses on the family, and they are not in agreement. Durkheim's nephew and colleague Marcel Mauss (1925) described the courses in his essay on Durkheim's unpublished work. Harry Alpert ([1939] 1961) appended a list of courses to his biography of Durkheim; this was adopted by Wallwork (1972). Last, Durkheim's biographer Steven Lukes (1972) appends a list of courses to his book (Appendix A:607-20; see also p. 179. A footnote [p. 617] discusses Lukes's sources and his estimate of their reliability).

In addition to uncertainty about what courses Durkheim presented, there is difficulty in determining which were about the family or contained material about the family. Sometimes, parts of courses are listed separately; other times, they are not. Material on the family might be included in a course labeled, for example, "La Morale." Mauss (1920) speculates that had Durkheim completed a book on "La Morale" based on his course, it would have included sections on "Domestic Morality," "Divorce," and "The Three Zones of Kinship" (p. 80).

Last, as Durkheim became more and more familiar with his material, he was less inclined to write out his course notes, as had been his preference and practice (Mauss 1925:9). He also was extremely busy in Paris with his teaching, graduate degree exams, the *Année*, administrative tasks, and simply the absorbing life of Paris. Thus, his earlier courses in Bordeaux are better documented than the later ones. Georges Davy, a student and later a colleague, did provide notes on the 1907-08 course on "Evolution of Marriage and the Family" offered at Paris. My best guess follows as to the course roster. It is based on Lukes, with inclusion of some of Mauss's information (which Lukes enters into his list but considers suspect). Readers are advised to consult the sources cited.

Bordeaux

1888-89   Cours public de sociologie: (1) La Famille, origines, types principaux

1890-91   Cours public de sociologie: Physiologie du droit et des moeurs: La Famille [Probably same as 1891-92, i.e., the family material was presented in the second half of the two-year course in sociology.]

1891-92   Cours public de sociologie: La Famille (à partir de la Famille patriarchale)

1895-96   Cours de sociologie: L'Histoire du socialisme [La Famille]

Paris

1902-03   L'Organisation domestique

1903-04   Physiologie du droit et des moeurs: Pt. II. Morale des groupes spéciaux de la société: Famille, groupes professionels, etc.

1905-06   La Famille

1907-08   L'Evolution du mariage et de la famille

1908-09   Physiologie du droit et des moeurs: La Morale Pt. I. Morale de la société. L'Organisation domestique

1909-10   Physiologie du droit et des moeurs: La Morale (suite) Pt. II. Morale des groupes spéciaux de la société: Famille, groupes professionels, etc. La Famille.

34. Sources for Durkheim's sociology of the family

a. The "Introduction" (Durkheim 1888a) and conclusion (Durkheim 1921) to Durkheim's family course were published separately, the latter, posthumously. They derive from different presentations of the course: the introduction from the first offering of the course in 1888 (Family: Origins and Principle Types), the conclusion from the course of 1892 (The Family, from the Patriarchal Family Onward), both presented at Bordeaux.

The body of the 1907-08 course given at Paris (Evolution of Marriage and the Family) was written up by Georges Davy (1925, [1931] 1950) from his notes. After the younger generation of sociologists, Durkheim's *Année* colleagues, had recovered from the War, they took up the task of assembling and publishing Durkheim's unfinished work. Mauss (1925) offers a brief summary of the 1892 course (pp. 13-14), but Davy took primary responsibility for summarizing Durkheim's family sociology. His summary of Durkheim's evolutionary theory integrates quotations from Durkheim's other work into the course summary as well as some comments from other anthropologists. He sometimes explicates a rival theory, then adds his own comments before presenting Durkheim's refutation. Davy's version of the course is thus one step removed from Durkheim's, but Durkheim's own views are always clearly labeled, and it is a useful documentation of Durkheim's evolutionary theory of the family. The fact that Mauss and Davy both present the same evolutionary stages lends confidence to their notes as accurate renditions of Durkheim's family course.

b. Durkheim published lengthy essays in the *Année* and elsewhere on ethnographic topics (for example, the incest taboo, Durkheim 1898c). He also wrote articles similar in method to *Suicide*, reflecting on government statistical data and their implications for policy (Durkheim 1888b, 1902c, 1906a).

c. A major source of Durkheim's ideas on the family are his many reviews of the work of others. Most, but not all, were published in *Année sociologique*. Typically, these take the form of brief exposition of the item under review followed by a critique and lengthy exposition of Durkheim's own views.

d. Selections from Durkheim's major works, notably *de la Division du travail social* ([1893] 1978) and *Le Suicide* ([1897a] 1930), contain important material on the family.

e. Durkheim had some important things to say when he participated in the debates of learned societies; these were usually transcribed and published. One society, l'Union pour la Vérité, conducted a year-long series of lectures and debates on "Questions Relative to the Economic and Legal Condition of Women" (*Libres entretiens* 1909). Some other sessions published in the *Libres entretiens* series are relevant to the topic of the family.

The substance of Durkheim's participation in the oral examinations of certain doctoral candidates is also on record, in keeping with the practice of publishing transcriptions of doctoral exams in *Revue de philosophie* or *Revue de métaphysique et de morale*. We have two that relate to the family on the topics of "Solidarity of the Family in the Criminal Law of Ancient Greece" (Durkheim 1904c) and "The Family in Ancient Israel" (Durkheim 1905b).

35. Aldous (1991), Bridenthal (1982), and Meštrović (1991) have all noted that anxieties about the survival of the family and what form it should take characterized the end of the nineteenth century as well as the twentieth. Aldous (1991) specifically mentions Durkheim (p. 660).

36. Kandal, Lehmann, and Sydie examine Durkheim's relationship to gender and feminism. Meštrović's interest is in masculine and feminine archetypes. Gender and feminism re Durkheim are discussed in detail in Chapter 7.

37. "Postindustrial" refers to a society in which the secondary sector of the economy (manufacturing), previously dominant, has become less significant than the tertiary sector (services and information). Similarly, "postmodern" presumes that a "modern" society, with its stable institutions and cultural values of rationality, objectivity, science, and technology, has been displaced by cultural fragmentation and inchoate and improvisational social relations. Claims to objectivity have been renounced in favor of the purely subjective. Theorists do not agree on the relationship of "postindustrial" society to "postmodernism." See Lyotard (1984) for a good brief discussion.

2

The Origins and Evolution of the Family

In order to understand the social phenomena of today to the degree
necessary to shape their development, it is not sufficient to observe
what is given in our current experience. . . . It is necessary to know
how it came about, that is, to have traced in history the manner in
which it is progressively composed. To have any chance of success in
determining . . . what will be the society of tomorrow, it is indis-
pensable to have studied the social forms of the distant past.

—*Durkheim (1899c:v)*

For casual students of Durkheim, his career begins with *The Division
of Labor* (Durkheim [1893]). But before that, he had published on
the family (Durkheim 1888a). Durkheim's theory of the family was part
and parcel of the intellectual controversy over the evolution of social
institutions that followed on the appearance of Darwin's ([1859] 1964)
On the Origin of Species.

Science and the Study of Society

As Durkheim began to write and teach, the origins of the family were
being furiously debated.[1] The second half of the nineteenth century had
seen a number of developments that stimulated interest in the origin and
development of social institutions. European literati had already discovered American Indians and portrayed them in such Romantic novels as
Atala (Chateaubriand [1827] 1905). Accounts by missionaries, merchants,

government officials, and other travelers and adventurers in America, Oceania, Africa, and Asia detailed their observations of exotic sexual, marital, and kin structures and practices. Many expatriates and travelers made some effort to collect and record data systematically, providing social theorists with rich (though not necessarily correct) sources of information. Archaeological finds of flint tools in association with extinct animals created interest in prehistoric man and encouraged the study of human society in an evolutionary perspective (Gruber 1968; Smith 1968; Stocking 1968).

Darwin's ([1859] 1964) *On the Origin of Species*, though controversial, had an enormous popular and intellectual impact and provided a framework for organizing ethnographic data into theories of the evolution of social institutions. The dominance of biological paradigms in the nineteenth-century study of the family has often been noted (e.g., Hutter 1981; Kingsbury and Scanzoni 1993). The tendency to create social typologies and arrange them in an evolutionary sequence existed before Darwin (Hutter 1981:18), but wide acceptance of Darwin's theory gave them legitimacy. Evolutionary theory provided a way of integrating reports of exotic sexual practices and social institutions into a reassuring narrative that would have the European conjugal family as its endpoint.

Changes in the social fabric as a consequence of industrialization and urbanization challenged the established political system. These changes raised questions about the permanence of marriage, the status of women, and the future of personal and family relations in a society that seemed to many to be destroying the old social bonds. In the last half of the nineteenth-century, fertility declined, divorce increased, and nonmarital births increased. Time-honored roles of men and women were threatened. The poverty and harsh living conditions of the new urban industrial class were apparent. As industrialization progressed, earnings came to be based on employment (rather than deriving from familial economic activity). The power and strength of the extended family eroded, while the emergent conjugal family appeared fragile and incomplete (van Leeuwen 1981:101-103). The family became more and more essential as a refuge from the mechanistic and impersonal larger society, yet its stability and viability came to seem problematic (Bridenthal 1982, esp. pp. 226-27; Collier et al. 1982:30-31; Hutter 1981:17; van Leeuwen 1981:101-103).

Scholars and policymakers sought understanding and found it in the new scientific theory of evolution as applied to social institutions. These studies of the evolution of the family in actuality addressed the present:

> Some are going to seek in yesterday's families models to propose for our imitation: that is what M. Le Play has specifically done with regard to the patriarchal family. The aim of others is, on the contrary, to bring out the

superiority of the current type and to glory in our progress. (Durkheim 1888a:272)[2]

As with other theories of the time, the latent purpose of Durkheim's own evolutionary theory of the family was to address contemporary social phenomena (Vogt 1976b:41):

> From that study of the past will emerge an explanation of the present. . . . However far back into the past we go, we will never lose the present from view. When we describe even the most primitive forms of the family, that will not only be to satisfy a quite legitimate curiosity, but to arrive little by little at an explanation of our European family. (Durkheim 1888a:263-64)

The Evolutionary Debates

These early anthropological writings represent the first social scientific accounts of the family. Competing theories flourished. They differed as to whether the original family was patriarchal (Maine [1861] 1888), matriarchal (Bachofen [1861] 1948; Morgan [1877] 1964), or embedded in a society that was highly egalitarian (Engels [1884] 1972).[3] They varied as to the original structure of relations between the sexes, whether it was group marriage (Morgan [1877] 1964; Engels [1884] 1972), "primitive promiscuity" (Bachofen [1861] 1948), a more limited polygamy (Maine [1861] 1888), or monogamy (Westermarck [1891] 1921). What all had in common was a framework of stages of development of family structures that typically culminated in the monogamous marriage and nuclear family of contemporary Western Europe.

Theories had political implications, with Bachofen's ([1861] 1948) theory of mother right and Morgan's ([1877] 1964) matriarchy seeming to justify feminist and socialist opposition to patriarchal domination of the family (Hutter 1981; Lasch 1977:25-26). Engels ([1884] 1972) romanticized the *gens*, the earlier large familial group, characterizing the American Indian *gens* as communal and democratic (1884:217-18). He saw the conjugal family as oppressive and looked to further revolutionary developments that would replace the economically based and patriarchal bourgeois family with a freer love: an emotionally based, not property-based marriage. Westermarck ([1891] 1921) defended the inevitability and superiority of the bourgeois family of contemporary Europe by claiming to find that monogamous marriage has existed always and everywhere, even among animals.

But where in all this is Durkheim? He is not visible in most recent accounts of nineteenth-century evolutionary theories (Collier et al. 1982;

Hutter 1981; Lasch 1977; Lee and Hass 1993), although he was in fact very active in the debate. Durkheim jousted with all of the competing theories of family evolution. Morgan's ([1877] 1964) *Ancient Society* had just appeared when Durkheim offered his first course on the family and new work of Bachofen's ([1880] 1996) appeared not long before that. From the second year of his appointment at Bordeaux, Durkheim made frequent reference to those writings and took a strong interest in the controversy. He wrote critical reviews of Bachofen's, Morgan's, and Westermarck's theories and those of other early writers on the family (Durkheim 1895b, 1898f, 1898h, 1907e). He was still going at it with Kohler over group marriage as late as 1910, terming Kohler's ideas "pure phantasmagoria" (Durkheim 1910c:360).[4]

Durkheim demolishes the theory of primitive promiscuity held by Morgan and others by pointing out that the wife-lending and religious prostitution practices used to illustrate promiscuity were in fact socially regulated (Durkheim 1895b:616, 1903c:360). He distinguished kinship nomenclature from consanguinity, demonstrating that collective kinship terms did not signify marriage forms, as Morgan claimed (Durkheim 1898h:313-319).

Against Westermarck, Durkheim argued the difficulty of inferring origins by examining the cultures of contemporary primitives. He pointed out that however simple such societies seem, "they have long since completely surpassed the first stages of human development" (1895b:615) and are not isolated from more advanced societies. "The most rudimentary societies [in existence today] are still complex" (Durkheim and Fauconnet 1903:477-78). Durkheim pointed to other errors in Westermarck's work: the unreliability of travelers' accounts used as ethnographic data, the invalidity of instinctual explanations, and the fallacy of using de facto couple attachments as instances of marriage, because marriage is by definition a socially regulated union (Durkheim 1888a, 1895b).

Durkheim typically complimented each theorist on his efforts to treat the family as an object of scientific inquiry (Durkheim 1888a, 1898h, 1907e; Durkheim and Fauconnet 1903). Conceding each some points, he acknowledged in Morgan the usefulness of kinship nomenclature as data and argues that critics had gone too far in stating that there was *no* overlap between kinship and consanguinity (Durkheim 1898h:316, 318). He complimented Westermarck on his assemblage of ethnographic data (Durkheim 1895b, 1898h:306). He rejected Bachofen's thesis of primitive matriarchy (Durkheim 1898c:22, 1898f:325),[5] but conceded that the position of women was probably higher in matriarchal societies than patriarchal ones (Durkheim 1902b:99). Durkheim did not praise or give much direct acknowledgement to Engels's work, but he shared Engels's respect for and use of Morgan's ethnographic fieldwork.[6]

Themes that define Durkheim's work on the family appear early and often in his course on the family and in reviews of other evolutionary theorists: (a) the distinction between consanguinity (blood lines) and kinship (socially constructed); (b) the inadequacy of biological explanations of social institutions; (c) the connection between social organization and family structure; (d) the utility of ethnographic data (with due attention to the fallacy of assuming that contemporary primitives equate to the peoples of earlier evolutionary stages); and (e) interest in totemism as a principle of social organization, with religion a key explanatory variable (Durkheim 1895b, 1898h).

It is thus difficult to account for Durkheim's omission from the intellectual history of nineteenth-century evolutionism. Also absent is the liberal centrist point of view he represents.[7] Current presentations of the evolutionary theories of the second half of the nineteenth century (e.g., Collier et al. 1982; Hutter 1981) see this period as one of confrontation between conservative (Le Play, Westermarck) and radical perspectives (Engels). But Durkheim, who was concerned about the social order and saw the family as essential, nevertheless welcomed the individuality permitted by freedom from the old familial control, as the epigraph to Chapter 1 indicates.

An Evolutionary Theory of the Family

The heart of Durkheim's (1895b) sociology of the family is his evolutionary theory of family structure, functions, and solidarity:

> It is the idea that the family has varied infinitely since the origin of humanity; that it has assumed forms essentially different from those it presents among historic peoples; that it, as well as marriage, has had the most humble beginnings; and that it is only very slowly and laboriously that one and another institution was established. (p. 622)

Durkheim did approach the sociology of the family in ways other than through evolutionary theory, particularly in his statistically based studies of suicide, fertility, illegitimacy, and divorce (Durkheim 1888b, 1897a, 1902c, 1906a). His concern with social solidarity (Durkheim 1893, 1897a) very much implicated the family institution. In his later years, Durkheim joined in the discussions of intellectual debating societies on the status and role of women and on sex education (Durkheim 1909b, 1911). These approaches are discussed in later chapters. But for the moment, let us examine Durkheim's less-well-known evolutionary theory of the family.[8]

An evolutionary theory must have a point of origin and a set of stages that progress according to a principle of development. Evolutionary theories tend to be teleological, that is, to posit as an endpoint the status quo or else a utopian vision of the society or institution—ideology or utopia, as it were (Mannheim 1936). Thus, evolutionary theories may be actually constructed in reverse, starting with the endpoint and designed to render it inevitable. In Durkheim's case and that of many nineteenth-century evolutionists, the end point was the conjugal family, newly emerged from the kin group. And the independent conjugal family needed defending. Conservative voices of alarm (Le Play [1855] 1877-79) remarked the decline of the extended family's power and control, as some continue to do today (Carlson 1993). Other evolutionists used their theories to critique contemporary society from the left. Feminists appreciated Bachofen's ([1861] 1948) presentation of an earlier—and allegedly better—matriarchal society. Engels ([1884] 1972) looked back to a freer past and forward to a freeing of the paired relationship from the gender stratification and economic domination of the institution of marriage.

Coexisting with a not-so-hidden political agenda was a genuine spirit of scientific inquiry. Imagine how exciting it was for newly self-identified social scientists to be presented with reports revealing exotic sexual practices and family forms! And before them, the task of making sense of it.

THE NATURE OF THE FAMILY

Durkheim appears to take up two general problems in his investigation of the family: (a) What is the nature of the family? (b) Where has it come from and where is it going? Concerning the first question, Durkheim attempted to single out the essential qualities of the family and to specify family phenomena. He characterized the family as a *social institution*, each of the joined terms having considerable significance and typical of his theoretical stance.

The Family as Social

Durkheim rejected the biological and psychological explanations of the family in vogue among his contemporaries. He pointed out that the family is a moral,[9] not simply a biological, association:

> It is necessary also, as we have already said, that there be rights and duties sanctioned by society uniting the members of which the family is composed. In other words, the family exists only insofar as it is a social institution, at the same time juridical and moral, placed under the protection of the surrounding collectivity. (Durkheim 1898f:329-30)

"[Kinship] is a *social* [italics added] bond or it is nothing" (Durkheim 1898h:318.

Durkheim refuted the proposition that kinship is based on consanguinity, taking a position well in accord with later anthropological thought (Schneider 1968). He gave examples of their divergence in the totemic clan and the Roman family as well as pointing to the exceptions of adoption and illegitimacy:

> Even today, the natural child not recognized is not, in the social sense of the word, kin to his ancestors; he has no family tie with them. Similarly, in Rome the child did not become a member of the family into which he was born by the sole fact of his birth; it was necessary in addition that the father recognize him by an appropriate ceremony, and by emancipation he could likewise put an end to all kinship, although consanguinity existed in full knowledge and view of everyone. . . . Kinship is essentially established through juridical and moral obligations that society imposes on certain individuals. (Durkheim 1898h:316)

Durkheim did not deny that there was some overlap of kinship and consanguinity (Durkheim 1895b:619). "But . . . the obligations are not graduated or classified exactly as the relationships of blood kinship" (Durkheim 1898h:317). As one example, a person may feel a closer relative of an infrequently seen member of the same clan than to a half-sibling of a different clan who has grown up in the same household (Durkheim 1898c:10).

Durkheim insisted on the nature of marriage as a social, not biologically based, institution. He asserted that instinct explanations are a "refusal of explanation" and a "method which explains the social by the psychological" (Durkheim 1895b:609, and see [1895a] 1956:100-111). Biological or psychological universals cannot account for variation in family forms: "Maternal love was the same among the Romans as the Germans" (Durkheim 1895b:609).

In defining the family in sociological terms, Durkheim set himself in opposition to the naturalistic explanations characteristic of many of his contemporaries. The nature of family ties continues to be an issue today, not only theoretically, in evolutionary psychology and sociobiology, but with real-world relevance, as biological and social models compete in the courts in legal conflicts involving adopted children (Bartholet 1993; Bartlett 1988; Dolgin 1993; Hill 1991).

The Family as an Institution

In analyzing the family, Durkheim was almost exclusively interested in the more formalized and stable, less ephemeral aspects of family and kinship—the family as a social institution.[10] He gave particular weight to those norms institutionalized in the judicial code. Referring to nuclear families within the clan, which tend to become distinct groupings, he insists,

> These little associations that one observes in the Australian clans are de facto associations, not associations of law. They depend on the inclination of the participants, form as they wish without being bound to any prior norm. They do not, therefore, constitute a social institution. One can see there seeds of the future, but that is all. (Durkheim 1898f:331)

He does concede normative force to socially sanctioned practices without legal status, because sometimes mores change in advance of the law (Davy 1925:81). Nevertheless, generally for Durkheim, the proper social phenomena of the family are formal rights and duties, and he frequently cites Roman law and the French Civil Code in his work.

STAGES OF EVOLUTION OF THE FAMILY

Durkheim was interested not only in the basic nature of the family but in its protean transformations throughout the course of history. To understand the family and its duties and rights, one has to examine the prior forms of the family that have led up to the end point, "the institution of today" (Davy 1925:82).

Durkheim posits an evolutionary theory of five stages, as the various forms of the family progressively emerge from the undifferentiated domestic-political clan. The evolutionary principle is one of structural differentiation. Over the course of history and prehistory, specialized institutions emerged to perform specific social functions, much as specialized organs of the body develop from an initial undifferentiated cell mass. Within a broad institutional category, such as the family, successive types evolve. The "phylogenetic schema," as Durkheim's nephew and collaborator Marcel Mauss (1925:14) termed them, include the following: (a) the differentiated clan-family, whether matrilineal or patrilineal; (b) the joint agnatic family; (c) the Roman patriarchal family; (d) the Germanic paternal family; and (e) the modern conjugal family. They form a series, arranged according to the "law of contraction" (Durkheim 1921:6), wherein the circle of kin becomes progressively smaller. "By laborious and complex transformations . . . little by little, from the bosom of the clan, indistinct and unorganized, [emerge] families which are more and more restricted, with well-defined geneaological trees and more formal organization" (Durkheim 1898f:331).

Accompanying each family type is a characteristic form of solidarity: Totemism[11] in the clan-family, the patrimony in the agnatic family, the authority of the Roman patriarch, the protection and advancement of family interests in the German paternal family, and the affectional ties of the modern conjugal family. In a general way, the tendency through time is to transfer family functions to other institutions: political and educational functions to the state and protection of interests to the occupational groups (Davy 1925). Let us look at these family types in more detail.

The Clan-Family

For Durkheim (1898f), "The clan is the family *par excellence*" (p. 330), and "the religion of the totem is certainly the center and focus of family life" (Durkheim 1898h:313, also [1912] 1979:148, fn 2). Durkheim saw the clan as an abstract type, although he relied heavily on examples from Australian and Native American tribes as well as Roman kin structures that he considered clanlike.[12]

In the beginning, social organization consisted of a large and undifferentiated political-domestic group that performed all social functions, of which the religious were most important.[13] Clans were organized around totems or putative ancestors, the "mystic principle" that also symbolized society and its origins. Marriage was exogamous and determined by membership in clans and their subunits. There were certain rights and duties of clan members, namely, the right to the clan name and entitlement to share in clan patrimony, religious cult practices, mourning, the right and duty of vengeance, and diverse other obligations. Clans also had a corporate civic responsibility and liability for the actions of their members. Clan members were both kinsmen and fellow citizens. In this milieu, individuals were not distinguished and did not hold property individually. Society was communal and egalitarian. Kinship was reckoned collectively, in clan terms, although blood kin might recognize each other in de facto social relations (Davy 1925:84-86, 95, 102).

Eventually, as clans began to form some attachment to territory (Durkheim 1905a), clan and family became differentiated; the clan was no longer a domestic organization. A large, amorphous, totemic-focused family system continued to function, differentiated from the territorial-political clan organization ([1893] 1978:161, 1898f). Over time, then, the clan-family evolved progressively from [1] the "political domestic group . . . [to the] [2] amorphous exogamous clan, a vast group of kin; [3] to the differentiated clan, families properly speaking, [of] patrilineal or matrilineal descent" (Durkheim 1921:6, Mauss fn 2; Davy 1925).

The Joint Agnatic Family

The joint agnatic family is a distinct form that emerged from the clan-family and from which, in turn, will emerge the patriarchal family. The agnatic family is a smaller group, and it is egalitarian. Shared property forms an important basis of its solidarity.

This family form differs from the clan by *not* being religious in character nor possessing a myth of totemic origin and kinship. Nor does this family comprise all of the extended kin. More restricted in size than the clan-family, it nevertheless remains somewhat large because it has political and defense functions in a society that has only a rudimentary state. Because of its smaller size and because kinship is often based on real consanguinity, ties are closer than in the clan-family (Davy 1925:103-104, 110).

There are several collateral branches of the family. Rather than a single head, each male heads a family within the "grand familial association." Governance and economic holdings are relatively democratic among the community males, the agnates. One male administers the family but is only the first among equals. The unity of the family is not dependent on the presence and leadership of a patriarch; rather, the brothers and their families remain together even after the death of their ancestor (Davy 1925:103-105). This family stage is essentially a corporate extended family, "the almost pure type of what Sumner Maine has called the joint family" (Durkheim 1910g:343), an "aggregate of collateral families, brothers and sisters, who live together with their descendants" (Durkheim 1898f:328).

Durkheim based his agnatic family on the Roman joint family, the *agnatio*. In part, Durkheim's evolutionary scheme represents an attempt to place family systems into a framework generated by Rome. He referred frequently to the Roman *gens*, which he considered an example of the clan-family. But despite the sense of the term *agnatic* as kinship through the male line and the association of this family form with Rome,[14] Durkheim considered that the joint family was more widespread and could be matrilineal as well as patrilineal.[15] He refers to

> proof that there existed in a multitude of societies a family very different from both those extensive and homogeneous aggregates [clans] . . . and the patriarchal family [that] one wished to make the starting point of domestic evolution. This is the maternal family. It is characterized by a very pronounced juridical dominance of kinship in the feminine line over kinship in the masculine line. It is the reverse of the agnatic family of Roman law. The child carries the name of his mother, inherits from her alone, legally has duties only to his maternal kin and rights only on them. Juridically his father is not his kin, whatever their actual relations and mutual affection (Durkheim 1895b:620).

Of course, observed Durkheim, just because a kinship system is based on matrilineal descent does not mean it is female dominant in authority; matriarchies are "an exceptional rarity" (Durkheim 1898f:325). Instead, maternal uncles and brothers replace fathers as authority figures in matrilineal families.

The Roman Patriarchal Family[16]

According to Durkheim, the operating principle of the classic Roman family was not the marriage relationship but *patria potestas,* or patriarchal power. Marriage had no implications for kinship but, rather, simply added a new member to the family of the paterfamilias (Davy 1925:87): "Kinship through women counts for nothing" (p. 107).

The father's authority over person and property was absolute. His wife was essentially his property. Women were subordinated to the male head in the same way that children were. The father and patriarch decided whom adult children would marry and held the power of life and death over them. "The entire life of the family was absorbed in the sovereign personality of the father" (Durkheim 1902e:377, 1907c; also see Davy 1925).[17]

In the Roman family, the economic communism, which characterizes all but the modern conjugal family system, was not visible. The power of the patriarch overwhelmed the kin group in this regard. Yet in another sense, it *is* family communism—just concentrated in the father as effective trustee of the family property (Durkheim 1910e:354).

The Roman patriarchal family was much more restricted in size and scope than the agnatic family. That contraction and the "monarchical" character of authority were the new features of the Roman patriarchal family (Davy 1925:107). It was essentially *one* family, for even adult sons did not have autonomous families—until the patriarch died. At that point, the sons' families separated, unlike the agnatic family households in which sons remained together.

Eventually, the Roman family was transformed: "The conjugal couple, at first lost in the family mass, becomes detached, becomes a group *sui generis* which has its own form and its special regulation" (Durkheim 1898i:343). The dowry of the wife became a "conjugal patrimony," which gave marriage an economic base independent of the patriarchally controlled extended family.

> To the nexus formed by the two spouses . . . are attached the children, who soon have rights to the conjugal patrimony and thus have, from thence forward, relations with their parents not previously known, since they are now independent of all *patria potestas* (p. 343).[18]

Changes over time in the Roman family made Roman marriage more similar to the Germanic. "This spontaneous rapprochement naturally facilitated their fusion" (Durkheim 1898i:340-41), to form the contemporary conjugal family, which otherwise would appear to spring directly from the Germanic family.

The (Germanic) Paternal Family[19]

"The paternal family" is the name Durkheim gave to the domestic institutions of the Germanic peoples.[20] It included the father and mother and all the generations issuing from them save for the daughter and her descendants (Durkheim 1921:2). As in Rome, the paternal family had a collective civic responsibility and family (economic) communism. Nevertheless, the family was constituted very differently in Germany than in Rome. The adult son could emancipate himself from his father and quit the paternal household (Davy 1925:111). That is, in the paternal family, patriarchal power did not dominate the lives of adult children so extensively as in Rome. Although the Germanic family was also premised on male dominance, it was more pliable.

The German family had an essentially bilateral kinship system more similar to that of modern Europe: "Patrilineal and matrilineal kinship were on the same footing among the Germans" (Durkheim 1898f:326). Durkheim attributes this to the paternal family's origin *not* in the agnatic kinship of the Romans but rather in "barbarian" tribal matrilineal kinship (1921:8, Mauss fn 1); it descended directly from the matrilineal clan-family (Davy 1925:111) Thus, a dual system ultimately evolved, as patrilineal kinship blended with the more ancient matrilineal kinship system.[21]

Davy points out that dual kinship, by placing the nuclear family in a similar relationship to both sets of kin, resulted in an equality of influence on the new household of the now-emancipated son (1925:111). As a consequence of bilateral kinship and the merger of patrilineal and matrilineal family systems, the Germanic family had a "tendency for the spouses to practice the regime of community property" (Durkheim 1904h:421; and see Davy 1925:111). Members could own property individually, although it might be administered by the family head (Durkheim 1921:8, 1903a).

Among German tribes, the engagement or agreement to marry represented the recognized beginning of a marital commitment, not the wedding. Cohabitation with consent rather than formal ceremony marked marriage. It is thus suggested that in Germany, "free union" existed alongside formal marriage as an accepted marital form, although of lower status (Durkheim 1921:14).[22]

Durkheim stressed the priority of the Germanic family system as an influence preceding whatever role Christianity played in shaping the modern conjugal family (Durkheim 1904i, 1913a, 1913d). The Roman family was more visible in the historical scholarship of Durkheim's time, but he asserts that

> It is impossible for us to understand the origin of the contemporary family if one does not know that it derives directly from the Germanic family and not the Roman family. For the latter, imprisoned in the narrow framework of the most agnatic organization that ever existed, could not get out of it by itself no matter the effort it had made to gradually free itself. (Durkheim 1898f:327)

The conjugal family emerged from a "contraction of the paternal family" (Durkheim 1921:2).

The Conjugal Family[23]

"Of all the familial groups, that which interests us above all and which it is most important of all to know and understand is that which exists presently under our eyes and in the midst of which we live" (Durkheim 1888a:259).

The nuclear family emerged only gradually from the extended family, being virtually nonexistent in the original political-domestic clan.[24] The evidence supports Durkheim in his description of a modern trend toward the greater freedom of the nuclear family from the extended family and closed community (Ariès 1962; Sennett 1970; Shorter 1975).[25]

His "conjugal family" is so called because "the only permanent elements are the husband and wife, united to one another by a free and individual choice, forming an autonomous family with their minor and unmarried children" (Davy 1925:116; Durkheim 1921:2). Durkheim's conjugal family would be quite at home in the later work of Talcott Parsons (1954, 1955a, 1965) or William Goode (1963, [1964] 1982). The latter, for example, describes the "Western conjugal family" as unique in its (a) emphasis on the married bond, (b) lessened dependence on help by extended kin, (c) neolocality, (d) free choice of mate, (f) multilinearity, and (g) intensity of emotionality, all characteristics mentioned by Durkheim (Davy 1925; Durkheim 1921). Because of the centrality of the conjugal couple to this stage, "free union" (a nonmarital cohabiting relationship) is unacceptable because it represents a challenge to the basic family (Durkheim 1921:14).

In Durkheim, the conjugal family is almost qualitatively different from earlier family types in that it is the first to be based on personal attachments rather than on shared family property or interests: "This time the old familial communism has almost totally disappeared. Each one of the members of this new family keeps his individuality and his own activity"

(Davy 1925:116). There is a residue of family communism in the parents' right of usufruct over the child's property during his minority, although with safeguards for the child and limits on the parents' testamentary discretion that favor the child (Durkheim 1921).

> Domestic solidarity becomes entirely personal. We are attached to our family only because we are attached to the person of our father or our mother, of our wife or our children. It was entirely otherwise in earlier times, when the ties that derive from things predominate in contrast to those that come from persons, when all familial organization had above all for its object to maintain in the family the domestic property and when all personal consideration seemed secondary beside this aim. (p. 9)

The authority of the modern French *père de famille* is far less than that of Roman *patria potestas*. While the child is dependent on the father and cannot dispose of his own person or property as yet, the father has a corresponding obligation to nurture and educate the child. His disciplinary actions are limited, and the state may intervene if they are inappropriate, even ordering the dissolution of parental power. Even when the child continues to live under the family roof after attaining majority, that has no legal consequences (Durkheim 1921).

On the child's marriage, the family connection no longer exists: "The child has his own personality henceforth, his distinctive interests, his personal responsibility" (Durkheim 1921:2). In fact, even in the family household, "each one of the members who compose [the conjugal family] has his individuality, his own sphere of action. Even the minor child has his, although it is subordinated to that of the father because of his lesser development" (p. 3).

Durkheim expected these voluntaristic family ties to be cemented by a new form of emotional solidarity meeting eternal human psychological needs. He is quite explicit in his expectation that the family will continue to exist because of its indispensability in providing psychological support and an opportunity for the expression of the whole self, in contrast to the other segmental relationships of modern society:

> [Other institutions or groups] take the individual only in a particular aspect and for intermittent manifestations of his activity. Consequently there remains a place for a setting that offers to his personal individual activity in its entirety the same protection and the same defense. . . . This setting is precisely the family. (Davy 1925:113-14)

PRIME MOVER: THE ENGINE OF FAMILY CHANGE[26]

What drives the evolutionary progression from clan to conjugal family? How do we get from beginning to end—and perhaps beyond?

The nature of the force impelling the evolution of the family is not entirely clear. In Davy's (1925) summary of the family course, it appears that the law of progressive contraction is an immanent and self-propelling force and that the differentiation of institutions is an inevitable process.

But remarks that in form seem to attribute causation, in fact describe results of the evolutionary process: The clan becomes a sedentary village, and totemism declines; political organization becomes more stable; family communism becomes less and less important and encompasses a more restricted group; marriage increases in importance vis-à-vis the corporate kin group. No specific features of the larger society are associated with this general process of transformation of one family form into another.

The Economy

In keeping with his antipathy toward Marx—(LaCapra [1972] 1985 refers to Durkheim's "ritual avoidance of Marx" [p. 22])—, Durkheim rejected economic determinism as an explanation of variation in family forms: "the same type of family is found, at least in its essentials, under very different economic systems" (Durkheim 1898f:328). For example, the Todas, Tibetans, and Jews were pastoral and the Malays agricultural, but all had fraternal polyandry. The pastoral Jews had a family system that was similar to that of urban Romans (Durkheim 1898f).

In rejecting economic determinism, Durkheim was shadow-boxing with Marx, who had died in 1883 but whose intellectual and political influence was pervasive during Durkheim's career. Durkheim did not directly acknowledge reading Marx or undertake a critical review of Marx's own writings. Yet it is clear from occasional brief references to Marxist rhetoric that Durkheim was familiar with the essentials of Marxist theory, including the writings of Engels (Marx's patron and colleague) on the family (Durkheim 1895c:80, 1906b:386, 1910i:365).

Durkheim's most focused response to Marx was a review of a book by economist Antonio Labriola ([1896] 1966; Durkheim 1897c). It was based on *The Communist Manifesto* (Marx [1848] 1988), which was included in French translation in an appendix. Durkheim took issue with the "hypothèse marxiste" that "economic materialism" is at the root of historical development. (Durkheim used the term *technology*, considering the level of technological development rather than capitalist ownership of the means of production the essential feature of the economy).

Durkheim agreed with the Marxists that one must explain social life and its historical development by looking for the deep structures in which it is rooted, not the vocabularies of motive of the actors. He denied Marxist influence in taking this position: "As for us, we arrived at [that idea] before having become acquainted with Marx, by whom we have never been influenced" (Durkheim 1897c:649-50). But he denies that modern technology or the organization of the means of production is that deep structure.

Durkheim does not write off economics: "We are far from claiming that the economic factor is only an epiphenomenon. Once it exists, it has an influence unique to it. . . . [But] it is secondary and derivative, [not] fundamental" (Durkheim 1897c:651).[27] Durkheim's rejection of economic determinism was not limited to Marxism but was more general. For example, he rejected Morselli's economic explanation of suicide (Durkheim 1888b). He argued against Greef that economics does not come first and solidarity later but rather the reverse (Durkheim 1886).

While Durkheim rejected economics as prime mover, economic phenenomena seem to enter by the back door in the concept of "family communism," or family-held property. The law of progressive contraction is seen to refer not only to the size of the kinship group per se, but also to the extent of shared property, basic to family solidarity in all stages except the last. However, the extent of family communism is a concomitant, not a determinant, of the course of evolution, and Durkheim did not undertake an overall analysis of the relationship of the economy— the mode and organization of production—to family structures and functions. Critics argue that he "never read Marx carefully" and addressed a crude and oversimplified version of Marxism. Critics have also asserted that his attacks on Marxism were motivated by a desire to maintain the hegemony of his version of sociology in a time in which "Marxism was the crucial intellectual development and socialism the key political development" (Gouldner 1970:116) as well as to avoid the controversy that would have risen from his acceptance of a Marxist perspective (Llobera 1981:230).

Social Morphology

In the "Introduction" to the course on the sociology of the family (Durkheim 1888a) and in "The Conjugal Family" (Durkheim 1921), Durkheim confronts the problem of prime mover directly. Here, the evolutionary force propelling social change is specified as an increase in the scale of the society:

> In the simultaneous growth in volume and density of societies, there is, in effect, the great novelty that separates contemporary nations from those of the past; there is probably one of the principal factors that dominates all·of history; there is, in any case, the cause that explains the transformations through which social solidarity has passed. (Durkheim 1888a:259)

In explaining the family, and in much of his work more generally, Durkheim looks to "social morphology" as a prime mover. The material aspects of society—population size, density, and distribution; transportation networks; the size and nature (urban or rural) of human settlement; ecological characteristics of territory—all these underlie social change. They do so because they shape social interaction, making "moral density" more or less intense. As social density increases, structural differentiation occurs, bringing with it not only specialization but also individuality (Durkheim 1888a, [1893] 1978, 1899b).

As the focus of social organization expands from clan to city to small national grouping to vast modern societies, society becomes correspondingly more differentiated. At the same time, social density and transportation networks bring people together. This increases social interaction among diverse elements of society, fostering, of necessity, an increased tolerance for individual differences, which then flourish. Such modern individuals will not easily mesh together into large, structured kinship units, which require instead a certain uniformity. Hence, we have the development of a new family form, the conjugal family, which is compatible with greater individuality. The marriage bond formed by the free choice of the spouses now becomes the center of gravity of the family.[28]

Religion

After 1895, Durkheim's interest shifted to religion as fundamental to social life, playing the role that Marx assigned to the means of production. Durkheim taught a course on religion in 1894-95, and he became aware of the work of the English anthropologists, especially Robertson Smith and James Frazer, who both wrote on totemism.[29] He began to see both the richness of ethnographic data as a source and the importance of religion in traditional societies (Durkheim 1907a:613; Gane 1992:94; Giddens 1972:12-13; Jones 1993:35; Lukes 1972:180-81).

While morphology may have initially given rise to what were then superstructural phenomena, religion included, those phenomena later came to have an independent existence so far as Durkheim is concerned. Yet

> While he argues the existence of real social phenomena largely independent of the original matrix of morphological characteristics, the latter are never entirely dismissed and they retain a fundamental place in his thinking. . . . [H]e never denied the importance of [social morphology]. (Andrews 1993:120)

Nevertheless, and in counterpoint to the Marxists, Durkheim (1897c) claimed that religion came first before all other social institutions:

Religion is the most primitive social phenomenon. . . . In principle, all is religious. . . . [T]he economic factor is rudimentary, while religious life is abundant and expansive. . . . [I]s it not . . . probable that the economy depends on religion more than the later depends on the former? (P. 650)

Durkheim's claim that religion is the most basic element shaping social forms was not overtly applied to analysis of the family other than that the family emerged from the undifferentiated totemic clan.

Multiple Causation

Given these twists and turns, it is not surprising to note that Durkheim seems to find that the "chaîne maîtresse" or "principle agent of social movement" can vary:

Nothing authorizes us to presume that there is a social phenomenon that enjoys such a prerogative over the others; . . . it is not proven that it would be always the same, in all times and places. The influence of religious practices was before much more marked than that of ideas; the influence of economic phenomena has varied in the reverse direction. The conditions of social life have changed too much in the course of history for the same institutions to have been able, always and everywhere, to keep the same importance. (Durkheim and Fauconnet 1903:475-76)

The question of what causes social change is very much connected to the question of whether or not evolution has concluded or is ongoing.

THE END OF EVOLUTION?

The totemic clan was the initial structure performing all societal functions, political, religious, and familial. From this undifferentiated clan-family, all other social institutions emerged through a process of structural differentiation. Durkheim's central idea is the evolutionary trend toward increasing differentiation in society that leads to fewer and more specialized family functions. The family becomes less extensive in membership, and extended kinship ties weaken, leaving the nuclear family as the basic unit:

The progress of the family has been to concentrate and personalize it. The family goes on contracting more and more, and at the same time, family relations take on a more and more exclusively personal character as a consequence of the progressive disappearance of domestic communism. While [the extended corporate] family loses ground, marriage, on the contrary, is strengthened. (Durkheim 1921:14)

In keeping with his "evolutionary optimism" (Jones 1986:59),[30] Durkheim appears to take the modern nuclear family for granted as an evolutionary endpoint. Logically, the evolutionary trend could be further extended in terms of decreasing size and loss of functions. Barrington Moore (1958), for example, extends the trends of individualism and free choice in family relations, decline in family functions, and reduction in structure, to reach the conclusion that the nuclear family is but a transitional stage so that the family will disappear eventually (pp. 160-78).

Durkheim places the conjugal family at the end of evolution, but at the same time, he does not conclude that further evolution is foreclosed. In arguing against Westermarck's ([1891] 1921) assumption of a constant conjugal family, Durkheim (1895b) states, "If the family has varied up to this point, there is no reason to believe these variations must heretofore cease, and consequently one must and one can try to foresee in what direction they will develop" (p. 622).

Moreover specifically, if the prime mover is social morpology, then fertility, population movements, conquests, violent or gradual infiltration, changes in population density, or shifts or differences in energy and density can destabilize any putative similarity among societies (Durkheim [1893] 1978:332-33).

> Since progress is a consequence of changes that occur in the social milieu, there is no reason to suppose that it will ever be finished. To come to an end, it would be necessary that at a given moment the milieu become stationary. (p. 332)[31]

In another sector of his work, as Durkheim tries to cope with the challenge to traditional gender roles posed by the republican idea of equality, he is forced to consider that the sexes might continue to evolve. He believes that women have become more differentiated from men (but also notes that where that is most true, in urban areas, they are also more included in social life; Durkheim [1897a] 1930:443-44).

In short, Durkheim could not resolve the dilemma of positing an endpoint, while acknowledging the possibility of ongoing evolution, any better than anyone else. On the one hand, he argued that the family will always be with us because of the needs it meets. But he also predicted that the power of the conjugal family to anchor its members to work and other constructive social contribution would eventually wane. As he saw it, in the society of his time, people were willing to work hard and live responsibly so as to accumulate property to pass on to their children. But Durkheim anticipated that inheritance would eventually be abolished and should be. He saw it as a feudal relic that wealth could be handed down but not the "property" of the middle and working classes, their training

and abilities (Durkheim 1921:10). If the last remnant of "family communism," the power to bequeath wealth and social status, were to vanish,
another motivation for work and social attachment must be found. The
small nuclear family, which dissolves on the death of the marital partners, was insufficiently weighty to anchor social attachment. In his early
teaching on the family, Durkheim proposed another solution: "It is the
professional group. I see only it that can succeed the family in the economic and moral functions that [the family] becomes more and more
incapable of performing" (Durkheim 1921:13).

Commentary and Critique

In later chapters, some of these points will be taken up in more detail, the
nature of solidarity in the modern family, for example. Yet it would be
well to pause here to think about what Durkheim's evolutionary theory
says about the family—and how this theory fits with the rest of his work.

AS EVOLUTIONARY THEORIES GO . . .

Durkheim's sociology of the family is closely connected to the themes of
structural differentiation and social solidarity presented in *The Division
of Labor* (Durkheim [1893] 1978). In fact, Durkheim began the "Introduction" to his family course by reviewing the previous year's discussion
of mechanical and organic solidarity (Durkheim 1888a:257-59).[32] The
conjugal family is clearly linked to *organic solidarity;* the *clan-family,* to
primitive society and *mechanical solidarity.*

In his evolutionary theory of the family, more evolutionary stages are
identified than the traditional/modern dichotomy of *The Division of Labor*
(Durkheim [1893] 1978). Strongly influenced by his mentor Fustel de
Coulanges ([1864] 1912), author of *The Ancient City,* Durkheim inserted
several evolutionary stages that were derived from the Roman family
between the traditional clan-family and the modern conjugal family. These
are the agnatic family and the patriarchal family. (He added the Germanic paternal family as well.) Scholars note that Durkheim's use of the
agnatic and patriarchal families (as well as the Roman *gens,* which he
equated to the clan) somewhat distorts the particulars and historical se-
quencing of these structures in order to fit his evolutionary format.[33]

As scholars have noted (e.g., Lukes 1972:189; LaCapra [1972]
1985:119), Durkheim did not attempt to establish historical links between one stage and another. In fact, these may not exist, as between the
Australian clan and the agnatic family, for example. This was a failure to

follow his own admonition that "genetic ties" as well as "resemblances and differences" must be explained and "genealogical trees" traced (Durkheim 1898f:331). Family forms must be "linked to one another according to a chronological and causal connection" (p. 319). The "genetic method of understanding, marking the place [of the family or society] in the process of change, is obligatory for the sociologist" (p. 327).

Durkheim seemed to defend against those who noticed this lack of continuity in his stages of evolutions by arguing that

> Development is not "rectilinear." New societies which replace extinct social types never begin their course at the precise point where the latter left off. How would that be possible? What the child continues is not the old age or maturity of his parents, but their own infancy. (Durkheim [1893] 1978:146)

Durkheim can be criticized, along with other evolutionists, for the rigidity that any evolutionary or stage theory presents. Durkheim rejected unilinear evolution in principle. In his view, societies could be grouped into "species" or types. That being so, a singular evolutionary process could not be presumed (Durkheim [1895a] 1956:76-78). These societal species, being distinct, could not be linked to one another in a linear fashion.

Levi-Strauss notes Durkheim's tendency toward unilinearity despite such statements (Levi-Strauss 1945:519, citing Durkheim [1895a] 1956:95-96). Strictly speaking, Durkheim's theory is *not* unilineal, because the patrilineal and matrilineal clan families give rise to separate evolutionary lines that emerge from the Roman and Germanic families to rejoin in the modern nuclear family. Yet statements such as "Since its origin [the clan] regresses without interruption" (Durkheim 1898f:331) and "family communism regresses in the most regular manner" (Durkheim 1921:9) do suggest unilinearity. The spirit of the law of contraction and the limited number of family types give his theory a unilinear cast that slights the empirical diversity of family types and the developmental sequences that existed historically.

Durkheim criticized others for their tendency to lump empirically diverse forms into abstract formulations (Durkheim 1898f:326-27), yet he himself presented a limited set of putatively historical types as stages of evolution, despite the wide knowledge he evidences of diverse cultures and customs.

Despite his criticism of others' tendency to assume that two disparate family forms are necessarily linked by linear development (Durkheim 1895b), Durkheim himself fell into an equally fallacious tendency to project the evolutionary trends backward. If the family in historic times has contracted its extent and reduced its functions, a linear projection

backward gives us a very extensive family encompassing all societal functions (i.e., the undifferentiated political-domestic clan-family).

There seems little justification for such a projection. The interpretation of such archaeological evidence as exists suggests that prehistoric
social organization of the hunting/gathering era took the form of small
local bands, aggregates of several nuclear families, with work and family
subgroups (Binford and Binford 1966; Friedl [1984] 1984:31; Leacock
1972:29). Winch and Blumberg (Blumberg and Winch 1972; Winch and
Blumberg 1974) present cross-cultural evidence suggesting that there has
been a curvilinear trend in familial complexity associated with increasing
societal complexity: nuclear families being characteristic of primitive hunt-
ing-gathering bands, extended families associated with more complex
agricultural societies, and again, the nuclear family with the advent of
industrialization.

In fact, Durkheim pondered this possibility. He reviewed a book that
asserted such a curvilinear pattern, which went from nuclear family and
monogamous marriage among animallike primitives to complex polygamous families and back to the nuclear family (Durkheim 1906b, especially
pp. 385-87). After reflection, Durkheim returned to his own formulation, arguing that while there are similarities between primitive and
modern family types, there are also striking differences. Moreover,

> Doubtless one can note curious analogies of the form social institutions
> present at the beginning of history and more recent times. . . . [But it is]
> impossible *a priori* that the same institution suits a wretched society of
> Australian blacks and a major European state." (P. 386)

If that were true, it would be to admit that there is no relationship between social institutions and their context, and that would be "the negation
of all sociology" (p. 386). Durkheim (1895c) also hypothesized that this
projection of an evolutionary return to more primitive times was simply a
form of avoidance of modern social problems (pp. 78-80).

And what of the future of the family? Durkheim extended his centrifugal trends forward in a linear fashion to make some scattered
predictions of the future, for example, the eventual abolition of inheritance. But while Durkheim debated the direction of evolution, he did not
extrapolate the so-called law of progressive contraction to its logical endpoint. Although he was accepting of the disengagement from kin and
individuation that had already taken place and did not see that as destroying "the family," he clearly did not want to anticipate a disintegration
of the family implied by its further loss of functions and membership:

> As the nation-state becomes more structured, the functions of the family
> become more specialized. In a mature society, its sole role is to ensure the
> physical and intellectual continuity of life. It is [the family] alone that can

carry out this task. And that is why, in spite of communist utopias, there will never be a state without a family. (Durkheim 1885:89)

At the same time, "There is no institution, even among those that pass for the most sacred, that I consider placed above dispute. . . . [O]ur conception of the family [is] destined to evolve and is already evolving under our eyes" (Durkheim 1906a:549).

DURKHEIM AND TWENTIETH-CENTURY FAMILY THEORY

Durkheim's theory is correctly labeled "evolutionary." It was formed in a time in which the evolutionary perspective on the family was most prominent. Evolutionary theory generally declined after World War I, replaced by functionalism and social psychology as important theoretical perspectives on the family. Durkheim's analysis of the family can be seen as an early version of the structure-functional theory of the family made so prominent in the 1950s by American sociologist Talcott Parsons. The focus of structure-functional theory is the activities, or functional requisites, necessary for societal survival and on the social institutions that perform them—in this case, the family.

Taken in general terms, ignoring the specificity of his stages, Durkheim is simply saying that there has been increasing differentiation in society, leading to fewer and more specialized family functions and a tendency for the family to be less extensive in membership. Kinship ties weaken, leaving the nuclear family as the basic unit. Durkheim calls attention to the voluntary character of the modern nuclear family; the free play of affectivity permitted by release from the larger kinship structure and the individuation of the family and its members; the transfer of economic, religious, and political functions from the family to other institutions, especially the state; functions shared by the family and other institutions; and the increase in the functional importance of the family as a source of psychological support, it being the only institution that encompasses the total, nonsegmental individual.

This is, of course, the Parsonian structure-functional model of the family (Parsons 1954, 1955a, 1965; also Ogburn 1933; shared by Goode 1963, [1964] 1982). Durkheim's reference to shared functions (that even when it loses functions to the state, the modern family still plays a role) anticipates Litwak (1965). Durkheim and structure-functional theory will be discussed in more detail in Chapter 4.

Durkheim's discussion of the trends leading to the conjugal family very much foreshadows Burgess and Locke's ([1945] 1960) "from institution to companionship." Burgess and Locke's seminal work defines the family as a "unity of interacting personalities," as the family in modern times comes to emphasize companionship more than institutional structures (p. vii; see also Lasch 1977:29-31). The social psychological take on the family, the interactional perspective, will be discussed in more detail in Chapter 5.

THE MERITS OF THE MASTER

Durkheim's work generally has "canonical status" in sociology (Turner 1986:xiii), but that cannot be said of his sociology of the family at the present time.

Nevertheless, despite the contradictions and weaknesses of Durkheim's evolutionary theory, Durkheim confronts issues still vital in sociology of the family: questions of the origins and future viability of family forms, the nature of marriage and kinship, and the changing preeminence of nuclear and extended families, among others. Although Durkheim's views were formulated in a different time and his expression of them may seem archaic, it is a theory that emphasizes social change. Durkheim's analysis can be relevant in the present era of striking changes in the family:

> We would suggest . . . that whatever their mistakes, these nineteenth-century thinkers *can* help us rethink the family today . . . partly because their concern to characterize difference and change gave rise to insights much more promising than their functionalist critics may have thought. (Collier et al. 1982:31)

It is even more compelling to think about the meaning of Durkheim's contribution in the light of the intellectual and social climate of his time. The family had been taken for granted in the medieval theodicy as a God-given form. In Durkheim's time, the family tended to be explained biologically, by animal analogies and instincts, or in terms of evolutionary teleology—in both cases, inevitable in form and function.

If we accept Durkheim's version of his debates with his intellectual opponents, he directed his efforts toward the establishment of a perspective on the family as a changing social institution whose purpose and function were the meeting of certain human needs. This was a most humanistic perspective. It was a view that tended to relativize and desacrilize the family, rendering both social change and scientific scrutiny acceptable.

Conclusion

In this chapter, Durkheim's evolutionary theory of the family has been presented. Postulates are that the family is an institution, with obligatory and regulated behavior and practices, and that it is socially constructed, not biological. The evolutionary sequence of family types consists of the following: the clan-family, which has emerged from the undifferentiated clan; the agnatic family; the Roman patriarchal family; the Germanic paternal family; and the conjugal family of modern times.

Durkheim's evolutionary theory has its faults, notably, a tendency toward unilinearity and the conversion of some historically unrelated family systems into sequential types. Read today, it has an archaic aura. Yet it contains a virtual blueprint for some features of subsequent structure-functional theory. The strength of evolutionary theories, including Durkheim's, is the focus on social change.

In the construction of his evolutionary theory, Durkheim made use of history and ethnography. In the next chapter, we look more closely at Durkheim's methods for studying the family.

Notes

1. A number of books were published earlier and around the time of the commencement of Durkheim's career: Bachofen's *Das Mutterecht* ([1861]1948) and *Antiquarische Briefe* ([1880] 1986); Giraud-Teulon's (1874) presentation of Bachofen's work in *Les Origines de la Famille* and *Les Origines du Mariage et de la Famille* (Giraud-Teulon 1884); Kohler's (1889a, 1889b) biography of Bachofen; L. H. Morgan's (1871) *Systems of Consanguinity* and his *Ancient Society* (Morgan [1877] 1964); as well as more general evolutionary theories (Frazer [1887] 1910; Lubbock [1870] 1912; Maine [1861] 1888; McLennan [1865] 1970; Spencer [1873] 1961; Tylor [1871] 1958). LeTourneau's ([1888] 1894) *L'Evolution du mariage et de la famille* and Westermarck's ([1891] 1921) *The History of Human Marriage* appeared soon after Durkheim began teaching at the University of Bordeaux.

2. Le Play did not consider himself an evolutionist. His *Les Ouvriers Européenes,* published earlier (1855) but released in a more widely circulated edition in 1879, was an empirical study of the contemporary family. Still, his description of the progression of family forms from the "patriarchal family" (extended family) to the "unstable family" (nuclear family) to the proposed "stem family" (Pitts 1968:87) has an evolutionary character, and Lasch (1977:27) includes him as an evolutionary theorist.

3. These terms refer to who has *authority* in the family, whether males, females, or both equally. A fourth term, "avuncular," refers to a family system in which the mother's brother (the maternal uncle) has authority over her children.

The latter pattern typically occurs in a kinship system that is *matrilineal* and *matrilocal*. These terms refer to how *descent* or kinship is reckoned and the *residence* of a married couple, respectively. *Matrilocal* describes a family in which residence is with the wife's family; *patrilocal*, with the husband's family; *neolocal*, independent residence of the couple; and *avunculocal*, residence with the mother's brother.

Kinship can be traced through the father's line (*patrilineal* descent), the mother's line (*matrilineal* descent), or through both sides of the family (*bilateral* kinship).

4. Josef Kohler was a German jurist and professor, a slightly older contemporary of Durkheim, whose primary interest was the comparative analysis of law ("Josef Kohler" 2001). But he also wrote an important book, *On the Prehistory of Marriage* (Kohler [1897] 1975) and was a strong advocate of the theories of Bachofen (Kohler 1889a, 1889b) and also Morgan (described in Durkheim 1898h).

For biographic information on Bachofen, Morgan, and Westermarck and discussion of their work, see the articles on each in the *International Encyclopedia of the Social Sciences* (Dörmann 1968; White 1968; and Granquist 1968, respectively).

5. This is a position supported by present-day scholarship (Bamberger 1974:266; Eller 2000).

6. Morgan did fieldwork, principally among the Iroquois (Hutter 1981:20-21; White 1968), but the others were "armchair evolutionists." Most of Durkheim's colleagues and students also did not do original fieldwork (Vogt 1976b:42), except Marcel Granet, who worked in China (Levy 1968).

7. *Liberal* is used here in its sense of a liberal democracy, rather than the economic liberalism of market determinism and atomistic individuals.

8. See Chapter 1 for a discussion of sources. The fullest presentation of Durkheim's evolutionary theory is his course on the family.

9. The French "morale" is very difficult to convert into English. It can have the sense of morality, as in normative expectations or ethics. Often, in that sense, it is translated as "ethics." It can also refer to the study of morality, a "sociology of morals." And finally, it is used in the sense of "social." It is the latter usage that most often fits the material that I translate here regarding the family. For a more detailed discussion of the meaning of "moral" in Durkheim's work, see Hall (1988, Chapter 1, especially pages 6-7).

10. By *social institution,* sociologists understand "widely recognized and relatively predictable and persistent patterns of behavior that have emerged over time to coordinate human activities toward meeting basic human and societal needs" (Ferrante 2000:364). The family as a social institution meets needs that vary by historical period and culture but which have included sexual regulation, reproduction, nurturant socialization, education, economic production and maintenance, emotional support, religious activities, health care, recreation, protection, welfare and meeting dependency needs, status placement, and political functions. Scholars debate which, if any, needs are universally met by the family (e.g., Murdoch 1949; Reiss 1965; Spiro 1960).

A related concept is *norm.* Norms are socially established and maintained rules of behavior, whether written or unwritten.

11. "The totem is the animate or inanimate being that serves as an emblem of the clan and gives it its name" (Durkheim 1898h:308).

12. A *clan* is a "social group based on assumed . . . descent from a common ancestor" (*Concise Columbia Encyclopedia* 1994:179). Such descent is often completely mythical. Durkheim wrote three lengthy articles on totemic clan societies (Durkheim 1898c, 1902b; Durkheim and Mauss 1903), as well as his *Elementary Forms of the Religious Life* (Durkheim [1912] 1979).

13. Jones (1992) finds Durkheim's assertion that this primitive family was constituted on a religious basis to be an important point, one that he attributes to the influence of Fustel de Coulanges (p. 35). However, this does not actually appear to be true of the Australian tribes cited as evidence (LaCapra [1972] 1985:258-60).

14. In his Roman schema, the *gens,* or clan, was succeeded by the *agnatio,* the joint agnatic family, and that was followed by the Roman patriarchal family. Durkheim's version of this succession involves some distortion of the historical time line (see Queen, Habenstein, and Quadagno 1988; Somerville 1982).

15. He refers to families of the Slavic *zadruga* type, "whether matrilineal or patrilineal" (Durkheim 1898f:331). Present-day scholars consider the *zadruga* to be agnatic, households of brothers (Mitterauer and Sieder 1982:13, 30; Quale 1888:179). But Durkheim intended the *zadruga* to be an example only, so the general point remains valid.

16. Durkheim also pointed to the Chinese patriarchal family (Durkheim 1921:6, fn 3, Marcel Mauss) and saw some resemblances between the Roman patriarchal family and the Malagasy and Jewish families (Durkheim 1898f, 1901b).

17. At least one Roman history scholar, Dixon (1992), takes issue with the interpretation that the law of *patria potestas* determined family relations and behavior. She sees a substantial gap between legal authority and actual practice.

18. This accords well with current scholars' views on the Roman family (e.g., Queen et al. 1988; Somerville 1982, chap. 4). Those accounts stress the importance of the Punic Wars, which drew men away from home and weakened men's authority over women and children.

19. Durkheim (1921) also referred to this form as the "paternal-maternal family" (p. 6, fn 2).

20. *Germanic* is usually used to refer collectively to the various "barbarian" tribes outside the Roman empire. These include Franks, Celts, Gauls, Anglo-Saxons, and other tribes controlling areas that extended beyond modern Germany.

21. Celtic mythology portrays a Bronze Age transformation from patrilineal to matrilineal kinship. For example, see the Welsh epic, *The Mabinogion* (1976).

22. Features that Durkheim attributed to the Germanic family are still considered accurate by today's scholars, although it is somewhat difficult to generalize, given the diversity of tribes and the changes induced by conversion to Christianity. Generally, the Germanic family (compared to the Roman family) was characterized by bilateral descent, a nuclear family, gender equality, more individual (not clan) holding of property, and strong pursuit of family interests (Quale 1988:174-79; Reher 1998:213, 226). With regard to the pursuit of family interests, one author compared the Germanic family system to the movie *The Godfather!* (Somerville 1982:58, and see generally chap. 5-7).

Glendon (1977) supplies some additional points about the Germanic family. She notes that among the Germanic peoples, marriage was a socially, but not legally, regulated institution (p. 308). Although one *could* have more than one wife, the Germans were relatively monogamous in practice. Old Germanic customary law recognized marital dissolution as actionable by agreement between the husband and the wife's relatives (p. 306).

23. George Simpson translated Durkheim's conclusion to his family course, "The Conjugal Family," into English (Durkheim 1921; Simpson 1965). Simpson sounds most surprised to find "the conjugal family" to be a Durkheimian concept, "predating current usage" (p. 527).

24. A *nuclear family* consists of a husband, wife, and their children, living in their own household. It is sometimes termed a *conjugal family,* being created by marriage and centered on the marital couple.

An *extended family* contains additional family members beyond a nuclear family. As a *household,* it is usually thought of as an older couple, one or more of their adult children, and their children. Other family members might be included also. The traditional extended family exercised *authority* over its members. The present-day extended family is more often thought of in terms of voluntary and selective *social interaction and mutual aid,* without coresidence or familial control over the nuclear family.

By "extended family," in their cross-cultural and historical comparisons, Durkheim and his contemporaries meant the traditional extended family, a corporate body, usually coresidential, that shared property and maintained authority over its members.

25. While the argument has been made that the nuclear family predominated in Western Europe and the United States well before the modern industrial era, recent research has supported the notion of the "decline of extended families" (Coontz 2000:283).

26. A term seldom used today, "prime mover" means "the original or most effective force in an undertaking or work" (*Webster's Third New International Dictionary of the English Language* 1976:1801).

27. For further discussion of Durkheim and Marx and/or the role of economics see Filloux (1970), Giddens (1978:16-17, 49-56; 1986:16-20), Llobera (1981), Pearce (1989, chap. 8), Vogt (1976a:317-21, 1976b:40-41), Zeitlin (1968, chap. 15). Giddens has put together some pieces by Durkheim that discuss socialism and communism (Durkheim 1986:120-53).

28. See Andrews (1993), Bellah (1959), and Turner (1995b) for extensive discussion of "social morphology" as an explanatory variable in Durkheim's work.

29. For detail on their lives and work, see the *International Encyclopedia of the Social Sciences* (Lienhart 1968; Peters 1968).

30. The term suits its use here, but in fact, Jones believes Durkheim later changed with regard to "evolutionary optimism."

31. Indeed, the French family is presently in the process of modification or at least pluralization due to a population shift. The massive migration from North Africa to France in the mid to late twentieth century has created a situation in which the Islamic laws and customs followed by immigrant families are in tension with the principles of French law regarding inheritance, real estate, polygamy, dowry, and marriage between relatives (Rude-Antoine 1986).

32. These terms are prominent in *The Division of Labor* (Durkheim [1893] 1978). It was his doctoral dissertation, in progress as he taught his first course on the family. As Durkheim analyzes the transition from traditional to modern society, he compares the basis for cohesion in a traditional society, "mechanical solidarity," to that in a modern society, "organic solidarity." Mechanical solidarity is "the similarity of all members of society in the values, beliefs, and understanding of norms," whereas organic solidarity occurs through specialization and diversity. People are no longer alike, but their interdependence, their need for each other's specialties, creates social bonds and a "social order based on interdependence and cooperation among people performing a wide range of diverse and specialized tasks" (Ferrante 2000:518).

33. Vis-à-vis the Roman family, there were some tensions between historical reality and the model of evolution to which Durkheim was committed. Durkheim himself occasionally varied from his ordering of family types. In an offhand remark in one review, he states that when the *patria potestas* declined, the son of the family began to claim property as his own and found an agnatic family (Durkheim 1901b:345). This suggests that the agnatic family follows the patriarchal family, while at the same time, Durkheim clearly sees the agnatic family and its equivalent, the Eastern European *zadruga,* as immediate successors to the clan-family (Durkheim 1898f) and *prior* to the patriarchal family. "Never has one seen the joint family born from a more limited family; all evidence proves that it is prior" (Durkheim 1898c:363, 1921).

Also somewhat mismatched was Durkheim's equation of the Roman *gens* to the clan. Indeed, the *gens* had religious as well as property trustee and guardianship functions. Yet it coexisted with the *patria potestas* family (Queen et al. 1988:4; Somerville 1982:37; see these sources for more detail on the Roman family).

3

Studying the Family

The sociologist . . . must confront the social facts, forgetting all
that he believed he knew about them, as if in the presence of an
unknown.

—*Durkheim (1909a:285)*[1]

W hat were the methods by which Durkheim studied the family?
What were the purposes he saw as valid? This chapter explores
Durkheim's methodological approaches to the study of the family: his
use of the materials of ethnography, history, law, and demography. Reflections on method were an intrinsic part of Durkheim's critical response
to others as well as central to his own teaching and writing. This methodological chapter thus connects with the evolutionary theory presented
in the last chapter as well as to the substantive content of the chapters
to come.

Durkheim's use of ethnographic data from Native American and Australian tribes seems vastly different from the painstaking analysis of
statistics, yet both approaches were present at the beginning. The "Introduction" to Durkheim's (1888a) Bordeaux course on the family, which
puts forth ethnography, history, and demography as methods of choice,
appeared in the same year as an early statistical work on suicide and
fertility (Durkheim 1888b). All these involved the metamethod of comparative analysis, comparison among societies, their subunits, or their
historical stages.

The Science of Sociology

Durkheim insisted on the *scientific* approach to the study of the family and other social phenomena. Analogies to natural science were frequent in his discussion of sociological methods: comparisons to "the naturalist" or "the physicist" (Durkheim 1888a:273), rhetoric about "geni and species" of family forms (p. 263). Durkheim opened his course on the family with a reference to Claude Bernard, French pioneer of the experimental method (p. 262). He went on to develop an analogy between the comparative method and the laboratory experiment, in which history serves as the "instrument of analysis" for society, as does the microscope in the physical sciences. Durkheim talks about analysis—discernment of the basic components of society—in the terms of natural science, comparing social units to cells and molecules (Durkheim 1909a:279-80).

According to Durkheim (1908), the scientist is oriented to establishing *general* concepts and explanations of social forms and relationships: "I have to abstract and leave many points aside" (p. 241). He noted similarities of the Roman *gens* to the Iroquois clan; concordances among the Roman and Germanic peoples; and additional similarities among the peoples of Greece, Italy, India, Ireland, and the Slavic nations (Durkheim and Fauconnet 1903:487). Durkheim (1907e) argued for the creation of a typology of societies (p. 384).

A scientific approach requires precise definitions rather than "commonsense meanings" or "everyday language" (Durkheim 1895b: 610). The sociologist must also maintain the detachment and objectivity of the natural sciences:

> The sociologist must begin by making *tabula rasa* of the notions that he has formed in the course of his life. He must take as a principle that he knows nothing of . . . [the social phenomena], of their characteristics or of the causes on which they depend. (Durkheim 1909a:284)

If instead, a social scientist relies on his own experience or values, idiosyncratic experience and ideology will shape interpretation, to the detriment of scientific discovery and interpretation:

> Thus, for a missionary imbued with Christian ideas on marriage, the facts of polyandry will be the symbol of a veritable domestic anarchy and the grossest immorality. On the contrary, a slightly revolutionary spirit . . . , carried away by his passion for the weak and his habit of taking up their defense, will judge these family types according to how the women are treated. (Durkheim 1888a:265-66)

Durkheim recognized that it is difficult to follow the precept to be objective when treating matters of everyday life and personal commitment: "Of necessity, we have some idea of things or we could not accomplish our daily tasks. . . . However, these notions, which are formed without method in order to respond to practical exigencies, are devoid of all scientific merit" (Durkheim 1909a:284-85).

Durkheim specifically argued against a political context for the study of society and family.[2] He wished ideology to be removed from the scientific study, for the scholar to be neutral in analyzing family systems. No family type should be considered better than another:

> In science, beings are not one above another. They are only different because their milieux differ. There is no manner of being and living that is better for us to the exclusion of all other, and consequently it is not possible to classify them hierarchically. (Durkheim 1888a:272-73, and see 1910a:187).

On the one hand, Durkheim seemed to espouse a "value-free" sociology of the family. At the same time, he saw a tight connection between social science and morality and privileged the modern nuclear family: "What is domestic morality if not the description and explanation of the family under the most perfect form, that is to say, the most recent at which we have arrived" (Durkheim 1888a:273).

The Comparative Method

Durkheim's perspective on the study of the family was what a later classification of family theories would name *the institutional approach* (Hill and Hansen 1960; Sirjamaki 1964). It is to use the comparative method to analyze the family as an institution in historical and cross-cultural perspective:

> The sociologist cannot consider only a sole people, still less from a unique period. [H]e must compare societies of the same type and also those of different types, in order that the variations which the institution presents or the practice which he wishes to understand, brought together with parallel variations in the social milieu, in the state of ideas, etc., permit him to perceive relationships which unite the two groups of facts and establish between them some causal link. (Durkheim 1909a:282)

Durkheim advances what is essentially Campbell and Stanley's (1966) "quasi-experiment": "The experimenter sets up those variations when they are not given, but if they are produced naturally, is it not permitted to call this operation by which one compares them an indirect experiment?" (Durkheim 1888a:262).

The logic of concomitant variation undergirds the process of drawing conclusions from historical and contemporaneous comparisons. One must compare cases to see where the features are consistently present or absent. That comparison tells us whether two "social facts" or patterns are causally connected (Durkheim 1898h:307, 1909a:281-82). Durkheim was quick to criticize what he saw as a common practice of piling up data without doing the work of analysis and critical evaluation (Durkheim 1895c:77).

He defended the comparative method against its critics at a session of the Société Française de Philosophie:

> When, with regard to marriage, I authenticate at different points of the globe identical formalities and ceremonies, comparable on all points, when I find that men and women live together in the same way, you think there is nothing there worth comparing? (Durkheim 1908:236-37)

Durkheim (1908) argued that conclusions about the relationship between social organization and the family could be drawn on the basis of "a number of well-observed and well-studied" cases that indicate covariance (pp. 236-37). The materials used by Durkheim in the comparative study of the family range widely: ethnographic data, history, law, and statistical data.

Ethnography

Many a strange kin, marriage, or sexual practice (foreign to turn-of-the-twentieth-century Europe, that is) was described and analyzed in the pages of *Année sociologique*. Durkheim did not engage in actual fieldwork, nor did most of the Durkheimians (Vogt 1976b:42).[3] Rather, Durkheim read ethnographic reports published in Europe and North America. He relied particularly on Lewis Henry Morgan's (1871, [1877] 1964) studies of the Iroquois and his material on Hawaiians and Polynesians, reports on the Omaha tribe by Dorsey (1884; also Fletcher and LaFlesche 1911), and Spencer and Gillen's (1899, 1904) fieldwork with the Australian tribes. Durkheim also reviewed books and articles on African (Durkheim 1904h), Asian (Durkheim 1898e, 1898g, 1905f), Pacific (Durkheim 1899d), and Eastern European cultures and their family systems (Durkheim 1898j, 1913c). (To appreciate the extent of his erudition, one must peruse the *Année sociologique*.) Durkheim was an ethnographic pack rat, storing up and making use of every scrap of ethnographic data that came his way, not always to theoretical advantage when it meant squeezing unique societies into the same conceptual box.

Durkheim followed contemporary practice in referring to primitive tribes as "*sauvages*" (Durkheim and Fauconnet 1903:490). He frequently compared the behavior and thought processes of children to those of "early man" and to adults in contemporary primitive societies (e.g., Durkheim [1925] 1974:113, 115, 143). But he also had some insight into the tendency of contemporary Western Europeans to assume their superiority. Durkheim attributed the limitations of primitives to their social milieu, their lack of opportunity and lack of exposure to modern ways, rather than to some essential inferiority. In principle, Durkheim saw no essential difference between primitive and "cultivated" man, no ceiling on developmental potential, though "centuries of culture" can leave different peoples with different aptitudes. "The exterior causes, physical or social, have been the principal sources of differentials among peoples. . . . Can one say that there are races destined to never surpass a certain level? Nothing seems less established" (Durkheim 1913b:33).

As fascinating as details of culture could be, Durkheim constantly criticized his contemporaries for piling up facts while not subjecting them to a theoretical interpretation. His principal use for the ethnographic materials, so far as the family is concerned, was to use them in establishing his evolutionary theory. They were also central to his writings on totemism and for his later related work on religion and its social meaning (Durkheim [1912] 1979).

Durkheim also took pains to establish the point that family is a social institution and not a set of blood relationships. For this reason, he was less interested in such ephemeral (as he saw it) or unregulated relationships as cohabitation. He seemed rather less interested in betrothal and marital customs, giving them less analytic attention except as they reflected the tension between kinship and consanguinity.

Durkheim avoided some of the pitfalls of the melange of traveler's reports and early anthropology in circulation at the time. He had been quite critical, or at least reserved, about ethnography early on because of the risk of fantasy in amateur travelers' accounts of exotic peoples and customs (Durkheim 1895c:77-78; Lukes 1972:180-81). He never confused contemporary primitive societies with early prehistory. He did not accept a common but mistaken claim that early prehistoric societies were matriarchal. This was based on a confusion between lineage and residence on the one hand (which might be matrilineal and matrilocal) and authority on the other, typically avuncular in matrilineal societies (Durkheim 1898c:22, 1898f:325).

Some critics question Durkheim's presentation of the anthropological literature. Jones (1986) characterizes Durkheim as "determinedly ignorant of the ethnographic literature" (p. 157). He also states that Durkheim's use of ethnographic evidence was quite selective. He echoes the criticism of others who say that Durkheim used the Australian data to illustrate theories rather than constructing theories to account for the data, that ethnographic data were forced into Durkheim's theoretical model rather than being taken on their own terms (pp. 153-54). Bellah (1959), on the other hand, notes that other respected field ethnographers, such as Radcliffe Brown and W. L. Warner, have a favorable opinion of Durkheim's work on Australia: "remarkable contributions. . . . Most anthropologists who have criticized Durkheim for being an armchair ethnologist have never set eyes on Australia" (p. 456, fn 49).

I am not qualified to pronounce on the merits of early anthropologists or the accuracy of Durkheim's presentations of their work. Rather, I am interested in what image of the family emerges from Durkheim's use of ethnography. And that is his evolutionary theory. Durkheim's studies of historically recorded societies relied more on formal history, law, and statistics for analysis of the family.

History

Durkheim is sometimes thought to be ahistorical because he took such pains to distinguish the work of historians from that of sociologists (Durkheim and Fauconnet 1903).[4] In reality, his comments were directed toward the use of history in a generalizing and theoretical way: "History can only be a science to the extent that it explains, and one can explain only by making comparisons" (Durkheim 1898b:ii).

History was needed to explore causation. The moment in which a causal act took place or a social form came into existence could only be captured in the past. History was also needed to supply the links between various stages in an evolutionary theory (Durkheim 1909a:280-81).

Durkheim relied heavily on historical studies in putting together his own family theory and defending it using classical, ancient German, medieval, and modern sources.[5] He took a special interest in the Roman family, influenced by his mentor Fustel de Coulanges (although he did not hesitate to criticize Fustel's work on occasion).[6] Perhaps, Durkheim also valued studies of Rome for another reason; they depended very much on the analysis of law, data he saw as especially valid. Moreover, the Napoleonic Code of 1804 (the foundation for the French *Code Civil*) was largely based on Roman law and demonstrated an admiration for the power that Roman law had given to the paterfamilias or head of the patriarchal family (Dixon 1992:18; Glendon 1989:98).

Critics have noted that Durkheim typically used history to construct types. He derived "theories of tendency" based on an arraying of these types rather than bringing "close historical analysis" to bear on theory (Abrams 1982:28). Of course, abstraction from history is precisely what he set out to do! But it is perhaps not coincidental that what emerges in Durkheim's evolutionary theory or in his presentations of other specific societies is a historical trend from family collectivism to individuality. What Durkheim (1905c) portrays of Rome is a fading away of the *gens* or clan and a loosening of patriarchal control; in Greece, it is the trend from family collective responsibility for criminal conduct or civil liability to a more individualized responsibility. Durkheim's interpretations of history seem theory driven.

Law

In the nineteenth century, jurisprudence and sociology were not such disparate disciplines as they are today.[7] Durkheim lectured to law students and argued the importance of sociology for their work:

> It does contain a certain number of truths which can guide the jurist in his practice. . . . Those who are charged with applying domestic law . . . have a need to know what is the current situation of the family; what changes have been produced; what others are in preparation. (Durkheim 1888a:279)

Durkheim relied on law as a indicator of the structure of the family in various settings. He cited Roman law, Catholic matrimonial law, and nineteenth- and twentieth-century European codes. Durkheim particularly cited changes in Roman law over time and revisions of the French Civil Code as evidence for changing family structures and attitudes toward the family. The late nineteenth-century revision of French family law drew attention to the role law plays in setting social norms and strengthening or weakening various family forms. Durkheim's focus on law may have been shaped by the tendency for French law to be more specific and more controlling of family behavior than Anglo-Saxon law, for example, and that made it a more perfect indicator of the relationships of kin versus spouses, husbands and wives, and parents and children (Glendon 1981, 1989).[8]

"The family of the civil code" is a construct still used by legal scholars (Glendon 1989:292). Durkheim's interest in law was not surprising, given the rapid changes in European family law that occurred at the end of the nineteenth century and the beginning of the twentieth (Glendon 1981). The Napoleonic Code adopted in 1804 was replaced by the new *Code Civil* in 1892.

THE FAMILY OF THE CIVIL CODE

As part of the profound changes wrought by the French Revolution, important and dramatic changes in family law were adopted in 1792-93. One provided that inheritance should derive to family members as individuals ("partage forcé"), rather than property being preserved and passed on in toto to a principal (male) heir. Other changes included limitations on paternal power, emancipation at age twenty-one, the equivalency of legitimate and illegitimate children regarding inheritance, and marriage as a civil contract, with divorce available in certain limited circumstances. One could also think of the establishment of state control over education as a change in the family, because in the past, the family and the church had had complete control over the education of children.

Most revolutionary innovations were abandoned with the waning of revolutionary fervor, followed by the ascent of Napoleon. In 1804, the so-called Napoleonic Code, or *Code Civil,* was adopted, which systematized French law. The *Code Civil* took family law in a conservative direction, restoring some traditional ordering to the family and other institutions. Civil marriage was retained, which gave secular rather than religious authorities control over marriage and made the point of state oversight of the family. But in the "family of the civil code," the husband was head of the household, parental permission was required for marriage till the age of twenty-one for women and twenty-five for men, parents still had the right to be consulted about an adult child's marriage decision even after majority, and the revolutionary adoption of inheritance rights and equal status for nonmarital children was rescinded. Divorce was completed abolished in 1816. Many provisions of the law (e.g., restrictions on inheritance that placed kin before spouse and the involvement of kin-composed family councils in some family decisions, particularly for parentless children) indicated a resurgence of substantial recognition to the kin group despite the emergence of the conjugal household as "the family" (Nisbet 1966:37-38; Glendon 1981:32-33, 114-15; 1989:33, 41-43, 71-73, 97; Rheinstein 1972).

France continued to struggle with these issues. Divorce was restored in 1884 but with many restrictions. The proposed alternative of divorce by mutual consent was a hot topic in Durkheim's era. This proposal and other tensions and changes in law represented societal choices as to (a) the relative strength of the nuclear family vis-à-vis the extended family, (b) the vision of the family as a blood line or a set of personal attachments, (c) the autonomy of adult children or their dependency and submission to patriarchal authority, (d) the incorporation of women into the family or their treatment as temporary passersby, and (e) the individualism that permitted divorce as well as restricting the authority of the head of household. Durkheim was particularly preoccupied with inheritance laws as indicative of kinship ties (and see Habakkuk 1955 for the significance of inheritance laws). He also wrote on divorce (Durkheim 1906a).

FAMILY PRACTICES, CUSTOM, AND LAW

Durkheim treated legal codes as a major source of data for the study of modern societies. The analysis of law is an important method of studying the family because, for Durkheim, it is established customs, not spontaneous behavior and de facto alliances, that are indicators of family forms and practices. And how does one identify such a custom?

> By the fact that it is a manner of acting . . . [that is] not only habitual, but obligatory for all the members of a society. . . . It represents not simply what is most often done, but what must be done. . . . The existence of a sanction is the criterion which prevents confusing the custom with simple habits. (Durkheim 1888a:267)

Simple behavioral acts may not represent an institutional form:

> We encounter remarkable proofs of attachment . . . between spouses or between children and parents, in families where . . . the domestic bond is still weak and loose. [It is] . . . movements of individual sensibility which inspires these acts of solidarity . . . but they could very well not correspond to anything in the organic type of the family . . . which depends not on particular temperaments but on collective necessities . . . imposed on each by the force of tradition. (p. 266)

Durkheim valued the objectivity of the judicial criterion. He found "fixed, crystallized" mores that had become "positive law for to which the public authority assures respect by precise and material sanctions" to have "a higher degree of objective character" and thus to be a "more generally valuable document." He argued that an objective legal indicator was particularly important in the study of domestic society, which is so much a part of personal life as to be less consciously perceived (Durkheim 1888a:268, see also [1893] 1978:28-29). Moreover, only when a behavior or attitude is put into law does it have a full effect (Durkheim [1897a] 1930:307).

A juridical criterion does have some clarity, and Durkheim has produced a creative analysis of the kinship implications of inheritance laws. But reliance on legal codes to read family phenomena can be limiting or even mistaken. At least one scholar argues that the Roman father's actual relationships with his children as revealed in empirical research were often very different from the paterfamilias model presented as Roman law (Dixon 1992:31). Dixon states categorically that "The picture of Roman family relations that might be formed by a summary of legal rights is not a sound basis for understanding ancient kinship and its underlying principles" (p. 59).

Legalistic definitions of social phenomena have other limitations. Durkheim did not consider that law as an institution might reflect the interests of the powerful rather than the ideals of a society (Cotterrell 1991; and see Scheppele 1994 for a history and typology of critical legal studies). Defining the family narrowly, in terms of the legal model, excludes atypical families or de facto families (such as "marital" unions not legally formalized; cohabitation; informal adoption; extramarital unions that create, in effect, a polygamous family, etc.).

To some degree, Durkheim acknowledged the problem. He admitted that his legal criterion excluded family phenomena that might be worth studying, and he left some room for customs not formally put into law: "But if it is a question of using mores only with prudence (because they have something more indecisive and ephemeral), when they are well established they can furnish very useful information" (Durkheim 1888a:268). Thus, Durkheim qualifies his insistence on a legal criterion somewhat but not with certainty or precisely enough to help a scholar distinguish more valid from less valid indicators.

> The rule which we have just stated is not without inconvenience. Law and mores express only social changes which are already fixed and consolidated; consequently, they do not give us information on phenomena which have not yet arrived or which are not bound to arrive at that degree of crystallization. . . . Now, among those [phenomena] which remain . . . in a fluid state, so to speak, there are some which are very important. . . . Similarly, a legal institution can long outlast its reason for existence, it retains its character although the social phenomena which it encompasses are modified. . . . But however real this inconvenience is, it must not make us renounce the method of prudence which I have recommended earlier, for it would be much better to neglect some facts than to employ suspect ones. (Durkheim 1888a:270-71)

If formal concepts of law do not grasp the empirical diversity of family life, demographic data may do this better. With a sigh of relief, Durkheim (1888a) turned his students toward the demographic study of the contemporary family, where "we will be able to grasp with certainty the phenomena of domestic life, even if they do not take a legal form" (p. 271).

Moral Statistics

Statistical analysis is used to implement the comparative method by examining variations in social phenomena by time and place. The idea that statistical data could point to social problems is a postulate of the "moral statistics"[9] movement: "It is possible to estimate the comparative health or illness [of a society]" (Durkheim 1888b:447).

Durkheim explored a number of family characteristics and issues through statistical analysis, for example, fertility (Durkheim 1888b), household composition (Durkheim 1900i), and divorce (Durkheim 1906a). He listed the following as statistical indicators that might reveal important trends relative to the "conjugal morality" of a given country: not only rates of adultery but also marriage rates; ages of spouses; circumstances and duration of marriages; the number of single, divorced, and widowed persons; living arrangements of children; number of children per family; number of children raised outside the family, adoptions, and so forth (Durkheim 1901a:434-35). These are the very indicators we see in our government documents today. The Durkheimians also examined the gender and family status correlates of such social pathologies as suicide (Durkheim 1888b) and crime (Richard 1900). Suicide rates are treated as "a known fact" that translates social malaise into numbers (Durkheim 1888b:447).

France's foremost social statisticians in the nineteenth and early twentieth centuries were the unique Bertillon family, for whom statistics were a family business carried on through the generations. Young Jacques, as a child, constructed statistical indicators of seasickness by noting how many times family members leaned over the rail while crossing the English Channel (Clark 1973:139). In 1883, Jacques Bertillon became director of the statistical bureau of Paris, a post he was to occupy for thirty years. He edited the *Annales de Démographie Internationale,* taught at several institutions of higher learning, and played a leading role in various national and international statistical associations. Jacques was only one member of this statistical lineage. His grandfather had taken up the work of Quételet in creating statistical methods; his father had proceeded him in teaching and as head of the Paris bureau; his brother, Alphonse, initially the family ne'er-do-well, eventually became well known for his applications of quantitative methods to criminal justice. Brother Georges, too, published a few

papers. Until the second and third generations of Bertillons began to insti-
tutionalize the formal teaching of statistics, it had been essentially a trade
passed down through the family and taught to its apprentices (Clark 1968a,
1973:136, 138-42, and chap. 4 generally).

Durkheim's best known use of statistics is in his book on suicide
(Durkheim [1897a] 1930), but there are many other examples in his work,
including a study of the relationship between fertility and suicide published in 1888 (Durkheim 1888b). In *Suicide,* he cited an enormous
number of statistical studies done by others, including the pioneering
work of Morselli ([1879] 1882). We may think of Durkheim as originat-
ing the accumulation of empirical data to address social problems, but in
fact, this was common practice well before his studies. The various European countries had established statistical bureaus early in the nineteenth
century for the express purpose of examining problems of the urban working class and to evaluate measures taken against poverty, crime, and disease
(Clark 1973:123). The sociologist Tarde provided data on suicide for the
Ministry of Justice in his capacity as Chief of the Bureau of Legal Statistics (Clark 1968b), and Le Play ([1855] 1877-79) compiled data based
on interviews with workers and their families. Jacques Bertillon (1880)
wrote a book on *Human Statistics of France: Birth, Marriage, and Death,*
and he published articles comparing suicide and divorce rates in various
countries. These were foundational to Durkheim's work (Clark 1968a;
also Giddens 1964).[10]

While Durkheim's effort was not novel in one sense, in another sense
it was. For the most part, these vast accumulations of data were simply
that; there was little effort at theoretical interpretation. Bertillon was
somewhat more analytical, but Durkheim's work was rather pioneering
in using statistical data in connection with theory, to test causal attribu-
tions (Clark 1973; Giddens 1978:41-42; Porter 1995; Turner 1986:133,
1996:355). For example, Durkheim looked for the social causes common to suicide and fertility. Ruling out ethnicity by comparison of Norman
fertility in France to that in Canada, he finds the common cause to be a
"weakness of the domestic spirit" (Durkheim 1888b:462).

Durkheim was enthusiastic about "moral statistics" because the stability of statistical data patterns seemed to make generally valid statements
about causal relationships possible (Turner 1996:356, 370).

> If one can establish that fertility growth is associated with a rise in the
> number of suicides, one would have the right to infer from that that a too
> great fertility is maladaptive. A reverse verification implies a contrary con-
> clusion. (Durkheim 1888b:447).

This is but one example of Durkheim's interest in identifying the social forces underlying the phenomenon of interest. Previously, much

"interpretation" of data had simply been an overlay of the writer's own ideology—conservative Catholicism, in the case of Le Play (Clark 1973: 124). Durkheim's work was more scientific in the larger sense, not only systematic but theoretical. His use of statistics parallels his use of history: not simply an accumulation of facts about the unique case, but rather, the use of data to understand social forces (Durkheim and Fauconnet 1903; Turner 1996:368).

Commentary and Critique

The one-hundredth anniversary of Durkheim's (1895) *Rules of Sociological Method* was celebrated by a special issue of *Sociological Perspectives* (Turner 1995a). Throughout this long interval, Durkheim's methods, statistical and otherwise, have been studied and critiqued. Durkheim could be said to be in tune with the current preference for multimethod approaches to social research. His study of the origin and development of the family in Chapter 2 relied on ethnographic and historical studies, the latter often grounded in law. Law of the Roman era and the French *Code Civil* revealed the gradual overturning of extended family authority and property in favor of the conjugal or nuclear family, (to be discussed in Chapter 4). Statistical data provided the foundation for analysis of social problems and policy dilemmas regarding fertility, divorce, and poverty (Chapter 6).

Critiques of Durkheim's methods are numerous in the literature, including the recent reconsideration of the *Rules* (Turner 1995a). His biographers chime in to make some critical points. LaCapra ([1972] 1985) notes that Durkheim's historical and ethnographic writings "play havoc with the relationships of logic and time," (p. 119) despite his statements about genetic links needed to establish historical continuity. The inevitability with which Durkheim looks at societies and finds a historical trend of structural differentiation and a corresponding transformation of social relationships from collectivism to individualism raises questions about whether his interpretation of history is dogma rather than being anchored in empirical science. Abrams (1982) concludes, speaking of the *Division of Labor* (Durkheim ([1893] 1978) that "Durkheim's type of historical sociology seems to have been something of a failure" because of its reliance on logic rather than being grounded in historical actuality. Yet he goes on to judge it a "fruitful and constructive contribution to historical sociology" in its general potential for theory and the development of historical scholarship (Abrams 1982:30-31).

With regard to law, Durkheim made a clear choice in favor of rule-based definitions of the family, which meant he left out much that others might have included in their studies. Many have criticized his statistical data and reasoning even in the context of his times. The use of statistics to infer causality and awareness of methodological problems in statistical inference was rather advanced at this time. But Durkheim often appeared to pay no attention to known pitfalls, and he made errors of both calculation and analytic strategy. It is also the case that his statistical approach simply lost ground to other modes of analysis without necessarily being mistaken (Besnard 1973; Giddens 1978:114-19; Porter 1995; Turner 1986:135-38, 1995b, 1996).[11]

The other side of the coin of Durkheim's multiplicity of methods is a methodological fragmentation of his work on the family, with varying methods applied to different problems. These are barely held together by evolutionary theory, resonance with his other work, and the endless repetition of his conclusions. The casual reader may notice the hop-skip-and-jump character of Durkheim's work on the family. The Durkheim scholar, though, sees that the quilt is stitched together, forming a whole with Durkheim's overall body of work.

While Durkheim's study of ethnography and history was not empirical, "the Durkheimians approached largely extant data with a fresh theoretical framework" (Vogt 1976b:42). The same could be said of their use of statistics, and Turner (1996) refers to the "methodological and conceptual novelty" of Durkheim's work (p. 374). A broad view of Durkheim's methodology gives us some important principles, still valid today. We accept that the family can be studied scientifically despite its emotional context and the "natural attitude" we hold toward the family (McLain and Weigert 1979; Schutz 1970). Durkheim's comparative method of analyzing ethnographic and historical data makes the statement that family and society are closely connected. While structure-functionalists, such as Parsons, did situate the family in a larger social context, there was also much sociology through the middle of the twentieth century that treated the family as a thing apart. Family sociology of the "marital adjustment" school[12] was something of an isolated niche, in little contact with the rest of the discipline. Many sociologists took little interest in the family and made no attempt to relate their focus to family relations.

Durkheim's focus on law supports an interactive view of law and society that fits nicely with contemporary interest in law and the family (McIntyre 1995). This kind of analysis was earlier known as the "institutional approach" to the study of the family. Although a few sociologists of mid-twentieth-century exemplify this approach (notably, Bernard Farber 1964, 1973, 1981), the institutional approach languished for many years while other twentieth-century sociologists largely concentrated their attention on family interaction and the family life cycle. The institutional perspective was declared dead in a 1971 review of conceptual frameworks on the family (Broderick 1971). At least, it was not distinguishable from the use of the comparative method in structure-functional theory (this theory to be discussed in more detail in Chapter 4).

The rise of social history in the 1960s devoted much attention to the changing shape of the family. With the more recent return of attention to political economy and to conflict theories that took a broad view of family and society, the kind of interests that Durkheim displayed in macrosocial change and connections of the family to other social institutions were much more in tune with the direction of sociology than they had been in the middle of the twentieth century. Current family policy concerns have focused attention on family law (Weitzman 1981, 1985 are but two examples) and so made Durkheim's preoccupation with family property and the legal regulation of family relations seem less quaint than they might have some thirty years ago. Durkheim's evolutionary perspective also emphasizes macrosocial analysis and social change.

We turn from methods back to substance in the next chapter, exploring the changing relationship of marriage to kinship and the role of the state as the third point of a family triangle. Theoretical perspectives to be discussed in Chapter 4 include structure-functional theory and Durkheim's application of a rudimentary systems theory to the waxing and waning of family forms.

Notes

1. For Durkheim, it was very much "the sociologist . . . he" or "the scientist . . . he." I have decided not to introduce gender-neutral terminology into quotations or in describing Durkheim's thought so as to avoid anachronism.

2. Gouldner (1970) asserts that Durkheim was guided in this by a desire to distinguish sociology from socialism (p. 135).

3. The term *the Durkheimians* refers to the cluster of sociologists around Durkheim. By and large, they were also connected to the *Année sociologique*. Detailed descriptions of this school of late nineteenth- and early twentieth-century sociology are presented in Besnard's (1983) *The Sociological Domain* and Clark's (1973) *Prophets and Patrons*. Clark also discusses competing schools of sociologists.

4. Vogt (1976b) describes the Durkheimians' predominant attitude toward history as "unfriendly" (p. 39), but that might be better stated as their attitude toward historians. Vogt is correct that the Durkheimians themselves "did little work in historical sociology" (p. 40).

5. Critics have pointed out that despite Durkheim's rhetoric about his articulation of the function and importance of history for sociology, his treatment of the division of labor is notably unhistorical. . . . "[I]t is clear that although he talks of historical law, he is in fact much more interested in the *logical* [italics added] connection between the two types of societies he has constructed than in their historical connection." (Abrams 1982:27)

He only notes concrete historical fact in discussing the "abnormal forms" (p. 27).

6. Durkheim thought that Fustel erred in not considering the Roman *gens* in the context of similar family types described by ethnographers (Durkheim 1898b:ii, 1905c:465).

7. A present-day scholar goes so far as to claim that "sociology . . . grew out of jurisprudence" (Scheppele 1994:383).

8. For a comprehensive discussion of Durkheim's sociology of law not limited to family law, see Vogt (1993).

9. For more detail on "moral statistics," see Clark (1968a, 1973). For a history and discussion of statistical developments in Europe and the United States as they relate to Durkheim's work, see Porter (1995) and Turner (1986, 1995b, 1996).

10. Despite the overlapping interests of Durkheim and Bertillon, Durkheim had mixed responses to Bertillon's work. On the one hand, in the "Introduction" to his course on the family, Durkheim (1888a) refers students to Bertillon's work and says that he himself plans to use those demographic data in his expository lectures (p. 271). In other writings, Durkheim (1906a) was quite critical of Bertillon.

Bertillon never joined with the Durkheimians in the *Année* school but rather, sat on the editorial board of René Worms's *Revue Internationale de Sociologie,* the organ of a competing, though less influential, school of sociologists (Clark 1968a:70, and see Clark 1973, chap. 5).

11. Turner (1995b, 1996) discusses in detail the level of statistical association accepted by Durkheim as probative and also other aspects of his statistical and methodological reasoning, with reference to Quételet, various German statisticians, Morselli, and to John Stuart Mill's rules of inference.

With regard to *Suicide* (Durkheim [1897a] 1930), scholars have continued to test Durkheim's theory against empirical data, with some confirmatory results (e.g., Besnard 1997; Danigelis and Pope 1979). *Emile Durkheim: Suicide One Hundred Years Later,* a centennial volume on his theory and research on suicide evidences Durkheim's inspiration of later scholars (Lester 1998).

12. By this I mean, for example, Burgess and Wallin's (1953) *Engagement and Marriage* and the like. Their focus was on microlevel empirical examination of the correlates of marital success.

4

The Family System

Kin, Conjugal Family, and the State

Marriage founds the family.
—Durkheim (1909b:280)

The forms of domestic life, even the most ancient and the most far removed from our mores, have not completely ceased to exist, but there remains something of it in the family of today.
—Durkheim (1888a:263)

Chapter 2 traced the family's development over time, Durkheim's evolutionary theory of the family. But what did the family look like to Durkheim analytically? In terms of its separate components, the family appears as a system in which kin, the conjugal family, and the state maintain a dynamic equilibrium.

Elements of the Family System

In the introductory lecture of his course on the family, Durkheim (1888a) identifies the elements of the family system as *kin, spouses, children,* and *the state*. He states that the next step in the study of the family should be an investigation of "how these elements function, that is, what relations unite them to one another, the complete system of these relations . . ." (p. 260).

To capture Durkheim's outline of the family system, it is necessary to present this section of the course in its entirety:

KIN

1. *Relations of the husband with his own relatives and those of his wife.*
2. *Relations of the wife with her own relatives and those of her husband*
   a. *with regard to persons.*
   b. *with regard to property.*
      (Emancipation by marriage; Dowry; Inheritance law; Guardianship; Kinship through marriage, its nature and consequences)
3. *Relations of the children with paternal and maternal relatives*
   a. *with regard to persons.*
   b. *with regard to property.*
      (Family council;[1] Guardianship; Inheritance law; etc.)

SPOUSES

1. *Relations of future spouses to the act establishing the family (marriage).*
   (Marriageable age; Consent; Absence of a prior marriage; Monogamy; Absence of kinship of the prohibited degree; etc.).
2. *Relations between the spouses with regard to persons.*
   (Respective rights and duties of the spouses; Nature of the conjugal bond: Dissolubility or indissolubility, etc.)
3. *Relations between the spouses with regard to property.*
   (Dowry system; Community or separation of property; Gifts; Inheritance law; etc.)

CHILDREN

1. *Relationships of the children with their parents with regard to persons.*
   (Paternal power; Emancipation; Majority, etc.)
2. *Relationships of the children with their parents with regard to property.*
   (Inheritance; Law on the reservation of a share of the estate for the child; The child's own property; Parental custodianship)
3. *Relationships of the children to each other.*
   (Currently, they reduce almost to inheritance law).

THE STATE

1. *General intervention of the state as it sanctions domestic law.*
   (The family as a social institution)
2. *Specific intervention in the relationships between future spouses.*
   (Solemnization of the marriage)

3. *Specific intervention in the relation between spouses.*
   (Substitution of the court for the husband in certain authorizations)
4. *Specific intervention in the relations between parents and children.*
   (Concurrence of the court in the exercise of paternal power; Security for the child; Draft bill on the forfeiture of paternal authority)
5. *Specific intervention in kin relationships.*
   (In family councils; In petitions for injunctions) (Durkheim 1888a:260-62)

Durkheim's presentation divides family relations into those of *property* and *persons*. This dichotomy occurred frequently in his analysis of the family and other institutions (Durkheim 1950) and follows the French Civil Code (Glendon 1989:97). In the "Introduction" to the family course, *both* aspects of family relations are specified primarily in legal terms. The reliance on law, rather than mores, to evidence elements of the family system, is necessary, according to Durkheim (1888a), because it is difficult to determine mores (p. 261, fn 1).

MAPPING THE SYSTEM

The family system contains three primary elements: (a) kin, (b) conjugal family, and (c) the state. In the conjugal family, children form a subsystem secondary to the spouses, their parents. There are also kin subsystems.

Durkheim saw the conjugal family to be the essence of the family of his time. And he saw the spouses as the only permanent members of that family in the sense that in the normal course of events, children would leave home, perhaps for further schooling or work and certainly to marry and found independent families. Although spouses could divorce or children could fail to follow the expected pattern, as a type, the married couple *is* the family in the long term. When one spouse dies (or the couple is divorced), that conjugal family is dissolved. For this reason, Durkheim detaches children from parents in presentation of the family system. As minors, they are subordinate to their parents. As adults, they part from parents to create their own conjugal families.

Durkheim lists all possible relationships among the parties. We can imagine a large blackboard, with lines drawn here and there. With reference to the conjugal family, we have the following relationships:

Husband to wife (and the future spouses to each other prior to marriage)

Husband to his kin

Husband to wife's kin

Wife to husband (during and prior to marriage)

Wife to her kin

Wife to husband's kin

Parents to children

Siblings to each other

Relationships between the conjugal family as a unit and kin are acknowledged in terms of "specific intervention in kin relationships" and also in some of the inheritance provisions. There is also the relationship of the state to each member of the conjugal family (Durkheim 1888a:260-62).

GENDER

It is interesting that in Durkheim's presentation of his initial course on the family, there is no direct note taken of gender. Reference to "the respective rights and duties of the spouses" contains no acknowledgment of gender differences. While the gender-differentiated terms *husband* and *wife* appear, the gender-neutral terms *spouse* (used in a context that gives its meaning as generic rather than male) or *parent* are more often employed. In sum, no substantive gender distinction is made with regard to roles and relationships in the family in this organizational chart of the family (Durkheim 1888a).

This is surprising, for "spouse" is a relationship that was definitely asymmetrical in French law before, during, and after Durkheim's time. The husband was "head of the family" until 1970. Between 1881 and 1907, married women's property laws were passed, giving women control over their earnings and inherited or gifted property, but women had to have their husband's permission to work outside the home until 1965. Even as parents, men and women differed in their legal status. Parental authority over children was clearly paternal and remained so until 1942. Even after parents' authority was conceptualized as joint, it was exercised by the father until 1970. He retained the sole right to administer the children's property until 1985 (Glendon 1989:88-89, 97-98, 111).

The gender-neutral labeling of husbands and wives, mothers and fathers in Durkheim's family course ignores the differentiation of men and women highlighted in his other work, including *The Division of Labor* (Durkheim [1893] 1978) on which he was working at around the same time.[2] Durkheim simply did not come to grips with gender in the early presentation of his family course (Chapter 7 gives fuller attention to Durkheim on gender).

THE CHANGING FAMILY SYSTEM

The story of the family in French history is the story of the tension between couple and kin epitomized by the epigrams introducing this chapter. The epigrammatic quotations from Durkheim's work describe the emergence of marriage as the foundation of the family, while kin still lurk in the background. Davy's summary of Durkheim's course describes an opposition, a primordial struggle, between marriage and the kin group, which does not wish to yield its ancient rights and authority (Davy 1925:81-82).

Durkheim wrote about transformations in the family system with a degree of detail that goes beyond his grand narrative of structural differentiation. System change is captured in analysis of the relative power of marriage versus kinship, parents over children, and the state in relation to other elements of the system. The transformation of the family presented in Durkheim's theory seems closely linked to the empirical details of changes in French family law. In presenting the preeminence of the conjugal family, Durkheim observed that changes in law in the 1890s gave spouses relatively more status as heirs than they had had previously, rather than treating them as extraneous to the family. From pre-Revolutionary times to Durkheim's era, the trend of French inheritance law was away from a corporate, kin-based construction of the family, in which children were family members while spouses were viewed as temporary guardians of family property. Both Davy's notes on Durkheim's 1892 course and Glendon, writing in the 1980s, stress the degree to which French law *remains* oriented to the family lineage. Nevertheless, Durkheim was correct in marking the *change* from former, more limited rights for the spouse (Davy 1925:79-82; Glendon 1981:11-23, 1989:246-49).

With regard to parent-child relations, Durkheim noted that changes in law fully emancipated adult children save for a need to respectfully seek parental advice about marriage. Previously, in pre-Revolutionary times and in the 1804 Civil Code, the law had provided parents (the father) with considerable power over adult children, including the right to approve their marriages. Over time, the age at which adult children *must* have parental permission to married was lowered (Glendon 1989:41-42, 97-98).[3]

Kinship

In beginning with kin, Durkheim linked his family system to evolutionary theory. Circles of kin represent survivals of earlier evolutionary forms:

> The modern family contains in it, in abridged version, all the historical development of the family, where, if it is not correct to say that all the familial types are found in the current type . . . , at least it is true of many. (Durkheim 1888a:263-64)

ZONES OF KINSHIP

Both evolutionary and system perspectives on the family highlight the modern dominance of the conjugal family. At the same time, kinship is retained. Around the central zone of the conjugal family are clustered secondary zones of kinship that are the remnants of former family forms.

The first zone outward from the conjugal family is composed of proximate ascendants and descendants. For ego,[4] these include his[5] parents and grandparents, brothers and sisters, and their descendants. This zone derives from the *paternal family* stage of evolution, which retains a role in modern times. These kin are secondary heirs who take the estate in the absence of children. They are eligible to be appointed to family councils, which act as parental substitutes and monitors of the marriage (Glendon 1981:15).[6]

The next zone outward contains more distant kin, counted to the sixth or seventh degree or more. This broader kinship derives from the male-based agnatic family. But now, extended kinship is bilateral. Ties to ego are weak; all that remains is the remote possibility of inheritance. The clan-family, which survived as an outer zone in previous stages, no longer exists, even vaguely (Durkheim 1921:5-6).

FAMILY COMMUNISM

Until modern times, kinship meant common economic interests. According to Durkheim (1921), all domestic societies except the conjugal family are based on "family communism:" Property and other economic resources are shared by the kin group (p. 3).[7]

Durkheim associated the clan-family and subsequent kin-based family forms with real property holdings that belonged collectively to the corporate family. The importance of landed property had less to do with its agricultural use than its sacral character as a symbol of the cult of the family (Durkheim 1950:181-83). In a traditional society, leaving the economic community of shared land meant leaving kin relations and was seldom done. "Under this [collective property] regime, persons are possessed by things at least as much as things [are possessed] by persons" (p. 193).

As the family contracts, says Durkheim, so does the extent of family communism. Presently, it exists only within the conjugal family and even there, only vestigially; it is no longer the basis of solidarity. The conjugal family is time limited, formed as it is by a marriage and dissolved on the death of one of the spouses. Because the conjugal family exists only during the lifetime of the spouses, there is no sense of family patrimony. Children are heirs, to be sure, but the community of marital property and some degree of testamentary freedom preclude the kin group from passing property intact through the bloodline. The property is not available to a wide circle of kin for their maintenance and benefit. Durkheim noted that even children could be partially (in France) or fully (in other European countries) disinherited in his time (Durkheim 1921:9).

Property and Persons

Family communism no longer works as it once did because of the individualism built into the conjugal family. In traditional society, property dominated personal life. Attachment to the land and family property for its symbolic as well as economic importance took precedence over individual desires and ambitions. But over a long and unspecified period of time, property became individualized, used to serve the needs of family members. A first step occurred in Rome, when property was formally concentrated in the hands of the paterfamilias (who held property in the name of the family, to be sure). Now, "man is above things" (Durkheim 1950:198).[8]

A second impetus for the individualization of family property came with the development of an industrial and commercial economy. In this economy, property was not only portable and easily divisible but also lacked a sacral character so far as symbolization of the family was concerned (Durkheim 1950:194-200).

Furthermore, in modern society, the "cult of the individual" characterizes social relations and moral values (Durkheim 1898a, 1950:68-78), and that also changes how the relationship of people to property is thought of. Family communism requires a sense of common identity that puts keeping the family patrimony intact above the interests and circumstances of individuals (Davy 1925:105-106). As the family circle contracts, individuality and personality emerge ever more strongly. With that centrifugal pull, property no longer coheres. In the conjugal family, all that remains of family communism is the parents' right of usufruct (usage) of the child's property until he reaches sixteen and the right of children to a specified inheritance share (Durkheim 1921:4, 8-9).

As Durkheim writes about the erosion of kinship and family communism, he seemed to give law a causal role in this process. Not only did the family circle contract by reason of changing social conditions (as described in Chapter 2), but the law itself played an important part in this transformation. When testamentary freedom appeared in law, it paralyzed the secondary zones of kinship by destroying family communism.

The Marital Community

"While communism disappeared from domestic society [i.e., kin], it re-appeared in the matrimonial society" (Durkheim 1921:12). In earlier family systems, spouses were treated as outsiders. Wives were entitled to economic support for the duration of the marriage and some protection as widows, husbands could manage the wife's property, but spouses were not co-owners of family property.

Development of a marital community of property is often attributed to the arrival of Christianity in Europe, elevating both marriage and the status of women. According to Durkheim (1904h), that is mistaken. The marital community emerged in the Germanic (paternal) family prior to the rise of Christian marriage (p. 438). Among the Germans, a woman was considered the partner of her husband (Durkheim 1913a:435). From the Germanic beginning, community property emerged as the "normal regime of marriage" (p. 436). Durkheim associated the community prop-erty regime with historical progress around the globe: "The more one advances in history, the more the society of spouses advances to first rank and becomes the essential and permanent element of the family . . . [in all] civilized countries" (p. 436).[9]

Durkheim's evolutionary scheme and family system models require the conjugal couple to be the new holders of family property. Community property as a regime of marital property is appropriate to evolving conju-gal solidarity. But in fact, the economic communism of marriage was quite limited in France. A surviving spouse was indeed entitled to half of the property, his or her share of the community. However, the other half of the property went to a retained share for children of the marriage and a residual estate that could be disposed of by testament. The husband or wife did not have to leave any of this portion of the property to the spouse. There were other restrictions on the community that disadvantaged the spouse: Real estate owned prior to the marriage or gifted to one of the spouses was not included (Davy 1921:79-82 reporting the law as of 1892). Durkheim himself noted with disapproval that "at least in our law, the husband is head of that [marital] society [which holds the common prop-erty]" (1913a:435, 437). To this day, French law severely restricts the portion of an estate that can be willed to a spouse.[10] From 1803 to 1917, kin from the fourth to the twelfth degree had priority over the spouse when there was no will (Davy 1925:82; Glendon 1981:24, 1989:246-48).

This is so striking a contrast to legal systems in other European coun-tries and the United States[11] that it suggests kinship remained very visible in France despite Durkheim's assertion of its weakening.[12] And note that Durkheim (1921) continues to use the word "family" for kin (p. 14). Is this contradiction of law (the persistence of kinship) and theory (the triumph of the conjugal family) an indication that Durkheim tended to give an analytic scheme priority over empirical reality? Or is the legal change, the weakening of kin power that did occur, so dramatic that it reasonably dominated the analysis?[13]

The tension between spouse and kin as heirs reflects the historic struggle of the conjugal family to emancipate itself from kin dominance. Durkheim's interest in inheritance fits his methodological commitment to law as an objective indicator of social phenomena (Durkheim [1895a] 1956:45). Certainly, the disposition of property is more measurable than the emotional climate of the family. On the other hand, Durkheim's reading of the law as evidencing the fading of family communism is somewhat suspect, given the remaining provisions in French law that continued to limit inheritance by spouses. In discounting those, he seemed to depart from his legal criterion. Still, spouses had more inheritance rights in Durkheim's time than they had had in the past.

Durkheim thought that inheritance would eventually be abolished completely. The French Revolution had abolished hereditary offices and titles; Durkheim expected wealth inheritance to follow. He favored the elimination of inheritance as a necessary condition for a merit-based society (Durkheim 1921:10-11). Contrary to his prediction and hope, this did not happen.

FICTIVE KINSHIP

A 1964, modification of French family law required that a judge not rely solely on kinship in appointing a family council but to consider the actual relationships people have had with their relatives. The judge may appoint "friends, neighbors, or any persons who seem . . . to have concern for the child" (Glendon 1981:20). The quasi-equivalence of kin and non-kin in this context brings to mind the concept of fictive kinship.

Durkheim (1899e) took considerable interest in "artificial kinship" (p. 321). In many societal settings, persons who are neither blood nor affinal kin are incorporated into the kinship system. Blood or affinal kin may have their family status altered, as in adoption of a son-in-law by his father-in-law. Present-day examples of fictive kinship are the godparent relationships of Catholic cultures, the "going for brothers [or] sisters" of African-American communities (Stack 1974), and complex networks of quasi-kin created by divorce and remarriage (Stacey 1990; Tiger 1978).

"Parrain" and "marraine" relationships (godparents or sponsors at confirmation) and those created by being honor attendants at a wedding were recognized by Durkheim (1899g) as creating kinship. He also noted other forms of fictive kinship described in ethnographic materials: the kinship of those joining the same pilgrimage, infants who share the same baptismal water or wet nurse, those who aid each other in escaping from a situation of danger, persons who agree to be brothers and sisters ("blood brothers"), or married couples who convert their relationship into a sibling one (Durkheim 1899e).[14]

Durkheim examined adoption in detail. Adoption has many purposes: to recruit candidates for hereditary offices, to provide an heir or to designate a preferred heir, to ensure a responsible party for kin-based religious rituals, to create parent-child relationships for their intrinsic emotional satisfaction, and, generally, to establish a family (Durkheim [1893] 1978:184-88, 1899f, 1905f).

There are significant limitations on fictive kinship, adoption at least, and Durkheim (1905f) drew conclusions about "the very great resistance that normal kinship appears to have placed in opposition to the encroachment of adoptive kinship" (p. 412). While clearly intrigued by fictive kinship, Durkheim continually returned to the notion that *all* kinship is constructed rather than consanguineal (Durkheim 1899e:323).

THE POLITICS OF KINSHIP

Much of Durkheim's sociology of the family highlights the struggle between the conjugal couple and kin for control of "the family (e.g., Durkheim 1913a; 1921; Davy 1925)." This is a battle he declares won by the conjugal family.

> The kin-based family, on the one hand, and the conjugal society, on the other, are two antagonists who could not develop side-by-side. If the first is strong, if it has a passionate sense of its unity—expressed in family communism—it opposes that anything of that patrimony pass into the hands of a stranger. For the [marital] community of property to become established, it is necessary that the society formed by the two spouses, instead of remaining absorbed in the group of relatives, disengages itself to constitute itself apart and become the principal center of family life. (1913a, p. 436)

Durkheim appears as one who valued the trend away from kin control. Perhaps he is more unromantic about the extended family than we might have thought from his concern about social cohesion, perhaps because he was closer in time to the coercive control of the kin group. In siding theoretically with the conjugal family against coercive kinship control, Durkheim ([1893] 1978) was taking a stand in favor of contemporary developments in the French family and family law—much as he spoke for the acceptance of modern society more generally.

The State

To include the state as a part of the family system may seem startling, and perhaps it is an overstatement of Durkheim's position. Yet his outline in the introduction to the family and his treatment of the role played by the state portrays the state's deep involvement in the basic structure of the family. "The conjugal family would not have been born from the patriarchal family [or paternal family or mix of the two] without the intervention of a new factor: the state" (Durkheim 1921:4).

The state is essentially a benign force in Durkheim's narrative. The state served as a lever to separate the conjugal family from kin and, within the conjugal family, to limit the authority of the patriarch over individuals, women and children in particular.

The detachment of the conjugal family from the larger kin group presented an opportunity for the emergence of desirable human sentiments and offered an appropriate setting for modern individuality: "The same reasons that have the effect of progressively restricting the family circle also permit the development of the personalities of family members" (Durkheim 1921:8). In his *Leçons de Sociologie*, Durkheim (1950) referred positively to "the cult of the individual" (p. 70) and linked the growth of the modern state to that of individuality. "Individualism increases with statism" (Durkheim 1900j:370). This is so because the state keeps other components of society from attaining sufficient power to oppress the individual. Of course, the state itself could potentially turn tyrannical and thus needed to be balanced by other forces (Durkheim 1902a).[15] (Individuality and autonomy will be discussed in more detail in Chapter 5).

Durkheim did not mean for this favorable view of both individualism and the state to mean the destruction of the family. "There are no rights except those of individuals and the state" was a principle of the French Revolution, implying the elimination not only of the church and other macro institutions of the *ancien régime* but even to some degree the family (Glendon 1989:298-99). This was not Durkheim's program. While he saw the conjugal family as insufficiently long lasting to be the basis of societal cohesion, it played an important role for its members and carried out crucial social functions. The conjugal family "has to exercise on the ensemble of our life a moral action of primordial importance. There is its true function" (Durkheim 1909b:281).

In a rather dispassionate way, Durkheim (1921) observed that "what is new and most distinctive [of the conjugal family] is the ever-growing intervention of the state in the domestic life of the family" (p. 4). "When formerly it was a stranger to domestic life, more and more it regulates it and supervises its functioning" (Durkheim 1909b:262).[16] Nevertheless, as a source of leverage against kin domination, the state appears in Durkheim's work on the family as a liberating force.

In pre-Revolutionary times, the state typically supported paternal power. Fathers had virtually unlimited power over minor children, including what education they could obtain. Paternal authority over children was true not only for minors but, in some respects, also for adult children, as fathers had to consent to marriage. In Durkheim's time (in 1907), parental control over marriage ceased to be operative, although a marriage could be delayed by legal maneuvering, allegations of other impediments to the marriage (Glendon, 1989:36, 41-43, 97).

The state could intervene where paternal power over minor children was deemed too harsh in application.[17] Paternal power had begun to attract state oversight even before the French Revolution. With the Revolution, state intervention into the family to counteract unlimited paternal power was put into law. Family councils were established, the age of majority was lowered, emancipation from paternal authority was recognized at majority, fathers were somewhat limited in their power to disinherit children, and education became compulsory so that a child's right to be education was not subject to parental approval (Hunt 1992:40-41, 66-67). Fathers were limited in their disciplinary rights over the person of the minor, and fathers exceeding normal limits might have their authority completely revoked (Carlson 1988:232-34). Durkheim (1921) itemized interventions authorized by law:

Correction of the father who goes too far in the exercise of his power

Presiding over family councils or boards of guardians

Taking charge of minor orphans who do not yet have a guardian

Issuing injunctions against specific paternal actions

Complete revocation of paternal power (p. 4; also Davy 1925:116-17)

At the same time that the state is a liberating force, it is also a stabilizing force. The state is responsible for what Durkheim considers a very significant characteristic of the conjugal family: the indissolubility of family ties.[18] In earlier family forms, ties of kinship could be broken by the family member who wished to leave (in agnatic or paternal families) or by the father (in the patriarchal family). "With the conjugal family, kinship ties are entirely indissoluble. It is the state that guarantees them, and thus removes from individuals the right to break them" (Durkheim 1921:4). A third function of the state (as we shall see in Chapter 6) is its ability to facilitate equality, to the benefit of poorer families and their children.

In analyzing the relationship of state and family, Durkheim anticipated Litwak's (1965) theory of "shared functions." In a modern society, other institutions have taken over many of the family's original functions. But

the family can collaborate with these specialized institutions. In a structurally differentiated society, state, other institutions, and family can work
together:

> Originally, the life of the family included almost all forms of social activ-
> ity: economic, religious, even judicial. Little by little the different functions
> left the domestic setting and were organized and developed outside: in the
> workshop, the factory, the office, the church, the court. However, the fam-
> ily kept something of its original role. If it is no longer directly foundational
> to these diverse manifestations of collective life, nevertheless, there are not
> any of them to which it is irrelevant. . . . All that touches [the economic,
> religious, political, and judicial life of the members, touches the family]. It
> has the task of aiding in the efforts that they make in these different direc-
> tions. (Durkheim 1909b:280-81; also Davy 1925:113)

All in all, Durkheim's presentation of the state's role vis-à-vis the family is an appreciative one. Even when the state intervenes in opposition to
paternal authority, that is viewed as enhancing family life by protecting
children from a harsh and damaging environment that violates social
norms. The observation that "the state has become a factor in domestic
life" (Durkheim 1921:4), part of the family system as it were, is seen by
Durkheim as supportive rather than confrontational to the family.

The Conjugal Family

We have examined two elements of the family system as it emerges in
Durkheim's perspective on the family: kin and state. Now, we go to the
heart of the family of his time, the conjugal family, "the most perfect form.
. . . at which we have arrived" (Durkheim 1888a:274). The conjugal family consists of the husband, wife, and their minor and unmarried children
(Durkheim 1921:20). There are three subsystems or types of relationships
in the conjugal family: husbands and wives, parents and children, and siblings. Of these, the conjugal relationship is the most central.

HUSBANDS AND WIVES

In the conjugal family, marriage assumes an importance it did not have in
previous evolutionary stages. Earlier, marriage served only to bring members into the family (Durkheim 1898i:342), rather tenuous members at
that. Now the marital couple *is* the essential family. Durkheim (1921)
notes the following in support of his claim that marriage has been sig-
nificantly elevated in modern society: (a) marriage is now a public act,

not a private contract; (b) it is entered into through certain legal formulas; (c) marriage is almost impossible to dissolve; and (d) monogamy is nearly perfect—that is, free unions have no legal force, thus no social importance (pp. 12, 14).

A qualitative difference between the conjugal family and earlier forms is that marriage is now a personal rather than property relationship (Durkheim 1921:14). At the same time, it is a personal relationship comprising *rights and duties,* not simply domesticity and emotional attachment. Durkheim seeks to capture the Janus-faced character of the family as part of the "personal or interpersonal sphere" *and* the "institutional sphere,"—"this two-edged formulation of the family in social space" (Morgan 1985:285-86).

A significant event was the appropriation by the state of the right to certify marital union (Durkheim 1909b:259, 261-62). One of the few family reforms of the French Revolution that remained unchanged under the Napoleonic regime and its royal and republican successors was compulsory civil marriage. Whereas marriage previously had two forms, formal legal marriage and informal free union, the latter lost its validity under the Civil Code (Glendon 1989:24-34).

Durkheim (1895b) made a sharp distinction between legal marriage and free union (what we would call cohabitation), arguing that

> One is a simple statement of fact [that a couple cohabits and maintains a sexual relationship] that the written or customary law neither recognizes nor sanctions, while the other by the simple fact of its existence creates legal obligations of the parties who form it, that is, rights and duties to which are attached organized sanctions. . . . [I]t often happens that free unions have the same duration without becoming regular marriages. . . . Lovers who remain united all their lives are not, for that, spouses. (pp. 612-13)

Similarly, Durkheim ([1895a] 1956) distinguished between monogamy in marriage in *fact* and in *law* (pp. 37-38).

PARENTS AND CHILDREN

Durkheim followed the spirit of the French Revolution in its opposition to paternal autocracy. Fathers were deemed important but as "good" fathers, who nurture their children (Hunt 1992:65-67, 163-64, 190 and chaps. 2 and 6 generally).

In Durkheim's time, the minor child was dependent on the father, who could control his person and fortune. The child had no civil status but was represented by the father and under his tutelage until age twenty-one and—Durkheim noted—even after his majority, so far as marriage is con-cerned.[19] But the father has a corresponding obligation to nurture and educate the child (Durkheim 1921:2).

Even in the child's minority, the state may intervene in his interest. And what is especially significant about the modern conjugal family is that once the child is married, the parent-child relationship is severed. Even if the child remains living with the parents, there are no legal implications. All that remains are an obligation to provide for parents in need and an entitlement to a fixed share of the family estate. The modern conjugal family has done away with the perpetual dependency characteristic of the patriarchal and paternal families and the parental authority over marital choice exercised previously under the Civil Code (Durkheim 1921:2-3).

SIBLINGS

Durkheim stated that in the conjugal family (in contrast to the joint ag-natic family), sibling relations are essentially limited to inheritance. He noted that there is no primogeniture; children share equally as heirs (Davy 1925:117).

The Lens of Later Times

Throughout a review of Durkheim's theory, comparisons suggest them-selves to present-day practices, political issues, and theoretical dilemmas. In what ways might Durkheim's theory of the family connect to concerns of today's family scientists and social theorists? There are some specific comparisons to consider. There is also the placement of Durkheim rela-tive to the later structure-functionalism of Parsons and a consideration of systems elements in Durkheim's theory of the family.

Topics in Durkheim's family sociology that resonate with mid- to late-twentieth-century interests include (a) the centrality of the couple, (b) the place of kinship in modern society, (c) the family economy in law, (d) property and persons, (e) the family and the state, (f) and family-in-law and family-in-fact.

CENTRALITY OF THE COUPLE

Like Durkheim, present-day scholars emphasize the centrality of the couple relationship. Given the limited time now spent in reproduction and child rearing, "marriage is becoming defined less as a union between parents raising a brood of children and more as a personal relationship between two individuals" (Skolnick and Skolnick 1999:12).

The demographics of Durkheim's time did *not* provide a lengthy child-free period at the beginning and end of conjugal life such as we have in the late twentieth and early twenty-first centuries. But Durkheim had other reasons for viewing the conjugal couple as the essential family, namely, the changes in French family law discussed throughout this chapter.

Durkheim's limited attention to sibling relationships is matched by contemporary sociology, which gives those family subsystems less attention than other family relationships.[20]

THE DECLINE OF KINSHIP

Has kinship vanished? Durkheim's family system retains "zones of kinship" while excluding these kin from influence over the nuclear family. How does this perspective on kinship fit present-day relations between kin and conjugal family?

Sociologists of the family at mid-twentieth century tended at first to accept Parsons's (1955a) conceptualization of the modern family as an "isolated nuclear family" (pp. 10-11). This term suggests a nuclear family bereft of kinship. But researchers pursuing the question through empirical studies found instead a continuing role for kinship. In the modern United States, the nuclear family is embedded in a kinship system of social interaction and mutual aid (Adams 1968; Kerckhoff 1965; Litwak 1960a, 1960b, 1965; Sussman 1965). Although not sharing a residence or even the same geographical area and not engaged in common economic activities, related nuclear units socialize with each other and exchange "significant services," although they "retain considerable autonomy" (Litwak 1965:291). The term *modified extended family* (or sometimes, *modified nuclear family*) was applied to this system: a central nuclear family in frequent interaction with kin. More recent research confirms the persistence of expressive and instrumental kin ties (Allen, Blieszner, and Roberto 2000; Lewin 2000).

But in fact, the comparison of the modified extended family to kinship in Durkheim's theory does not work. Durkheim's analysis of kinship was a legal one, focused on the domains of succession and authority. We have little sense in his zones of kinship of any similarity to the modified extended family of informal social interaction and mutual aid among kin. Moreover, when Durkheim reported the decline of kinship, he really meant the degree to which the family was organized around kin. The essentially voluntary sociability and mutual aid of modern kin is not the same thing as a corporate family. Parsons (1965), in fact, stated that his use of the term "isolated nuclear family" referred to the structural autonomy of conjugal families and the absence of a corporate body of kin, not to a complete absence of kin ties. And in the modern family, activation of kinship ties is essentially voluntary.

Thus, the present-day modified extended family does not exemplify the kin solidarity and family communism Durkheim had in mind when speaking of kinship (Lasch 1977:142-43; Parsons 1965:35; Schneider 1968:72-75).[21] The place of kinship in society—whether or not kinship is the framework for the economy, social functions, and other activities—and the nature of voluntary social and assistance relationships among kin are two different things (Adams 1968:176-78). Durkheim is right that kinship no longer frames the family.

Durkheim's analysis of the changing family is supported by present-day legal scholarship.[22] The rise of the nuclear family and decline of kinship seems factually indisputable and politically incontestable—how many present-day North Americans or Europeans wish to recreate a familistic veto over marriage choice? Yet there are expressions of regret today at the decline of kinship in its more powerful historic form.

How relevant this transformation is to present-day controversies is indicated by conservative laments at the passing of kin control. The conservative advocacy organization, Focus on the Family, advocates parental control over courtship (Ryun and Ryun 1995). The return of economic interdependency between generations has also been called for, to be achieved by the abolishment of Social Security in favor of direct support of the elderly by their children (Christensen 1993). More generally, concerns are expressed that dissolution of the kin group (and individualism within the nuclear family) has left the field to autonomous individuals on the one hand (Glendon 1989) and a looming state apparatus on the other: "Under these accumulated pressures the family has faded in legal and cultural significance. Meanwhile, both the state and the individual have stated claims to heightened importance" (Carlson 1988:239).

Some social scientists and liberals have also regretted what they see as nuclear family isolation from kin and community. Critics in the 1960s valorized the communal life of preindustrial times as against the private nuclear family, which was seen as essentially pathogenic (Cooper 1971). Scholars noted that the privacy and domesticity of the modern nuclear family removed children from important social contacts and experiences (Sennett 1970:229-37) and precluded communal investment in children and assistance to parents in child rearing. (See Lasch 1977, chap. 7; Skolnick 1996, chap. 5, for more complex overviews of these critiques and responses to them).

THE FAMILY ECONOMY IN LAW

In the United States, courts will not intervene in ongoing marriages to resolve internal disputes about family finances and expenditures (*McGuire v. McGuire* 1953). Control of family property by one or another marital partner becomes legally transparent only on divorce or death.

There are two basic models of marital property: separate holdings or community property. Durkheim has described the emergence of community property in the continental European family. Historically, Britain retained a separate-property system, and this British system dominates the United States. Only a small minority of American states, primarily those with a French or Spanish cultural heritage, have a community property regime.[23]

In distributing marital property in a divorce, the separate-property states now largely ignore formal title in favor of equal or equitable distribution of marital property, a de facto community property regime. But as in Durkheim's time, community property may be less than it seems for the partner who is more dependent, typically the wife. When couples lack accumulated wealth (most couples), the only tangible item of property is the family home and perhaps a pension, and not all couples have those. Of more importance to postdivorce economic security is future earning capacity. However, no states consider earning capacity to be marital property. Some jurisdictions have compensated spouses who contributed financially to their partners' professional education (Buehler 1995:105-11; *Postema v. Postema* 1991).

Control over marital property and disposition of property after marital dissolution was a feminist issue in the nineteenth and early twentieth centuries. With the Second Wave women's movement, these issues have again become important in feminist legal theory and in the social sciences.[24]

With regard to inheritance today, just how dominant the conjugal family is over kin can be seen by using Durkheim's methodology of examining law. By and large, people in present-day European and North American societies take for granted the favorable position of spouse as heir, and the laws have moved to reflect that (Glendon 1989:238-40). A spouse has pride of place among potential heirs of an intestate spouse, although usually not as sole heir where there are surviving children. Wills virtually always name the spouse as sole or principal heir. Yet it is interesting that the kin-spouse tension in inheritance resurfaced in some legislation proposed in Quebec in 1987 that would have permitted surviving spouses only lifetime usufruct (usage) of an estate, which would go ultimately to the child. The argument was that the child needs protection against the excessive individualism of modern times (Connel-Thouez 1987). Evident here is a certain mistrust of the spouse, the child's parent.

Succession and inheritance continue to play an important role in perpetuating economic inequality. Like Durkheim, present-day scholars have noted the tension between equality of opportunity, on the one hand, and liberty and individualism on the other, as it plays out in inheritance. In the present-day United States, for example, eighty percent of household wealth results from intergenerational transfers (Kao, Hong, and Widdows 1997:358; McNamee and Miller 1989:8, 1998).

Inheritance law can seem quaint, boring even, to present-day sociologists, who until recently were more interested in family interaction or family functions than in family property.[25] McNamee and Miller (1989) bemoan the "sociological neglect" of inheritance (p. 7). Nevertheless, in the last twenty years, there has been a resurgence of interest in the law of family money in its many forms. Scholars explore inheritance law and practice and the social implications of inheritance using exchange theory, kin selection theories of altruism, human capital theory, social constructivist theory, rational transfer theory, functional theory, conflict theory, Bourdieuian theory, and neo-Gramscian theory (Cheal 1988; Emigh 1994; Kao et al. 1997; McNamee and Miller 1991; and see Miller and McNamee 1998).

One researcher has tested "Durkheim's Prediction About the Declining Importance of The Family and Inheritance" to see if there is a tendency to will property to persons other than family members. But overwhelmingly, family members remain favored heirs. Recent research in the United States found that over 90 percent of bequests are to family members (Glendon 1989:238-40; McNamee and Miller 1998:196; Schwartz 1996).

French law in Durkheim's time required equality among offspring in bequests from parents; indeed, this was a heritage of the French Revolution. Present-day research on inheritance in the United States has explored the question of equality among children as heirs and found that despite laws that treat children equally with regard to intestate inheritance, the poorest adult child is the most likely to benefit from money transfers from parents (of all kinds, not only bequests; "The Poorest Adult Sibling" 1994).

Patterns of inheritance have important social implications. Schwartz (1996) suggests that

a shift *away* from family inheritance would motivate younger members of families to achieve the education and skills necessary for them to secure and maintain good jobs, careers, and esteemed adult statuses in modern society, in part because they would realize that they could no longer depend on inheriting wealth through their families of origin. However, this shift could also weaken intergenerational bonds within families and lead to widespread societal instability if younger family members no longer "behaved" and no longer assisted older members in times of need. At the least, intergenerational relations within families could become indifferent or attenuated; at most relations could become hostile and destructive. (p. 506).

Durkheim's interest in inheritance law was not misplaced. Inheritance law and practice is important as a social phenomenon because of its links to class and gender inequality; family boundaries; competition between the family of orientation and family of procreation; parental control and parent-child relations; the "postmodern family" (Stacey 1990), in which complex marital relations complicate inheritance (Hill 1995); and, generally, with regard to the relationship of money to love.

PROPERTY AND PERSONS

Following the distinction in French family law, Durkheim used property-person rubrics in presenting his analyses of family change. He gave inheritance meticulous attention as an indicator of the tension between kinship and marriage. But the kin-conjugal struggle in the United States today is not so much over property as persons. Grandparent visitation laws passed in fifty states are none other than the assertion of kin rights in the children of the conjugal family (Bohl 1997; *Brooks v. Parkerson* 1995; Greenhouse 2000; Nichols 1997; *Troxel v. Granville* 1999). Similarly, the Elián Gonzalez case pitted a father against his kin, who asked, "Why aren't we given the opportunity to speak for him?" ("Elián Decision" 2000).[26]

Property and persons can merge rather than being separate dimensions as they were in Durkheim's work. Present-day scholars collapse the person-property distinction by arguing that "all property relations involve the construction of connections between persons and things" (Clignet 1995:275 citing Strathern 1985:202). Gifts made in wills express testators' feelings about a recipient and the relations between the two. At the same time, testators may make decisions about family property in a more analytical way. They may consider the productive potential of property, may reciprocate past assistance, or have concerns about the economic needs of children (Clignet 1995; Kao et al. 1997).

The Family and the State

Durkheim appears largely positive about the emancipation of the conjugal family and the role of the state in this process. This fits his commitment to the ideals of the French Revolution, to the French republic and secular state, and to public education as the locus par excellence for the formation of good citizens.

Current American social critics have a less benign view of state intervention into the family, conservatives (Carlson 1988:239) and liberals (Coontz 1992, chap. 6) alike. But Durkheim was content with a kin group, conjugal family, and modern state in an equilibrium that served the interests of the family. He did not view the state as in opposition to the family. We see nothing in Durkheim comparable to a late-twentieth-century conservative's polemic titled "The State's Assault on the Family" (Carlson 1998) or the more scholarly critiques of state intervention in the family by Donzelot (1979) and Lasch (1977). Durkheim's career was in large part devoted to public education and hence to a socialization of children in which the state plays a great role. He did not share present-day American conservatives' suspicion of public education (Wolfe 1998:125-26); on the contrary, the development of secular public education was a life's work.

FAMILY IN LAW AND FAMILY IN FACT

In today's postmodern society, the definition of "family" seems less clear than it did to Durkheim. Stacey (1990) and others argue that there is no statistically or culturally normative family form today and that social science and social policy must recognize that fact. It is qualities of identity, intimacy, caregiving, and commitment, whether formal or informal, that identify a family. Families can be anchored in homosexual as well as heterosexual adult relationships, in affinity as well as biology or law (e.g., Stacey 1990, 1993).

Conservative or centrist critics and social scientists do posit the nuclear family and permanent marriage as culturally normative even if not empirically universal. They call for a strengthening of the nuclear family and marriage rather than adaptation to divorce, cohabitation, and nonmarital parenthood (Gallagher 1996; Popenoe 1993).

In sum,

> Public definitions of the family have been broadened by those on the political left to recognize a range of forms [citations deleted]. At the same time others on the political right have embraced a more narrow definition, characterizing only married parents and their children as families [citations deleted]. Both broad and narrow definitions often carry with them the freight and fervor of ideology, characterizing as much what families should be as what they are. (Moen and Forest 1999:634)

These policy scholars "take an economical, inclusive view of families, an approach we feel is necessary to fit today's realities" (Moen and Forest 1999:634). Judges and government officials must do more than debate family structure; they must make legally binding decisions as to what counts as a family today. In struggling with this question, some have departed from the traditional definition of blood, marriage, and adoption to use common residence, economic dependency, length of attachment, and generally intersecting lives as criteria.

Durkheim recognized this dilemma in studying the family: whether to employ an inclusive definition of family as families-in-fact or the more limited but clearer legal criterion. In ethnographic data involving premodern, often non-European, family systems, Durkheim would accept customs as indicators of family phenomena. Not so in modern European and American societies, which had well-developed legal codes. There, he mostly insisted on a legal criterion. He saw this as a case of Type I versus Type II error and preferred to err on the side of excluding customary practices that had not yet cohered into law even if they might represent what was to come.

This choice was debatable in his time. On the one hand, there were arguments for recognizing free unions, for example, in law as well as research. But the thrust of opinion was for closing in on formal marriage as the only recognizable form. Today, the empirical and cultural situation has changed, and nonconventional families are numerous. The debate as to what is a family remains a two-sided one.

Theoretical Affinities

Durkheim's family theory raises some interesting questions at a broader level, that is, in terms of macrotheoretical approaches to the family. To what extent was Talcott Parsons's family theory drawn, consciously or unconsciously, from Durkheim? Second, on the basis of his work on the family, can Durkheim be considered a systems theorist?

DURKHEIM AND PARSONS

Sociologist Talcott Parsons was a definitive sociological voice at mid-twentieth century. His book, *Family Socialization and Interaction Process* (Parsons and Bales 1955, coauthored with Robert Bales), was a well-accepted vision of the modern family until the feminist movement and other social change challenged his premises of gender roles and family life. Developments in sociology challenged his intellectual hegemony.

A structure-functional theorist, Parsons addressed the transition from a traditional to modern industrial society. Like Durkheim, Parsons describes a transition from an extended family performing numerous functions to a nuclear family unfettered by kinship ties. Parsons uses an onion metaphor, but he essentially describes the Durkheimian zones of kinship that surround the conjugal family. Kinship is bilateral, the strong corporate kin unit has passed into history, and women have higher status in society and the family. Yet men and women have differentiated family roles: Males are instrumental; females, expressive. Inheritance is important for what it tells us about the family (Parsons 1954, 1955a).

There are differences between Parsons and Durkheim. Parsons puts his analysis of the modern family in terms of the American family. When he refers to the European family, it is to the traditional extended-kinship system, not the modern conjugal family. And Parsons's theory is much more complex and developed in more detail. It includes a psychological level of interaction and child development within the family. Unlike Durkheim, Parsons acknowledged the tension between a *bilateral kinship system,* in which men and women are treated equally, and the strongly *differentiated roles* of the sexes in society, which placed family status in the hands of the male and left the woman in a situation of "strain." (Parsons 1954:191-94).[27] Yet parallels to Durkheim's work are evident.

It is hard to say whether these similarities result from Parsons's reading of Durkheim or reflect a convergence based on observation of the same historical developments. Other sociologists of Parsons's time do report the same transition from traditional to modern society (Goode 1963; Ogburn 1933). On the other hand, Parsons was the foremost American interpreter of Durkheim; it was he who made Durkheim known to American sociologists. Yet Durkheim's family theory goes unacknowledged in Parson's own work in this area.

Steeped in Durkheim's work, I am inclined to see him as an unacknowledged forerunner of Parsons. Certainly, his early role as a structure-functional theorist of the family was not made visible by Parsons and deserves to be known now.

SYSTEMS THEORY

Durkheim is usually considered a structure-functional theorist (Turner 1998:12-13). Turner also categorized Durkheim as an evolutionist (p. 82); this theoretical perspective is indeed prominent in his work on the family. Was Durkheim a bit of a systems theorist as well? One does not think of Durkheim as such. But in fact, there are elements of systems theory in his sociology of the family.

In the "Introduction" to his course on the family, Durkheim (1888a) presented "the complete system of these relations whose totality constitutes family life" (p. 260). His presentation of the changing relations of kin, conjugal family, and state very much fits the definition of a system as a "set of elements standing in interrelationship among themselves and with the environment" (Von Bertalanffy 1975:159 in Whitchurch and Constantine 1993:326). Although Durkheim's theory does not include the concepts of feedback mechanism and self-regulation, there is a sense of balance or equilibrium among the elements. As one changes, so do the others.

The classification of Durkheim's work as rudimentary systems theory depends, of course, on what one means by systems theory. While the system idea is ancient, a proximate source is Von Bertalanffy's general system theory (Broderick 1993, chap. 1).[28] In applications to the family, systems theory has often been equated to the family process theory that developed out of family therapy. In family science, the seminal work was probably Kantor and Lehr's (1975) *Inside the Family*. Durkheim is certainly not a family process theorist. He does *not* focus on the social psychological interior of the family nor observe "real families in real-time interaction" (Broderick 1993:15).

Still, in Durkheim's theoretical perspective, the family displays features characteristic of systems: "The components in a system are *interdependent* . . . [and] the behaviors of the components exhibit *mutual influence,* meaning that what happens with one component generally affects every other component" (Whitchurch and Constantine 1993:32). Durkheim's family system displays other qualities of systems theories: hierarchy, boundaries, equifinality, and equilibrium states. Systems theories do tend to eventuate in *taxonomies,* another feature of Durkheim's sociology of the family (Whitchurch and Constantine 1993:332-336).[29]

Hierarchy

Durkheim gives attention to hierarchy in reporting some modification of traditional family hierarchies. He notes virtual elimination of parent-child domination so far as adult children are concerned. He concedes some individuality and autonomy to the minor child, who has some limited control over property now, some protection from abusive parental power, and an expectation of respect for his individuality within the family.

More ambiguously treated was the gender hierarchy. In his many reviews of ethnographic work, Durkheim explored the status of women, finding greater or lesser subordination in societies too numerous to mention. With regard to the modern conjugal family, Durkheim (1888a) presents spousal and parental rights and responsibilities in a gender-neutral way in the "Introduction" to his family course. Yet he does recognize women's legal disability with regard to control over family property.

Despite the theoretical equality provided by a community property re-gime, the husband, not the wife, exercised control of the marital property. (Durkheim's overall perspective on the status of women, his struggle to reconcile differentiation with equality, is explored in Chapter 7).

Last, Durkheim documents the changing, declining authority of the extended family over kinsmen.

Boundaries

A continuing theme in Durkheim's work is placement of the boundary around the family—who is included? A master image is that of an amor-phous circle of kin, gradually resolving into a set of concentric circles. The conjugal couple emerges ever more strongly in the center. The outer rings pale; the outermost, the old clan-family, fades completely. Inherit-ance law provides an objective indicator of these boundaries, though lagging somewhat behind normative change.

Another boundary axis in Durkheim's work is that of lineage: reckon-ing kinship through the matrilineal or patrilineal line. In the modern conjugal family, maternal and paternal kinship are equally important.

Equifinality

Durkheim's family theory infers "*equifinality* or the ability of a system to achieve the same goals through different routes" (Whitchurch and Constantine 1993:334). While equifinality was not a strong motif, Durkheim (1895b) did take a nonjudgmental stance toward cultural and historical variation such that more than one family type can accomplish the same end: "Domestic society has been able to rest on very different bases" (p. 622).

Equilibrium

This is a strong theme in Durkheim's work, as the three elements of the family system—conjugal family, kin, and state—maintain a shifting bal-ance. Change in one unit affects the others. As the corporate kin body loses power and control over persons and property, the marital couple gains. When it emerges in the course of European history, the state pro-vides the leverage that will free the conjugal couple from kin control. The system rebalances. Kin remain as part of a family system but with a loss of control over what had previously been subordinate elements: the con-jugal couple and their children. The state can also intervene in the conjugal family, supporting paternal power—or contravening it to protect the children from abuse. To prevent the state from becoming so strong that it overwhelms the family, other social forces must develop to balance state power.

Durkheim's family system maintains an equilibrium, but it is a moving equilibrium: an "evolution of structural states," each in short-term equilibrium (Winton 1995:61). In Durkheim's work, the system moves in one direction only. It follows the assumed course of history toward emancipation of the nuclear family from kin and of the individual members of the family (children) from the nuclear family unit. Thus, Durkheim as systems theorist connects to Durkheim as evolutionist.

Durkheim's sense of equilibrium and mutual influence in the family system did not rise to the level of specific feedback mechanisms. In fact, there would be no negative feedback mechanism in this evolving and changing system, which did *not* maintain a steady state. In the terms of Whitchurch and Constantine (1993), Durkheim's family system would exhibit "morphogenetic" change (p. 336). Durkheim would likely agree with them that a particular component (in this case, the state) can have a strong impact on system change.

Systems Theory and Structure-Functional Theory

Perhaps, the attempt to classify Durkheim as a systems theorist is a bit forced. But noting the systems' theoretical elements in Durkheim's work, however pale they may be, can be seen as part of a growing convergence between structure-functional theory and systems theory.

System is a concept in structure-functional theory (Winton 1995:46), but the connection of functionalism to system theory was not made for some time. Now, understandings of these theories have changed. The *Sourcebook of Family Theories and Methods* (Boss et al. 1993) continues a distinction between the two, with separate articles. Yet voices are heard that point to an overlap between structure-functional theory and systems theory (or the replacement of the former by the latter), often placing Parsons at the juncture between the two (Broderick 1993:7-15; Kingsbury and Scanzoni 1993:195; Klein and Jurich 1993:51; Morgan 1985:132; Trevino 1999). Klein and White (1996) note a similarity, although they do not go so far as to classify Parsons as a systems theorist (p. 153). A previous distinction between the two theories—that structure-functional theory tends toward stasis, while systems theory is dynamic—is mitigated by noting the potential for system change even in Parsons's work. He stated that his focus on stasis system analysis was simply a foothold for a study of social change whose time had not yet come (Broderick 1993, citing Parsons 1951).

Conclusion

Kin, conjugal couple, and the state are interrelated in the family system of Durkheim's analysis. In the modern era, the conjugal couple emerged from the corporate kin group as the family par excellence. Thanks to the leverage of the modern state, the nuclear family was now independent of kin control. The state supported not only the autonomy of the nuclear family but also the individualism of its members. That individualism extended to some degree of personal autonomy for the minor child and complete autonomy for adult children. Zones of kinship surrounded the conjugal family but with a lesser role to play than in the past. Of course, the state itself could intervene in the family, and Durkheim's overall perspective included the need for intermediate groups to anchor individuals to society and to counterbalance the power of the state.

Durkheim did not systematically address the interior psychodynamic and interactional workings of the family in his evolutionary theory (Chapter 2) or in his exposition of the elements of the family system (in this chapter). Yet in his discussion of "the conjugal family" in the concluding lecture of his course (Durkheim 1921) and in his analysis of education and socialization (e.g., *Moral Education;* Durkheim [1925] 1974]), Durkheim did take some note of the emotional life of the family, its psychosocial functions, and the individuality of its members. We explore this aspect of Durkheim's work on the family in the next chapter, together with the question of social solidarity so prominent in Durkheim's thinking.

Notes

1. In 1790, the Revolutionary Constituent Assembly wished to reduce paternal authority and so established "family councils." Rather than a father having sole authority over children (adults as well as minors), assemblies of relatives would play a role in family decision making about children—their education, marriage, and so forth. The family council was also supposed to mediate or adjudicate disputes between parents and minor children (Hunt 1992:40-41).

2. He did an initial plan of *The Division of Labor* before he went to Germany to study in 1885-86 (Giddens 1978:14). The "Introduction" to his family course was published in 1888 but would have been prepared earlier.

3. Specifics and dates of the various modifications of these laws are too detailed to include here. With regard to marriage, parental consent was not required for those over twenty-one after 1907. But adult children seeking to marry were still required to approach their parents with request for approval. These "*actes respecteuses*" varied in required number depending on age of the adult child. For those required to make three *actes respecteuses,* each a month apart, the delay of marriage could be significant, but parents could not actually prevent a marriage after 1907 (Glendon 1989:41-42).

4. The term *ego* indicates the individual who is the starting point for the calculation of kinship.

5. It seems anachronistic to employ gender-neutral terminology when summarizing Durkheim's work and so I have not.

6. The family council was, as discussed in Note 1, a sort of kin court. Anchored in pre-Revolutionary customs, it was incorporated into Revolutionary legislation and continued in the Napoleonic Code of 1804. Two important functions of this kin body were guardianship (appointing, supervising, removing guardians; approving major decisions by the guardian; providing family consent to marriage or emancipation where perhaps not approved by the father) and intervention in a troubled marriage. A family council composed of relatives of both husband and wife served as a conciliation court for couples in conflict. Certification of council attempts at reconciling the couple was required before a divorce could be obtained (Glendon 1981:15; Rheinstein 1972:203).

7. In making this distinction, Durkheim pondered holdings in the patriarchal family, because property seemingly belonged to the patriarch. But he concluded that property was still held communally, with the paterfamilias serving as symbol and representative of the corporate family (Durkheim 1921:3, Mauss fn 3).

8. In discerning a trend toward the dominance of persons over property, Durkheim did not anticipate or consider the "commodification" of persons and relationships that play a prominent role in present-day sociological theorizing (Bartos 1996).

9. Durkheim did recognize that England had a separate property regime, which he ascribed to its unique history.

10. For example, if there are two children, two-thirds of the residual estate goes to them. Of the remaining disposable estate, the surviving spouse may have only the usufruct of one-quarter of the estate where there are *any* descendants, ascendants, brothers or sisters, or illegitimate children conceived during the time of the marriage. If there are no descendants and so forth, the spouse may take one-half of that portion of the estate, while collateral relatives to the fourth degree take the remainder. The spouse's entitlement is reduced by an amount equal to life insurance plus any substantial gifts made during the marriage (Glendon 1989:246-49).

11. Until around 1960, inheritance law in the United States also gave kin some priority when a spouse died intestate. Even though spouses are favored by those making wills, then and now, revised law still recognizes the interests of children (and in some states, of parents and grandparents) in addition to those of the spouse. This is more likely in states influenced by the French Civil Code (Hill 1995:63, 73).

Sociologists writing on American kinship have consistently remarked on the tension between the standard American model of kinship, which gives high priority to the spouse, and inheritance laws more likely to respect children in intestate situations (Farber 1981:57-58). For a more detailed discussion of inheritance theory and practice, see Clignet (1995).

12. Mary Ann Glendon (1989) wrote that "although French law does increasingly promote individual freedom in marriage, it still bears more traces than [British, American, or German] . . . systems of an older social order" (p. 77; and see Rheinstein 1972:202-03, 212, 215, fn 18).

13. Davy's (1925) summary of Durkheim's course takes a stronger line on the persistence of kinship in inheritance in the face of the normative status of the conjugal family. There, the contradiction is resolved by concluding that "the law remains behind the mores" (pp. 80-81). The death notice gives the spouse prominence, while "the regular heirs are the children . . . as representatives and continuers of the family" (p. 81). At the same time, Davy's analysis of the law as of 1892 acknowledges the gains of the spouse and conjugal family over time, as well as the equality of men and women in inheritance law (pp. 80-82). Which emphasis, which nuance represents Durkheim himself is difficult to say, save that in his

other work, he validates the legal over an informal normative criterion and the conjugal family over kin.

14. This exists in Catholic canon law as a "brother-sister marriage." Couples who have a canon law impediment to a valid Catholic marriage may apply for permission to be married or to continue their marriages, although they must not maintain conjugal sexual relations. Henry and Claire Booth Luce were alleged to have had a brother-sister marriage after her conversion to Catholicism (as Henry was divorced and thus not an eligible marriage partner for a Catholic).

15. Durkheim's preferred form of the state was parliamentary democracy because of its capacity to communicate and include citizens in the political process (Durkheim 1950:68-78, 92-130; and see Durkheim 1902a and Vogt 1993:82-93).

16. See Donzelot's (1979) *The Policing of Families* for a detailed history and critique of the relationships of the family to the state and philanthropic associations. As noted in the discussion of law in Chapter 3, in France, the state has historically been permitted a high level of intervention and supervision of the family.

17. Durkheim generally spoke of the increasing role of the state in *modern* times. But he did point to a Roman example of state intervention serving to limit abusive paternal power (Durkheim 1904j).

18. Durkheim did not mean that a marriage was indissoluble by divorce but rather that marital dissolution required review and approval by the state. Durkheim's views on divorce are discussed in detail in Chapters 6 and 7.

19. Durkheim's "The Conjugal Family" was published posthumously in 1921 but was taken from the family course as presented in 1892. Thus, it was written prior to the 1907 change in law that permitted free choice of marriage to adults of both sexes.

20. Much research today is focused on sibling relations in later life and in regard to the care of elderly parents (Goetting 1986b; White and Riedmann 1992). Bedford (1995) offers a detailed review of research that discusses costs and benefits of sibling relations, changes in sibling relationship over the life cycle, and the effects of gender and other characteristics. Sibling relationships are typically less intense than parent-child relationships (Adams 1995:327-28).

21. See Lasch (1977:142-43) and Skolnick (1996:106-108) for a more detailed and nuanced discussion of the debates about the place of kinship in the contemporary United States.

22. Mary Ann Glendon summarizes direction of family law from early modern times:

> Western family law, in the sense of norms anchored by the state . . . [was] characterized simultaneously by a gradual strengthening of legal ties within the husband-wife family, and a progressive attenuation of bonds linking the members of the family unit to the wider kinship group. Over time, the circle of family relationships that give rise to legal relationships grew smaller and more marriage-centered, while legal reinforcement of those connections that cause people to think of themselves as related to each other within a larger group gradually diminished. (Glendon 1981:11)

23. Variously numbered at eight (Wadlington 1995:22), nine (Areen 1992:290), or seven plus three others with community property features (Buehler 1995:105).

24. Lenore Weitzman's (1981) *The Marriage Contract* was the first sociology book I know of to address the legal and economic aspects of marriage and divorce, with special emphasis on gender inequality and the failure of law to address social and family change. Since then, interest in family law has mushroomed among sociologists and family scientists. Marital property is one focus of this interest (Buehler 1995; Cherlin 1998; McIntyre and Sussman 1995).

25. Adams (1995) does take "property holding and inheritance" to be a significant family function (p. 315). Economist Gary Becker's (1960, 1981) work and the exchange theory of Peter Blau (1964) initiated a return of interest in the family as an economic institution.

26. Five-year-old Elián was one of the few survivors of a group of Cubans whose boat capsized as they attempted to reach the United States to seek political asylum. His mother and stepfather died, but he still had a father in Cuba and also kin in the United States. After a prolonged legal and political struggle between the father and his relatives, Elián was returned to his father.

27. Durkheim's theories of women and gender differentiation will be discussed in Chapter 7.

28. Von Bertalanffy was an Austrian biologist working just prior to World War II who is credited with the development of general system theory (Whitchurch and Constantine 1993:326, 349).

29. Whitchurch and Constantine (1993) take the components of the family system to be *individual* family members. But because they also make a point of different levels of analysis, I see no reason not to consider higher-level components (i.e., kin, conjugal family, and state) as systemic if they display these features.

5

The Interior of the Family

> The family . . . sustains the individual in each moment and under all
> aspects of his existence.
>
> —*Davy (1925:113)*

Durkheim's perspective on the family presents a formal family structure. He finds family in the "objective" terms of legal regulation
and normative practices—the institutional rather than relational side of
marriage and the family.

Is there a place in Durkheim's work for the psychosocial interior of
the family? Durkheim's family interior is lightly furnished, but it does
exist—in discourse on solidarity, domesticity, affectivity, gender, socialization, and individuality. These topics vary in terms of Durkheim's
attention, from extensive pages on solidarity to brief and offhand references to emotions. They bring together some contradictory aspects of
Durkheim's thought: his concern for solidarity and regulation in the family, his positive view of individualism, and his appreciation of the
spontaneity and warmth of the modern family.

An examination of these topics as they occur in Durkheim's corpus
raises questions: (a) How can Durkheim adopt a legal and institutional
perspective on the family when family is so obviously an emotional
realm? (b) How does Durkheim theorize conjugal roles and relationships? (c) How can the family *not* play the major role in the socialization
of the child? (d) Is the tension between individualism and solidarity
adequately resolved in Durkheim's analysis of the family? These questions do not have complete or definitive answers, but we begin to explore
them in this chapter.

Solidarity

Scrutiny begins with Durkheim's macrosocial concern for societal solidarity, the ties that hold a society together. In the *Division of Labor* (Durkheim [1893] 1978), and earlier (Durkheim 1888a), Durkheim famously wrote of the transition from mechanical to organic solidarity as society modernized.

In the evolutionary past, family and society were the same thing. All social and economic activity had the clan-family as its setting. Gradually, territorial communities and kinship diverged, and kin groups devolved into smaller family units. Social functions came to be carried out by specialized institutions, the state emerging with special responsibilities and strong powers. The process of structural differentiation transformed the basis of social solidarity from similarity to an interdependence created by specialization and exchange.

Durkheim argued the viability of a modern society sustained by organic solidarity. Yet he still questioned the power of the larger society to inspire the sacrifice and loyalty previously anchored in family and kinship. The intensity of a dense kinship network is missing in the exchange relations of organic solidarity. The state is too distant to serve as a point of attachment. The conjugal family of modern times is too small and too impermanent to be the glue that firmly attaches the individual to society. If inheritance were to be abolished, as Durkheim expected, the motivation to work for one's children's future would be lacking. What would replace it as an attachment to motivate social responsibility and work, a group not so big and remote as political society? Intermediate groups other than the family should be created to bond individuals to society (Durkheim [1897a] 1930:434-40, 1902a, 1921).

The future of family as well as societal solidarity concerned Durkheim. Throughout most of the span of family evolution, totem or patriarch and always the family patrimony had served to hold the family together:

> Before, domestic solidarity was not just a collection of individuals united by mutual affection, but it was the group itself, in abstract and impersonal unity. It was the family name, with the memories that recreated . . . a history of its own to which its members attached themselves. [It was] the fields; the situation; the reputation. All that tends to disappear. (Durkheim [1897a] 1930:433)

The family patrimony is now reduced to the marital community of property. There are no other holistic family economic interests in an economy where careers are those of individuals, and the possibility of passing on wealth is limited. But "the individual is not a sufficient goal for himself.

When he takes himself as the endpoint, he falls into a state of moral misery that leads to suicide" (Durkheim 1921:11).

The size of the family unit has an impact on family cohesion:

> It is not . . . to the unique nature of the feelings that parents have for their immediate descendants that one must attribute this preservative virtue [of family size]. . . . [F]eelings . . . cannot be powerful if the family is disintegrated. . . . The intensity such feelings attain depends on the number of consciences that feel them in common. . . . Likewise, when the family is not very extensive, few relatives are together at any one time; domestic life languishes and there are moments when the home is deserted. (Durkheim [1897a] 1930:213-14)

In modern times, the conjugal family has essentially only two members, husband and wife, insufficient mass to muster an emotional hold:

> Even when couples are not sterile, our home is empty of children during the major part of our existence. The needs of their education, then their social situation and marriage take them away from us very quickly. The family is reduced, for a great part of our life, to the conjugal couple only (Durkheim 1909b:270).

And then it dissolves completely.

If family solidarity is no longer based in "things" (family patrimony) or attachment to a large corporate kin group, what might hold the small modern conjugal family together? Now, "we are attached to our family only because we are attached to the person of our father, our mother, our wife, our children" (Durkheim 1921:9). Using statistical data to explore the cross-cutting effects of marital status and parenthood, Durkheim ([1897a] 1930) concludes that it is the "family society" (parents and children), not the "conjugal society" of husband and wife, which protects against suicide. This is especially so for women; men do have an additional benefit from marriage (pp. 191-97).

There are some emergent forces that strengthen the conjugal family. In an era of increasing state intervention, marriage can be dissolved only with the permission of the state (Durkheim 1909b:261-62). Monogamy becomes law and more or less fact. The question remains:

> Is domestic solidarity weakened or reinforced by [the changes in the family induced by evolution and declining family size]? It is very difficult to answer this question. On the one hand, it is stronger since the bonds of relatedness are today indissoluble, but on the other hand, the obligations to which they give rise are less numerous and less important. What is certain is that they have been transformed. . . . We cleave to our family because we are attached to the persons who compose it. . . . With the

loosening of [family] communism, things ceased more and more to bind domestic society. Domestic solidarity becomes entirely personal. (Durkheim 1921:8-9)

Durkheim *was* concerned about social cohesion, turning to the occupational groups as mediating structures, given the insufficiency of the family in this regard. He *did* see the conjugal family as unsuited to the task of socialization (Durkheim [1925] 1974). Does this mean he found the conjugal family qua family inadequate in principle?

While ambivalent about its solidarity, Durkheim nevertheless had a favorable opinion of the conjugal family and was appreciative of the family as an emotional setting for its members. He viewed the transition from "things" to "persons" positively (Durkheim 1950:194-205) and referred to the conjugal family as "the most perfect form" (Durkheim 1888a:273). Perhaps most important to its stability is that despite its loss of functions to other institutions, the conjugal family becomes an essential refuge and support in a competitive, impersonal society (Durkheim 1921:10-12).

Domesticity

The family, in Christopher Lasch's (1977) words, is a "haven in a heartless world" (p. xix). With the extensive industrialization of the nineteenth century, the family underwent a transformation from corporate kin group, locus of many functions, to private domain of domestic tranquility. The separation of work and family led to thinking of society as split between public and private realms, with "domestic life as an emotional refuge in a cold and competitive society" (Lasch 1977:6-8; see also Berger and Kellner 1970; Hutter 1981:85-86; Sennett 1970).

Despite some misgivings, in the ensemble of his writings, Durkheim was as positive about the value of the family *foyer*[1] in this modern era as he was accepting of other social change, challenging the pessimism of LePlay, Tönnies, and other conservatives (Aldous 1972:1192; Durkheim 1888a:273).

The family remains the seat of moral discipline and fosters the altruism required of parents bringing up children. Davy's (1925) presentation of Durkheim's course is lyrical about the role of the family. It offers

the man and the woman the most favorable opportunity for the most intimate and . . . permanent physical and moral union, the unequaled communion of anguish and hope of two beings together bent to the task of their flesh. . . . [The family forms] for them and for their children that "interior" in the intimacy of which they preserve memories, plan projects, unconsciously weave day-to-day happiness, and with a united heart accept misfortune when it comes. . . . [It is] that place of renewal where effort is eased and the will acquires new strength . . . [for] an end which goes beyond egoistic and temporary pleasure. . . . [The family is] that refuge where the wounds of life find their consolation and errors their pardon, . . . a center of morality, energy, and sweetness; a school of life, love, and work . . . that could never lose its role. (Davy 1925:113-114)

In this description of the conjugal family, we find Durkheim's perennial theme of obligation and moral order. We also find the family as emotional refuge, a seat of affections, and locus of happiness.

Affectivity

For the most part, Durkheim did not directly address the more ineffable aspects of family life in his work. But he left very visible clues in what he takes for granted or briefly mentions. What Durkheim found wanting in the family as a basis for solidarity or socialization can be thought of as a photographic negative; printed, it reveals family affectivity. The conjugal family is unworkable as the source of solidarity in society because it is the based on the free choice of marital partners in which "passion" plays a role (Davy 1925:86). The conjugal family cannot effectively socialize children beyond the years of early nurture because of the warm emotions parents have for children. This precludes a more detached insistence on their fulfillment of normative expectations (Durkheim [1925] 1974).

Durkheim ([1925] 1974) contrasted the school, a site of collective life of a group that differs and is apart from the family, with the family's "outpouring of hearts" and "overflowing feelings" (p. 199). The interior of the family is a place of freedom, spontaneity, and individuality:

The family . . . is a very small group of persons, who know each other intimately, who are in constant personal contact. Consequently their relations are not submitted to any regulation that is general, impersonal, or immutable. Instead, [families] have . . . something free and easy about them, that makes them resistant to rigid determination. Domestic duties have something of the particular, which would not be able to be fixed once and for all in definitive rules applicable to all in the same way. They are capable of bending to the diversity of personality and circumstance. It is a question of temperaments, of mutual accommodation facilitated by affection and familiarity. (P. 124).

With this description, Durkheim captured the emotionality of the family, the family as primary group (Cooley 1909). This is a sense of the family as private backstage space where people can be themselves (Goffman 1959). It suggests that family and domestic life can never be completely rationalized.

Negative as well as positive emotions are associated with the family. Durkheim observed, for example, that while married men have lower rates of suicide, they have higher rates of homicide than single men (Durkheim [1897a] 1930:404-407). It is startling to read the following sentence: "While family life has a restraining effect on suicide, it rather stimulates murder" (p. 404).

In context, this statement is less jarring and more explicable. Durkheim does *not* here refer to intrafamilial conflict or domestic violence, as we might think. Referring to his evolutionary theory, Durkheim means to say that in earlier times, the collective intensity of large kin groups and the absence of a protective state gave rise to violent defense of family safety and interests, to vendettas (Durkheim [1897a] 1930:406-407).[2] But still, he does speak of the dualistic quality of family feeling in words that resonate with present-day perspectives as to the Janus-faced character of the family:

> The family has been in the past the maker of law and custom whose severity has often gone to extremes of violence; at the same time that it is the milieu where men have learned for the first time to enjoy expressions of feeling." (Durkheim 1902a:xxx)

Durkheim mentions family affect only in passing; he does not develop a sustained analysis of the emotions at the interior of the family. Where he does offer some analysis of the emotional realm, it departs from present-day thinking in significant respects. He reverses the comparison of past and present generally held by today's family scholars. We tend to see emotionality as a prominent feature of the family in modern times (e.g., Shorter 1975), whereas traditional families met practical needs and were characterized by affect that was more detached, even negative (Stone 1979:76-89). For Durkheim, the large, kin-based family of the past generated *more* emotional intensity because of its sheer size and homogeneity, the collective behavioral phenomenon of reverberating emotional currents. Durkheim's delineation of the emotional differences between traditional and modern families seems to be driven by the mechanical-organic solidarity schematic.

Somewhat contradictorily but more in line with his general take on the modern family, Durkheim (1900b) notes that the *fewer* the children, the more intense the parents' affection for each. Even so, parents' attachment to their children must be socially constructed, as paternal feeling does not appear in all societies: "It is the social organization of the relations of kinship which determines the respective feelings of parents and children. They would have been otherwise if the social structure had been different" (Durkheim [1893] 1978:341).

In yet another distinction, the married couple's love for each other is seen to be different from that expressed in other family ties. In explaining the incest taboo, Durkheim (1898c) contrasts love in the family of origin with the more passionate, sexual, pleasure-oriented, and voluntary character of couple love, noting "the eternal antithesis between passion and duty" (p. 67).

> Our relations with our brothers, sisters, and parents[3] are tightly regulated by moral stipulations ["la morale"]. . . . Assuredly, sympathy and particular inclinations are far from being banished. However, domestic affections have this distinctive property; they are always colored with respect. Love here is not simply a spontaneous movement of private sensibility, it is, in part, a duty. . . . One does not have the right to not love ones parents. . . . [T]he feelings that brothers and sisters express for one another does not depend only, or even principally, on their individual qualities. . . . It is the family which requires that they be united. (pp. 59-60)

In contrast, sexual relations are dominated by spontaneous inclination and pleasure, not obligation, role, or moral integrity:

> The man and woman who unite seek in this union their pleasure, and their association depends exclusively, at least in principle, on their chosen affinities. They associate with each other because it pleases them, while brothers and sisters must please each other because they are associated in the bosom of the family. Love in this case [sexual relationship] can be itself only on the condition of being spontaneous. It excludes all idea of obligation and regulation. It is the domain of liberty, where imagination goes unimpeded, where the interest of the parties and their pleasure are almost the dominant law. . . . This, of course means it is not under the domain of morality. This is not so true of that regulated union that constitutes marriage. With marriage, sexual relations affect family and so the family puts a certain regulation on this form of sexual transaction, to put it in harmony with domestic interests, though that regulation does not affect sex per se, just its consequences. (Durkheim 1898c:60-61)

Marriage begins as the choice of the partners, from the same feelings of mutual attraction as free union. Once chosen, a marriage then creates duties (Durkheim 1898c:60-61). These obligations are solidified by the arrival of children: "The moral influence of the family is not really felt until the conjugal couple becomes a family, properly speaking" (p. 61).

One senses overall that Durkheim is rather suspicious of feelings. They inhibit rational action. They inspire violence. They are indeterminate and ephemeral. They are essentially asocial. For Durkheim, then, they are not so central. There are abstract references to sentiments, but missing is the emotional family of lived experience. Dominant are the family structures of law and mores with which Durkheim is much more comfortable.

Gender

The legal rubrics of Durkheim's (1888a) "Introduction" to his family course obscure gender, but gender is prominent in Durkheim's discussion of marital roles and relations in *The Division of Labor* (Durkheim [1893] 1978) and *Suicide* (Durkheim [1897a] 1930).

THE FAMILIAL DIVISION OF LABOR

In the *Division of Labor,* Durkheim ([1893] 1978) connects domestic law to the familial division of labor: "Who is charged with the different domestic functions? What is a husband? A father?" (p. 91). The juridical organization of the family evolved to distribute functions among different family members by age and sex and dependency. The division of labor unites the family. Durkheim acknowledges that we do not usually think of the family as made cohesive by the division of labor but rather by sentiments and beliefs held in common. "There are, in effect, so many things in common among members of a familial group that the special character of tasks that come to each one of them easily escapes us." Yet "far from being a . . . secondary phenomenon, this familial division of labor dominates . . . the development of the family" (pp. 91-92).

When Durkheim directly confronts data on such phenomena as divorce and suicide, he presents an analysis based on gender as well as marital status. He articulates a theory of complementary roles that may have inspired Parson's (1955a) instrumental and expressive roles.[4] But where Parsons saw primarily consensus and functionality, Durkheim is more willing to acknowledge differences in the benefit to men and women of their family status and roles. Making a number of comparisons in suicide rates by gender, age, marital status, and parental status, he finds a "coefficient of preservation" of marriage that is significant for male mortality but that has mixed results for women (Durkheim [1897a] 1930:181, 186-207, 1906a): "Generally speaking, the wife profits less from family life than the husband" (Durkheim [1897a] 1930:196).

Durkheim is thought of as a functionalist and consensus theorist, but a closer look at these data and some other materials suggest that exchange theory and conflict theory are latently present in his work on the family. The status of women in family and society will be more thoroughly discussed in Chapter 7, but let us examine here some indications of these theoretical perspectives.

EXCHANGE THEORY

Exchange theory is a broad theoretical perspective that sees human relationships as anchored in the rewards and costs incurred in the exchange of resources (Homans 1961; Scanzoni 1970; Thibault and Kelley 1959). These can be economic assets or noneconomic resources, such as affection, personality, beauty, skill, deference, and so forth.[5] Economists who have applied exchange theory to the family hypothesize that specialization provides a more advantageous exchange for the parties. Thus, gender role differentiation in marriage should facilitate the well-being of a family (Becker 1981). There are elements of exchange theory in Durkheim's work.

Durkheim sees men and women as essentially different, more so in modern than traditional society, as structural differentiation leaves its mark on gender as well as other aspects of society (Durkheim [1893] 1978:20-25). Because they are different, husband and wife can exchange resources to their mutual benefit. What is important about that is that the exchange process leads to marital solidarity:

> If the division of labor produces solidarity, it is not only because it makes of each individual an exchangist . . .; it is because it creates among men a system of rights and duties which links them to one another in a stable fashion. (Pp. 402-403)

While sexual attraction and love require "a certain harmony of thoughts and feelings" (Durkheim [1893] 1978:19),

> It is no less true that what gives to this affection its specific character and what produces its particular energy is not similarity but dissimilarity of the natures it unites. However, it is not a contrast pure and simple that makes their feelings for each other blossom, but only differences that imply a need for each other and make each complete can have this virtue. . . . In other

words, it is the sexual division of labor which is the source of conjugal solidarity. (P. 19)

The sense of being made whole by the other goes much further than exchange in a quasi-economic sense. To think that is to misunderstand what exchange relations imply and the identification that results from them:

> The image of the one who completes us becomes as inseparable from our self as our own. . . . It becomes an integral and permanent part of our consciousness . . . to such a degree that we cannot do without it." (p. 25)

Turn-of-the-twentieth-century marriages would have been typically characterized by *specialization* of roles.[6] But the status and roles of women were hotly debated at this time, and the continuation of woman's traditional role was in question. In taking his part in debates on the roles of women (*Libres entretiens* 1909), Durkheim mounted a strong defense of complementarity. Now, Durkheim found *equality* generally a necessity for exchange relations in the division of labor (Durkheim [1893] 1978:403), but such equality was unlikely to have characterized marriages founded on gender traditionalism. Such ambivalence about equality when gender was involved is to be analyzed in more detail in Chapter 7. But we can note Durkheim's occasional recognition of the conflicting interests of men and women in the family.

CONFLICT THEORY

Conflict theory, which takes many forms, including feminist theory, depicts a society in which groups compete for scarce resources. Power and conflict in society are explicitly acknowledged, in contrast to other theories, such as functionalism, which offer a vision of society as ordered and consensual.[7]

The dichotomization of conflict and order in classical sociological theory typically assigns Marx to the conflict pole and Durkheim to social order and consensus. It has been widely accepted but has recently been challenged. Connell (1997) calls this a "textbook cliche" (p. 1539), while Giddens (1976) terms it "not useful" and "a myth" (pp. 706, 714, 716). None other than Parsons (1968) acknowledged that "Durkheim was no mere extoller of the virtues of solidarity" (p. 316). Durkheim himself states that "it is not necessary, nor even possible, that social life be without strife" (Durkheim [1893] 1978:357).

While noting the solidarity produced by gender difference, Durkheim seems willing to concede that there is a conflict of interest between men and women with regard to the institution of marriage. According to Durkheim ([1897a] 1930), data on suicide indicate that the regulatory function of marriage benefits men more than women (pp. 174-208).[8] The "coefficient of preservation" (the degree to which being married reduces the rate of suicide) is greater for men than women (p. 189). "Conjugal society is harmful to women and aggravates her tendency toward suicide" (p. 196). Thus, permissive or restrictive divorce laws affect husbands and wives differently so far as their impact on suicide is concerned. A married woman is less likely to commit suicide where divorce is more freely available (in cases of unhappy marriage), so where marriage is supported by strict divorce laws, "it is she who has made a sacrifice" (p. 311). "The interests of the spouses in marriage are manifestly contrary" (p. 442).

Durkheim ([1897a] 1930) attributed the differential effect of marriage and divorce to the nature of each sex: men need control; women, freedom. Men, being more evolved, so to speak, need marriage, which "regulates the life of passion." Women, who are more biologically programmed, have little need for social regulation: "it is a burden without great advantage" (pp. 304, 306, 307). Thus (speaking of suicide rates among the widowed), "She can more easily do without a man than a man can do without her" (Durkheim 1901i:439).

Socialization

Socialization is the process by which individuals develop human qualities and capacities, acquire a self-concept, learn the culture, and establish behavioral conformity to social norms. It is normal for the topic of socialization to appear in a writing on the family. The historian, social critic, and sometime Marxist Christopher Lasch (1977) terms the family "the chief agency of socialization" (p. 3). In functionalist theory, socialization is the residual and irreplaceable family function, remaining after other functions have been handed off to specialized institutions (Reiss 1965).[9] With rare exceptions, present-day sociologists and psychologists concur in viewing the family as the normal setting for basic socialization, continuing in importance throughout adolescence.

FAMILY, SCHOOL, AND STATE AS AGENTS OF SOCIALIZATION

The family's warmth and support are seen by today's scholars to facilitate socialization by motivating children's compliance and identification with parental values and norms (e.g., Straus 1964):

Because of its enormous emotional influence, [the family] colors all of a child's subsequent experience. . . . If the reproduction of culture were simply a matter of formal instruction and discipline, it could be left to the schools. But it also requires that culture be embedded in personality. Socialization makes the individual want to do what he has to do; the family is the agency to which society entrusts this complex and delicate task. (Lasch 1977:3-4)

Durkheim differs. In Durkheim's sociology, the family is *not* an appropriate agent for the important task of moral education. This is precisely *because* of the family's warmth; the affectivity characteristic of the family *precludes* its effectiveness as a socializing agent. Durkheim fears that indulgence is the normal attitude of the parent. To socialize the child into the norms and expectations of society, as well as for formal intellectual learning, separation from the family is necessary, and the state must play a role.

Durkheim (1922) is well aware that this is controversial:

The rights of the family are placed in opposition [to those of the state]. The child, it is said, first of all belongs to his parents. It is thus they who have the right to direct his intellectual and moral development according to their views. Education is thus conceived of as something essentially private and domestic. . . . But it is not necessary that [the state's] role remain so negative. If . . . education has, above all, a collective function, if it has as its object to adapt the child to the social milieu in which he is destined to live, it is impossible that society be disinterested in such a process. . . . When education is an essential social function, the state cannot ignore it. (pp. 59-60)

DISCIPLINE AND AUTONOMY

Durkheim sought a balance between discipline and autonomy in the socialization process. He could be said to favor the "authoritative" approach to child rearing (Baumrind 1971). Authoritative parenting combines firm expectations and disciplinary follow-through with parental warmth and the avoidance of harsh physical punishment. Ultimately, the socialized person must identify with social expectations and with society and want to do what is required. Personality must be developed, not repressed, if the child is to become an adult who will make a contribution to society. Thus, it is important that moral education recognize personhood, in Durkheim's terms ([1925] 1974), *"the spirit of autonomy,"* as well as *"the spirit of discipline"* and *"attachment to groups."* One must

leave to the pupil some initiative, some liberty, some movement. It is necessary that he begin to work, as he plays, with his whole heart, with his
whole being, with . . . ardor and vivacity . . . spontaneously, freely, and
naturally. (Buisson and Durkheim 1911:553)

At the same time, the child must learn to "acquire a taste for discipline
and order in his conduct" (p. 553).

All of these aspects of moral education can be better accomplished by
schools than the family. One of the problems with family socialization is
that each family has a unique milieu, providing a narrow slice of life, and
if only one person in the family engages in the child's moral education,
his experience will be even more limited. He will be pressed into a narrow and idiosyncratic mold and his autonomy compromised. Limited to
the family, the child will not be able to develop his individuality (Durkheim
[1925] 1974:122).

True, the family can begin the formation of good habits and a structured life, but this is more effectively done by the school. The school has
previously existing rules to which the child must conform. It is a situation closer to that which he will encounter in the larger society (Durkheim
[1925] 1974:123-26). Moreover,

> The school group is closer to adult society than was the family. . . . In
> addition to being more numerous, the individuals, students and teachers,
> who compose it are brought together, not by personal sentiments . . . but
> for reasons that are entirely general and abstract. . . . For all these rea-
> sons, the rule of the school is not capable of bending with the same flexibility
> as that of the family . . . it cannot accommodate to . . . temperaments. The
> regime of the school has something more cold and impersonal, it is more
> addressed to reason and speaks less of sensibility, it demands greater ef-
> fort. (p. 126)

The school is more extensive than the family group of friends, and it
resembles political society in not being based on kinship or personal choice.
Yet at the same time, it is small enough to have personal relationships
that attach one to the group. This "collective life" of the class enlarges
his consciousness and "awakens in the child the feeling of solidarity"
(pp. 194-95, 207-209).

Durkheim specifically weighed in on what has continued to be a controversial aspect of discipline: the use of corporal punishment by parents
or school. He argues that corporal punishment is not really a practice of
the family, past or present, that it developed primarily in schools
(Durkheim [1925] 1974:160). He sees it as a barbaric practice suitable
only for training animals.

INTERNALIZATION

The ultimate goal of the socialization process so far as society is concerned is the internalization of social norms and values, that is, their incorporation into the psyche. Hynes (1975) cites Parsons's (1960) comparison of Durkheim to Freud, Cooley, and Mead in their "convergence on the idea of internalization" (Hynes 1975:98; also Parsons 1955b:55, 110).

Durkheim (1922) imagined a personality that would include a socialized component and an individualized realm:

> In each of us, one can say, there exist two beings which, though separable only by abstractions, are nevertheless distinct. One is composed of all the mental states that belong only to ourselves and to events in our personal life: that is what one could call the individual being. The other is a system of ideas, sentiments, and habits that express in us, not our personality, but the group or different groups to which we belong. Such are the religious beliefs and moral practices, national or professional traditions, collective opinions of all sorts. Their ensemble forms the social being. (pp. 49-50)

Like psychologists or sociologists who are better known than he for their theorizing of socialization and child development, Durkheim (1922) attributes both socialized and unsocialized aspects to the person. It is this dual nature that creates a need for socialization:

> The child, on entering life, brings only his individual nature. Society finds itself then, with each new generation, faced with a virtually clean slate on which it must start anew. It is necessary that . . . to the egoistic and asocial being just born, [society] must add another, capable of leading a moral and social life. (pp. 50-51)

Individuality

Durkheim's socialization emphasized the school *because* it is *social*, the agent of society. The family, on the other hand, is valued as a setting for individuality. "It is the individual personalities that form the family that we love, and in first place, our children" (Durkheim, 1900b:560).

That Durkheim was more favorable toward individualism than his reputation promises was first asserted by Giddens (1972:6-10, 1986:23).[10] Durkheim (1898a) wrote a long piece on individualism, analyzing its various forms. Pristine utilitarian individualism is "a religion of which man is, at the same time, the worshiper, and the God." But there is another, more palatable, even desirable, form of individualism, "the glorification

not of me, but of the individual in general." This moral individualism
generates empathy for mankind and "a great thirst for justice" for all. It is
a belief system that "ensures the moral unity of the country." "The indi-
vidualist who defends the rights of the individual, defends at the same
time, the vital interests of society. . . . The religion of the individual is a
social institution" (pp. 8-12). Durkheim once again bridges antinomies
and defends modern values by his reformulation of the common understanding of a concept.

Revisionism with regard to individualism in Durkheim has not been
so clearly applied to his perspective on the family. This is essentially because *Suicide* (Durkheim [1897a] 1930), with its concern for the benefits
of family solidarity, is more widely read than the posthumously published "The Conjugal Family" (Durkheim 1921).

The conjugal family presents a new organization of the interior of the
family. The old family communism having disappeared, "each of the
members [of the family] has his own individuality, his own sphere of
action. Even the minor child has his, although it is subordinate to that of
the father because of his lesser development" (Durkheim 1921:3). This
development of individuality in the family became possible as the social
stage grew larger. As nation-states formed, the great circle of kin lost
power. As the family circle contracted,

> the personalities of members of the family emerged. . . . Differences spe-
> cific to each individual, each member of the family, became more numerous
> and more important. . . . Each one took his own character, his personal
> manner of feeling and thinking. (p. 8)

Solidarity Again

"If the communism that has created the family disappears, does not the
increasing individualism risk destroying it?" (Davy 1925:116). Durkheim's
answer, according to Davy,[11] is that the family, though restricted in size,
"will still continue no less effectively to exercise a regulatory action on
the totality of our being" (p. 114).

Davy's assertion that for Durkheim, the conjugal family serves to regulate individuals is challenged by another of Durkheim's colleagues.
Maurice Halbwachs (1918)[12] presented a more pessimistic version of
Durkheim's work, concluding that "domestic life is languishing" and that
"members more and more consider that the family is the means of satis-
fying, more conveniently and completely, their individual desires" (p. 403).
I would challenge his tone. This does not sound like Durkheim, and the

specific quote about languishing family life is a referent to the decline of kinship, not to the efficacy of the conjugal family (Durkheim [1897a] 1930:213-24). But Davy may give too optimistic a reading of Durkheim's perspective.

While never altering the particulars of his theory, Durkheim himself seems to have expressed different views about the future of the family in different writings. There is the warm reception of affective individualism in "The Conjugal Family" (Durkheim 1921). When Durkheim turns in this piece to address the problem of solidarity and to advocate occupational groups as the solution, the tone regarding family change is nonthreatening, in contrast to the concern about domestic anomie expressed in "Divorce by Mutual Consent" (Durkheim 1906a). While the two pieces are, of course, not dealing with exactly the same issues, the receptivity toward individualism in the former without concomitant expression of a strong fear of anomie is remarkable but in line with other works, such as *Moral Education* (Durkheim [1925] 1974).[13] In his "Introduction" to the family course, Durkheim (1888a) states that "the family of today is neither more nor less perfect than that of old. It is different because the circumstances are different" (p. 273).

Despite the warm portrayal of the conjugal family, the conclusion that it will continue, and the assertion that it suits modern society, Durkheim did have his doubts. How is the solidarity of the family to be maintained, given its shrinking size, loss of functions, and growing autonomy and individualism? In the conjugal family, solidarity is basically affectional. That is tenuous; according to Durkheim, there should be other supports or constraints. While individualism, as well as an affect-based conjugal family, were positive values for Durkheim, his view of the family could be summed up as "love is not enough." He specifically rejected what he saw as a common view among his intellectual contemporaries—that the family is entirely a private and individual matter (Durkheim 1900j).

Family ties have an important protective effect for the individual in addition to their social import. The regulation of marriage prevents suicide by reducing anomie (Durkheim 1909b:277). Nevertheless, the trend in suicide rates in recent years had been upwards for all marital statuses (Durkheim 1888b, [1897a] 1930, 1906a). So Durkheim wished to have an external "rule" to support this largely affective unit (Durkheim 1909b). He acknowledged the necessity, even desirability, of divorce in cases of severe conflict and dysfunction, but argued against divorce by mutual consent even where there were no children: "It is not correct today to say that children are the sole purpose of the family. They are an element; they are not everything. And consequently, the necessity of matrimonial regulation . . . does not depend on their presence or absence" (p. 270).

Law is not the only underpinning of the conjugal family. At various times, Durkheim cited the essentiality of the family as a haven from demands of the public world, the family's role as an advocate of private individual and family interests, and its place as the locus of holistic personality in contrast to the other, segmental relations of modern society (Davy 1925:113-14). Moreover,

> common life is attractive at the same time that it is coercive. Doubtless, constraint is necessary to lead man to go beyond himself, to join to his physical nature another nature. But to the degree that he develops a taste for his new existence, he comes to need it. (Durkheim 1902a:xvii)

It provides the conditions of happiness (Durkheim 1909b:277).

Subject to Debate

Almost one hundred years later, questions addressed by Durkheim are still subject to debate. Durkheim had firm opinions about some of the topics of this chapter, while in other areas, he was less sure or expressed contradictory views.

SOLIDARITY

Durkheim's ambiguity about whether solidarity in the modern family is strong or weak has registered with those Durkheim scholars who have paid attention to the family (e.g., Wallwork 1972:95-98). It is a theme that reaches from Durkheim's time to ours, emerging in the frequent debates in academic, policy, and media settings about the "decline of the family" (or not). Glendon (1989) notes that

> the modern law of the on-going family has internalized a high degree of tension between the idea of the family as involving cooperation and community, on the one hand, and as facilitating the personal fulfillment of its members on the other. (p. 143; and see Cladis 1992:2 and chap. 1 and 2 generally; Giddens 1971:99)

These values are indeed in tension in the nations of the developed world.

On the whole, Durkheim was accepting and confident about the modern conjugal family—as a setting for human development and happiness, as a locus of dedication to others. But he saw divorce as a threat (if the law were to be modified to permit divorce by mutual consent). And he worried about the feminist movement and changing gender roles. (These topics are pursued in Chapters 6 and 7, respectively).

EXCHANGE

The degree to which exchange based on complementarity facilitates couple solidarity is not dogmatically affirmed today, as it was by Durkheim, but remains under consideration. Economist Gary Becker's (1981) late-twentieth-century version of the benefits of specialization and exchange in marriage is still enormously influential (Nock 1998, especially pp. 133-34; Oppenheimer 1997:432-33), but various research suggests limits and qualifications to this premise.

Social psychologist George Levenger (1974) developed a stage theory of the progression of couples from pure exchange and a detached evaluation of costs and benefits of the relationship to a powerful identification with the other and an inability to separate the other's well-being from one's own. There is some similarity to Durkheim's reasoning in that Levenger takes the position that exchange per se does *not* equate to solidarity but that an exchange relationship may develop over time into a stable relationship with joint outcomes and emotional attachment.

A recent article explored "what binds heterosexual couples together" (Brines and Joyner 1999:333). The researchers looked at couple cohesion from an exchange perspective that conceptualized partner bonding as a function of interdependency in the "specialization and trading model" (p. 335). Both "integrative bargaining" (under conditions of equal power) and "competitive bargaining" (unequal power) are possible, but only the former leads to "positive emotions" and "increased stay behavior" in married and cohabiting couples (p. 336, citing Lawler and Yoon 1993). Equality is especially important to cohabiting relationships. While specialization enhances the cohesiveness of marriage, it is not so essential to conjugal couples because marriage per se seems to encourage joint investment quite apart from couple exchange. Marriage also provides the couple the capacity to tolerate departures from traditional exchanges when marital roles become more similar through increased wage earning of the wife. In other words, marital cohesion feeds back into the process and permits flexibility in gender roles.

Last, a review of research on "the specialization and trading model" as manifested in women's employment suggests that there are limits to the functionality of sharply differentiated couple roles. Chief among them is the risk of the couple/family unit losing a set of essential skills if one partner dies or departs (Oppenheimer 1997).

SOCIALIZATION

Lasch (1977) views "the expropriation of child rearing by the state and by the health and welfare professions" as a dangerous aberration, which he seems to blame on Durkheim without naming him. Lasch criticizes the social science that "insisted that man is wholly the product of society" and that "the principle of 'interdependence' governs all of modern society" (p. xxii).

Indeed, Lasch (1977) is right about Durkheim. And Durkheim's views may be surprising to us, especially given the frequent characterization of him as "conservative." Today's family conservatives resist the control of the state (Carlson 1988) and to some degree oppose the common public schools. In today's family theory and research, we may find specific families or types of families or family patterns considered inadequate to the task of socialization, but never is the family institution found to be unsuitable in principle.

But for Durkheim, after the preschool years, socialization of the child *must* take place in extrafamilial settings, especially the school. The family is too soft for the important task of making the child a member of society. The dominance of the state over the family as socializing agent par excellence reflects the heritage of the French Revolution—the importance of secular citizenship and a mistrust of the private family. The French resolution of state-family conflict over control of education is very different than the outcome in the United States, which reserves to parents the ultimate authority to direct their children's education (*Meyer v. Nebraska* 1923; *Pierce v. Society of Sisters* 1925; *Wisconsin v. Yoder* 1972).

This sense of the family as *too* warm, *too* supportive, *too* hesitant to insist on normative behavior is parallel to Parson and Fox's (1952) conclusion that the family is too nurturant to administer a therapeutic regime to a family member occupying the sick role. The same affective/affectively-neutral dichotomy[14] appears in Spiro's ([1958] 1965) study of socialization in the Israeli kibbutz. There, communal socialization divides the parental role between the kibbutz worker, who has responsibility for the physical care, socialization, and education of children day and night, and the parent, who spends uncluttered time with the child for a few hours a day. The parent does play an important role in the child's identity and humanity but is not the principal socializing agent. The parent is an after-hours companion and gives love unconditionally. When socialization is the responsibility of community agents, parents may and do indulge their children freely without needing to monitor and discipline their behavior.

At the same time that Durkheim urged discipline and an abstract educational regime that did not give too much to individual temperaments or situational vicissitudes, he was firmly opposed to the extreme of discipline—corporal punishment. Durkheim viewed corporal punishment as inhumane and as crushing the autonomy that was one aspect of moral development. Moreover, he thought it ineffective in developing the spirit of discipline, as it interfered with the attachment to groups that facilitated socialization. Perhaps, his view was unusual in its day, as there has continued to be strong advocacy of corporal punishment in our time by some academics as well as by ordinary families and by some conservative family advocates. The preponderance of research suggests that this form of punishment is either ineffective or only effective in limited circumstances. In terms of social policy, the trend in major industrial nations is against corporal punishment (Straus 1994).

THE FUTURE OF THE FAMILY

Some current commentators sound wholly alarmed, for example, Lasch (1977), who says "the family has been slowly coming apart for more than 100 years" (p. 22; and see Gallagher 1996; Whitehead 1996). Others claim the family is "here to stay" (Bane 1976) or has simply transformed itself, and this is not so unusual historically (Coontz 1992; Stacey 1990). Advances, as well as problems, are part of social and family change, a point with which Durkheim would agree.

Some scholars try to take a comprehensive and neutral look at the family, especially so far as change affects children (Booth and Amato 1997; Hewlett and West 1998). Finding some improvements but also much cause for alarm, they discuss what policies are required to enhance the lives of children and the parenting work of families. In the next chapter, we see Durkheim address family policies for family problems.

Conclusion

This chapter brings together what can be found in Durkheim's work on the interior of the family, on solidarity, domesticity, affectivity, gender, socialization, and individuality. The texture of the chapter is pebbled. As in a cobblestone street, the units (topics) are of different sizes in terms of the amount of attention Durkheim gave to them. When fitted together, there is a bumpy inconsistency as one tries to find a sure surface on which to found conclusions.

Durkheim on the interior of the family is rather vague and mostly unempirical. Although he speaks often of emotions, of familial warmth, of individuality in the family, one finds it difficult to imagine this family interaction in concrete terms. The presentation is mostly in terms of abstract dichotomies of individual and social, public and private, kin and conjugal relations. There is little flavor of the real lives of families as appears in the work of Laing and Esterson (1970), Kantor and Lehr (1975), and anthropologist Jules Henry (1971), for example. One must acknowledge that Durkheim remains "the metaphysician" of his university days so far as the interior of the family is concerned.

Notes

1. *Foyer* does not have an exact equivalent in English, yet it is such an evocative word in French. *Foyer* captures the sense of the family home, its space and decor, its emotional warmth, loyalty, sustenance, and privacy. *Hearth* is perhaps the English translation that comes closest to the French image.

2. Durkheim refers to the French island province of Corsica, which has a regional culture very similar to that of Sicily. Before Italy was consolidated into a nation-state, protection and order in southern Italy were provided by the family. This is the origin of the *mafia,* whose turn toward crime was facilitated by the sense that those outside the family were fair game in a society with no sense of national unity.

3. The French word *parents* can mean either parents or kin. The context of this section does not make clear which it is, and my choice of "parents" is thus arbitrary.

4. A statement by Parsons (1955b) might seem to acknowledge that; "It is a well-known principle of differentiation of social structures, that competitive pressures can be eased by qualitative differentiation of roles (this was probably first stated by Durkheim)" (p. 96). However, Parsons here speaks of parents and children rather than husbands and wives.

5. For applications of exchange theory to the family and to emotions, see Sabatelli and Shehan (1993) and Lawlor and Thye (1999).

6. While the Durkheims had a traditional division of labor, if one biographical article is to be believed, the family economy very much depended on Mme. Durkheim's inheritance. Mme. Durkheim also played a supportive part in Durkheim's career, proofreading and correcting articles for *Année sociologique,* as well as performing other tasks of the academic spouse.

7. Farrington and Chertok (1993) offer a good overview of conflict theories of the family. There is also the classic Engels ([1884] 1972) work: *The Origin of the Family, Private Property, and the State.*

8. The conclusions stated here were not necessarily true of all geographic areas, as Durkheim notes. He reports a variety of data on gender differences in rates by marital status that vary by time and place and defy easy summary.

Present-day social scientists find much to criticize in Durkheim's analysis of data on suicide. However, what is of interest in this chapter's presentation of Durkheim's views is what he concluded about gender differences in the effects of marriage, not the validity of the analysis on which it is based. See Besnard (1993a) for a critique of Durkheim's statistical analysis and his interpretation of the data.

9. Weigert and Thomas (1971) do not agree, positing that while nurturant socialization in the form of "self-investiture" is essential, it might be accomplished outside the family, even technologically, in the unknown future.

10. For further discussions of individualism in Durkheim, see Cladis (1992), Fenton (1984:44), Lehmann (1993:239, 242-43); and Vogt (1993).

11. Recall that Georges Davy was an *Année* colleague of Durkheim's who joined the staff in 1910. His notes on Durkheim's course on the family are widely cited (e.g., in Lukes's 1972 definitive biography of Durkheim [p. 179]).

12. Halbwachs joined the staff of *Année sociologique* in 1905. He received his doctorate in 1913 and was eventually made Professor at the University of Strasbourg. His work generally is among the most respected of Durkheim's disciples (see comments by Clark 1973:211 and Karady 1981:39).

13. *Moral Education* was published posthumously. Consensus as to the actual date of writing is 1902-03, although 1899 has also been proposed (Besnard 1993b).

14. "Affective" and "Affectively neutral" are one of four pairs of "pattern variables," dimensions used by Talcott Parsons to analyze societies and relationships (see Abercrombie, Hill, and Turner 1994:304). As the words imply, the distinction is between a relationship of emotional attachment and one of emotional detachment and objectivity.

6

Family Problems, Public Policy, and Social Justice

Durkheim's works manifest an abiding interest in the practical implications of social scientific knowledge.

—*Giddens (1978:11-12)*

Wasn't family policy invented in the United States in the 1970s? Or perhaps Europe in the 1930s?—A chapter on Durkheim and family policy may come as a surprise to readers.

We do know that Durkheim wrote much about divorce as he pondered societal and familial solidarity. Yet despite the statistical detail, his gaze seemed directed toward the higher plane of theoretical analysis. Less known is Durkheim's involvement in ground-level debates on policy related to the family and not only with regard to divorce.

Durkheim on Family Policy

Durkheim was consistent in his view that sociologists and other academics should only rarely enter politics or be directly involved as policymakers. "The work of the sociologist is not that of the statesman" (Durkheim 1902a:xxvii). While intellectuals have something to add to a legislative body, few are needed in this role. And not being men of action, they are less able to conduct practical governance and policy. Moreover, "it must not happen that in the lecturer of today one suspects the candidate of tomorrow" (Durkheim 1904a:706).

SOCIOLOGISTS IN ACTION

Yet intellectuals do have a role to play:

> Writers and scholars are citizens; it is thus evident that they have the strict
> duty to participate in public life. . . . It is by the book, the conference, the
> works of popular education that our action must be exercised. We must
> above all be *advisers, educators.* (Durkheim 1904a:705)

That was an important part of the discipline for Durkheim:

> Durkheim frequently asserted that sociology should . . . find its justifica-
> tion in practice: that a sociology which had no relevance to practical
> problems would be a worthless endeavor. It is one of the major tasks of
> sociology to determine the nascent direction of change which a society at
> any given time is experiencing, and to show which trends "should" be
> fostered as the coming pattern. (Giddens 1986:26; see also Filloux 1993)

Durkheim showed his interest in policy quite early in his career, writing on the fertility problem and suicide (Durkheim 1888b). In Paris, he
was very active in several societies that held regular forums on the questions of the day. Presentations and discussions at meetings of the Union
pour la Vérité and la Société Française de Philosophie were recorded,
transcribed, and published in *Libres entretiens* and *Bulletin de la société
française de philosophie.*

"The family became a 'problem' that needed study for a 'solution'"
(Bridenthal 1982:226). As France and other countries debated what to
do about divorce, illegitimacy,[1] and low fertility, scholars in various nations of Europe stepped forward with their analyses. Statistical branches
of the state or city, often headed by well-respected scholars, collected
data as a foundation for policy-making purposes (van Leeuwen 1981:98),
just as Congress and state legislatures today commission studies of problems they plan to act on.

Durkheim wrote about policy issues in occasional pieces, typically based
on demographic data. He reviewed books and articles that addressed
policy, again, usually grounded in empirical data. How much influence
Durkheim had on policy, what influence he wanted to have, is uncertain
at this remove. Durkheim did not himself enter the political process except on two matters: the Dreyfus case and World War I. Yet he did not
speak and write from an exclusively theoretical point of view; he cared
about the policy issues. His purpose in intellectual analysis was "present
and practical" (Jones 1986:115).

Public intellectuals play an important role in France, then and now.
Durkheim and the Durkheimians had a great deal of influence, and un-
doubtedly his opinions were duly noted, especially after his move to Paris

in 1902. His university position made him responsible for the education of lycée instructors who in turn influenced their pupils. Durkheim served on important committees in the University and the Ministry of Public Instruction. He was personally friendly with some important public figures. Some called Durkheim a "secular pope" (Jones 1986:20). At the same time, Durkheim's antagonists in debate were quite confident and were sometimes politically or intellectually influential and very committed to their positions.

VIEWPOINTS ON POLICY

At the turn of the nineteenth century into the twentieth, France had some notable family problems that generated strong debates on social policy. These debates much resemble those of our most recent turn of the century. For example, although the absolute numbers of divorces at that time were much lower than the figures we worry about today, the trend was upward. On divorce as well as on other matters, "the concerns voiced by conservatives and radicals in the nineteenth century have their counterparts in the twentieth century" (Hutter 1981:31; also Bridenthal 1982:230-31). The issues were very similar to Barbara Whitehead's (1996) recent summation of the divorce dilemma: the "classic problem: how to expand individual freedoms without encouraging individual license" (p. 13). Tension between the goals of preserving "family" as institution, meeting the needs of actual families and their members, and respecting an emerging voluntaristic conception of the family marked these debates.

The politics of the day involved socialism in its various forms, a challenge to the bourgeois secular republicanism of the Third Republic. Durkheim is considered by some to be a socialist of sorts, a fellow traveler at least, though not so by others (see Chapter 1). In his work, Durkheim did express a general concern for social justice. That concern about inequality comes from secular republicanism as well as the influence of the socialism to which many of his friends and colleagues subscribed. There are references to the original values of the French Revolution in Durkheim's analysis of family policy issues, such as illegitimacy. The republican values he clearly held—*liberté, égalité,* and *fraternité*—confronted a society marked by sharp inequalities.

In addition to the lens of social justice and republican values, Durkheim drew on a medical metaphor to consider family problems, looking for the "healthy" state of affairs. The health metaphor is pronounced in *Suicide* (Durkheim [1897a] 1930), where the suicide rate is used as an indicator of social health (also Durkheim 1888b:447). Jones (1986) characterizes Durkheim as seeing "sociology as analogous to medicine and the sociologist as a kind of physician" (p. 80, fn 32). Durkheim sought to learn the distribution (epidemiology) of sickness and health and then to make a diagnosis and find a treatment (Giddens 1978:12; also Jones 1986:50). Problems were characteristically framed in terms of a normal-pathological dichotomy: "There is for all phenomena of life a normal zone, below or above which it becomes pathological" (Durkheim 1888b:460).

Turn-of-the-Twentieth-Century Family Problems

What family problems were visible in Europe at the turn of the twentieth century? As part of the evolution of the family from kin group to nuclear family, from institution to companionship (Burgess and Locke [1945] 1960), community and kin control gave way to a more individualistic ethic. This transformation of European society presented thoughtful, policy-oriented intellectuals with urgent social problems.

Policy on divorce had been contested on the public stage in France for a long time. Dilemmas of illegitimacy (hardly a new phenomenon) now focused on child welfare, the poverty of unwed mothers, and paternal and state responsibility, rather than on the putative sinfulness of the mother. France saw an early drop in fertility, and the French defeat in the Franco-Prussian War stimulated further concern about demographics and the power of numbers. The decline in household size was a related matter. Child labor, poverty, the abuse of women, prostitution, desertion, juvenile delinquency, and women's entry into the labor force were other phenomena with implications for family viability (Fouillée 1897; Hutter 1981:27; van Leeuwen 1981:111).

In the next section, some of these family policy issues are examined: divorce, nonmarital births, cohabitation, and fertility and household size.

DIVORCE

Divorce law reform was as contentious an issue in turn-of-the-twentieth-century France as it is in present-day America. From the late eighteenth century through the nineteenth and on to Durkheim's time, divorce law and policy had been the object of struggle between conservative and liberal forces, the latter often ambivalent about divorce.

History of Divorce in France

In pre-Revolutionary France, which had an established Catholic church, formal divorce was not possible.[2] The French Revolution liberated marital partners; divorce became available on request of husband or wife on various grounds from 1792 onward, although hedged about by a cumbersome procedure. However, even before Napoleon's accession, there was post-Revolutionary agitation against divorce. It was not acted on definitively until promulgation of the Napoleonic Code in 1804. This Civil Code retained divorce, including, in principle, divorce by mutual consent. But where the parties did not agree, divorce was essentially fault based and more difficult to obtain, especially for women plaintiffs. With the restoration of the monarchy in 1816, divorce was abolished altogether (Hunt 1992:41-42, 161-62; Rheinstein 1972, chap. 8).

The rational-secular values of the Third Republic were conducive to a reconsideration of the divorce option. Feminists and radicals were first to advocate for divorce, but the cause was taken up by moderate republicans and the final compromise reflected their interests. On one hand, they saw a liberty principle in divorce, and as secularists, they rejected traditional church control over the family. On the other, republicans were concerned about the stability of the social order. After years of struggle over divorce policy, a law was passed in 1884 to make divorce available in certain circumstances (Fletcher 1991). It was a fault system of divorce. However, judges soon began to interpret the law so liberally that divorce was essentially available on the request of both parties. It followed that formalization of "divorce by mutual consent" was again proposed (Rheinstein 1972, chap. 8). Feminists such as Marianne Weber (1907) advocated divorce by mutual consent.

The Divorce Debate

Debate about divorce in Durkheim's time centered on what policy the state should adopt: whether to permit divorce by mutual consent, to retain the status quo, or to press for enforcement of the fault-based law.

Durkheim did not oppose divorce in principle: "Nothing is further from our thought than to put in question the principle of divorce, that in certain conditions spouses must be permitted to escape from marriage. That does not even appear to be contested" (Durkheim 1906a:549).[3]

Yet divorce is the social problem that Durkheim revisited most frequently and spoke publicly about most often (Besnard 1993a:172) and not only in his book on suicide. Durkheim did oppose divorce by mutual consent. He stated his views and argued with others in the Union pour la Vérité debate on "Mariage et divorce" (Libres entretiens 1909) and in an article for Revue bleue on "Divorce by Mutual Consent" (Durkheim 1906a), and of course, his book on suicide had devoted much attention to the topic. Besnard (1993a) believes that Durkheim's emotionality around divorce colored his whole theory of social regulation (p. 172).

Durkheim seemed concerned that he would be taken to be a reaction-ary in the face of a wide consensus in favor of expanded legal divorce. He took pains to specify that his opposition to divorce by mutual consent was not some sort of automatic conservative reaction: "To the degree that one can know oneself, I do not feel myself to have a reactionary spirit" (Durkheim 1906a:549). Indeed, regarding divorce, "it is difficult to say whether it is positive or negative, morally speaking" (Durkheim 1901a:434).

Durkheim (1906a) challenged the argument that "it is in the interests of parents—and a little also, they say, in the interests of children—that the right to separate when their union has become intolerable is demanded for spouses" (p. 549). Other arguments presented in support of divorce by mutual consent included that marriage is a contract. That being so, its dissolution ought to be decided by the parties, not the state. It was also argued that divorce by mutual consent should at least be available to couples without children.

Durkheim argued that while the upbringing of children was an impor-tant element, the absence of children did not obviate the need to restrict divorce. Marriage has a regulatory function that benefits both the par-ticipants and society generally, and this is enough to justify state oversight (Durkheim 1909b:258-59, 261-62, 270, 277-80). The position that mar-riage is a contract that can be broken by the partners is answered by an argument similar to that of the *Division of Labor* (Durkheim [1893] 1978). Contracts do not exist in a vacuum but are embedded in a social context; hence, the state must concur in a marital breakup (Durkheim 1909b:258, 261-62). Moreover, the marriage contract is not narrowly a matter of the couple but also affects third parties, for instance, children, and even when there are none, the two extended families (Durkheim 1906a:552).

Durkheim's greatest concern about divorce was for society generally. Divorce by mutual consent would be a "very dangerous influence" on marriage. He cites comparative data (from *Suicide*) as proof that "the practice of divorce strongly affects . . . the state of marriage." What might seem to be in the interest of individuals would be a "grave social malady" because it would undermine the institution of marriage (Durkheim 1906a:549-50).

Freedom of divorce would also be bad for the individual, for the spouse's happiness is dependent on conjugal discipline (Durkheim 1906a:554). It is not so much that those divorcing commit suicide at high rates but rather, that married persons commit suicide more frequently where divorce is more easily attainable. Where divorce is common, the protective effect of marriage is less. The theoretical argument is that of anomie:

> Marriage, by the rule to which he submits his passion, gives to the man a moral foundation that increases his force of resistance. In assigning to his desires an object that is certain, definite, and, in principle, invariable, it prevents him from frustrating himself in the pursuit of novel, ever-changing ends, that, once attained, leave behind only fatigue and disenchantment. It prevents the heart from agitating and tormenting itself vainly in the search for impossible or deceptive pleasures. (Durkheim 1906a:552)

A too great availability of divorce undercuts the antianomic function of marriage: "Regulation to which one submits oneself only when one so fancies is not regulation" (p. 552).

Durkheim concedes that the advantages he is talking about largely fall to men. Married women benefit less than men, perhaps not at all, from the regulation of marriage represented by restrictions on divorce (Durkheim [1897a] 1930:189, 196; 1906a:551-52).[4] According to Durkheim (1909b), women do not need this legal regulation, being more affected by "mores and opinions" with "more severity" (p. 279). In other words, informal social controls are sufficient to ensure women's stability; legal restraints are less important to women's well-being.

While not considering it the only reason for preventing divorce by mutual consent, Durkheim (1906a) did point to the impact on children. Yes, "it can happen that in the interest of a good domestic order and the children, it is better to dissolve the conjugal society than to let it continue to no one's profit" (p. 553). Durkheim considers that these cases will be few. More likely are

> Menages which are simply mediocre, where the spouses do not have for each other all the sympathy that would be desirable, and where, however, each has for his duty sufficient feeling to acquit his function usefully, at the same time that that attachment to a common task, approaching each other in mutual tolerance, renders life more endurable and sweeter [than it would be outside of marriage]. (p. 553)

Who Decides? The Particulars of Divorce Law

The form divorce takes is very important for a policy goal of balance between (a) a needed mechanism for leaving bad or dangerous marriages and (b) the maintenance intact of most marriages. There is a significant difference between a *judge* applying specific legal standards to conclude that a marriage has failed and the *parties* receiving a divorce on application, with the judge a mere registrant of their decision. "In the one case, the divorce is granted only if it is just; in the other, it is granted automatically because it is asked" (Durkheim 1906a:552). Durkheim (1906d) argues that the parties are subjective, focusing on their hurts; the judge is objectively better able to evaluate the potential functionality of the marriage (p. 442).

In Durkheim's time, a putatively "fault" legal doctrine was rather subject to manipulation in an actual divorce process. Adultery and criminal conviction were clear-cut causes of action. But three-year separation (which might be backdated) and, especially claims of "excessive maltreatment and grave harm" had an indeterminancy that permitted a judge to grant a divorce on flimsy or contrived evidence. According to Durkheim, judges used their discretion to grant divorces rather freely for what were essentially minor slights—"indelicacy; lack of regard," incompatibility of temperament—thus "creating causes of divorce that the legislator had not envisioned" (Durkheim 1906d:438-39). Estimates were that perhaps 70 of 100 applications received favorable rulings, and in one series of forty cases, only one was denied (*Libres entretiens* 1909:283).

One of the arguments made in favor of adopting divorce by mutual consent was exactly this de facto freedom of divorce. One author claimed that cultural pressure for divorce was just too great to resist and so the 1884 law might as well be changed, because it could not be enforced. Durkheim agreed that "certainly the judge only follows the mores," but he went on to question, "are the mores healthy?" Is this phenomenon "normal or not"? (Durkheim 1906d:440). In his view, to shape the law by public opinion would be most consequential, as it would give formal societal approval to an undesirable practice (Durkheim [1897a] 1930:307). The law still makes a moral statement even when it is evaded. Judges must be encouraged to uphold the law, and legislators must not effectively abandon their responsibility. Durkheim would not prohibit divorce entirely. Rather, he wanted to ensure that divorce would not be obtained solely at the discretion of the parties. He would let divorce remain more difficult and less resorted to rather than change the law to make it available by mutual consent. A judge must make a decision about the viability of the marriage and the necessity of divorce.

Durkheim did see some difficulty in finding a legal formula to sort reasonable from unreasonable divorces. He considered that perhaps the problem could be solved by specifying more precisely the standards for a judicial finding of marital mistreatment or harm. He even expressed the thought that abandonment of the domicile when there are children could be made a criminal offense. He quickly dropped that idea (Durkheim 1906a:553-54), but it does serve as an indication of how strongly Durkheim opposed divorce by mutual consent.

This discussion of the divorce debate emphasizes arguments critical of unregulated divorce and in favor of greater restrictiveness because that is essentially Durkheim's position. He was well aware that certain of his contemporaries held a voluntary rather than institutional conception of the family. Their views were evident in the debate on divorce (*Libres entretiens* 1909) as well as in their thoughts on "free union" or cohabitation.[5] Durkheim's views on nonmarital childbearing, while mixed, were more welfare-oriented than punitive.

COHABITATION AND NONMARITAL BIRTHS

Durkheim's concern about illegitimacy was for children, their proper socialization and moral education. It was also about marriage. To accept free union would be to equate a situation without obligation to one with strong and clear moral obligations. This confusion would undercut the institution of marriage. It would mean less protection for children and less security for the marital partners. "Free union is a conjugal society where obligation does not exist. Thus it is an immoral society. And that is why children raised in such milieu present such great quantities of moral defects" (Durkheim 1921:14).

FREE UNION

In Durkheim's essentially progressive theory of family evolution, free union—what we would call cohabitation today[6]—was not only a less desirable form of conjugal union but an outmoded one associated with an earlier stage of the family: "The more the family is organized, the more marriage has tended to be the only condition of parenthood" (Durkheim 1921:14). Marriage is not only more desirable, it is the only moral form because it creates obligations, the most important of which are put into legal form.

What Durkheim described in terms of the dominance of legal marriage remained true in France until 1972, when the distinctions between legitimate and illegitimate children were definitively erased. Before then, "there is no family in law but the legitimate family. No legal bonds exist between members of the so-called natural family" (Mazeaud, Mazeaud, and Mazeaud 1967:39, quoted in Glendon 1989:259).

Yet free union was quite prevalent in nineteenth-century France because of the unavailability of divorce and the requirement that younger adults consult with or gain approval from parents for their marriage (Glendon 1977:85). Some feminists also advocated for free union to replace what they viewed as patriarchal marriage, while others were concerned that free union would lead to the exploitation of women (Fletcher 1991, chap. 1). In practice, free unions were *sometimes* treated as something approaching marriage. There might be property settlement on dissolution or compensation in the form of damages awarded for seduction under false promise of marriage or for later abandonment (Glendon 1989:255-59).

Many scholars of Durkheim's time, and of course, Durkheim himself, wished to support marriage and eliminate free union. Some were impeded by a reluctance to join conservatives in religiously or traditionally based critiques of free union, so they sought alternative ways to rationalize their point of view. One scholar made the argument that marriage benefits women because in marriage, a woman's personhood is respected. In free union, on the contrary, the principal motive is sexual desire and not "her character . . ., her spirit, her will. If he loved her completely, he would unite with her whole being, he would make her the companion of his life, his wife." In free union, the woman

> is diminished and she cannot accept this diminution, which is an outrage, without failing in her duty to herself. Marriage is thus the only form of sexual union to which the woman can lend herself without failure, for it is there alone that she plays her role as a human person. (Summarized by Durkheim in 1900j:367)

Durkheim was having none of this essentially therapeutic and self-realizing rationale for marriage. He presented it to show "the manner in which the cultivated spirits of our time conceive the family and its role in society" (Durkheim 1900j:370). He found this line of argument too individualistic, too lacking in recognition that the family is normative and institutional. "There is no family without law, without a domestic morality, and that law and that morality are imposed on the familial group by the surrounding society" (p. 370).

Nonmarital Children and Child Support

Illegitimate children might be born to a relatively stable free union, or they might be the product of an man's brief or ongoing liaison. While the establishment of paternal responsibility for out-of-wedlock children could threaten a particular marriage or the marital institution, Durkheim believed that one had to be concerned about the welfare of children of unwed parents. A punitive or nonsupportive stance would be to punish innocent children, future citizens of France, for the failings of their parents. Moreover, republican France had initially committed itself to abolishing distinctions based on birth status (Durkheim 1902h:380, 1907d), and a 1896 law placed recognized natural children on an equal footing with those born in marriage so far as inheritance was concerned (*Libres entretiens* 1909:267).

The policy dilemma was how to provide support to female-headed families so as to take care of children, while not at the same time encouraging further unwed births. French law in Durkheim's time permitted the voluntary acknowledgment of paternity but prohibited the investigation and establishment of paternity against the wishes of the natural father.[7] This prohibition had been put into the Civil Code by its original drafters. Despite the republican desire to erase the distinction between legitimate and illegitimate children in a spirit of citizen equality, revolutionaries were ambivalent about changes in the family. Permitting the courts to establish paternity against the wishes of the natural father might "disturb the domestic order." There was a fear of the "invasion of the family by strangers." When the distinction between legitimate and illegitimate children was erased, a protective barrier was deemed necessary. As the revolutionaries brought down most other social institutions, they needed the family to be "a sacred thing, a base of social order." Anything that could "alter the purity, compromise the sanctity" of the family was "intolerable and prohibited, even at the price of individual suffering" (Durkheim 1902h:380-81, reporting the views of others).

Whether or not the law should be changed was a policy issue of sufficient interest to European policymakers that considerable research on the impact of paternity laws was undertaken, especially in Germany. Durkheim was skeptical about some of the arguments for permitting the establishment of paternity and child support. He thought them insufficiently supported by the data presented. One author argued that prohibiting the establishment of paternity contributed to the rise in illegitimacy (men did not have to worry about such complications of their nonmarital sexual activity). Durkheim did not think empirical data on marriage and illegitimacy rates supported this point. Nor did he think that if illegitimacy were reduced, juvenile crime would decline, another argument made in favor of change. Some data comparing rates of illegitimacy to marriage rates suggested that if women could legally pursue the establishment of paternity, marriage would follow. Generally, though, Durkheim (1903d) thought that the data available on illegitimacy and its correlates were too limited in geographic reach to be of use. He did believe there was statistical support for one conclusion: that infant mortality is higher for illegitimate children and especially so in jurisdictions where the juridical establishment of paternity was not permitted:

> This result is not at all surprising. . . . [T]he [higher infant mortality] of illegitimacy . . . is due to the state of misery, physiological and otherwise, in which the unwed mother finds herself when she gives birth. It is natural that where she has no recourse against the father of her child, that misery is greater still and produces more disastrous effects. (Durkheim 1903d:417)

Overall, Durkheim concluded that the legal right of the unmarried mother to identify the father and claim support would not make the difference people assumed it would. That is, changing the law might not reduce illegitimacy: "These entirely utilitarian considerations [of whether the father can be made to pay support], these calculations, cannot have a very profound effect on a phenomenon which depends, above all, on such profound physical and moral states" (Durkheim 1901g:442).

But for Durkheim, both social health and the principle of social equality pointed toward changing the law. Society has always sought to find institutional mechanisms to protect "natural children" and attach them to society. Durkheim noted when he wrote on this topic in 1902 that among major European countries, only France and Italy prohibited the nonvoluntary establishment of paternity (Durkheim 1902h:379). "The prohibition [of juridical paternity establishment] is abnormal" (Durkheim 1903d:418), a "singularity of our law" that one regards with "astonishment" (Durkheim 1902h:380).

For those opponents who feared the impact on the family of permitting an unwed mother to identify the father, the 1896 modification of the Civil Code to permit recognized natural children to inherit seemed a further threat. "The more that legislation attenuates the difference between the situation . . . of the legitimate and natural children, the more it diminishes . . . the moral authority and prestige of marriage" (M. Jules Dietz in *Libres entretiens* 1909:267).[8]

Durkheim disagreed:

> The fact that one extends to natural children certain of the advantages of marriage is evidence not that marriage is depreciated, but that one finds it unjust to make children bear the consequences of the mistake committed by their parents. (*Libres entretiens* 1909:267)

Correlates and Causes of Nonmarital Births

Scholars of Durkheim's time explored the causes of nonmarital births, seeking the key to prevention. Durkheim (1901g) pointed out that the proportion of unwed births can be high, not necessarily because of sexual deregulation but because marriage rates might be low and thus marital fertility also (p. 441).

He denied a direct effect of the economy on illegitimacy, arguing instead that social crisis in the form of either economic or political upheaval produced an effect on society that is really one of morale (Durkheim 1901c). This change in morale affects both illegitimate and legitimate births. Thus, "the variations in illegitimate births take on an entirely different signification [than that of sexual license]; they are symptomatic of the variations through which passes the mental and moral state of the country" (Durkheim 1901g:443).

Family Types and Child Outcomes

Scholars and policymakers in Durkheim's time, like those today, were interested in the outcomes for children in different family settings. The adult functioning of illegitimate children in different circumstances was explored, often measured by fitness for military service. Data on unwed mothers in various postbirth settings were analyzed in a comparative approach similar in concept to analysis of variance. Some unwed mothers remained single, whereas others remarried. A distinction was made as to whether the marriage was to the father of the child or not (usually not). Some mothers had died.

There were implications for public policy and child welfare services in these studies. For example, children who were placed in public care when their mothers died had better outcomes than those whose mothers lived but remained single. Results for stepfamilies were mixed, depending on the study. Durkheim (1906c) reviewed a German outcome study that he finds somewhat limited in both data and analysis. What is interesting is not so much the validity of the study or Durkheim's critique but that studies published in the early 1900s attempted to do analyses parallel to today's.

FERTILITY AND HOUSEHOLD SIZE

Durkheim expressed succinctly the French national concern about its birth rate: "An insufficient natality is a collective malady; a society is not healthy if it does not include enough living elements" (Durkheim 1900b:558).

The Population Problem

French anxiety about the birth rate dates from earlier than the nation's defeat in the Franco-Prussian War. The demographic transition began quite early in France. Fertility fell from 1800 onward, so France had low fertility for a longer period than most societies (Caldwell 1999; Weeks 1999:522). Military considerations were an important aspect of concern about fertility. But a sufficient population was also thought important to meet needs for labor and for political power and colonial development. A certain natural vitality and strength of culture and economy were associated with a strong and growing population in the minds of many; a weak birth rate meant a weak nation. For traditionalists and Catholic sectors of the public (often overlapping categories), large families of children were the essence of family life. Liberals and socialists were also committed to population growth as an important social goal (Johnson 1994:133-35).

Durkheim shared national concern about fertility, expressing surprise that one scholar could deny the "continued weakness of our fertility" (Durkheim 1905d:616) when "it is evident . . . that the number of our births is below normal" (Durkheim 1900b:559). (Durkheim [1888b] also concluded from his reading of the research that too high a birth rate could also be pathological because of the more difficult "struggle for life"; p. 460).

Durkheim was sufficiently interested in the population problem to have written an early article exploring the statistical relationship between fertility and suicide (Durkheim 1888b).[9] He reviewed much of the statistical-demographic work of Bertillon (e.g., 1902c)[10] and others and the interpretations made of those data by their contemporaries.

Causes and Correlates of Low Fertility

Consistent with his general theoretical perspective, Durkheim argued that the long-term downward trend in fertility could not be explained by economic trends (Durkheim 1902g, 1903a, 1905d). Nor was impaired fecundity or infertility an explanation.[11] Although the number of children per family dropped, childlessness had remained unchanged since mid-nineteenth century, suggesting that fecundity was constant (Durkheim 1902c). The decline came from a decrease in families with three children. Families of four remained numerous, but the shift by many couples to two- or even one-child families was the proximate cause of "the precarious state . . . of our population" (Durkheim 1900b:559).

Fertility (number of children born) varied by age at marriage, the age difference between husband and wife, the length of the marriage, and other variables (Durkheim 1902g, 1903f, 1905e). Rural residents and Catholics typically had higher fertility, but in Durkheim's opinion, data were far too limited and regionally varied to warrant firm conclusions about religious or rural-urban differences. He did accept as proven that a convergence on two children was typical of urban Europe, Germany at least (Durkheim 1902g). And he agreed that data confirmed the common impression that better-off families had fewer children (Durkheim 1902c, 1905e), a pattern that continues today (Weeks 1999:194, 209). "It is the poor who have more children" (Durkheim 1904g:655).

None of the explanations commonly offered for low fertility were convincing to Durkheim. As he saw it, variations in fertility did not match patterns of economic development or demographic characteristics of a region (Durkheim 1900c). He did not clearly articulate a theory of the demographic transition that would have explained declining fertility and the inverse relationship between family size and social class in terms of economic opportunity and opportunity costs.[12] By process of elimination (a common strategy in his reasoning), Durkheim concluded that the root cause of lowered fertility lay in cultural or "moral" factors, the "collective temperament of the group" rather than the material situation (Durkheim 1902g:437).

This was not specified in detail, and Durkheim's (1900b) theory of fertility remains rather underdeveloped. He did see changes in culture associated with modernization as part of the process, chief among them, individualism:

> We agree . . . that the inadequacy of our fertility is due above all to moral causes and that the principle of those causes consists of a certain development of the spirit of individuation. . . . A change was produced in the domestic order . . . which renders it less appealing to us to have large families. (P. 560).

In his discussion of fertility, Durkheim seems far less approving of individualism than in some other writings. Here, he paints a picture of individualistic self-isolation. Where families are more meager and thus less intensely unified, individuals are less close to one another. This "weakening of the domestic spirit" is "letting the cold wind of egoism enter, which ices hearts and beats down courage" (Durkheim 1888b:463).

While rejecting explanations linked to economic development, Durkheim did connect a desire for small families to economic ambition, a facet of individualism. Here, he approaches a theoretical explanation similar to that of the demographic transition, although he made no connection to infant survival or broad transformations in the economy. It is simply that people came to "prefer material ease to the pleasures of life in common" (Durkheim 1888b:462).

Durkheim does grasp that the parent-child relationship and the value of children had changed. In the past, people had many children so as to perpetuate the family in its collective identity: "above all one wished to prevent the name of the elders from perishing, to not leave empty the family home" (Durkheim 1900b:560).

> Today we practice domestic life entirely differently. The abstract personality of a family society is no longer the object of the same sentiments, . . . it is the individual personalities which form it, and especially our children. Now, the interest in our children is not that they be numerous. So that we can cultivate them with care, it is good that our efforts not be dispersed over a great number of heads. (Durkheim 1900b:560-61)

Thus, Durkheim normalizes small families, accepting the intense socialization practices (and emotional relationships) of the modern middle class. Indeed, he himself had two children.

Still, in the modern family, children leave home eventually. The declining motivation for high fertility is not incidental but is something that was lost in the transformation of the family and will not be easy to replace (Durkheim 1900b).[13]

Population Policy

Most proposed solutions to the fertility problem were economic. Le Play, a conservative and traditionalist social scientist, blamed declining fertility on the change in inheritance laws that required equitable distribution of estates among offspring (Pitts 1968:86). To maintain some coherence of property, it was now necessary to have few heirs. Because Durkheim was opposed to inheritance in principle because of its perpetuation of inequality, he would not wish to address the fertility problem by returning to a system that would concentrate family wealth in one heir.

Jacques Bertillon (1880) proposed that fertility be encouraged through *faveurs budgetaires* in the form of tax reductions for large families. Durkheim concluded that while this had the virtue of being equitable, it would not work as population policy. Because a higher economic level meant fewer children, improving the family economy would be likely to lower rather than increase fertility (Durkheim 1902c). Moreover, in Durkheim's view, fertility is affected most by "a state of the spirit that one cannot cut into by financial means" (p. 436).

Household Size and Composition

Household size is not the same as fertility. While the two often go together, it could be that the household could be empty of children no matter how many were born. Children could and did leave home early to emigrate, to pursue their educations, and to establish themselves in business or other occupations. At the same time, single adults or married children could live with parents, or other persons, such as domestics or retirees, might move into a household. There are also nonfamily living arrangements, such as prisons, hospitals, educational institutions, convents, and military barracks (Durkheim [1897a] 1930:209; 1900i).

Statistics pointed to France's singularity in terms of decrease in household size. This was due not only to lowered fertility but also to an increasing tendency to live alone. In fact, this tendency toward single or single-parent living was greater in France than any other European country save Finland (Durkheim 1900i:572).

When a marriage was broken by death or divorce, single or single-parent living might be the result. This was especially true for women, who seemed to have an "aptitude for the solitary life" (Durkheim 1900i:573). According to a study Durkheim reviewed, there were twice as many women as men in single-headed households. No mention was made of age per se. However, among those young enough to be rearing children, the sex difference was even more pronounced.

"It seems that [women] can more easily isolate themselves as live in groups, and that, once alone, circumstances dictate what kind of life they adopt" (Durkheim 1900i:573). Thus, while they might choose to live alone as single parents, unmarried women were also more likely than others to be in households in which other relatives were present. This tendency to fill in the gap in the family provided, for Durkheim, a hopeful note. He saw the persistence of the family, a preference for family living, in the tendency for the family group to reconstitute itself when one of the spouses was missing. But because, in Durkheim's formulation, sheer mass had the effect of increasing solidarity, the trend toward diminution of the family household caused him some concern.

Durkheim was concerned but had no salutary solution to the problem of diminished fertility and household size, given that it was anchored in evolutionary change in family and society.[14] Instead, he turned his attention to other ways of creating solidarity in modern society, through occupational groups.

EQUALITY AND SOCIAL JUSTICE

Underlying Durkheim's views on some family problems, notably the situation of nonmarital children, is a tacit sense of social justice. Scholars debate his commitment to equality and social justice (Cladis 1992; Connell 1997; Fenton 1984:43-47; Filloux 1993; Gane 1992; Giddens 1978:109, 1986; Jones, 1986; Lehmann 1995b, especially the conclusion; Lukes 1972:78, 115, 157; Meštrović 1988:5, 7; Pearce 1989; Schoenfeld and Meštrović 1989; Vogt 1993; Young 1994; Zeitlin 1968). Generally speaking, equality for Durkheim meant merit, equality of opportunity. This did not preclude an inequality grounded in individual talent and accomplishment so long as access to roles was not limited by hereditary advantage and rewards could be based on performance. Neither inequality resulting from differences of talent nor the difficulty of measuring "merit" troubled Durkheim. Nor did he devote much attention to absolute levels of poverty or connect social and economic inequality to structures of class power and systemic advantage.[15]

Durkheim's policy focus with respect to inequality was on inheritance law. Inheritance of wealth perpetuated class advantage and contradicted the equality among citizens that was an ideal of the French Revolution.

Durkheim saw inequality to be in decline, given that families could no longer pass along hereditary offices and honor. He anticipated that inheritance would be completely abolished in the near future. Not so, of course, and the degree to which individuals can inherit family wealth unimpeded (by taxes) is a significant policy issue in the early part of the twenty-first century (Naughton 2001).

Meritocracy was Durkheim's major theme, but there was a minor one that recognized the injustice that could result from his version of equality as meritocracy. Durkheim (1910a) acknowledged that "in fact, we are unequal in physical strength, intellectual power, and will power" (p. 191; translation W. D. Halls). Gane (1992:9), in particular, references *Leçons de Sociologie* (Durkheim 1950:220) to conclude that Durkheim thought advanced societies should strive for greater equality by compensating for the unequal distribution of talent (but see Schoenfeld and Meštrović 1989). In *Leçons de Sociologie*, Durkheim writes,

> If justice alone is in question, these inequalities of merit will still persist. But where human sympathy is concerned, even these inequalities cannot be justified. For it is man, a human being, that we love . . ., not man a scholar of genius or as an able man of business. . . . Charity is the feeling of human sympathy that we see becoming clear of even these last remaining traces of inequality. . . . This, then, is the very acme of justice. (Durkheim 1950:219-20; translation C. Brookfield)

Durkheim does not believe that society has attained a state of consciousness where empathy is sufficient and egoism restrained enough that men will work without an "exact recompense," permitting instead "a complete leveling to equal values." But in the future, what is now charity to soften a distributive justice system based on merit may become a "strict obligation, that may be the spring of new institutions" (Durkheim 1950:220).[16]

Family Policy and Social Values

In the realm of family policy, we have the perhaps novel view of Durkheim as policymaker, champion of the illegitimate child, conceding the need for divorce, concerned about being perceived as reactionary, and concerned in principle about social justice. We also have the familiar gloom about the negative impact of modern changes in marital stability and fertility. We have concern and caution on issues that reflect the tension between individuality and solidarity.

Durkheim's expressed views on family policy have not been seen as a whole in any volume that I know of. Yet some general themes emerge from the concrete issues. These are themes that reflect typical tensions in Durkheim's work. His family policy perspectives do not resolve those tensions, for Durkheim's key value commitments—to the French Revolution and to community—do not always complement each other. Revolutionary values of equality and liberty may be associated with social effects that are not so desirable. Present-day scholars and policymakers struggle with the same complexities.

SCIENCE, MORALITY, AND POLICY

One can characterize Durkheim's sometimes contradictory approach to policy issues by noting that he combines the roles of scientist and moralist. Lukes (1972) puts this in less neutral terms as an "alliance of sociological acumen with strict Victorian morality" (p. 533).

Sometimes, morality dominated science. For example, in his zeal to insist on limitations on divorce, Durkheim minimized his discovery as a scientist that marriage was not so advantageous nor divorce so disadvantageous for women. Sometimes, morality and science merged. Durkheim's use of a "health" standard for society masked what was often a moral view with a seemingly objective criterion for social behavior. The health metaphor is one used by present-day social scientists concerned about the viability of marriage and the family (Popenoe and Whitehead 1998-99; Waite 2001:465) and other social problems (Rockett 1998). In her comparison of the evaluation of social institutions to the evaluation of medical or public health measures, Waite (2001) is explicit about the need to advance value criteria (p. 466).

As Traugott (1978) notes, "Durkheim was a moderate rather than a reactionary" (p. 37), a "liberal" in the context of the Third Republic (p. 36).

> It is his almost obsessive desire to discover a measured and temperate course of action that has sometimes been mistaken for a frank conservatism. . . . [d]espite his liberal politics. . . . [T]he conservative tone [is] most apparent in his discussion of moral issues. (P. 37)

Turner (1993) credits Durkheim with an appreciation of "the problematic character of social intervention." This was not typical of the times, for most social scientists, social critics, and politicians had every confidence in their abilities to chart directions for society (p. 14 with reference to Besnard 1993a). Concern for the latent effects of policy intervention still exists today. Glendon (1989) worries about "the law's occasional power to adversely affect family life and doubts about its ability to have more than a weak effect in supporting or strengthening families" (p. 312).

Divorce, fertility, cohabitation and nonmarital births, and affiliation, that is, sharing family life or living alone, were family issues that occupied Durkheim. These continue to be important policy issues in our time.

Divorce

The similarity between divorce debates at the beginning and the end of the twentieth century is striking. Durkheim's argument that too-easy availability of divorce undermines the security and happiness of marriage is one that has been made very explicitly in late-twentieth-century critiques of divorce law and practice (Gallagher 1996; and see Glenn 1996:31; Whitehead 1996:181). Durkheim's views opposing divorce by mutual consent, but not ruling out divorce altogether, could be seen as a centrist position in his time and ours. Like communitarian[17] as well as more conservative perspectives, it places family responsibility (defined as continuing a marriage) above individual choice and happiness.

Presently in the United States, the reform of divorce law that began in the 1970s is being challenged, drawing on much the same kind of argument that Durkheim offered. The major element of the reform was that all states enacted procedures for no-fault divorce; there did not have to be a proven "guilty" party in terms of a limited set of "grounds" for divorce. This meant not only that couples could divorce by mutual consent but went even further. Now, divorce can be obtained unilaterally. In all states, divorce is permitted on the basis of "irretrievable breakdown" or "irreconcilable differences," which can be alleged by either spouse and do not require proof of fault or agreement of the other party.[18]

Divorce rates rose rapidly in the United States from the mid-1960s to the early 1980s, and have since stabilized but at a high level. Concerns expressed by those scholars and policy advocates who would like to reform the reforms include (a) loss of the social-control function of marriage for young males; (b) the postdivorce depressed financial circumstances of women and children; (c) the estrangement of many fathers from their children; (d) the problematic behavioral, educational, occupational, and marital outcomes for children; (e) the possible deinstitutionalization of marriage; and (f) a generally high level of unhappiness in and after marriage in a "divorce culture" (Whitehead 1996; and see Gallagher 1996;

Glenn 1996; Popenoe 1990, 1993; Popenoe and Whitehead 1998-99, 2000:14; Wallerstein and Blakeslee 1989; Wallerstein, Lewis, and Blakeslee 2000; Whyte 2000). Moreover, marriage provides clear advantages in practical terms and enhances well-being in many respects (Nock 1998; Waite 1995).

Other scholars and commentators (e.g., Acock and Demo 1990; Cherlin 2000; Coontz 1992; Stacey 1993) disagree with those cited earlier as to the negative effects of divorce, their inevitability, or their significance in terms of child outcomes. The research of Judith Wallerstein is particularly criticized. Scholars who believe that the negative impact of divorce has been overstated place divorce in historical perspective. They note that while divorce rates were low in the past, the high mortality rates common prior to the twentieth century led to marital dissolution, remarriage and stepfamilies, and higher rates of orphanhood than exist today.

Still others find that divorce is beneficial in a minority of cases, while problematic in a majority (Booth and Amato 1997). And last, at least one scholar reviewing the literature finds that "marriage is typically an asset for men, regardless of the quality of the marital union," while the outcomes for women depend on marital quality (Nock 1998:14), a conclusion somewhat reminiscent of Durkheim's note taken of the greater impact of marriage on men.

There is no serious move to completely eliminate divorce in the United States today, but those who believe divorce is too readily available propose various restrictions and also argue for a set of promarriage policies. Policy proposals include: (a) restoration of "fault"; (b) a lengthy waiting period, perhaps three years; (c) a two-tier divorce process, with a more extensive process for divorces involving children; (d) prioritization of children's needs in allocation of property and support responsibilities; (e) a more general child support reform; (f) "covenant marriage" (a two-tier system of marriage that would commit the couple to a more stringent divorce process, with fewer grounds) or other premarriage commitment; (g) encouragement of premarital counseling; (h) removal of alleged "marriage penalties" in tax policies and benefits programs; (i) parenting plans to focus attention on postdivorce family functioning; and (j) publicizing research that would convince the public of the risks of divorce (Hewlett and West 1998:242-43; Waite and Gallagher 2000:188-99; Whyte 2000). Several books have appeared that point to the benefits of marriage (Waite and Gallagher 2000) or that criticize college textbooks for insufficient positive attention to marriage (Glenn 1997a, 1997b).

Most of the advocates for a more restrictive divorce law acknowledge that divorce is necessary in some cases. Throughout American history, "the challenge for a democratic people was to uphold the freedom to divorce without inspiring promiscuous divorce" (Whitehead 1996:13). Concern is directed toward divorces that are thought unnecessary and avoidable. These would involve marriages that do not have severe problems, such as violence, but simply experience a decline in romantic feeling. They would be marriages in which the couple is no longer so happy but conflict is remote enough so that they can provide a good home for their minor children (Booth and Amato 1997; Wallerstein and Blakeslee 1989; Whitehead 1996). The sense Durkheim had that a less-than-good marriage might nevertheless have benefits for the partners and especially for the children is very much a part of the contemporary critique of divorce. Booth and Amato (1997) found in their research that approximately one third of marriages were characterized by a dysfunctional level of conflict prior to divorce, while in two-thirds of divorced couples, the marital tensions between the partners were not so overtly disruptive or disturbing to the children.

Liberal scholars, in contrast to conservatives and communitarians, tend to argue that (a) the impact of divorce on children has been exaggerated, (b) most divorces occur after a lengthy period of trying to save the marriage, (c) efforts to support divorced families financially and otherwise would do more to aid children than legal restrictions on divorce, (d) some number of divorcing parents can continue to coparent effectively postdivorce, (e) legal arrangements regarding custody and visitation need attention more than divorce per se, and (f) family structure is less significant than family relationship quality. Moreover, restoration of fault, implementation of waiting periods, or other impediments to divorce might have unexpected negative consequences (Acock and Demo 1994; Ahrons 1994; Bartlett 1999; Cherlin 2000; Coontz 1997, chap. 4, 1999; Pollitt 2000; Thompson and Wyatt 1999; and see "Divorce, American Style" 2000, commentary by David Blankenhorn, Judith Wallerstein, and Katha Pollitt). Policy proposals would include attention to the economic and social needs of postdivorce families and to measures such as joint custody that are believed to enhance coparenting.

Durkheim would be most easily aligned with the current reformists who wish to restrict divorce to cases of severe dysfunction, provable in court by convincing evidence rather than a partner's assertion of irretrievable breakdown. Durkheim does depart from current American concerns about divorce, which have the welfare of children as their primary focus. His greatest concern was "marital anomie." Durkheim feared that the unchecked freedom to divorce offered by the French Revolution had proven unsuccessful then and would not provide a happy life in his time. It would facilitate the divorce of couples who might otherwise have made a go of it with at least moderate satisfaction. And it would diminish the benefits of marriage.

But like Durkheim, today's critics of divorce may be fighting a losing battle. Although divorce by mutual consent was *not* formally adopted in

France until quite far along in the twentieth century, the effective availability of divorce continued throughout Durkheim's lifetime and after (Glendon 1989:159-73). Durkheim (1906a) noted ruefully,

> We do not fool ourselves, unfortunately this idea of the rule and its utility is far from being widespread and popular. Opinion sees in all regulation an evil, to which one must sometimes resign oneself, but also necessarily try to reduce to a minimum. (p. 554)

Regulation of people's personal lives is not well received in a cultural moment when (it is alleged) rights outweigh responsibilities (Glendon 1991; also Glenn 1996:31).

Fertility

Durkheim's concern for a too-low fertility rate would have seemed quaint and outdated until recently, when there has come to be a certain alarm about dramatically falling birth rates in Europe, Japan, and North America (Erlanger 2000; Wattenberg 1987). Labor force and markets are motifs also articulated in the earlier French panic, but military concerns are not an issue at present. What is new at the turn of the twenty-first century is the anticipated need to support and care for the growing numbers of elderly citizens.

The smaller family of Durkheim's time attracted Durkheim's attention in terms of its interaction and socialization process. In talking about the more intense socialization of children permitted by a smaller family, Durkheim foreshadowed Nobel economist Gary Becker's (1960) explanation of fertility differentials in terms of the "quality" of children—children are more costly of time and money in the upper and middle classes because more is expected from them. A large research literature has developed on the "value of children," comparing traditional to modern societies. Children are now valued for emotional reasons, not economic ones (Goetting 1986b; Hoffman and Hoffman 1973; Hoffman and Manis 1979; Zelizer 1985).

Cohabitation and Nonmarital Childbearing

In Durkheim's time, marriage seemed to be driving out free union—or so it was hoped, as more people were enabled by economic advancement and the availability of divorce to regularize their unions through marriage. Presently, cohabitation has emerged as a strong challenge to marriage, even more so in some European countries than in the United States.[19]

"Illegitimacy" has lost its legal disability, but nonmarital births continue to cause concern, if not in moral terms, then in policy ones. In fact, Durkheim's focus was more on policy than morality, the economic viability of single-parent families and outcomes for children. In present-day France (1994/98), 40 percent of births are nonmarital (compared to the U.S. 33.8 percent in 1998). Many European countries have rates greater than 30 percent (United Nations 2000:36, chart 2.7; Ventura et al. 2000:8).

The discussion of cohabitation and nonmarital births in Durkheim's time and ours highlights some of the tensions that arise in family policy. The question of whether families framed in terms of divorce and remarriage, cohabitation and nonmarital births, should be treated as normatively inadequate or supported as alternative family forms is as heated now as it was then. Family policy has typically foundered on the definition of "family": "Public discourse on the family typically takes the shape of emotional and polemical debates by some, hinging, at least in part, on divergent definitions by some and the assignment by others of a privileged position to families with traditional marriages" (Moen and Forest 1999:634).

Durkheim's position was clear: The conjugal family, the bourgeois nuclear family, was that privileged family model. In terms of gender (as we shall see in the next chapter), he could not move beyond that lens. But for nonmarital children, for single mothers, for those in frightful marriages, he had a sympathy that made him look for humanitarian solutions rather than taking a judgmental position.

Individualism or Community?

Living in families or "bowling alone"? An article with the title "Bowling Alone" (Putnam 1995) attracted enormous attention with its assertion that social solidarity is vanishing in the present-day United States (also Putnam 2000). People prefer individualistic activities and lives to the pleasures and duties of community. Bellah et al. (1985) had earlier expressed a concern about excessive individualism and loss of community that also created a stir when it was published.

These messages pick up on a theme that has been heard since at least Durkheim's time—that modern society and the accompanying decline of kinship, small towns, and ethnic communities are leading to an excessive individualism and spells alienation from social institutions as well as informal social ties.

Some years ago, Barrington Moore (1958) speculated that the trend toward a smaller and smaller family would lead to the evolutionary endpoint of the solitary individual. This resonates with Durkheim's (1900i) concern about "the tendency of the elementary group to reduce itself more and more until it attains its extreme limit" (pp. 572-73). Certainly, the decline of fertility in France and the proportion of people living alone concerned him in this way.

The thesis of "Bowling Alone" (Putnam 1995) has been challenged and data proffered that suggest Americans are no more alone than they used to be, just doing different things together (see Ladd 1999; Talbot 2000; Wolfe 1999 for varied responses to Putnam). Durkheim hoped that alternative ways of connecting people in society would indeed develop in modern society, notably the occupational groups. The realization of hopes for solidarity in modern society, and what policies might support that hope, are not yet so clear.

Conclusion

Durkheim had an interest in the practical policy use of sociological theory and research. He entered into dialogue with policymakers and intellectuals on family policy issues related to divorce, cohabitation, nonmarital births, and fertility. These policy questions were analyzed in the context of individualism versus community, science and morality, and equality and social justice. These same themes appear in present-day family policy debates. So do the same family issues.

With regard to equality and social justice, Durkheim showed some awareness of the contradictions of merit and equality in society. He expressed a vague future hope that meritocracy plus charity would give way to a pure social equality.

The twenty-first-century reader may be most struck by Durkheim's imperfect resolution of the contradictions of inequality concerning the status of women. One of the issues facing turn-of-the-twentieth-century Europe was the "problem" of women and the feminist challenge. Sex and gender are the focus of the next chapter, as we explore Durkheim's views on women and feminism and on sexuality and sex education.

Notes

1. We now refer to nonmarital births rather than "illegitimacy," but the turn-of-the-twentieth-century debate was conducted under the latter rubric, with its aura of disapprobation. Because that reflects the perspective of the times, it seems appropriate to use the term.

2. However, marriages could be annulled or a separation from bed and board obtained. Also worth noting is that French Protestants had access to divorce following the Edict of Nantes (1598). This accorded Protestants religious rights, thus the acceptance of divorce in Protestant teaching was honored. The revocation of the Edict in 1685 proscribed non-Catholic religions and so the authority of Protestant churches to grant divorces was vacated.

In another important pre-Revolutionary development, secular courts gradually took over administration of the law of marriage from the Catholic church (Rheinstein 1972:197-98).

3. Durkheim (1906a) posits a consensus that he admits does not include Catholic traditionalists (p. 549).

4. Durkheim was consistent in finding men to be the beneficiaries of marital regulation (through the limitation of divorce), while varying in what he said about women. Sometimes, he reported no impact of divorce availability on women's suicide rate; sometimes, he found that strict divorce law had a negative effect on women. And while he generally found that married women had lower suicide rates than single ones, for childless women the reverse was true. Some variation in Durkheim's presentation of data on suicide can be attributed to varied demographic sources and analytical problems. However, Jennifer Lehmann (1995a) makes a theoretical interpretation of Durkheim's change in interpretation of his data as representing an attempt to rescue his gender theory from the dilemma of harming women in order to preserve an advantage for men (pp. 921-24). Besnard (1993a) also gives theoretical weight to this variation in a discussion of "fatalistic" suicide). Durkheim's theoretical perspective on women is discussed in more detail in Chapter 7.

5. For a detailed discussion of the politics and law of divorce in nineteenth-century France, see Fletcher (1991).

6. "Common-law marriage" is another type of informal union under American law. Legally speaking, what this means is that a couple "holding themselves out" as married for a certain length of time, which varies by state, was considered to be married. British in origin, it was abolished there but survived in the U.S. frontier setting, where clergy or state officials were not always available to perform formal marriages.

In the past several decades, common-law marriage has been eliminated from domestic law by the vast majority of American states. However, cohabitation under certain circumstances ("express . . ." or "implicit contract") may lead courts to attribute obligations to the partners, while not necessarily considering them to have been married. Regardless of marital status, parents are *always* obliged to support children of the union (Areen 1992:76-77; Krause 1986:48-50, 55-61).

The term *common-law marriage* comes from the Anglo-American common-law legal tradition in which custom and case decisions gradually accumulated to form, for all practical purposes, a legal code. In modern times, the formal acts of legislative bodies add provisions to this body of law, and case law continues to develop.

France has a *continental* rather than common-law system. Continental law refers to the legal system based on the Napoleonic Code of 1804, which characterizes most European law outside the British Isles. It is also the framework for state law in Louisiana. In the continental legal system, formal codes of law are developed holistically. They may be added to or modified by legislation. There are some differences in legal procedure between continental and common-law legal systems, but they are not relevant here.

Not having a common-law system, France never had "common-law marriage." However, informal free unions were sometimes recognized in a similar way. Glendon (1977) argues that the conceptual distinction between simple and temporary cohabitation and a more established free union did not really exist in France (p. 107, fn 24, and see her chap. 3 generally).

7. Marital fathers are as natural in the biological sense as nonmarital fathers, of course. However, *natural father* was the term of choice for nonmarital fathers in Durkheim's time and in his writings.

8. He was an attorney at the French Court of Appeal.

9. See Johnson (1994) for a methdological critique of Durkheim's work on suicide and natality.

10. Jacques Bertillon was a leading figure in France's statistical agency. His father, Louis-Adolph Bertillon, had earlier been active on this demographic problem (Johnson 1994:136).

11. *Fecundity* refers to the biological capacity for reproduction, while *fertility* refers to the actual number of children born. *Infertility* and *subfecundity* refer to not being able to have children or the number of children desired, respectively. Because infertility and subfecundity are diagnosed by the inability to conceive and deliver a desired child within a specified time interval, the cause is indeterminate and could be biological or other.

12. Demographic transition theory posits that as industrialization occurred, families developed higher economic aspirations, children were more likely to survive, their education became important for advancement, and the nuclear family became independent of the extended family, so children were no longer needed for continuation of the lineage. Urbanization and secularization changed attitudes, including a shift from fatalism to a sense of control over life and nature. All these contributed to a desire for and the effective implementation of smaller family size. See Weeks (1999, chaps. 3 and 6) for a detailed explanation of demographic theories relevant to the issues discussed here.

13. See Davis and Blake (1956) for an analysis of why traditional societies and extended kinship produce high levels of fertility.

14. See Davis and Blake (1956) for a still-relevant discussion of why traditional societies and extended families provide structural pressure and support for high fertility.

15. In *Leçons de Sociologie* (lectures given at Bordeaux in 1890 through 1900 and repeated at Paris in 1904 and 1912; Kubali 1950:1), Durkheim does confront the class system: "There are two main classes in society, [rich and poor], linked by all sorts of intermediate classes" (Durkheim 1950:213, translated by C. Brookfield). The framework for Durkheim's discussion of class is contract. The issue for him is whether equitable contracts, which reward merit and services, can really be negotiated between parties whose resources are unequal. His conclusion:

> In principle, the system operates in conditions which do not allow of justice. . . . It is true that over the centuries, the injustice could be accepted without revolt because the demand for equality was less. Today, however, it conflicts only too obviously with the attitude that is found underlying our morality. (Durkheim 1950:213-14, translated by C. Brookfield)

Nevertheless, Durkheim did not link himself with any contemporary movements toward equality, save for indirect links to socialism and resistance to anti-Semitism in the Dreyfus case. With regard to socialism, he opposed the idea of a state-planned economy prominent in both socialism and Marxism. He did not subscribe to the labor theory of value (Durkheim 1950:199-200, translated by C. Brookfield), which implied that more economic rewards should go to the working class (Durkheim 1910a:189, 191, translated by W. D. Halls).

16. See Filloux (1993) and Schoenfeld and Meštrović (1989) for a more detailed discussion of these issues.

17. The communitarian movement is relatively new as a formalized policy and political perspective. Communitarians advocate that more weight be given to community needs and values and less to individual rights. They believe that society has become imbalanced since the 1960s in this regard (Glendon 1991). A general statement of communitarian principles can be found in Etzioni's (1993) *The Spirit of Community;* the organizational arm of the movement is the Institute for American Values.

Communitarians writing about the family include David Blankenhorn, Maggie Gallagher, Mary Ann Glendon, Norval Glenn, David Popenoe, and Barbara Dafoe Whitehead. While communitarians would, I believe, define themselves as centrist, liberal critics see them as more conservative. For critical perspectives on the movement and its family policy, see Walker (1998) and Stacey (1993).

18. Although, in principle, some evidence must be offered to show that the marriage is not viable, the simple assertion by one of the spouses that the marriage is over suffices, by definition, to prove irretrievable breakdown. A judge must agree and grant the divorce, but refusal would be a rare event. In effect, in the present-day United States, not even mutual consent is required; the divorce can be obtained at the will of only one of the parties.

"Fault" has not totally vanished from the divorce process. Fault standards remain in some state laws, alongside a no-fault process, and may be invoked by a spouse. Informally, the appearance of fault can also affect awards of alimony, property, and child custody, even when not formally relevant. And sometimes, fault does remain in the state legal code, applicable to these elements of divorce.

19. Current data (1992/96) indicate that cohabitation is widespread among younger French adults: sixty-three percent of twenty to twenty-four year olds and thirty-three percent of twenty-five to twenty-nine year olds. Eighteen percent of thirty to thirty-four year olds are cohabiting. This compares to thirty-three percent of the older age group who are cohabiting in Sweden. Comparable American data are not available, but Canadian figures are similar to those for France (United Nations 2000:27, chart 2.6).

7

Women and Sex

Challenges to the Family Order[1]

Woman must seek equality in the functions which are in keeping
with her true nature.

—*Durkheim (1900e:391)*

It is because men and women differ from each other that they seek
each other out with passion.

—*Durkheim ([1893] 1978:19)*

In 1963, Betty Friedan spoke of "the problem that has no name" (p. 15).
In turn-of-the-twentieth-century France, it had a name: "the problem
of the sexes" or "the woman problem." It had a theory: feminism. And it
had a proposed solution: equality. All of these were subject to debate.

Durkheim was in the midst of this disputation about the status of
women. He wrote reviews of feminist work and other scholarship on
women. He took part in debates among scholars, journalists, lawyers
and judges, activists, and other public figures. His own work on suicide
and other sociological problems required theoretical reflection on women
and discussion of gender roles.

This chapter presents Durkheim's perspective on women, his theory
of gender. In a separate section of the chapter, Durkheim's analysis of sex
and sexuality are discussed.[2]

Introduction

Books and articles *about* Durkheim's perspective on women are more extensive than what he himself wrote, substantial though that is. This chapter explores both in social context. For one, there is the social and political milieu of the time in which Durkheim wrote. We need to look at the history of feminism in France and examine what Durkheim's contemporaries thought about women, equality, and feminism.

Present-day interpretations of Durkheim's work also take place in a social context. Durkheim on women is burnt-over territory. Beginning with Besnard's (1973) reconsideration of *Suicide* (Durkheim [1897a] 1930), we have books, articles, and papers by Besnard (1973, 1993a, 1997), Danigelis and Pope (1979), Erickson (1992, 1993), Gane (1983), Johnson (1979), Kandal (1988), Lamanna (1990), Lehmann (1990, 1991, 1994, 1995a, 1995b), Roth (1989-90), Shope (1994), Sydie (1987), and Wityak and Wallace (1981), as well as critical reviews of Jennifer Lehmann's (1994) *Durkheim and Women,* which continue the discussion (Besnard 1996; Challenger 1996; Cladis 1995; Gane 1995; Meštrović 1996; Orrú 1995; Tiryakian 1995). This flurry of activity was likely stimulated by the late-twentieth-century resurgence of feminism after a period of latency,[3] a development that coincided with renewed interest in Durkheim on the part of social scientists and other scholars. The result is a critical perspective on Durkheim's writings on women that is largely feminist.

Robert Alun Jones (1974) discussed two ways in which theory can be evaluated: historicism and systematics. One may read a classical theorist against present understandings and find him or her useful or else wanting by virtue of errors, blind alleys, irrelevance, time boundedness, or even offensiveness to present-day sensibilities. Jones argued instead for a *historicist* approach to social theory, understanding the theorist's work as situated in his or her historical times and intellectual context.

I decline to choose between these two options. In responding to Durkheim's writings on women and gender, a historicist approach is essential, although it does not give us a definitive answer to the question, Was Durkheim antifeminist in the context of his times? But like literary works, intellectual positions and works of scholarship can change their meaning as the audience changes. What is the sense of Durkheim's writings on women at the turn of the twenty-first century? In a present-day context of gender theory and gender politics, what do scholars say about Durkheim?

Feminism in France

Durkheim was intellectually active in the midst of the feminist movement of the late nineteenth and early twentieth centuries. He entered an ongoing debate that had started at the time of the French Revolution. Revolutionary leaders were puzzled about how to integrate women into the principles of "liberty, equality, and fraternity" and how to respond to women's political activism during and after the Revolution:

> Did they have equal rights in property inheritance, did they have equal rights in the family, could they participate fully in politics? In short, were they citizens in the full sense of the word? What was their role to be in the new revolutionary family? (Hunt 1992:89)

By and large, that role was *not* full citizenship. Despite their formal commitment to equality, "republican men . . . expressed great uneasiness about women acting in public ways" (Hunt 1992:81). Women's revolutionarily inspired activist groups and writings were suppressed. The legal disability of women continued throughout Durkheim's lifetime, and only after World War II did French women get the vote. But "Liberal political theory and the exclusion of women did not go neatly together" (p. 204).[4]

In the nineteenth century, socioeconomic and cultural change reinforced emancipatory ideologies and provided a foundation for social movements, including feminism. There was an important General Congress of Feminist Societies in Paris in 1892, the first conference in France to use the term *feminist*. Government representatives participated (Boxer 1981; Scott 1996). The nineteenth century saw the emergence of a class of bourgeois women with the leisure and education to aspire to political involvement and to articulate the feminist movement's theoretical underpinnings (Fletcher 1991; Kimmel 1987; LeGates 1995).

"The theory of the political, social, and economic equality of the sexes" (LeGates 1995:494) is one definition of feminism. But the feminist movements of nineteenth-century Europe and North America did not speak with one voice. In that era (as well as ours), there was a distinction between "equality" feminism and "difference" feminism. "Equal rights" feminism treats men and women as essentially similar, seeking for women the roles and opportunities formerly available only to men and in general, advocating for equal and similar treatment irrespective of sex. "Social" or "cultural" feminism accepts the existence of differences between men and women, whether presumed to be biological or social in origin. In that perspective, social policy and law should meet the unique needs of women, which may be different from those of men. Women's distinctive contributions to society—notably their moral virtue, social concern, and family roles—should be recognized and honored.[5] There was some shift toward cultural feminism during the nineteenth century. The argument that women's family roles and special qualities disposed them toward a moral leadership and interest in social welfare that would be of benefit to society had great appeal. And equality feminism and cultural feminism were not so polarized in the nineteenth and early twentieth centuries as they are now, at the beginning of the twenty-first. Nevertheless, intellectual and political disputation often involved the question of similarity or difference between the sexes (Cott 1986; Hunt 1992:199-204; LeGates 1995:502-505; Moses 1984; Sapiro 1994, chap. 14; Scott 1996).

During the Third Republic (1871-1940), Catholics and other conservatives continued to affirm traditional roles. Socialists and republicans alike struggled with "the woman question." Neither party was much help to feminists, offering only minimal and inconsistent support. Working-class movements were divided about women's employment, believing it favored bourgeois women who wanted to work at the expense of a family wage for the working-class husband (Boxer 1981:60-61, 65-68; Scott 1996; Slaughter and Kern 1981:4-7, 66-88; Stetson 1987). In fact, the mainstream feminist movement was fairly moderate. The majority of French feminists highlighted, rather than rejected family and family roles, but they wanted some changes made. They were inclined to accept the premise of gender difference. But they did not intend to accept unequal treatment based on those differences (Boxer 1981; Scott 1996; Shope 1994:27-28).

Feminist issues at that time included access to higher education, the professions, and other work; women's control over their own earnings; "maternal authority" (the right of the married woman to share authority over the children with her husband); divorce; elimination of prostitution; the plight of single mothers; maternity leave and other supports for employed working-class or poor mothers; maternity homes; equal legal treatment of women in terms of guardianship and in the aftermath of adultery; woman's legal autonomy (the right to contract and to pursue legal action without husband's authorization); and the right of unmarried mothers to seek paternity identification and child support (Boxer 1981; Cova 1991; Durkheim 1901e; Fletcher 1991; *Libres entretiens* 1909; Moses 1984; Scott 1996; Shope 1994).[6]

In France, the dominant political tension regarding women was one of mismatch between the French Revolutionary values of equality and the disadvantaged position of women in law as well as custom, in the home as well as in the public realm of political and economic activity. There was a contradiction between a modern society, economy, and demographics (the falling birthrate) and an exaltation of the maternal role and domesticity for women.

Voices made the case that inequality was no longer justified. Lourbet (1900), for example, in *The Problem of the Sexes*, took the position that the subordination of women may have been justified in an earlier time when physical force played an important role, but now, when intellectual faculties dominate, there is no reason a woman should be destined for inferiority (in Durkheim 1901h). Like many, however, Lourbet (1900) thought that women should be deeply involved mothers.

Catholics and other conservatives held the line and tried to push the clock back. But that was not the world of the sophisticated secular intellectual, the socialist worker, or even the educated bourgeois woman. What was on the table in those circles was what response to make to *feminist* ideas and proposals? How far to go with *equality:* conceptually, juridically, and normatively?

Durkheim's Venues

Durkheim was deeply engaged in consideration of women's status and role. While his "Introduction to the Sociology of the Family" (Durkheim 1888a) refers to "spouses," obscuring the differences in their authority in the family, gender is prominent in the *The Division of Labor* (Durkheim [1893] 1978) and *Suicide* (Durkheim [1897a] 1930). Feminism is directly addressed in reviews in *Année sociologique*.[7] And Durkheim makes a vivid appearance in a debate on the status and roles of women that occupied the Union pour la Vérité for the better part of the 1908-09 calendar year (Durkheim 1909b).[8] Here, he was surrounded by feminists! The Union board had voted "feminism" as its topic for the 1908-09 series (*Libres entretiens* 1909:5), more fully stated as "Questions Relating to the Economic and Juridical Condition of Women." Debates were lively. Their tone is captured by this remark, made in response to the antifeminist observation that husbands could act for their wives in important decisions: "He demands to be master, while the woman only asks reason as mistress" (Mlle. Gabrielle Louis, Editor of *La Française,* in *Libres entretiens* 1909:8-9).

Durkheim participated in the fifth debate of the series on marriage and divorce. There were four women participants, two described as "women of letters" and two with no institutional or occupational designation.[9] In other debates, participants included officers of the National Council of French Women and editors of *La Française*. Speakers alluded to reports and legislative lobbying by feminist organizations.

One does not have to be a woman to be a feminist, and more than one male participant expressed his commitment to the equality of women (while usually not anticipating that women would relinquish their maternal role). Monsieur Dietz, a judge in the Court of Appeals, pointed out that times had changed. Some women contribute to the household through their earnings. Those who relinquish employment to remain in the home must not be seen as inferior. A woman's work is "equivalent to that of the father and must merit for her the same rights" (in *Libres entretiens* 1909:20). But ambiguity in the commitment to women's equality was more typical of male participants in these debates. M. Brunschwicg spoke against the "tyranny" of the subordination of women. Yet he took the position that men and women were not the same, they were complementary (*Libres entretiens* 1909:6). Paul Desjardins, secretary of the Entretiens stated his views:

> We must always, in the feminine, consider the human. . . . We must consider what is common to men and women and substitute that rule for a romantic exaltation of the sex which is [said to be] "weak, detestable, and charming." (p. 244)

Women should be treated equally, according to the common law: "In that we are clearly feminist." Yet a claim by woman for herself without regard to children, family, or society is unacceptable. "Feminine individualism is monstrous and inhuman" (in *Libres entretiens* 1909:244).

Durkheim did *not* declare himself a feminist, in this debate or elsewhere. He expressed great interest in the feminist movement as a category for sociological analysis (Durkheim 1900g) and thought that it would not be a transitory phenomenon (Durkheim 1900e:391). Durkheim addressed the feminist movement directly in his reviews of books on the subject. He refers to the feminist movement as "unconscious" or "unaware," meaning, I believe, that he thinks feminists do not realize the import of their demands. He calls attention to *women* who have made points critical of feminism (p. 391).

The particular Union debate in which Durkheim participated concerned divorce, the proposed adoption of divorce by mutual consent (discussed in Chapter 6). Durkheim defended the status quo, which permitted judges to grant a divorce in certain situations. Feminists on the panel (as well as some judges) favored divorce by mutual consent. Durkheim defended the current system as not disadvantageous to women and as necessary for an ordered society, referring frequently to the necessity of *"règle"* or regulation. Women participants did not hesitate to dispute the well-known Durkheim. One asked rather confrontationally, "What is this rule [règle] ... with a capital R?" (Mme. L.M. Compain[10] in *Libres entretiens* 1909:281). She implied and some others agreed that Durkheim had invoked a vague metaphysical deus ex machina in support of his position. (In response to the sharp question, Durkheim did explain more fully what he meant by *règle,* which was law and well-established custom).

DURKHEIM AND MARIANNE WEBER

Durkheim (1910i) confronted feminist Marianne Weber indirectly through a review of her 1907 book *Wife and Mother in the Different Economic Societies.*[11] Marianne Weber was the wife of sociologist Max Weber. She was a well-known scholar in her own right and a leader of the feminist movement in Germany who spoke publicly on women's issues.[12]

Marianne Weber's feminist theories were presented in her 1907 book and in a later work (Weber 1919), which criticized the ideas of another major sociologist of the time, Georg Simmel ([1890-1911] 1985).[13] The juxtaposition of their views on women highlights the issue that faced intellectuals confronting feminist demands for female equality: how to reconcile the principle of equality with putative differences between the sexes. Simmel's theory (as interpreted by van Vucht Tijssen 1991) has elements of cultural feminism, based on the premise that there were profound differences between men and women. Women had strengths that men lacked. While men did indeed create "objective culture"—the products of civilization, including the arts—women had the intuitive capacity to integrate objective culture with subjective experience. Simmel intends to make the point that women are superior to men. But Weber[14] is not persuaded by this bow to women's special qualities. Simmel praised women for qualities that effectively constrained their lives by excluding them from public life.

Weber (1919, as interpreted by van Vucht Tijssen 1991) presents an innovative resolution of the dichotomy between similarity and difference. She offers the metaphor of overlapping circles: Men and women have "a core of shared capacities" (van Vucht Tijssen 1991:210, citing Weber 1919). Weber's conceptualization of sex differences implies not only that women could and should participate in public life and create objective culture but also that men can and should contribute to the relational and caregiving side of life, developing the more "subjective" side of their personalities in the process. Weber expected that, in the long run, women would attain equality in the public sphere while not losing their humane feminine qualities.

Durkheim, of course, was no longer living when Weber's 1919 book was published. Yet her views were well known because of her public career. Durkheim's and Weber's ideas about gender came into conflict in Durkheim's review of Weber's 1907 book (Durkheim 1910i). His response to Weber's ideas brought out his own views on women more clearly.

Durkheim (1910i) bows in respect before criticizing Weber's perspective. She has "been serious in how she has informed herself" and has used her sources "with a judgment and critical spirit to which it is fitting to pay homage" (p. 364). But (and it is always "but" with Durkheim when it comes to the position of women), there are some serious faults in her thinking. In her critique of male dominance, Weber oversimplifies historical periods by combining quite diverse societies; she has a simplistic two-stage family theory; she tries to cover too much, and in general, "it seems useless to discuss a thesis which contradicts so many known facts" (p. 366).

Durkheim moves on to examine the connections Weber makes between the history of women and the history of the family. According to Weber (as summarized by Durkheim in 1910i), the evolution of the family

> has only profited the masculine part of humanity. . . . Heads of individual families have always been men. . . . The importance of military functions gave social primacy to the strong sex. Only, what has resulted from that is a subordination of the woman, which still exists. (pp. 366-67)

Durkheim does not disagree that male sovereignty continues into the modern era. But he is not inclined, as Weber is, to see this as a survival, a simple prejudice that must be done away with now. Weber foresees an eventual complete legal assimilation of men and women, wife and husband, in which "neither of the two spouses has rights superior to the other" (p. 367). She notes that, more and more often, the woman earns her living and contributes to family maintenance through this work or work in the home (van Vucht Tijssen 1991). Weber points to socialization rather than nature as a reason for the visible differences between men and women. She urges that women be brought along educationally and professionally to the point of complete public as well as private equality.

As to Durkheim's (1910i) opinion of Weber's pitch for gender equality, "We are far from contesting that the legal status of women calls for important reforms." But over and over, Durkheim insists on the "complexity of the problem" (p. 367). Why can Weber not see that the patriarchal family of Rome, not to mention its successor, the modern European conjugal family, is an *advance* in the status of women? Rather than enslaving women, this evolution of the family brought the husband more tightly into the domestic sphere. True,

This domestic regime has given birth to the woman's legal minority in civil life. But on the other hand, . . . family life is much more intense and more important than in previous types [of families]. The role of the woman . . . to preside over that interior life, has taken [on] . . . more importance and has elevated the moral[15] position of wife and mother. . . . The husband and wife are brought together, are more constantly in contact because the center of gravity of masculine life has ceased to be external to the home, as it was in the past. The more the family holds the attention of the man, the more he feels himself to be his wife's partner and the more he loses the habit of seeing her as inferior. (P. 368)

Durkheim argues that respect for woman has increased throughout history, as formal marriage has become more central to family and society. He gives this a quasi-religious cast in comparing the *foyer* or home to an object of religious worship: the woman benefits from the "religious respect that the foyer inspires." If this is undone, if the sacred character of the home and marital union is transformed into a society of tentatively coupled individuals, that will lower the status of women by her loss of "feminine grandeur" (Durkheim 1910i:368).

One might think that what she loses on one side, she will gain on the other, by means of a more considerable role that she will play in civil society. But will the gain represented by the conquest of rights . . . compensate for the important losses? (Pp. 368-69)

Despite his expressed esteem for women, Durkheim was not even close to the profeminist position of some men of his era who saw that the equality of women had the potential to facilitate better family relations because a liberated woman had more to offer (Kimmel 1987).

A Contradictory Theory of Gender

If we use Kimmel's (1987) classification of men's responses to turn-of-the-twentieth-century feminism as (a) antifeminist, (b) masculinist, and (c) profeminist, we might place Durkheim in the antifeminist category. The signal indicators of antifeminism, according to Kimmel, are agreement that differentiated sex roles should be maintained because they are functional and that gender inequality rests, at least in part, on biological difference. These viewpoints are credited to Durkheim, and indeed, he did not favor complete political-legal equality for women or autonomy in marriage. "Scientific" evidence was offered for the assumption of biological difference. Historian Joan Scott (1996) talks about the "naturalizing effect" of the data on sex differences in brain size cited by Durkheim, who "provided a good example of this position, one that was widely subscribed to at the time" (pp. 96-97).[16]

Still, Durkheim's views are more variegated, more complex, and more recognizant of the power of the principle of women's equality than is sometimes recognized, yet full of contradictions. In Durkheim's view, societal solidarity required normative social structures. But the heritage of the French Revolution demanded citizen equality, and modernizing social change led to expectations of some degree of individuality and voluntarism in personal relations. Durkheim held commitments to both solidarity and liberal equality, not in a balanced way but with excruciating tension. He did not proceed to a profeminist resolution of this tension, but his views are too complex to be neatly contained in an antifeminist box. Let us take a closer look at Durkheim's theory of gender.

THE FACTS, JUST THE FACTS

Durkheim approached "the woman question" in two contexts: ethnographic scholarship and contemporary policy debate. His first concern was to establish a valid ethnographic and historical portrait of the status of women.

The ethnographic interest appeared in numerous book reviews in which he considered "the condition of women" in Babylonian, Jewish, Anglo-Saxon, Malagasian, German, Chinese, Japanese, African, and other societies (e.g., Durkheim 1900d, 1900f, 1900l, 1901b, 1901k, 1903b, 1903e, 1905g; Durkheim and Bianconi 1913). In some of these, women had considerable independence from their husbands in terms of legal process, commercial transactions, or government power (Durkheim 1905g; Durkheim and Bianconi 1913).

Durkheim was quite critical of some of this work. He refers to an *American Journal of Sociology* article by Thorstein Veblen on "barbarian" women as "not very up-to-date on the state of the question" (Durkheim 1900l:392). Durkheim takes issue with a stage theory of gender presented by Gaston Richard, an *Année* colleague. Following a primitive stage in which men and women are relatively *equal* (though both subordinate to the collective), *patriarchy* emerges. Men have a privileged situation, and women are inferior. Last, in the third stage, in modern times, individualism results in "a more and more complete *assimilation of the two sexes* from the moral, legal, and political point of view" (as summarized by Durkheim 1910f:369). Durkheim criticizes Richard and others for "passing in review" a series of diverse societies and forcing them into an artificial, unsupported, and not very well-thought-out theory (Durkheim 1904f, 1910f).

In addition to ethnographic studies, Durkheim was interested in more current "facts" relevant to the status of women. His many books, articles, and reviews pertaining to policy questions made use of statistical data on a wide range of topics in addition to his well-known work on suicide. For example, he reviewed an article that examined German statistics on differences in employment by gender and marital status (Durkheim 1901f).

Durkheim also reviewed books specifically about feminism or advocating women's equality. In these reviews, Durkheim is sometimes noncommittal, describing but not commenting. In some, he criticizes the methodology of the work, stating that it is, for example, vague and general (Durkheim 1904j, 1913a. His review of a Spanish book on "*Feminismo*" is more opinionated. But the author did make a point about the women's movement with which Durkheim agreed: that public opinion would be a more important determinant of women's status than legal codes (Durkheim 1900g).

THE EQUALITY PRINCIPLE AND THE PRIVILEGED WOMAN

Equality was in the air. Marianne Weber was not the only advocate of gender equality reviewed by Durkheim. A typical presentation of the equality argument (by a male, incidentally) stated that

> the feminine sex is not condemned by her congenital nature to be in the state of inferiority in which the mores and law maintain her. Inequality of the sexes is not a primary and natural fact; it is due to the empire that man has arrogated to himself by force, scorning justice. Marital and paternal power are a product of violence. (Summarized in Durkheim 1904k:418)

The author under review calls for the full integration of the principle of women's equality into the world view of the members of society.

Often, Durkheim's attack on such views is indirect, a critique of the particulars of the analysis. There are times when Durkheim accepts the idea of equality rhetorically, while conditioning it in such a way that it vanishes. Woman must look for equality in accordance with her "true nature" (Durkheim 1900e:391). "The family is, par excellence, the feminine field of action" (Durkheim 1904e:430). But Durkheim essentially took the position that there was no status or equality problem for women. Women have seen much improvement in their situation over historical time and may have attained equality of a nonjuridical sort. From the sixteenth century, women began to acquire culture "equal or superior to that of men of the same class" (Durkheim 1904e:431).

This involved a trade-off. As women were accorded more deference and salons emerged as forums for women's intellectual and political discourse, the legal and political condition of woman declined. Women's civil incapacity became institutionalized. This was first justified straightforwardly as husbands' privilege (i.e., patriarchy). Later, a seemingly more palatable rationale came to the fore: the benefit to the weaker sex of the protection offered by male authority. If women's contracts and purchases lacked legitimacy, they could be rescinded. Women were protected from the effects of foolish acts by their civil incapacity. (Women could petition the courts for redress against overbearing husbands; Durkheim 1904e). Durkheim agreed with the definition of the situation as advantageous for women.

Durkheim was well aware of societies in which women were the equal of men and independent of them in many respects. For example, in Malagasy (present-day Mozambique), each spouse freely administered his or her own property. Women could go to court on their own (Durkheim 1901b). But Durkheim argued against civil independence as a criterion for the status of women. He went so far as to argue that women *gained* in social position in the Roman patriarchal family! There, he says, the legal minority of women came about to protect the integrity of family property. Woman's alleged subordination results from the fact that "she has won [inheritance] rights that she did not have earlier." And more generally, "the servitude to which woman is sometimes submitted comes in reality from the fact that her condition has improved" (Durkheim 1899h:314).

Durkheim's defense against an equality feminism was that it would be a retreat from a woman's privileged position. If women gained public rights and civil participation, they would lose a valuable and elevated position in the home (Durkheim 1910i). The moral role of woman is greater in *domestic* society, more important and stronger organizationally (Durkheim 1904e). Yet in criticism of Anna Lampérière's (1898) book on the social role of women, Durkheim took issue with her assignment of women to roles of "organization and assimilation," presumably in the home. Not only did this plan leave out single women and childless widows, but "is it so certain that [the woman] should be more and more shut up in the interior [of the home]?" (Durkheim 1900e:390-91). I would have to agree with Durkheim (1899h) that "one sees how complex this question is" (p. 314); it was certainly so in his thinking.

FAMILY UNITY AND FEMALE AUTONOMY

For Durkheim, the status of women was bound up with concerns about the solidarity of the family. The equality of women was a threat to the family if it meant autonomy or equal power in the family:

Nothing appears more questionable. The independence of the wife vis-à-vis the husband often comes about from the laxity of the conjugal bond. Now, it can only be loose when the two spouses are more or less strangers to one another; this is the great obstacle to the moral equalization of the two sexes. (Durkheim 1899h:314)

The "laxity of the conjugal bond" that would presumably have to accompany the emancipation of women rendered Durkheim cool toward the equality principle. For the conjugal family to be strong, the partners needed to be unitary. Because they could not both lead at once in the same realm, the husband's power had to be greater than the wife's, or they had to have separate domains of authority, or both. "The matrimonial bond could not tighten and the family concentrate without the result being a juridical subordination of wife to husband, for that subordination is the necessary condition of family unity" (Durkheim 1904e:432). In the future, it might be possible to have a more complex conjugal union in which each had his or her juridical (legal) individuality, but that would take time and could only happen later (p. 432).

The association of women's equality with an unacceptably weak conjugal bond is a theme that occurred elsewhere in Durkheim's writings (e.g., Durkheim 1900j, 1907b). If feminism is defined as seeking "increased autonomy for women" (Black 1989:18), then Durkheim's position is antifeminist. Other intellectuals reviewed by Durkheim constructed the dilemma differently. Bryce began at the opposite end of the connection between solidarity and equality. If the equality of women is "just" and cannot be turned back, then perhaps marital solidarity could be maintained by strengthening the moral sentiments supporting marriage. In this review, Durkheim (1907b) presents Bryce's egalitarian position and assertion that marital solidarity can survive without stating his own acceptance or rejection (p. 437).

A related threat to the family from feminism had to do with giving up the idea of a private family sphere presided over by a woman devoted to that task and that task only:

The author [of *The Problem of the Sexes*, a book by Lourbet that Durkheim was reviewing] does not touch on the great difficulty. The equality of the two sexes can become greater only if the woman inserts herself more in public life. But how then will the family be transformed? Profound changes will be necessary, from which there is perhaps no place to withdraw, but which it is necessary to anticipate. (Durkheim 1901h:364)

While women's independence of action might be a threat to family solidarity, family solidarity could be a threat to women's well-being. In *Suicide*, Durkheim ([1897a] 1930) presents as empirical fact that marriage did not appear such a benefit to women. Where divorce was more frequent, suicide rates of women were lower (pp. 298-300): "Divorce protects her" (p. 307). "Marriage, currently, profits the man more than the woman" (Durkheim 1900h:563). In *Suicide* (Durkheim [1897a] 1930), he spoke of the impact on women of a too severe marital regulation, which "closes the exits and prohibits all hope, even legitimate" (p. 306).

Later, in "Divorce by Mutual Consent," Durkheim (1906a) rescinds his conclusion about the negative effect of marriage on women. Now, he finds an error in his earlier interpretation of the statistics on suicide rates. He had previously found married women in Paris (where divorce rates were high) to be less inclined to suicide than single women and noted generally that the effect the availability of divorce had on women was a slight increase in immunity to suicide (Durkheim [1897a] 1930:299-300). Now, he concludes that the relative advantage of married women in Paris was not owing to anything about marriage and divorce; rather, young single women alone in the city were exposed to conditions that carried the risk of suicide. "It does not seem that the practice of divorce affects female suicide appreciably" (Durkheim 1906a:551). He held to this conclusion and stated in the Union de la Vérité debate that women do not lose in marriage even if they fail to gain: "Whether divorce is easy or difficult to obtain, [the woman's tendency toward] suicide is the same" (Durkheim 1909b:279).[17]

If Durkheim could say that women were not damaged by the regulation of divorce he favored and feminists generally opposed, this made Durkheim's task of confronting feminism a bit easier. Now, Durkheim could have his cake and eat it, too; regulation did not hurt women after all.[18] (See Copley 1988, chap. 5, for an extended discussion of feminism and divorce.) The conclusion that marriage did not seem to make a difference in women's suicide rates is a specific case of a more general law that Durkheim (1906a) formulated:

> The state of marriage affects the moral constitution of the woman only weakly. . . . She is a little outside of the moral effects of marriage. As she does not profit much from it, she also does not suffer from it. (p. 188)

STRUCTURAL DIFFERENTIATION

Not only would family unity would be threatened by female autonomy, it would also be threatened by a too great similarity of men and women.

> It is the sexual division of labor which is the source of conjugal solidarity. . . . The separation of the sexes has been a major event in the evolution of sentiments. . . . One can see that [the division of sexual labor] has devel-

oped in exactly the same direction and the same manner as conjugal solidarity. (Durkheim [1893] 1978:19-20)

Durkheim laid out a theory of gender that fit his theory of structural differentiation in the division of labor. Men and women were becoming increasingly different with evolutionary progress from primitive to civilized times (Durkheim 1901h:364). Durkheim presents structural differentiation in several contexts. In a sociological vein, it is the evolutionary development of a gendered *division of labor*. Ethnographically, we witness the evolution of separate male and female *cultures*. And sometimes, Durkheim presents women as *outside of society* altogether.

Evolution of the Sexual Division of Labor

In the past, women and men were not all that different physiologically: "Woman was not the weak creature that she has become today" (Durkheim [1893] 1978:20). "One of the traits that today distinguishes the woman, her gentleness, did not appear to have belonged to her earlier" (pp. 21-22). "The difference in the force of the man and that of the woman was relatively smaller than it is today" (p. 20). Functions were similar: "The two sexes led almost the same existence. . . . [In] a great number of savage peoples, the woman participates in political life" (pp. 21-22).

This was a common Victorian perspective, gender differentiation as part of the story of evolution from savagery and barbarism to civilization (Russett 1989, chap. 5).[19] In Durkheim's ([1893] 1978) version,

> Women long ago gave up war and public affairs to concentrate entirely on the interior of the family. . . . Today, among civilized peoples, the woman leads an existence entirely different from that of the man. One would say that the two great functions of psychic life are dissociated, with one sex monopolizing the affective functions and the other, intellectual functions. (p. 23)

In Durkheim's view, the division of labor benefited women. In the past, primitive women, as well as men, worked productively but in a burdened way in a brutish culture. With civilization, woman was freed of these burdens and has a higher status, though it is not identical to that of man. Reviewing a book on Anglo-Saxon marital relations, he reports the author's finding that "the rise in the status of women began in the upper classes of society, to spread to the others only subsequently and very slowly." While the lower-class woman is in a state of "moral abjection," the noblewoman is given great respect and presides at feasts and distributes presents. She lives a life of "luxury, art, and imagination" (Durkheim 1901k:358).

Two Cultures in Primitive Society

When Durkheim addressed the division between men and women ethno-graphically, he sometimes contradicted his theory of primitive similarity and a common life of men and women. Among some primitive peoples, he found a profound separation of the sexes that could go as far as differ-ent languages (Durkheim 1898c:461, 1901d, 1904d). In a review of Frazer's work, Durkheim concludes that in primitive societies "women formed a group apart in the overall society" (Durkheim 1901d:365). Durkheim develops the separate-culture theme in various ways besides language: the aesthetic realm, dwellings, the experiences of everyday life. While discussing clothing differences, he refers to "the vast system of prohibitions which, in all civilizations, separate the sexes materially and morally" (Durkheim 1910h:380).

Durkheim connects the primitive separation of the sexes to blood ta-boos, religious in origin and intensity. In the original matrilineal societies, women were carriers of totemic identity. Their blood thus had a religious aura, and they were almost universally kept apart from men in tribal soci-eties in situations involving blood—for example, childbirth. Durkheim refers to "a sentiment of religious horror" that was renewed each month by the woman's menses. This came to influence the whole of life: food types, eating arrangements, occupation, dance, and so on, ending in "a profound separation of the two sexes" and "a sort of antagonism that exists between the two parts of the population" even in the most ordinary circumstances of everyday life (Durkheim 1898c:44-46, 1903b, 1904d:439).

> A sort of barrier exists between the two sexes. . . . [If the] man has func-tions that are forbidden to the woman even though she would be capable of fulfilling them and vice versa; if in our relationships with women we have adopted a special language; special manners; etc., it is in part because thousands of years ago, our fathers made of blood in general and of men-strual blood in particular the representation that we have described. (Durkheim 1898c:68)

Durkheim also noted the productive role of women in tribal societies. But in explaining the (relative) female autonomy and power in primitive societies, he found "particularly important" the "magical character with which the woman is frequently invested" (Durkheim 1906e:380).

Woman as Outsider[20]

In some of his work, Durkheim carries the separation of the sexes so far as to treat women as complete outsiders to civilization. He supports his claim that women are less affected by marriage by asserting that women are generally "outside the social order" (Durkheim 1910b:493). Speaking of the rise in suicide accompanying modernization, he notes that the suicide rates of women are lower because women have participated less than men in the progression of civilization; "they more often reprise certain traits of primitive natures" (Durkheim [1893] 1978:227).

Women are also less likely to engage in criminal activity.[21] Being *outside* society, they are *sheltered* from deviance. "The woman in the city is more outside of serious social life and consequently suffers the effects [of crimogenic pressures] less" (Durkheim 1910d:512). Writing approvingly of a book on women and crime, which he called "a portrait of woman without partiality," Durkheim echoes the author's list of female traits: "more impulsive, less capable of controlling herself and restraining herself, her reactions are easily violent, she has even a sort of penchant for the cruelty that civilization progressively dampens without totally getting rid of it" (p. 493). Lehmann (1995a) and others have noted the contradiction in Durkheim's explanations of deviance. Usually (for men), deviance is a consequence of underregulation or insufficient integration. Women avoid deviance by *not* being integrated into or regulated by society, by being outside society.

Durkheim maintains that because women are, in effect, less evolved, they do not need to be so sexually and maritally regulated as men. Because of a woman's more instinctive nature, "to find calm and peace, she needs only to follow her instincts." While restrictions also bear somewhat heavily on men, they profit more from this limitation of their horizon, which prevents the anomie to which they are vulnerable. At this point, Durkheim ([1897a] 1930) acknowledges men's privileged status in society: "Besides, the mores accord him certain privileges which permit attenuation, to a certain degree, of the rigor of the regime" (pp. 306-307).

Some of Durkheim's remarks on women as outsiders are quite demeaning by present-day standards and, I would argue, by those of the times. Most liberal turn-of-the-twentieth-century commentators who opposed feminist egalitarian reforms paid lip service to women's equality or their motherhood or fineness of spirit, all the while providing a rationale for keeping women in their place. But Durkheim does not hesitate to comment that "In a general way, a woman's mental life is less developed" (Durkheim [1897a] 1930:306). Speaking of the social adjustment of women to widowhood, he offers this frequently quoted statement:

> She lives more than man outside the common life. . . . Society is less necessary to her because she is less impregnated with sociability. She has few needs for that. . . . With some devotional practices, some animals to care for, the old single woman has her life fulfilled. . . . [Man] is a more complex being. (pp. 231-32)

Durkheim seems to see men as more vulnerable than women. In a review of an article expressing concern about "the deplorable condition of widowhood" and the poverty of widows, Durkheim (1901i) responded somewhat testily that it is widowed men who are more disadvantaged; they have higher mortality rates. Durkheim's insistence on social arrangements more beneficial to men may be explained subjectively by his hints that men are more socially fragile; objectively, that is, from the outside, feminists would see patriarchy.

BIOLOGICAL DIFFERENCE OR SOCIAL CONSTRUCTION?

How, then, are women and men different? What accounts for the putative differences? As noted in Chapter 2, Durkheim's dominant theoretical perspective is one that presents institutions as socially created, not naturalistic. But with regard to men, women, and their talents and roles, he falls back on biology. The Victorian consensus on inherent differences between men and women clearly influenced Durkheim. Because science of the times claimed to substantiate inherent differences in intellect and behavior between men and women (Fouillée 1893; Russett 1989), one might expect the scientifically oriented Durkheim to pay attention, and he did. In *The Division of Labor,* Durkheim ([1893] 1978) cites Lebon's studies of brain size: "The volume of the cranium of man and woman, when one compares subjects of equal size, weight, and age, presents considerable differences in favor of the man and that inequality keeps growing with civilization" (p. 21, quoting Lebon). While masculine brains grow and develop, women's have remained stationary or regressed in size (p. 24). It is interesting that even in Durkheim's era, there was strong research undercutting the supposed conjunction between brain size and intelligence. But that research was not readily accepted (Russett 1989:164-65).

Durkheim had to be well aware of these countervailing views. He reviewed books by LeTourneau, who argued that the "mental inferiority of the contemporary woman is a product of history," meaning that it was socially created. As quoted by Durkheim (1904f), LeTourneau called for "putting the two sexes as soon as possible on a footing of equality in marriage, in the family, and in society" (p. 434). But, asks Durkheim, "Will this equality of rights suffice to end an unequal heredity? . . . Legal equality should follow mental equality rather than preceding it" (p. 434).[22]

Writing in other contexts, Durkheim argues for the force of history over biology with regard to the sexes. In his analysis of suicide, Durkheim sometimes makes the point that the "influence of sex [on suicide and homicide] is much more an effect of social than organic causes" (Durkheim [1897a] 1930:389). Criticizing the explanation of sexual taboos in

Crawley's *Mystic Rose,* which was published in 1892, Durkheim (1902d) makes the point that animal nature (biology) pushes the sexes *toward* one another, not away, which is contrary to the observed sociohistorical trend as Durkheim sees it. "The mystery [the taboos keeping male and female lives apart] is a product, not of animal nature, but of history" (p. 355). Durkheim (1898c) also seemed to negate biological explanations regarding sex differences in "The Prohibition of Incest and Its Origins." Here, he attributes the separation of the sexes to the blood taboo, which has disappeared but left certain cultural patterns in its wake.

> We would not have known these needs if reasons long forgotten had not determined the sexes to separate and to form in some way two societies— for nothing in the constitution of one or the other renders such a separation necessary. (pp. 68-69)

Social causes of gender differences, whether structural differentiation (a *sociohistorical* explanation) or the emergence of sexual separation in totemic tribal societies (an *ethnographic* explanation), still leave women in a state of subordination and exclusion. Can that be overcome?

CULTURAL LEADERSHIP: CONTRADICTIONS RESOLVED?

The contradiction between Durkheim's theoretical commitment to social construction and his biological determinism is not the only inconsistency in Durkheim's thinking about women. Men and women *have* to be different according to the premise of increased structural differentiation in modern society. That poses a contradiction to his liberal republican value of equality.[23]

One way that Durkheim could resolve the tension between difference and equality was by assigning women a public sphere of their own, the aesthetic realm of high culture:

> It is not entirely proven that [the opposition between men and women] . . . must be maintained. Doubtless . . . it was less marked at the origin than it is today. But one cannot conclude that it is destined to develop without end. . . . Assuredly, we cannot suppose that woman will ever be in a condition to fulfill the same functions as man in society. But she can have a role of her own, which will be more active and more important than that of today. The feminine sex will never again become more similar to the masculine sex; . . . on the contrary one can foresee that it be further differentiated. Only, more than in the past, the differences will be socially utilized. For example, to the extent that the man, absorbed more and more by utilitarian functions, is obliged to renounce aesthetic functions, can those not revert to the woman? The two sexes will come closer, while

differentiating themselves. They will be equally involved in society, but in a different manner. (Durkheim [1897a] 1930:443)[24]

To serve the purpose, the aesthetic realm had to be characterized as clearly feminine. Women had already become involved in cultural activities, posing the threat for Durkheim of convergence with men. Durkheim needed to explain why "in certain classes, women occupy themselves with art and literature, like men, so one might believe that the occupations of the two sexes are tending to become once again homogeneous" (Durkheim [1893] 1978:23). He argued that woman brought her own nature to these activities, and "her role remains very special, very different from that of man. Moreover, if art and letters begin to become feminine matters, the other sex seems to let them go to give themselves especially to science" (p. 23).[25] The apparent rehomogenization is, in actuality, the emergence of a new differentiation, part of the evolutionary change in women's role from brute economic production to a more refined, more differentiated role.

> From the times of chivalry . . . woman acquired a prestige which she had never had until then; she became the incarnation of the aesthetic and even moral ideal, the representative par excellence of all the fineness, all the elegance, of civilization. (Durkheim 1904d:439)

It is arguable that leadership in the cultural and aesthetic domain still left women inferior to men. Scholars have generally considered the aesthetic realm to be stigmatized by Durkheim (Gane 1983:259; Lehmann 1994:70-72; Roth 1989-90; Sydie 1987, chap. 2). Men are moving out of this realm into the more highly valued domain of science. The aesthetic domain is linked to the animalistic level of sexuality; it is "nature," not "culture" in the sense of the social (Sydie 1987, chap. 2).[26] In his course on education, Durkheim ([1938] 1969) presented the aesthetic as the opposite of reality, as natural rather than social, as distraction from the task of "moral activity" (p. 240). Thus, regardless of Durkheim's attempt to present the channeling of women into the aesthetic domain as a version of equality, it can be seen instead as extremely negative, a further denigration of women. One can raise some faint objections to the negative characterization of the aesthetic realm by noting that aesthetics are sometimes linked to religion and to intellectuality in Durkheim's rhetoric (Durkheim 1898c, 1910h:382-83, [1912] 1979:544-47; Lukes 1972:469-70).

Finding women a realm of their own seems something of an afterthought rather than a convincing commitment to the equality of women. It does suggest that Durkheim was troubled by finding himself in opposition to the advancement of women (as feminist leaders defined the situation). He made other efforts to reconcile his views and social concerns with the movement to emancipate women.

THIS WILL PASS

Durkheim [1897a] 1930) speaks about the situation he has outlined regarding divorce (pp. 289-311). At times, he acknowledges that a restrictive divorce policy benefits men but has a negative impact on women. The question is, "Is it necessary to sacrifice one of the two sexes, to choose between two evils, the one that is less grave?" (p. 442). Perhaps not.

The difference arises because of the unequal participation of the two sexes in social life, because one is "a product of society, while the other remains such as she has been made by nature" (Durkheim [1897a] 1930:443). Thus far, a reiteration of vintage Durkheim on women. But returning to the troubling thought that his policy preference for restrictions on divorce favors the interests of men over women, Durkheim notes that if inequality in social participation is reduced, restricted divorce would no longer be "accused of serving only one of the parties" (p. 444). With this development, the impact of divorce would now be the same for both sexes. In making this observation, Durkheim evidences some concern that his position on divorce will be perceived as sexist. He did not want to be cast as a reactionary in the debate on the status of women, hence his somewhat contorted efforts to find a solution that fits his theory while also being acceptable politically.

The cultural-realm solution accepts differentiation as inevitable. But it does bring women into the public arena, and the rhetoric is at least more positive in speaking of woman's "more important" role in society. Durkheim ([1897a] 1930) goes farther in a sort of throwaway statement in a footnote:

> One can foresee that this differentiation [of the sexes] would probably not have the severely regulatory character that it has today. The woman would not be excluded categorically from certain functions and relegated to others. She would be able to choose freely, but her choice, being determined by her aptitudes, would generally bring her to the same class of occupations. It would be considerably uniform without being obligatory. (p. 443, fn 1)

A glass half empty or half full? Durkheim's most egalitarian perspectives—woman's public role in the arts and the option for certain (unusual) women to choose unconventional (male) occupations—are both heavily qualified by their association with negatively valued realms and a quasi-biological determinism. Moreover, Durkheim ([1897a] 1930) issues a cautionary advisory to

> those who today advocate rights for women equal to those of men, not to forget too much that the work of centuries cannot be abolished in an instant; that juridical equality cannot legitimate such evident psychological inequality. We must employ all our efforts toward reducing that inequality. (p. 444)

IN SUM: SOLIDARITY, EQUALITY, AND THE DIVISION OF LABOR

Durkheim believed not only that the division of labor was efficient (Durkheim [1893] 1978:24), but much more important, that the solidarity it produced made society possible. This was as true of conjugal society as it was of society generally (pp. 19-26). Yet marital solidarity seemed to require sacrifice on the woman's part and a refusal of feminist claims to equality. In insisting that women's roles never become the same as men's, that female autonomy be rejected, and that male authority in the family be preserved, that divorce be limited as to grounds and regulated in process, Durkheim took positions antithetical to dominant feminist positions of his time.[27] He spoke *against* equality for women when posited as similarity and against formal legal equality.

In coping with the contradiction to his republican and generally egalitarian values, Durkheim sometimes offered women a domain of their own, spoke of an equally respected position for women in society, and occasionally alluded to future possibilities. But Durkheim also made his case against feminism by going beyond arguments of social necessity to attribute negative qualities to women. One might have made a positive interpretation of Durkheim's concession that women need less regulation than men. But it does not come out that way, not in statements like "her mental life is less developed" (Durkheim [1897a] 1930:306) and in comparisons to primitives (p. 227; and see Lehmann various and Wityak and Wallace 1981).

The Late-Twentieth-Century Debate About Durkheim

The status of women was subject to debate in the late nineteenth and early twentieth centuries. Our time, the turn of the twenty-first century, is similarly a locus of debate about the roles of women. It is also characterized by disputation about Durkheim and women. Was Durkheim antifeminist? Was Durkheim antiwoman?

CRITICAL PERSPECTIVES

Numerous critical articles and books have appeared from the 1970s onward (itemized at the beginning of this chapter).[28]

Lehmann (1995a), who has written the most extensively on this subject, attributes "deliberate theoretical strategies" to Durkheim (p. 921). She claims to know Durkheim's "true motivation" and "nonfeminist agenda"; Lehmann (1994) goes beyond a critique of Durkheim stated as a negative proposition—"The betterment of women's lives is not Durkheim's object" (p. 71)—to speak of "Durkheim's unequivocal antifeminism" (p. 124). One wonders at this deep and certain knowledge of motive perhaps not derivable from his written work.[29] Gane (1983) speaks of "deeply irrational misogyny" but rolls that back to "profound fears" and "ambiguous paternalism" (p. 246). Admittedly, Durkheim supplied much evidence on which to base these charges.

Other critiques focus on nature-culture themes (with woman as "nature") and also note the equation of women to primitives and children by Durkheim (Sydie 1987; Wityak and Wallace 1981; and others). Virtually all writing about Durkheim and women takes note of the truly outrageous statements he made about women's capacities.

Besnard (1993a) places Durkheim's gender theory into the context of the proposed divorce reform of his time, which caused him great anxiety about the future of the family. But Besnard (1973) also sees "a sort of incompatibility between Durkheimian sociology and women" (p. 28) and refers to "certain prejudices of Durkheim in regard to women" (p. 61). Many critics focus on Durkheim's treatment of divorce in the *Division of Labor* (Durkheim [1893] 1978), *Suicide* (Durkheim [1897a] 1930), and "Divorce by Mutual Consent" (Durkheim 1906a). Durkheim first writes of women's "sacrifice" on behalf of men and social stability and then denies it (Besnard 1973, 1993a; and others).

Discussion of Durkheim as conservative, liberal, or radical forms part of the critique; Lehmann (1994) finds elements or interpretations of all these political perspectives in Durkheim's work, and see Gane (1983).

A number of critics note contradictions in Durkheim's theory of gender. Gane's (1983, 1995) critique is complex. He sees Durkheim as a gender traditionalist with contradictions that are not resolved. In his analysis, Gane includes Durkheim's ethnographic writings on totemism, incest, and other ethnography, as well as his theory of structural differentiation and perspective on divorce and suicide. In his anthropological writings, Durkheim (e.g., 1898c) grounds his view of gender in putative customs of taboo, a different line than the positing of biological differences (in brain size, for example) that appears in his books or the structural necessities of organic solidarity. In some writings, Durkheim (e.g., 1900e) did not enunciate a need for male dominance, just differentiation between the sexes.

DIMENSIONS OF GENDER

Complexity and contradiction are almost inevitable in Durkheim's writings on women, given the structuring of his argumentation in terms of a number of dimensions. There is first the *social versus biological* mode of explanation of human behavior and social structure. There are two different social theories: a social evolutionary theory of structural differentiation and an anthropological theory of two cultures arising out of religious taboos. In his family sociology, generally, Durkheim rejects biological explanations and definitively asserts that social institutions are not biologically grounded, not "natural." But when it comes to women, we see references to brain size. There are also remarks to the effect that inequality is historically grounded, not inevitable.

Another dimension is that of *society versus the individual*. Durkheim valued both but more often chooses the societal pole. He welcomes "the cult of the individual," which frees the individual from corporate family control. He is considerably more open to individualism than he is typically given credit for, but he is ambivalent. Durkheim's is a socially created individual. An individualism that threatens the family is rejected.

A third continuum is that of gender *similarity or difference*. Durkheim definitively rejects the premise of similarity between the sexes. It does not fit his theory of increasing structural differentiation in modern society. It threatens an organic solidarity of the conjugal couple based on complementarity.

The first two dimensions connect to Durkheim's position on women with some uncertainty, because his views do vary. With regard to the last dichotomy, Durkheim is clearly positioned *against* feminism and the equality of women defined as similarity. By this standard, he *is* antifeminist—unless one gives great weight to his vague, anxious, and heavily qualified comments about possible futures.

WAS DURKHEIM ANTIFEMINIST?

Nineteenth-century feminism was divided between "difference" feminists and "equality" feminists. A complementary view of gender roles was common, perhaps the dominant position among late-nineteenth-century and turn-of-the-twentieth-century feminists (Shope 1994:35). Marianne Weber (1907, 1919), for example, acknowledged the desirability of some continued differences between women and men. Even the most critical present-day commentator, Jennifer Lehmann (1994), conceded that exploring the historical context led to "the realization that Durkheim's theory of separate sexual spheres of ability and activity was not necessarily or inherently as antifeminist as it might appear today and in the Anglophone political discourse" (p. 29; see also Shope 1994:35). But she also states, correctly in my view, that Durkheim was not just a product of his time (Lehmann 1994:30).

Durkheim seems antiwoman, as well as antifeminist, in his willingness to sacrifice women's well-being in marriage and divorce to social benefit (as he saw it). His placing woman outside society and demeaning her basic capacity for thought, agency, and adult responsibility cannot be ignored. When women's hardship in poverty and widowhood is suggested, Durkheim shifts the focus to men's vulnerability, away from women's needs. On the other hand, some of his social-policy concerns were very supportive of women, particularly his attention to single mothers and their children. And he acknowledged that there might be women trapped in hopeless marital situations who would benefit from divorce.

Durkheim's reference to feminine grandeur and a higher status of women in "civilized" times are intended to be in support of women, but these "pedestal" approaches tend not to be very appreciated in our times. This is a "rhetorical strategy of elevating women while at the same time delimiting their scope" (Kimmel 1987:277-78).

Some have a view of Durkheim as caught in his times and, by those standards, not so antifeminist. Durkheim did "support those reforms in legal position that did not erode the sexual division of labor" (Offen 1984:666-67).[30] In fact, a later twentieth-century historian (Degler 1980) is willing to argue that although separate spheres are now perceived as repressive, their actual effect was often an improvement over the *soi-disant* economically productive past, even for bourgeois and upper-class women. Self-directed work in the home could be a release from the drudgery of a farm or workshop and an improvement in material conditions. It provided a sphere of female control that engendered respect and some autonomy: "Domesticity was an alternative to patriarchy" (p. 28). Separate spheres also provided women some power to act in the public realm, justified by assertions of female moral superiority.

Johnson (1979) agrees with Durkheim that men and women live in different social worlds, a point she applies to contemporary trends in attempted suicide. Shope (1994) sees Durkheim as a supporter of equality but in the form of gradual reform and acceptance of differentiation. Tiryakian (1995) argued that "Durkheim's views of women might be judged as patriarchal by 'evolved' standards, but they were common currency in the Victorian age, among liberals as well as conservatives" (p. 1376).

In sum, Durkheim is sometimes defended from criticism of his views on women on the assumption that he was simply a man of his times—what more could be expected? I think, on the contrary, there were many currents of feminism available in the culture of the time and known to Durkheim. Such views were held by other intellectuals with whom he came into contact, personally or through their writing, male as well as female. And how could he ignore the accomplishments of the learned females with whom he had occasion to exchange ideas?

Durkheim's commitment to gender differentiation could have been, but was not, coupled with statements about equality. The latter was a common position in Durkheim's time. Moreover, Durkheim was not willing to explain the lesser involvement of women in public roles and intellectual activity as a socially produced difference. Instead, he presented sex differences to mean an virtually intrinsic inequality—perhaps grounded in past cultural and social experiences but not easily remediable. He thus foreclosed gender equality in his time. Infrequent statements to the contrary are heavily qualified. Perhaps, Besnard (1973) is right that Durkheim was so focused on the threat that divorce reform posed to the family that he could not think straight (pp. 59-60).

Lehmann's view is that Durkheim's dominant theme of gender was one of "sex as caste" and the "welfare of society," to be sure, but also "the liberation of men" (Lehmann 1990:183, 1995b:578). In a similar vein, Sydie (1987) reads "society" as "men" (p. 46). I believe it is impossible to know Durkheim's actual motivation as *consciously* patriarchal, as Lehmann (1990) posits it, referring to "his actual objectives" and "true motivation" (p. 183) being "the interests of men" (Lehmann 1995b: 576). Certainly, a *political* standard could be invoked against Durkheim, measuring him against presentist standards of equality feminism, as Lehman does, and this does not require claiming insight into mental states.

How valid a political critique of a social theorist is depends on one's view of the sociological perspective or of intellectual approaches more generally—whether a critical perspective or a "value-free" model of social science. It also depends on one's politics. While liberal (not to mention radical) feminists would be much in conflict with Durkheim's views, communitarians should welcome him. Durkheim's conviction that social good should be prioritized over individual desires and his concern that divorce and independence within marriage are significant threats to family and society are exactly the positions taken by present-day communitarians (e.g., Gallagher 1996; Glendon 1991 and elsewhere; Hewlett and West 1998; Popenoe 1988, 1993; Whitehead 1996).

Likewise, a critique of Durkheim from a feminist point of view depends on one's definition of feminism, which cannot be limited to equality feminism.[31] A perspective somewhat in line with cultural or difference feminism might be teased out of Durkheim's work by disregarding pejorative statements and making contemporary applications.

Despite the offensive statements about women that do appear in his work, I take the position that Durkheim's gender theory is primarily driven by his systematics, not by his social position as an advantaged or patriarchal male in historical context. Men and women *had* to be different for his project of theory development to be convincing. His theory of structural differentiation and solidarity grounded his insistence that solidarity required an interdependency of men and women based on difference. His commitment to theoretical abstraction was stronger than his republican political philosophy.

Durkheim's Gender Theory in Our Time

Durkheim's discussion of women and men can be suggestive and relevant to present-day gender issues. The more things change, the more they remain the same.

WOMEN'S EQUALITY

Present-day perspectives on gender roles often take forms that were powerful in the past. The split between equality and difference feminism today tracks nineteenth-century debates over separate spheres and the question of where feminism would be placed in the context of women's family roles and unique moral tone.

Discussion about gender roles today resonates with the revived interest in biological determinism and gender essentialism. It is argued that traditional male and female roles are "*natural*" and that behavior is basically biologistic. Differences between the sexes in family roles and behavior are ascribed at least partially to biology, even by some sociologists (Booth and Dabbs 1993; Rossi 1984; Udry 2000). Evolutionary psychology is a powerful influence in anthropology and psychology, and sociobiology is becoming more visible in sociology. Biological theories of gendered behavior have survived countervailing evidence and strong challenges. Symbolic anthropologists have pointed to a nature (woman) and culture (man) dichotomy as a very persistent underpinning of gender inequality.

Political conservatives tend to treat gender differences as biologically based and thus as givens in public policy.

The moral sensitivity of women and/or their commitment to family responsibility is presented by cultural or social feminists as a reason for acknowledging gender differences and respecting them in social policy (Fineman 1991; Gilligan 1982). Cultural feminists claim an equality that takes account of those differences.

Present-day functionalists are concerned about the increasing similarity of gender roles, particularly regarding women who take up the "male" role of heavy career involvement. Will there be adequate coverage of family and children's needs? Popenoe (1988), who claims to welcome gender equality in principle, finds changing gender roles a contributing factor to family instability. He is less concerned about gender similarity per se than he is about the lack of one adult whose primary realm is the family (p. 289; see comments by Cowan 1993 and Stacey 1993). Of course, that one person has typically been female. Advocacy of the necessity of functional interdependency based on differentiated gender roles can be quite thoughtful (e.g., Nock 1998). But equality feminists continue to express suspicion of a separate-but-equal solution to the "problem of women."

DOMESTICITY AND GENDER ROLES

Writing on Durkheim from a late-twentieth-century perspective, Meštrović (1991) seizes on the *foyer* theme, the idea of the desertion of the home in modern times (pp. 181-83, citing *Suicide*). Meštrović considers structural differentiation to have drawn women, as well as men, out of the home and into the workplace. Whereas Durkheim looked at the risk of an empty home, for Meštrović, risk becomes reality in the late twentieth century with the truncation of family time that results when both spouses devote more attention to public rather than private life. (Indeed, "spending more time with the family" is at the top of the list of what survey respondents believe would help strengthen the family; Mellman, Lazarus, and Rivlin 1990:89). Meštrović takes Durkheim's "pessimistic assessment" as a description of how "economic anomie contributes to domestic anomie." Working couples abandon the home out of economic necessity. Meštrović proposes that, as a society, we examine the possibilities for resolving work-family tensions, looking at such models as Japan and Sweden (pp. 181-82).

Meštrović (1991) writes of two-earner couples, while in the place cited, Durkheim himself writes about the problem of low fertility and small family size that lessens the intensity of family feeling and leaves the home sometimes unoccupied. Still, Meštrović's analysis is interesting and gives a different cast to Durkheim's reluctance to endorse a similarity version of gender equality:

> It is not true that Durkheim wants to restore the past based on some conservative or Romantic biases. Rather he sought to purify and distinguish what he thought should have been the normal forms of the modern development of the workplace and family from the anomic forms that predominate. (p. 183)

Meštrović (1991) implies that work-family tensions are hard on everyone, without directly addressing gender. But a concern for *foyer* that does not address the problem of women's historically greater responsibility for the home (Hochschild 1989) obscures a latent gender equality issue. Present-day sociologists do not always confront this tension directly (Popenoe 1993), or they may acknowledge it regretfully (Glenn 1993).

What to do about domesticity has been a challenge for those wishing to liberate women from household responsibilities. Because of their personalized quality, not all domestic functions can be replaced by market purchases and institutional structures (Boulding 1977:71; Brown 1982:154-55; Glendon 1989:112). Hayden (1981a, 1981b) does point to late-nineteenth- and early-twentieth-century efforts to socialize domestic work that might have been somewhat successful had they received political support. The current expansion of child care and food services does suggest considerable movement away from domestic provision of those functions by families.

The other side of the complementary-roles coin, the burden on men of masculinity and the provider obligation (Bernard 1986; Goode 1982), and the possibility of changed roles was not directly explored by Durkheim. Men's roles in the family and their articulation with employment are of considerable interest today.

A concern that something would be lost with a straightforward adoption of gender equality was pervasive in Durkheim's time. Now, "there is anxiety, not without foundation, that the equality of women could result in the complete loss of the human qualities long associated with 'woman's sphere'" (Bellah et al. 1985:111). Women are associated with what we would today call "care-giving" and the maintenance of a private sphere in which communal values are dominant. The fear that these would vanish with the adoption of equal rights for women was common in the nineteenth century, just as feminism and family change are sometimes thought to be a threat to caring in the twentieth century. Today's communitarians would be close to Durkheim's views. A somewhat related theme is that a woman who chases the rainbow of career success and an individualistic lifestyle will find herself deeply unhappy (Crittenden 1999; Gallagher 1989, Graglia 1998).

SOCIAL CONTROL OF MEN

The family was essential for men, in Durkheim's view. Without the family, a man was more inclined to suicide and no doubt other pathology. Durkheim saw men as needing the social control of marriage more than women. Today also, certain conservatives present a promarriage, antidivorce social-control case based on men's volatility and potential for deviance, now thought to be essentially biological in origin. George Gilder's (1973, 1974, 1986) books argue that marriage is necessary to civilize otherwise antisocial men: "The man still needs to be tamed" (Gilder 1986:47).[32] This view is presented in a more positive tone in Steven Nock's (1998) *Marriage in Men's Lives*. He argues that inequality and dependency in marriage benefit not only men but society because of their contribution to marital stability, a very Durkheimian position.

MEN'S ROLES IN THE FAMILY

Durkheim argued that gender differentiation was accompanied by men's increasing interest in the home. This came about because of the greater respect for women in civilized society. Durkheim's idea that men in modern society are moving toward greater domestic involvement and collaboration with their wives contravenes the usual comparisons of traditional and modern society. Historians see a preindustrial setting as one in which men and women both were involved in the home, although engaged in different activities (Skolnick 1996:90). With industrialization, work (and men) moved away from the family homestead, while women remained there until late in the twentieth century (Bernard 1986; Huber and Spitze 1988).

Another way of looking at Durkheim's view that men were being drawn more closely into the family is to bring this proposition closer in time. In early industrialization, men did indeed withdraw from the family. But in the early twentieth century and perhaps earlier, a model emerged of marriage as a shared home life, indeed, a shared life. In this post-Victorian "companionate marriage" model of marriage, which came into full bloom in the 1920s, spouses retained specialized roles: husband as provider, wife as homemaker. But central to the marriage was that they would be romantic partners in courtship and companions in marriage (Skolnick 1991, chap. 1).

Durkheim seemed to grasp this coming social change with his assertion that men were becoming more domestic and more interested in what
had formerly been a female world, although he put in into a historical
account that seems far off the mark. Durkheim did not go so far as to
proclaim equality even within the family, but the point he grasps—that
men returned to the home to be alongside women—is a valid one and
does represent a significant change that would seem to represent an improvement in women's status.

Sexuality and Sexual Relations

Sexuality and gender stratification are treated in separate sections in this
chapter because I believe Durkheim's work on each to be somewhat distinct. Durkheim invoked biology in analyzing gender roles, and naturalistic
themes appear in Durkheim's discussion of men, women, and sexuality.
But for the most part, sexuality and sexual relations were social for
Durkheim.

Sex was a limited interest in terms of his writing and recorded speaking. There was no course offered, no substantial articles were written.
Book reviews are often very short; that of Havelock Ellis's important
work, for example, is less than a page (Durkheim 1902f). However, sections in the *Année* on "La morale sexuelle" and "Statistique de la moralité
sexuelle" indicate Durkheim's interest in sexuality. Especially in "The
Prohibition of Incest . . ." (Durkheim 1898c) and in a Union pour la Vérité
debate on sex education (Durkheim 1911), Durkheim discussed sexuality at length.

SEX AND SOCIETY

Sex was linked to social phenomena and social institutions: religion, the
family, and marriage. Sex education must include "the sentiments, ideas,
and institutions which give these relations their specifically human form
. . . the double aspect of the sex act" (Durkheim 1911:38). Durkheim's
social scientific exploration of sex included both ethnographic materials
from so-called primitive cultures and his policy approach to modern
society.

In his ethnographic analyses of then-labeled primitive societies,
Durkheim focused on taboos and the separate gender cultures that grew
out of them. Sexuality and sexual relations were closely connected to
magicoreligious elements in society. Durkheim had less to say about sexuality and sexual relations in modern Europe, and he did not link women's

sexuality so closely to their status and role in modern society. Here, he had other concerns: structural differentiation and familial solidarity.

Sex *could* disrupt the social order, and men were particularly vulnerable. Thus, restraints on individualism were necessary, even if they were damaging to women. But a feminist, Marxist, or conflict theoretical analysis linking control over women's sexuality and reproductive capacity to oppressive societal restraint was not on Durkheim's analytic agenda.

Durkheim was one of many in his time who wished to bring sex into the realm of scientific analysis and rational educational practices. On the one hand, he seems entirely unemotional as he discusses sexuality, treating it as any other object of scientific scrutiny. On the other, it was more often the emotive power of sexuality that interested him—its potential for disrupting the social order. The nature of sex is "mysterious," "exceptional," "troubling," and "disconcerting." It "shocks, offends, repulses us at the same time that it attracts us" (Durkheim 1911:34). It is "immodest," the "negation of modesty," it has "an immoral character." At the same time, it has an "associative power," "allies human beings," and so it is "moralizing" and "incomparable" (p. 35). The combination of the sacred and the profane in sexuality gives it explosive force.

SEX, PASSION, AND MARRIAGE

Sex and love bring the couple together in marriage. "The feelings of the future spouses . . . are identical to those manifested in free union"; the "same nature" and the "same instincts" (Durkheim 1898c:61).

There is an inherent tension between sex and family:

> [Sexual] [l]ove can be itself only on the condition that it is spontaneous. It excludes all idea of obligation and rule. Sexual relations are voluntary and a search for pleasure. Sex is the domain of liberty, where imagination goes unfettered, where the interest of the parties and their pleasure are the dominant law. (Durkheim 1898c:60-61)

To combine sex and family by marrying a sibling would be to mix "goodness and pleasure; duty and passion; sacred and profane" and could produce "moral chaos." Yet normal marriage does combine sex and family, as partner choice is grounded in sexual attraction. But this sexual love relationship is transformed by marriage and especially by the arrival of children (p. 61). "Marriage . . . comes about because sexual relations affect the family and the latter, in turn, reacts back on it and imposes certain rules, destined to put it in harmony with domestic interests" (p. 61). Without rule, there is no morality; without marital regulation, sex is anomic (Durkheim [1897a] 1930:308).

Marriage was "rudimentary" in primitive societies. Primitive marriage did not require monogamy and exhibited little conjugal solidarity (Durkheim 1893:22). Gradually, with the evolution from primitive to modern society, marriage was more and more formalized as an institution and monogamy more and more compulsory. As "civilization" emerged, sexual relations were more and more, in principle, confined to marriage (Durkheim 1898c:59-61).

The incest taboo precludes marriage between close kin. This protects family relations from being overwhelmed by sexual seeking, but it also means that marriage, the sanctioned sexual relationship, can be truly rewarding. If one married one's relatives, "marriage or sexual life would not have become what it is." Individual choice would play a smaller role, and that would leave "a lesser role for the free play of imagination, of dreams, the spontaneity of desire, for marital partners would be fixed from birth" (Durkheim 1898c:63). Because marriage regulates sex, sex has gone beyond the physical, with "sentiments of all sorts that civilization has little by little grafted on to a base of physical appetite. . . . Love is more mental than physical" (Durkheim [1897a] 1930:303).

Sex, Intimacy, and Marriage

Sexuality creates intimacy between the partners. In sex, one individual is an instrument of pleasure for another, yet usually, the sacral and autonomous character of another person is respected. The unique combination of profanity with spirituality gives the sex act its force.

> To touch a holy thing without employing respectful precautions. . . . There is . . . a sort of profanation in not respecting the boundaries that separate men [sic], violating limits, in unduly penetrating another. . . . [I]n the sex act, that profanation attains an exceptional intensity because the two persons in contact swallow up one another. Never is the abandonment of that reserve, which is another aspect of our dignity, so complete. . . . [But] that profanation, in effect, produces . . . the most intimate communion that can exist between two conscious beings. Through the effect of that communion, the two persons who unite become one. The limits that previously circumscribed each of them are displaced. . . . A new personality is born which envelopes and includes the two others. (Durkheim 1911:46)

In marriage, the profane sex act is sacralized, and profanation disappears (pp. 46-47). This connection of sex and intimacy is a perspective that would be at home in the psychology and sexology of the late twentieth century. So also is the notion that a committed relationship provides the best setting (e.g., Masters and Johnson 1974).

SEX AND CREATIVITY

Exogamy freed sex from the constraints of family morality. But sex changed so that, in time, it became "complicated and spiritualized." Intellectual and emotional currents that chafed under severe moral rules became conjoined to sex, and "thus it is that ideas relative to sex are closely tied to the development of art, poetry . . . all the individual or collective manifestations where imagination is a great part" (Durkheim 1898c:66).

SEX, SCIENCE, AND MORALITY

Durkheim's typical merging of morality and science emerges in the Union de la Vérité debate on sex education in which he participated. "The necessity of [sex education] is not contested by anybody." Nor are the recommended practices of sexual hygiene in dispute. But hygiene and moral principles are two different things. A sex education that focuses only on the concrete risks of nonmarital sex is insufficient; those risks are in fact obvious (Durkheim 1911:33). This is said in response to a debate protagonist who wishes to confine sexuality to a "biological act" (p. 36) and another who thinks there is too much overlay of outdated and religion-based abstinence rules in sex education (p. 44).

While there are no "domestic altars or family divinities" in modern Europe, "the family is impregnated with religiosity" (Durkheim 1898c:60). That means that the family is characterized by a respect typically given to religious deities; it is sacred while sexuality is profane. Sex education must capture the "collective sentiment" of the sacralization of sex as a "grave, solemn, and religious act" (Durkheim 1911:34). The mystical quality of sex is more than a survival or prejudice nor is it dependent on the views of a particular religious denomination. "The sex act is not just any act, but on the contrary . . . [by] its strangeness, it has a place entirely apart in moral life" (p. 35).

A sex education that treated sexuality as physiology, as a "biological function comparable to digestion and circulation" (Durkheim 1911:35), might remove the mystery from sex, rendering it profane and deleting the more complex nexus that has come to surround it: "To . . . make the moral aspect of the sexes felt by the young man, it is perhaps necessary to make use of scientific knowledge only with discretion and reserve" (p. 33).

Durkheim is not overtly challenging a scientific education that clarifies for the two sexes the physical nature of the act. "I am far from wishing to exclude reason from sexual relations" (Durkheim 1911:38). He presents himself as a scientist, a scientist of the social as well as the physiological. But he does not wish the moral and sacred character of sex to be written off as bourgeois prudery (p. 35). Durkheim believes one can logically justify a moral rule of abstinence without resorting to religious justification and prohibitions by pointing out that sex outside of marriage is disturbing to family organization (p. 45). But that is somewhat abstract. Better to convey "this troubling, singular character of the sex act" (p. 46).

Most of Durkheim's comments in the debate on sex education were focused on "young men," on the need to convince them of the virtues of premarital abstinence. The focus on young men would make it seem that Durkheim did not expect young women to be sexually active. At some points in the debate, he did address "the two sexes" (Durkheim 1911:36) or "young men and the adult in general" (p. 33). His debate antagonist, M. Doléris, who took the position that sex is a solely "biological act" (p. 36), did speak of girls' sex education, of giving them a complete education.

SEX AND GENDER

Gender differences do manifest themselves with regard to sex. More naturally sexual, women's sexuality is more under control by nature (Durkheim [1897a] 1930:306). Men need more sexual regulation (i.e., marriage).

Gender differentiation, social as well as physical, is essential to sexual relations. It is difference that inspires desire:

> That mystery with which, whether wrongly or rightly, we love to cloak the woman, that unknown quantity that each sex has for the other, and which creates perhaps the principal charm of their interchange, that special curiosity which is one of the more powerful stimulants of amorous intrigue, all sorts of ideas and practices which have become one of the refreshing diversions of existence is, however, difficult to maintain if men and women mix their lives too completely. (Durkheim 1898c:68)

SEXUAL ORIENTATION

I have not encountered any discussion of homosexuality in what I have read of Durkheim on family and sexuality. Given that Durkheim does address sexuality and sexual relations, this is surprising. I could not find reviews of books on homosexuality by other writers in the *Année,* either.[33] Does this represent avoidance? There is no way to know. Still, I find it noteworthy that in a review of Havelock Ellis's book, *Studies in the Psychology of Sex,* Durkheim (1902f) does not comment on his section on homosexuality or "sexual inversion," as it was commonly termed.[34]

Homosexuality was quite visible in the scientific writings and in literature in the late nineteenth and early twentieth centuries. In law, while
homosexuality was widely treated as a crime in other European countries,
the French civil code proscribed only "public" acts. (The police were quite
inventive in their efforts to trap gay men into an "offense against public
decency.") Scientific study operated in an uneasy tension between positive
science and Victorian morality. Public attitudes were condemnatory and
in support of criminalization until the 1880s. Yet those pioneers in psy-
chiatric medicine, Charcot and Magnon, led the way toward definition of
homosexuality as a clinical medical matter, not always with improved
outcomes for the gay man, who could be confined to a mental hospital.

The point is that there was much public discourse on homosexuality.
Yet in Durkheim's writing, sexual relations were always addressed in a
heterosexual context, whether marital or nonmarital.

Conclusion

In this chapter, "women" and "sex" have been given separate sections.
The first sections are about gender, with a focus on women. The last
section is on sexuality and sexual relations, with little attention to women.

The dominant focus of the chapter is feminism. French feminism is
described early in the chapter, followed by accounts of written and oral
exchanges about feminism to which Durkheim was a party. In Durkheim's
time, feminism was an active and visible social movement in France, and
feminist organizations had an active public policy agenda.

Durkheim's theory of gender is presented, its themes summarized as
best they can be, given the spread of Durkheim's writings in this area,
with all their contradictions. His views are discussed and evaluated from
a historicist perspective, their place in the social context of the late nineteenth and early twentieth centuries. Attention is also given to the current,
late-twentieth- and early-twenty-first-century, debate about Durkheim's
perspective on women: Was he antifeminist? How antifeminist was he?
Durkheim's analysis of women and gender is next related to present-day
feminism and sociology of the family.

Last, a separate section of the chapter examines Durkheim's social
perspective on sexuality and sexual relations.

What—besides the obvious—unites the major topics of gender and
sex in Durkheim's analytic approach? In both, a social control theme is
visible. The relationship of art and creativity to both sexuality and the
feminine links these sectors. Last, ethnographic materials linking gender
roles and the status of women and sexuality to cult and taboo is a common feature.

In presenting present-day critiques of Durkheim's writing on women, the problem of how to evaluate Durkheim's work comes to the fore. This chapter addressed the major question of Durkheim's work on women in a historicist, as well as present-day, context. The next and last chapter is devoted to a summing up of Durkheim's work on the family more generally: its scope, its strengths and weaknesses, its social context—one might say, the systematics of Durkheim on the family.

Notes

1. In principle, this chapter should be titled "Sex and Gender" rather than "Women and Sex." But what is distinctive about Durkheim's analysis of gender is what he said about women.

2. Present-day usage by sociologists commonly distinguishes between "sex" (biological characteristics and processes) and "gender" (sociocultural aspects of boys,' girls,' men's, and women's lives), and I follow that. Victorians did *not* make this distinction (Russett 1989, "Note on Terminology," n.p.). I believe that it was only clearly defined recently, in the context of "women's studies" academic writing and other feminist works. Agreement on the distinction between sex and gender is not universal across disciplines among those writing in English today, let alone usage in other languages.

3. In the United States, this second wave of feminism began in the 1960s. Key markers are Betty Friedan's (1963) book, *The Feminine Mystique,* civil rights activists' responses to sexism in the movement (Evans 1979), formation of the National Organization of Women and the establishment of state commissions with their constituency of liberal middle-class women, and consciousness-raising groups that tended toward more radical perspectives (Freeman 1995; Sapiro 1994, chap. 14). In Europe, Simone de Beauvoir's (1949) *The Second Sex* was an important marker.

For accounts of North American and European feminism in the nineteenth and twentieth centuries see Black (1989), Boxer (1981), Copley (1988), Cott (1986), Cova (1991), Degler (1980), Fletcher (1991), Freeman (1995), Hause (1987), Hause and Kenney (1984) Kandal (1988), LeGates (1995), Moses (1984), Offen (1984, 1987, 1988), Scott (1996), Shope (1994), Slaughter and Kern (1981, chap. 3), Stetson (1987), and Tilly (1981).

4. The history of the French Revolution and women is fascinating! Hunt (1992) provides an account that is well worth reading. Chapter titles—"The Band of Brothers" and "The Bad Mother"—convey the sensibility of this work, and Chapter 6 is also quite relevant to French family issues in the late eighteenth through twentieth centuries.

5. For a discussion of these two strands of feminism, conceptually and as they play out in the contemporary United States, see Black (1989, Introduction and chaps. 1-3), Fineman (1991), Weisberg (1993), and Williams (1991). Equality feminists are suspicious of differential treatment of women even when labeled as supportive, while cultural feminists reject the abstraction of liberal feminism, which they see as disadvantaging women who do not fit the independent career woman model.

6. Women had entered the labor force in increasing numbers in the nineteenth century. At the turn of the twentieth century, forty-five percent were employed (Offen [1987:183] reports 38 percent for 1911). But women had to have their husband's consent for employment. Needless to say, jobs to which women had access were of lower status. They were barred from professional schools and also labor unions (Shope 1994:27). These issues were of concern to feminists.

Protective legislation had feminist proponents and opponents, as did divorce by mutual consent. Divorce was a major feminist issue throughout the nineteenth and into the twentieth century. "Free love" was advocated by some feminists, but this was an extremely divisive issue. It was rejected by most feminists, who were more concerned about reinforcing monogamy and male commitment to the family (Boxer 1981; Cova 1991; Fletcher 1991; *Libres entretiens* 1909; Moses 1984; Scott 1996; Shope 1994; Slaughter and Kern 1981).

Although feminists received only limited support from socialist and republican politicians for a feminist agenda, nevertheless, some important legislation passed. In 1880, a law was passed that created girls' secondary schools, permitted single women to exercise "paternal authority," and created theoretical equality between husbands and wives in this regard (an equality of spouses so hedged with exceptions that it was inoperable). Between 1881 and 1907, a series of French statutes gave married women the right to dispose of their own property. By and large, legal change was not the direct result of feminist or socialist political efforts but rather represented the response of moderate republican politicians to social pressure. It seemed reasonable to extend to all citizens the legal protection of a woman's economic resources already attainable by the wealthy through private contract. Advances included a limited divorce law (passed in 1884) and changes in inheritance law (1896) improving the status of illegitimate children (Glendon 1989:111; Shope 1994:31).

7. By my count, there are reviews by Durkheim of books or articles that contain material on women in all but one volume (V) of *Année sociologique*. *Année sociologique* sometimes ran a section on "the female worker." Books on women in the trades and in department store sales were among the books reviewed by others (e.g., Bourgin 1913b, 1913c). *Année sociologique* also reviewed the work of American women sociologists and progressives, such as Sophonisba Breckenridge and Edith Abbott (Bourgin 1913a; Ray 1913).

8. Union pour la Vérité was an association of academics, liberal clergy, and politicians. It was a debating society that organized discussions of timely topics by a slate of personages with relevant expertise and interests. Whatever panelists' affiliations were, they were *not* to be committed in advance to positions of a particular church, party, or philosophy but open to a freewheeling exchange of ideas (Lukes, 1972:535-36).

Durkheim is known to have participated in one of the sessions, that on "Marriage and Divorce." How many others he may have attended is unknown. The exchanges were published as *Libres entretiens* and so were accessible to readers as well as participants and attendees. Topics of the 1908-09 series included "Maternal Authority," "Woman's Work in the Home," "Woman's Work in Competition with Men's Work," "Women in Public Employment?", "Marriage and Divorce," and "Woman and the Moral Police" (i.e., the vice squad in confrontation with prostitutes; *Libres entretiens* 1909).

9. I believe one of these women, Jeanne Chambon, to have been a novelist. A Mlle. Chambon published *Les nièces de tante Luce* in 1910. The eight male participants (in addition to Durkheim and the presider) included lawyers, editors, professors of law, and judges. One person was not identifiable as to gender but was probably male.

10. A "woman of letters," she was the editor of *La Française* and of the review *Ideés Modernes*.

11. Meštrović (1991:180) has it as *Wife and Mother in Legal Development 1904*.

12. Max Weber, a German sociologist of the same era as Durkheim, though a little younger (1864-1920), is considered to be another of sociology's "greats." His career began brilliantly, and he had various university appointments, but due to recurring bouts of depression and general malaise, he was often not in an academic position. Nevertheless, he produced an important body of work. He was more directly active in political matters than was Durkheim. See Bendix (1968), Green (1974), and Morrison (1995, chap. 4) for a detailed account of his life and work.

Max Weber's wife, born Marianne Schnitger (1870-1954), was a cousin, who lived with the family for a time during her education; they married in 1893. Max, who had earlier held more traditional views, came to support feminism publicly through her influence. Yet it was Marianne who did the heavy lifting of speaking and writing on feminism. She produced several important books on women and the family (Weber 1907, 1919). She also wrote a biography of her husband, which provides considerable insight into her own life (Weber 1927). Marianne Weber has not received much attention from biographers save for their interest in the troubled Weber marriage and Max's relationships with other women (Green 1974). See Gane (1993, chap. 9), (Green 1974), and van Vucht Tijssen (1991) for material on her life and work.

13. Georg Simmel was a German sociologist, considered by many to be a founding father of sociology along with Durkheim, Weber, and Marx. See Mayntz (1968) for a detailed account of his life and work. Simmel published a series of essays between 1890 and 1911, which appeared in book form only in 1985 (in Germany). See van Vucht Tijssen (1991) for more detail on Simmel's views on gender.

14. References to "Weber" without a first name are to Marianne Weber unless otherwise indicated.

15. Recall the multiple, complex meanings of *moral* in Durkheim's work. In this usage, moral has the sense of social value more than relating to sin or character fault.

16. Scott places the postulate of gender role difference *before* the corollary assumption of biological differences. That is, norms of socially desirable roles drove the science of sex differences rather than the other way around. This seems likely in Durkheim's case.

17. See Besnard (1973, 1993a), Gane (1983), and Traugott (1978:271, fn 3) for discussion of Durkheim's change of mind and errors with these data.

18. It is important to note that Durkheim's objection was to divorce *by mutual consent,* not to divorce in all cases: "Oh! pardon: I admit divorce; I have spoken [here] of a relative indissolubility. I believe absolute indissolubility impossible" (in *Libres entretiens* 1909:293). For Durkheim, having the divorce decision effectively made by the judge and based on sufficient evidence of serious marital dysfunction served to regulate the institution of marriage. In analyzing Durkheim's position, the distinction between divorce by mutual consent and divorce in general is not always made.

19. This stage theory was the basis of Engels's ([1884] 1972) work on the family, also. He has a completely different political analysis, of course, finding the family under bourgeois capitalism (civilization) to be oppressive to women.

20. The term is from Mike Gane's (1983) article, reprinted in Gane (1992, 1993). An excellent article, one of the best on Durkheim and women, it develops the "woman as outsider" theme in convincing detail.

21. While Durkheim noted a pattern of high male crime rates (still true), he also commented that there are some murders more commonly committed by women: infanticides, abortion, and poisonings and half of domestic murders. Even as Durkheim speaks of male criminality, he seems to be simultaneously arguing that women commit a substantial amount of crime, that even more female crime would be recorded if the crimes women typically commit were not so invisible, being domestic. He added that women's crime rates are affected by leniency in the judicial system (Durkheim [1897a] 1930:389-90).

22. Jacques Lourbet (1896), in *La femme devant la science contemporaine,* discussed "the problem of the sexes" on a "scientific terrain" (p. v). He attacked a number of scholars, including Fouillée and Lebon, noting that brain size and reproductive organs were not good indicators of intellect and function because some animals looked better than humans on these indicators (p. 112). "Science [cannot] demonstrate the irremedial inferiority of the woman" (p. 14). Lourbet pointed out that all the arguments against the woman reduce to

this syllogism: The man, *free* for thousands of years, has produced *s;* the woman, slave during the same time, has not produced *s;* thus, the woman will never produce *s* (pp. 155-56).

Let us see what woman produces when she is free, concludes Lourbet. I cannot find any Durkheim commentary on this work, but Durkheim did review Lourbet's, *Le problème des Sexes* (published in 1900), briefly and rather negatively (Durkheim 1901h).

23. It would seem also to contradict his life experience. Mme. Durkheim, quite strong on the domestic front, was also an able assistant to her husband in his intellectual work. On the other hand, Gane (1995) claims that "Durkheim was an unreconstructed patriarch, who went to considerable lengths to give privileges to his son over his daughter" (p. 69).

24. It is hoped that it will not be too confusing to the reader that *culture* is used in two senses in this section. One is with reference to what are termed *cultural activities:* music, art, dance, literature, drama, and the like. The other sense is that of the contrast between "nature," what is deemed biologically given, and "culture," the realm of socially created and structured behavior and products.

25. This notion that women's entry into an occupation is associated with the exit of men is one that recent research finds to be empirically true of the modern United States. The status of an occupation, and its rewards, tend to drop with the entry of substantial numbers of women. Men, who have more options, move to other economic arenas (Reskin and Roos 1990).

26. Sydie (1987) develops the nature-culture, woman-man theme in her analysis of classical works in sociology. Also see Besnard (1973, 1993a:176) and Sherry Ortner's (1996) work in anthropology on the dichotomization of gender and the persistent structural disadvantage of women linked to their categorization as "nature" rather than "culture."

27. This statement is a generalization. As a reading of the sources referenced in this chapter would indicate, feminists did vary in their theoretical and policy positions. There were also women who were antifeminist activists and spokespersons.

28. I cannot do justice to each of these critiques in the space of this chapter. Readers are advised to read the original sources.

29. See critical reviews of her book *Durkheim and Women* (Lehmann 1994) by Besnard (1996), Challenger (1996), Cladis (1995), Gane (1995), Meštrović (1996), Orrù (1995), and Tiryakian (1995).

30. Offen herself includes the word *only* in her sentence, suggesting insufficient support, and she is critical of Durkheim and others for not going farther.

31. Although it is my own politics.

32. A somewhat Durkheimian social-control theme shaped a Supreme Court decision in an important sex discrimination case involving California statutory rape law. The male partner was prosecuted but not the female. To a sex discrimination challenge, the court responded that women are naturally circumscribed in their sexual conduct by the anticipated consequence of pregnancy (biological), while men need legal (social) limits (*Michael M. v. Superior Court of Sonoma County* 1981).

33. I searched the sections on deviance and criminality, given that homosexuality was often so viewed at that time. I also checked the indexes of some collections and books on Durkheim. This was not by any means a thorough and comprehensive search.

34. This review is unsigned but is attributed to Durkheim by Lukes (1972). What Durkheim found of interest in Ellis was his discussion of modesty.

8

Conclusion

Do I contradict myself?
Very well then I contradict myself,
(I am large, I contain multitudes.)
                    —*Walt Whitman,* "Song of Myself."

D urkheim's work indeed contains multitudes of ideas, and they are sometimes contradictory, vulnerable to attack on many grounds. He was a man of his times. He was also an academic maverick, and so convinced of the rightness of his sociological theories that he was not very open to revision. Why then read Durkheim?

Why Read Durkheim?

Durkheim on the family is of interest because his times were, in many ways, our times. Parallel policy questions were on the table in these two turn-of-the-century eras. Durkheim's sociology of the family is also of interest because it is foundational to certain strains of present-day or recent past perspectives on the family. His work engages conceptual and real-world issues that are presently high profile.

Despite criticism, Durkheim continues to inspire. His classic *Suicide* (Durkheim [1897a] 1930) and his other major books have passed the one hundred year mark and are still going strong as inspirations for theory and research (e.g., Besnard 1997). Traugott (1978) acknowledges that "sinking feeling" that classicists such as Durkheim have done it all. "His numerous anticipations of what we think of as contemporary theory are at once a measure of the power of Durkheim's thought and of its formative influence upon the modern discipline" (pp. 3-4).

INATTENTION TO DURKHEIM'S SOCIOLOGY OF THE FAMILY—WHY?

Durkheim's work on the family is relatively invisible. The qualifier is important because, over the years, note has been taken of this feature of Durkheim's corpus. Several decades of debate on Durkheim's writings on women has meant excursions into areas such as divorce and gender roles that are quite central to the family. Historians of French feminism have also been over this territory.

Yet family review volumes do not include Durkheim as a sociologist of the family. Most family sociologists and most social theorists do not think of Durkheim in these terms. Given that Durkheim is a primary founder of sociology and that his other work remains dominant in the field, why does his sociology of the family not have equal stature?

I address this question with everyday language and commonsense reasoning rather than in the formal terms of sociology of knowledge. One important barrier to American sociologists' exploration of Durkheim's sociology of the family is that not all of it is translated into English, and not all sociologists read French. The scope and organization of Durkheim translation affects what is known about his work. First to appear in English were his four major books (Durkheim [1893] 1978, [1895a] 1956, [1897a] 1930, [1912] 1979). It took many years for other books to be translated. *Moral Education* (Durkheim [1925] 1974) was an especially important lack.

George Simpson published a translation of the conclusion to Durkheim's family course ("The Conjugal Family"; Durkheim 1921) in 1965. This was a very important piece but appeared to be an isolated moment in Durkheimian time. In 1978, Mark Traugott added the "Introduction" to the course on the family (1888a) and the important article on "Divorce by Mutual Consent" (1906a). Remaining untranslated is the extended description of Durkheim's course on the family by a former student, Georges Davy (1925). Durkheim's (1909b) participation in the "Marriage and Divorce" debate of the Union pour la Vérité is little known.

A great vacuum has existed regarding Durkheim's many and extensive book reviews, published in the twelve volumes of *Année sociologique* and elsewhere. Some have appeared in various compendia but not organized around the topic of the family. Some translations (Nandan 1980a) have been strongly criticized (Besnard 1982).

The checkerboard pattern of translation and fragmented presentation has shaped a view of Durkheim that is incomplete and different in gestalt from what a fuller presentation would afford. For example, including Durkheim's evolutionary theory of the family (Davy 1925) enhances the importance of the *Division of Labor* (Durkheim [1893] 1978). It throws the conjugal family, the end point of familial evolution, into greater prominence and gives it a more positive cast. For Durkheim, an appreciation of the emotional strength and support of the modern family and the opportunity it offers for individual development coexisted with anxiety about its solidarity. But it is only the latter that we hear about in his major books. Durkheim's assessment of modern individualism is often taken to be uniformly gloomy, when, in fact, personal autonomy was valued by Durkheim (1921, [1925] 1974; and see Giddens 1978).

If we read Durkheim's (1906c) review of an article in a German sociology journal, we find him exploring statistics on the socialization outcomes of unwed births. He discovers that unwed parentage per se is not disadvantaging if the mother eventually marries. Despite his concern about the single mother who remains unmarried, his pragmatic acceptance of the morally suspect birth that turns out all right places Durkheim in a more liberal or at least more pragmatic stance toward the traditional family than we might have expected.

Even aside from the shifting emphases set up by translation arrangements, the corpus of Durkheim's work is scattered. Although he himself intended a major work on the family, that never happened. Due to his untimely death, Durkheim never wrote a single volume to systematically develop his ideas on the family. Important pieces were published posthumously rather than during his lifetime. Given the inaccessibility of some of Durkheim's writings on the family and the scattered character of his work in this area, many family scholars would not have had direct contact with it unless they were also interested in classical theory. They might be familiar with what are essentially Durkheim's ideas but not associate them with Durkheim.

Moreover, the Durkheim we knew for some time was a Parsonian version of Durkheim. Later scholars followed Parsons in his apparent neglect of Durkheim's writings on the family (perhaps only apparent, at that). Younger generations of scholars, who may have little interest in the now out-of-favor Parsons,[1] may be equally uninterested in exploring Durkheim's work because they associate the two.

Meanwhile, in the middle period of the twentieth century, sociology of the family was often atheoretical[2] in the sense that microlevel empirical studies were not connected to broad theoretical perspectives. Sociological theory appeared in textbooks on the family (e.g., Adams 1971; Reiss 1971), but family sociologists were unlikely to read primary sources. They often had little intellectual interchange with their faculty colleagues in other areas and little interest in macrosociology: stratification, political economy, social theory, social movements, and the like. Evolutionary theory was considered long dead, an embarrassment, really. Its potential for high-lighting sociohistorical change went unrecognized, overshadowed by archaisms, inaccurate periodization, and rigid stage theories.

Durkheim's interest in law and policy on the family also did not match the direction of the field. Prominent now, these interests did not begin to reemerge in American family sociology until the 1970s. For many years in mid-century, empirical studies of "marital adjustment" epitomized the field (e.g., Burgess and Wallin, 1953). Interactional and family develop-ment perspectives focused attention on the interior of the family. In this microsocial context, work anchored in another time, another place, may not have drawn attention.

Structure-functionalism was powerful, to be sure, but Durkheim's part in this paradigm of the family went unremarked. While functionalism *is* a macro-perspective, the consensus politics and positivist outlook of this framework precluded the kind of political economic and historical work on the family we see today, work more resonant with Durkheim's focus of interest. Huber and Spitze's (1988) article on "Trends in the Family" in the *Handbook of Sociology* illustrates the return to a macrosocial, indeed, evolutionary, perspective on the family.

HISTORICISM AND SYSTEMATICS

The question "why is Durkheim's family sociology not known?" implies that it should be, that it has something to offer.

Classical theorists can be read in two ways: historicism (the context of the time) and systematics (contributions to a body of systematic theory) (Jones 1974; citing Merton [1957] 1968). While not rejecting systemat-ics, Jones (1986) argues the case for historicism. Theorists are better understood and appreciated when they are examined in historical con-text. Moreover, in the historical context, the theorist may find forgiveness, so to speak, for normative offenses or intellectual misjudgements. Or scholars may find further grounds for criticism. Still, we learn from ex-amining classical sociological thinking, "warts and all" (p. 158).

Both ways of reading classical theory have something to offer. In dis-cussions of Durkheim's theories in previous chapters, the historical intellectual context has been prominent. It is exciting to read the ex-changes between Durkheim and his colleagues—and antagonists. Dusty pages in the library, yes, but containing the lively ideas of keen thinkers confronting each other in an intellectual network that was probably more cohesive than all but the most specialized associations of the present. How vivid was their intellectual world! It is a world we would recognize in many respects.

One might think a turn-of-the-twentieth-century scholar would seem completely remote to our time, given the changes that have taken place in the family. In an era of concern about divorce rates, single parents, and the successful socialization of youth, family scientists might assume "the family" to be so transformed that older perspectives have nothing to tell us. Well, the trends we are concerned about today were apparent in the Europe of Durkheim's time. Expressions of anxiety about the family were quite similar. Durkheim's analyses of policy issues often reflected a tension between individualism and communal solidarity still at issue in family politics today.

His work is relevant theoretically as well as being connected to present-day empirical problems. It represents a particular framing of sociology of the family that has lost somewhat in popularity but is still relevant at an abstract level. Whether or not one accepts Besnard's (1973) wry assessment that "the current flowering of studies on Durkheim can surprise and even irritate those who see in the rupture with the 'founding fathers' a condition of the progress of sociology" (p. 27), Durkheim's heritage is a force to be reckoned with.

Durkheim welcomed the nuclear family when some others wished to turn the family clock back. He was optimistic about the future of the family when some others were pessimistic. In the context of his times, his views on divorce and on women were liberal only by comparison to conservative traditionalists. But Durkheim was more open to change in law and policy in other areas.

SUMMARY OF CHAPTERS

Much in the previous chapters brings forth the historical and intellectual context of Durkheim's work on the family, a historicist explication of Durkheim. The substantive chapters also make comparisons to present-day sociology of the family and family issues.

Chapter 1 presents Durkheim's life and times. His biography is one of anchorage in a close-knit Alsatian Jewish family and community, from which he moved into the secular intellectual world of the Ecole Normale Supérieure and the French university system. Durkheim was intellectually active during the Third Republic (1870-1940). On the one hand, this was a period of political instability, with numerous changes of government and the occasional coup threat. On the other hand, in its centrism, it was a remarkably stable political system. The ideas of the French Revolution—liberty, equality, fraternity—and leftist, working class, and feminist movements were offset by the essential social conservatism of moderate republicans, the bourgeoisie, and much of the working class. The extreme conservatives of traditional Catholic sectors and right-wing parties, those who would return to pre-Revolutionary structures and values, were vocal but mostly ineffective politically. Still, *"les deux Frances,"*—the traditional social order, on the one hand, and the emancipatory movements, on the other—were both visible in struggles over policy and law reform. And those who were generally favorable to reform and egalitarianism were often reluctant to let go of the traditional family, at least in its nuclear form.

Politically, Durkheim was active on only two matters: the Dreyfus case and France's World War I effort. But he was quite influential with regard to public education as well as on family matters. His views were based on his evolutionary theory of the family (Chapter 2), which presented the modern nuclear family, now free of kin control, as the model.

As described in Chapter 3, statistical and ethnographic data, history, and the analysis of changes in legal codes were Durkheim's methods for studying the family. While structure-functional theory was most foundational to Durkheim's work, especially the concept of structural differentiation, elements of systems theory, exchange theory, and conflict theory also appear (Chapters 4 and 5). Chapter 4 examines the changing balance among kin, conjugal family, and the state. In Chapter 5, the degree to which Durkheim interested himself in the interior and less formal aspects of the family is considered.

Chapter 6 takes up Durkheim's views on family policy issues of his time, such as divorce, fertility, cohabitation, nonmarital births, and the support of single mothers. The feminist movement was a vocal force in late-nineteenth- and early-twentieth-century France. Durkheim engaged feminist ideas in public forums and in written reviews of feminist work (Chapter 7). "The woman question" appeared to be most difficult for Durkheim, as his theoretical commitment to structural differentiation and solidarity came into conflict with the egalitarian ideals of the French Revolution and his often liberal political spirit.[3] Present-day sociologists, historians, and feminists (frequently overlapping categories) have given Durkheim's ideas on women much critical attention.

Rather than repeat in detail the historical situating of Durkheim's work described earlier, I devote the rest of this chapter to a brief examination of (a) Durkheim's influence on present-day sociology of the family, (b) what Durkheim did *not* do as a sociologist of the family, (c) how sociology of the family fit with his other writing, and (d) strengths and weaknesses in Durkheim's work. In examining Durkheim's sociology of the family in the context of the present, I make comparisons to U.S. sociology and family issues, as that is the body of research and the social context with which I am familiar.

Durkheim's Contributions

A SOCIOLOGY OF THE FAMILY

Durkheim's most basic contribution is a sociological perspective on the family. Durkheim's was "the first truly modern sociological study of the family" (Craib 1997:81). As the first to hold a chair of sociology in the French university system and as the French founding father of sociology, Durkheim's interest in the family pointed to the inclusion of "family" in the domain of sociology. He was intense about the family; family mattered.

His was a revolutionary perspective on the family in the context of the times. We can appreciate the significance of Durkheim's sociology of the family in noting the sharpness with which it departs from earlier and contemporaneous theories of the family and the degree to which his paradigm continues to be employed more than one hundred years after he taught his first course on the family. He insisted on the family as a social institution at a time when many others took a naturalistic or religious perspective on the family or advanced empirically invalid evolutionary schema.

Durkheim defined his approach as scientific, analytic more than ideological. He directed his efforts toward the establishment of a perspective on the family conceptualized as a changing social institution. The family was seen to meet human needs rather than evolving mechanically from lower-order forms or resulting from some suprahuman purpose. In spite of Durkheim's sometime reputation as a sociological conservative and idolater of society, this was a most humanistic perspective. It was a view that tended to relativize and desacralize the family, rendering both social change and scientific scrutiny acceptable.

While certain commentators find Durkheim's "social metaphysic" troubling (LaCapra [1972]1985:181), the social constitution of the family deserves emphasis today, when biological explanations of human behavior receive increased attention and gain intellectual respectability (e.g., Booth, Carver, and Granger 2000; Degler 1991; Nielsen 1994; Rowe 1994; Udry 2000). However carefully qualified by their authors, biological explanations are typically understood by the public as a simplistic biological determinism (A.M.P. 1997; Brody 1998; Goode 2000a, 2000b; Konner 1988).

A SCIENCE OF SOCIETY

Durkheim brought the family into the realm of science. Many social philosophers had examined the family in intellectual study, often mixing
prescription with analysis. Durkheim made the overt case for treating
family as an object of scientific study like any other. His interest in the
family and his leadership in the field brought "family" into sociology.
Possibly, this would not have happened without his insistence, as the
family had been thought of as too removed from the public arena to be
worth scientific study and too sacred to be so treated.

Durkheim exhorted his students to be objective in their study of the
family. Theory and research should not be shaped by political views or
preconceptions. Instead, a scientific empiricism and value-free analysis
was called for. Durkheim did not always follow his own precepts, nor
was he aware of the limitations of his standpoint. Yet his definition of
the field of family sociology was clear and an advance in his time.

A NORMATIVE MODEL OF THE FAMILY

Durkheim's view of the family was in no way pluralistic. For each evolutionary stage, including his time, there was *one* model of the family. Other
forms would make it into his work only as deviance. For example, he did
acknowledge the existence of "free union" (cohabitation) but declared
this *not* "family" by virtue of its lack of regulation.

Durkheim did give attention to single-parent families as a *social problem,* recognizing this family form as a child-rearing setting. Whether this
represents acknowledgment of a multiplicity of family types is hard to
say. Given mortality rates and some divorce, there must have been many
step-families in Durkheim's era. But he does not specifically mention this
family form. Homosexuality, let alone homosexual partnerships and families, were not in Durkheim's purview.

For the most part, Durkheim used a juridical criterion for defining the
family, which is one reason his framework of family types included only
one form at a time. This legalistic approach excluded de facto families. In
premodern settings, he did have to look at mores rather than law, but he
was ambivalent about this. He was reluctant to recognize emerging family forms, preferring to wait for their crystallization into legal form. His
tendency to give minimal attention to less-structured forms of family
behavior is one of the most significant limitations of Durkheim's approach,
for it excludes much that is interesting to contemporary sociologists.

In sum, Durkheim, like later structure-functionalists, took the modal
form of family, the normative form, as his focus of study. The normative

form was not only the ideal, it was the only legitimate form of family. While present-day sociologists are far from converging on so restrictive a view of the family, the clarity of Durkheim's presentation and his legitimation of the conjugal family was an important contribution.

EVOLUTIONARY THEORY AND SOCIAL CHANGE

Durkheim's most visible theoretical perspective is an evolutionary one. This approach was common to scholars of his era, although he distinguishes his from others' theories. More convincing in many respects than those others, Durkheim's evolutionary theory nevertheless has the faults of evolutionary or developmental-stage theories. He has a tendency to fall into unilinearity (Levi-Strauss 1945:519), even while criticizing others for ignoring the variety of family types or the plethora of concrete family systems (Durkheim 1895b:610). The assumption of one-way development and the compression of historical (and prehistorical) variability into types arranged in stages permeates his theory. His lack of attention to processes of development and historical links between one stage and another, which in fact do not always exist, is a related problem.

These are aspects of Durkheim's thought that give his theory of the family an archaic cast. Sociologists and anthropologists no longer feel so confident in the sort of speculation about primitive family forms characteristic of turn-of-the-twentieth-century intellectuals. So why is it included as a contribution to theory? Because Durkheim, like other evolutionists, had a vision of society and family that gave social change an important place; this was lacking in some other family theories dominant during the mid-twentieth century.

STRUCTURE-FUNCTIONAL THEORY

If we look beyond surface details for the basic structure of Durkheim's theoretical position, we find the foundation of the structure-functional theory of the family. Durkheim asserts a historical trend toward structural differentiation. The family performs fewer and more specialized functions, and other institutions develop and take over such functions as education, religion, and economic production. Families become smaller, no longer the large clans or even substantial extended families of the past. As kinship ties become less important, the nuclear family becomes independent of kin. It is now the basic family unit. Abstracted from ethnographic "facts" and the indefensible set of family stages, this is the structure-functional model of Parsons (1954, 1955a, 1965; shared by Goode 1963; also Ogburn 1933).

In his mid-1950s writings, Parsons analyzes the family in terms of a trend toward increasing structural and functional differentiation. Durkheim's family theory is cast in a more evolutionary mold, but in essence, it has also chronicled the gradual diminution of kinship as the organizing principle of society. We end in modern times with a stripped-down nuclear family, freed of the restrictions of the kinship collectivity. The family is a haven from the outside world rather than the locus of all social life. This nuclear family is held together by bonds of emotion. Yet gender differentiation of spouses is strong—the instrumental-expressive dichotomy—and it is essential to the solidarity and functionality of the family (Parsons 1954, 1955a, 1955b; Parsons and Bales 1955).

Parsons does not cite Durkheim's work on the family. The structure-functional perspective has always been credited to Parsons, for better or for worse. Yet Parsons presents an essentially Durkheimian perspective. Similarities abound. Durkheim outlined concentric zones of kinship. Parsons (1954) writes of "the 'onion' principle, "which implies "proportionately increasing distantness" within each "circle" of linked conjugal families (p. 182).

Parsons is the preeminent figure who brought Durkheim's sociology to the attention of American social scientists. It seems that this did not include Durkheim's sociology of the family. Yet we see something of it in Parsons's repertoire, Durkheim unacknowledged. Whether Parsons himself was not so aware of his source, whether the perspective was so immanent in others' work or historical developments that it did not seem to Parsons to be distinctively Durkheimian, this lack of acknowledgement is a puzzle I have not been able to solve.

That said, the Parsonian structure-functional perspective is superior in some ways to that of Durkheim. The Durkheimian theme of differentiation that we find in Parsons is perhaps more neatly formulated by the latter as a typology. Parsons deals with categories of societies (i.e., "primitive" and "advanced"), rather than imputing dubious sequences of quasi-historical societies, as Durkheim did. There is a traditional-modern society typology implicit in Durkheim's work, though ("primitive-civilized"). Both typologies suffer from excessive abstraction by comparison to the rich social histories published subsequent to Parsons's work in the 1950s.

Yet Parsons's rendition of the family is considerably more developed than Durkheim's. The latter's basic construction of the family is more abstract and schematic, less detailed than Parsons's, despite Durkheim's pervasive use of ethnographic and statistical data. And Parsons introduces stratification by class and race into his discussion of the American family (e.g., Parsons 1965) as well as more particulars about the kin structure and the nuclear family. On the other hand, as generations of

graduate students will testify, Parsons's detail, including his incorporation of psychoanalytic perspectives, can clutter his sociological theory to
the point of incomprehension.

There are echoes of Durkheim in the work of other structure-
functionalists. Resonances may be just that: independent invention by
others who were not Durkheim scholars—intellectual currents, not bor-
rowings. But I think the similarities should be noted. "From institution
to companionship" is the theme of Burgess and Locke's ([1945] 1960)
take on the family. One could argue that Durkheim's evolutionary trend
toward the conjugal family is similar. This is a less strong case given that
Durkheim's family remains firmly institutional. Goode (1963), in his discussion of the industrial revolution and the goodness of fit between the
conjugal family and the modern industrial system, is considerably more
specific about processes of change and historical linkages than Durkheim.
Nevertheless, the ideas are basically similar. And Durkheim anticipates
Litwak's (1965) "shared functions."

Parsons on Durkheim is not the same as Durkheim on Durkheim. This
is no less true in regard to the family. Parsons was selective in his introduction of a Durkheimian perspective. Later scholars, who have done
much to correct the limitations of Parsons on Durkheim, have nevertheless followed Parsons in his apparent neglect of Durkheim's writings on
the family—most not realizing that much of the structure-functional paradigm of the family, outlined for us by Parsons, is really Durkheim's thought.

EXCHANGE AND CONFLICT THEORIES

Given even less recognition than his influence on Parsons are Durkheim's
early, though rudimentary, thrusts at exchange theory and conflict theory.
Durkheim-as-consensus-theorist has seemed the only view possible. Now,
in the voluminous writings on Durkheim and women, note is being taken
of how he set up a vision of conflict between men's and women's interests
in marriage. With the lens of contemporary feminism, that is what stands
out in *Suicide* (Durkheim [1897a] 1930), although Durkheim did later
labor to obscure and deny this gender conflict. There are other remarks
on conflict in his work, including an acceptance of conflict as inevitable
in society.

Exchange in marriage was clearly part of the Durkheimian theory of
the conjugal family. He posited a gender-differentiated exchange as the
foundation of marital solidarity. The view that interdependency (the economic dependency of women on men) is essential to stable marriage is
still powerfully heard and widely accepted despite some evidence to the
contrary (Oppenheimer 1997). The fact that this proposition is still important testifies to Durkheim's theoretical insight.

THE CONJUGAL FAMILY

Durkheim stressed that the nuclear family system places marriage in a position of strategic importance; it becomes the principle structural foundation of the family. Durkheim's emphasis on marriage went so far as to be dismissive of the well-being of children as *the* reason for opposing unrestricted divorce. The couple outlasts their child-rearing years, and it is the impact of divorce on the partners themselves that is the most essential point. In contrast, in today's argumentation for more restrictive divorce, it is the well-being of children that is especially at issue.

The emphasis on marriage, on the conjugal couple, was the focus of the companionate model of marriage that emerged around or a little after Durkheim's time. Durkheim's theory of sexual separatism was certainly at odds with this model, but his structural differentiation was not. Elements of his perspective on marriage—the conjugal couple's complementarity, voluntary choice of partners, sexual intimacy and passion in marriage, and the drawing of men into family life—are isomorphic with the companionate model of marriage that came to be preferred around the 1920s, in the United States, at least (Skolnick 1991). Sociologically, this development became visible somewhat later in Burgess and Locke's ([1945] 1960) *From Institution to Companionship*. But it was present in Durkheim's work well before that.

The complexity of Durkheim's thought can be seen in the tension between regulation and voluntarism in the family. In "The Conjugal Family," Durkheim (1921) speaks eloquently of individuality in the family. He speaks of the family as an association of individuals, each with his activities and property rights. He even seems to minimize the legal disability of the minor or any differentiation between husband and wife, in other words, to overlook differences of status, role, and authority within the family. This was far from Durkheim's bottom line. But it is a facet of Durkheim's thought.

FAMILY LAW AND POLICY

Durkheim was a very visible actor in advocacy of policies he thought necessary and viable, although he carefully distinguished the roles of scientist and academic from that of policymaker. In the context of the times, he was a liberal who welcomed modernization and moderate social change. Liberal reformers in many European societies were proposing and often realizing increased freedom of the individual from familial social control by means of legislation on property, emancipation, the status of women, divorce, and illegitimacy. Many of the issues treated analytically by Durkheim and others were implicitly or explicitly connected to debates on social policy.

Durkheim approved of a strong role for the state vis-à-vis families. Not only was education-socialization to be under the aegis of the state, but the state could also intervene to protect children and intervene on behalf of young adults seeking autonomy in their marital choices. He also saw the state as protector of female-headed, single-parent households in that the difficulties of raising children alone could be ameliorated by state-secured child support.

Law interested Durkheim more generally. Methodologically, it served as an indicator of family patterns. Structurally, it *was* the family. Durkheim preferred to take the family writ in law as his object of study. There are numerous references to the French Civil Code in his work.

American sociologists took little interest in family law during the interwar years of the twentieth century. The "institutional" conceptual framework, which gave law more weight, was dismissed from the list of conceptual theories in Broderick's (1971) *Journal of Marriage and the Family* decade review. In the past twenty-five years, law has emerged as an important area in family studies, in part, because family has become so much more visibly regulated by law. Sociologists have moved to take an interest in the law of divorce reform and child custody; domestic violence and termination of parenthood; adoption; reproductive technology; gay and lesbian parenthood, and alternative families more generally; and the family economy in law. Durkheim's interest in law now seems more relevant and less archaic than it might have before the mid-1970s.[4]

THE FUTURE OF THE FAMILY

Another Durkheim persona to highlight is the Durkheim who is sanguine about the future of the family. What is the future of the family? Durkheim makes some scattered predictions of the future by extending linear trends forward, notably in anticipating the eventual abolishment of inheritance to create a so-called meritocracy. But he did not extrapolate the trend toward the reduction in size and functions of the family beyond the conjugal family.

Barrington Moore (1958) did extend the trends of individualism and free choice in family relations, decline in family functions, and reduction in family structure, to reach the conclusion that the bourgeois nuclear family is but a transitional stage and will disappear eventually, leaving only the solitary individual. Those who are confident about the future of the family as we know it are

> projecting certain middle-class hopes and ideals onto a refractory reality. . . . [T]he burden of proof falls on those who maintain that the family is a social institution whose fate will differ in its essentials from that that has befallen all the others. (pp. 161, 178)

Some present-day sociologists and others are much concerned that this will happen and is happening, although they hope to forestall this disaster or correct it (Glendon 1989; Popenoe 1993; even Cowan 1993 and Stacey 1993, in some respects).

Durkheim did *not* expect a decline in the family as an institution. He clearly did not wish to anticipate a disintegration of the family based on its loss of functions and membership. He was quite accepting of the disengagement from kinship and individuation that had already taken place. He resolved his theoretical problem of the contradiction between an evolutionary perspective, which implies further evolution, and the normative advocacy of stable family institutions in a fashion parallel to the substitution of organic for mechanical solidarity in *The Division of Labor* (Durkheim [1893] 1978). In modern society, new forms emerge and stabilize. Durkheim most often views the modern nuclear family as an evolutionary endpoint, composing part of a stable, normal society. Despite his concerns about solidarity, to read Durkheim is to come away with a relatively optimistic view of the future of the family.

What Durkheim Didn't Do

A theme of the preceding section is Durkheim's contribution to systematic theory and to pragmatic applications of sociology of the family. To point out what Durkheim did *not* include in his study of the family is not so much to indicate deficiencies, which a partisan can easily excuse in terms of the level of expectation one is permitted to have of a single person. It is rather to throw into relief developments in the sociology of the family over the period since Durkheim died or to note other perspectives on the family.

KINSHIP RELATIONS AND MUTUAL AID

Durkheim had much to say about kinship; this was not a neglected topic. His focus was the liberation of the conjugal family from kinship and the reduced functions of the kinship group. True enough. But the almost forty-years-old revisionist view of kinship in industrial society—that there continues to be considerable emotional attachment and mutual aid among extended family members (Adams 1968; Litwak 1965; Sussman 1965; Sussman and Burchinal 1969)—is not part of Durkheim's discussion.

He does recognize the existence of secondary zones of kinship, but they are seen as functionally irrelevant. Perhaps, he does not speak about the affection, influence, and mutual aid that are important and significant extended-family phenomena because they lack the formality and obligatory quality he requires of social facts. This is ironic in view of his own attachment to kin. His letters contain accounts of family events and visits that sometimes delayed his professional projects (Durkheim 1973). His nephew Marcel Mauss's involvement in the *Année sociologique* was a striking overlap of kinship and occupation.

MATE SELECTION, MARITAL ADJUSTMENT, AND THE FAMILY LIFE CYCLE

Some key concerns of mid-century sociologists did not appear in Durkheim's work. Mate selection and marital adjustment were prominent in the interests of sociologists of the family in the 1950s. Family development theory, the "family life cycle," was equally prominent. These have receded as a focus of the discipline because of the development of other interests, interests more isomorphic with those of Durkheim—family law and policy, for example.

Courtship process; certain aspects of mate selection, particularly heterogamy-homogamy; and revised versions of the family life cycle do remain significant, though less prominent, topics of family science research. By earlier configurations of the field, their absence in Durkheim was notable (Bynder 1969:533). Durkheim did attach great importance to the fact that children eventually left the family, but often in his work, "children" seem generic and the conjugal family unchanging.

Bynder remarks on the absence of "love" as a topic of interest in Durkheim's sociology of the family. In fact, Durkheim did attempt to grasp the nature of love in his many discussions of sexual passion and familial love and commitment. He distinguishes familial love, with its aura of duty, from the sexual passion that is the foundation for marital choice and facilitates intimacy, under proper circumstances. These two resemble the "eros" and "agape" of John Alan Lee's typology of love (Lee 1973).

SOCIALIZATION

Durkheim devoted great attention to socialization—but not to family socialization. Although he mentioned the family's collaboration with the state, he believed true socialization—the development of morality in the child—to be the province of the state through the public schools.

One has little sense of a child's interaction with parents. What is stressed about the parent-child relationship is that it is broken on the child's adulthood. Only the issue of parental control over minors and possible intervention of the state receives much attention.

Relevant to socialization, though, is the issue of corporal punishment. Opposed to corporal punishment, Durkheim did devote considerable attention to disciplinary methods and the rationale for renouncing physical coercion as a socialization practice.

SOCIAL PSYCHOLOGY OF FAMILY LIFE

In Durkheim's attribution of a support function to the family, the *foyer* or haven aspect of the family, there is a sense of the family as a small group of people in interaction. Chapter 5 pulls together as much of the interior of the family as can be found in Durkheim's work. He is not particularly interested in pursuing the interaction approach or in developing the social psychology of the family any further than to note the performance of such a function. Indeed, to give great weight to informal social processes would be to undermine the objective definition of the family and the legal criteria of family phenomena so important to him.

That Durkheim's "family" is a modern family is, I believe, unchallengeable. That is to say, it is *not* "postmodern." He takes for granted that the normal family contains a husband, wife, and usually children of the marriage. Durkheim's legal criterion for specifying "family" drew a line around the nuclear family as well as the kin-based family of the past, excluding families based on cohabitation, homosexual relationships, or intentionality. He did not remark on stepfamilies, which must, however, have been very common. Single-parent families were within his purview, though primarily as a social problem. He takes getting married for granted and treats the "anomie" of singlehood ("sexual anomie") and widowhood ("domestic anomie") as well as that of overly loose marital ties ("conjugal anomie") as problematic.

FAMILY AND ECONOMY

In considering the relationship of family to society, Durkheim slighted the economy. He did not consider the relationship of families to the economy on either a macro- or microsocial basis. This is a slight overstatement in that there was an occasional examination of family pathology (so-called) by income levels. And family communism, collective family property, served as a basis of family solidarity in the earlier stages of family evolution.

But the kind of work-family interface that is so central a research and policy topic in contemporary America and elsewhere is not found in Durkheim. This is not surprising in the case of women, who were supposed to have no such dilemma. But even for men, work (that is, jobs) is not addressed in conjunction with analyzing family life. Unlike Parsons, Durkheim did not conceptualize a family-society linkage through the husband's occupational role (Parsons 1955a). Nor did he analyze the potential for role conflict, not to mention the linkages and conflicts for women that interest us today. Durkheim *did* review books on women workers, however. It is not evident from the reviews whether the workers were single or whether the scope of the book included married women workers.

Durkheim addressed the linkage of the family to social structure in the absence of corporate kin groups with broad functions. His concern for the "egoism" of individual nuclear families did take economic form. He anticipated that the decline of family communism apparent in the limited property holdings and transfers of the single-generation-bilateral-neolocal-conjugal family would diminish man's motivation for work and prove threatening to the society. The development of occupational groups as regulators of economic and social life was to solve this problem.

He also examined the family economy in the sense of control over the family's economic resources. This was a central part of his analysis of kinship. He gave considerable attention to marital property regimes and also to inheritance.

SOCIOCULTURAL DIVERSITY IN FAMILY LIFE

In regard to modern society, Durkheim's concern was with ideal types of family structure; in actuality, this meant the Western European bourgeois nuclear family. He did not deal with class variation to any degree except in relation to fertility or the poverty of single-parent families. Sometimes, employment was treated as a variable, but there was no class typology of family life. Durkheim did look at urban-rural differences in suicide rates by marital status, and religion was part of his analysis of suicide, also. Durkheim used data from other countries, and within France, he compared provinces, paying special attention to their juridical status vis-à-vis various laws and policies. But he did not attempt to define subcultural family types analogous to today's "African American family," "Latino family," and so on. Essentially, the nuclear family Durkheim examined and took for granted was the urban European middle-class family.

It goes without saying that these were Caucasian families, for France did not then have the racial and ethnic diversity it does today. Such minority groups as existed were pressed toward cultural assimilation. Jews were a noticeable minority presence but tended to be secular and assimilated. Regional variations in culture existed, but probably the most notable of those was removed when Alsace-Lorraine was annexed by Germany after the Franco-Prussian War. France had and continues to have an assimilationist politics.[5]

So in Durkheim's work, variation might exist but only as pathology. There was no sense of legitimate variation in family forms within the nation of France or its colonies. Only in putative evolutionary history do we see variant forms. With regard to primitive, rather than modern, families, it was a different story. There, what we might call orientalism was in view, fascination with the exotic.[6] Cultural variation in sexual practices, gender roles, marriage, and family forms revealed by ethnographic study were considered simply interesting. By definition, the so-called primitive was not threatening, having been displaced by civilization.

A BROADER LOOK

Of course, there are many and broader aspects of sociology of the family we could point to as lacking in Durkheim's work. But it would be rather anachronistic to fault him for, say, not using statistical techniques yet to be developed! On the other hand, he has been criticized for insufficient use of those available to him.

Similarly, postmodern theories (e.g., Stacey 1990), gender theories that deconstruct the family (e.g., Thorne 1982), symbolic anthropology (e.g., Rosaldo 1974), phenomenological sociology of the family (McLain and Weigert 1979), and other theories that do not credit an objectively "real" family are at the opposite pole from Durkheim's work and the positivistic assumptions in which it is grounded. That is not who Durkheim is.

The Sociology of the Family and Durkheim's Other Work

What is striking to the reader of Durkheim's sociology of the family is how integral it is to his other work. Durkheim gave his work on the family a centrality that has often been overlooked by scholars. The first published mention of mechanical and organic solidarity occurs in Durkheim's (1888a) "Introduction to the Sociology of the Family," based on a course on the family he offered at Bordeaux in the 1887-88 school year.[7] In this same publication, the occupational groups are first proposed as a solution to the problem of linking individual and family to the larger society. The intertwining of concepts from *The Division of Labor* (Durkheim [1893] 1978) with Durkheim's family sociology is significant to those who believe that *The Division of Labor* is Durkheim's "fundamental work" (Giddens1972:12; also Münch 1988:25).[8]

There are also connections with Durkheim's later work. One scholarly work noted that there is more data on the family in *Suicide* than on any other factor (Danigelis and Pope 1979:1083). The theme of anomie found in *Suicide* repeats Durkheim's interpretation of empirical research on fertility, written earlier (Durkheim 1888b). The *Rules of The Sociological Method* (Durkheim [1895a] 1956), with their emphasis on the comparative method and on law, are foreshadowed in Durkheim's course on the family, and family is discussed in the *Rules*. The totemic basis of the primordial family is the counterpart to totemism in *Elementary Forms of The Religious Life* (Durkheim 1912). Positive statements about individualism similar to those in *Moral Education* (Durkheim [1925] 1974) appear in Durkheim's (1921) discussion of "The Conjugal Family." In sum, the family was a model, nexus, or echo of his work in other areas. If one looks at Durkheim's general work on society with family in mind, one sees the institution of the family as a crucial element in his conceptualization of society.

The Value of Durkheim's Sociology

STRENGTHS AND WEAKNESSES

Durkheim's work does not go without criticism, yet the plethora of recent books on Durkheim suggests his continuing impact and importance to sociology.

Criticisms of Durkheim's work include misuse and misinterpretation of data and inadequate statistical techniques (Besnard 1993:172, 181; Pearce 1989:118-19; Turner 1986, and others) and armchair theorizing in lieu of actual ethnographic field work. Durkheim's totemism, foundational to his theories of kinship, sexuality, and incest, can be criticized both theoretically and empirically (LaCapra [1972] 1985, chap. 6; Levi-Strauss 1945; Seligman 1950). Harry Alpert (1974), the first English-language biographer of Durkheim, points to numerous weaknesses or errors in Durkheim's "science and scholarship," including

> being high-handed in the use of evidence, theoretically dogmatic, confused, ambiguous, misleading to himself and others, violating his own methodological rules, not taking advantage of the statistical tools available to him, and using a polemical and metaphorical style that confounded rather than clarified; . . . [c]onceptual confusions and ambiguities, conflation of significant distinctions, overstating his case, resort[ing] to the logical error of begging the question . . ., and failure to avoid the logical pitfalls of the argument by elimination. (p. 199, referring to Lukes 1972 as well as his own views)

Durkheim also had a knack for criticizing in others things he did himself, notably collapsing diverse ethnographic materials into simplistic categories or indefensible evolutionary sequences. Yet Alpert notes that Durkheim continues to "command attention" (p. 199).

What kind of thinker was Durkheim? For one thing, he was immersed in a network of inquiry and reflection. Sharing Durkheim's wide reading gives us an awareness of the intellectual ferment and creativity of the late nineteenth and early twentieth centuries. Practically every philosophical and social question of interest today was addressed in the pages of *Revue philosophique* and *Année sociologique* by Durkheim or his colleagues. Even when Durkheim sharply disagreed with other intellectuals, he was in dialogue with them. However, this disputatious milieu could lead to exaggeration. Hadden and Borgatta (1969) note that, in early anthropology and sociology (1860-1900), "the academic climate fostered development of theories . . . and involvement with ones own personal theory which may have caused statements to become absolute that were intended in the formulation to be tentative hypotheses" (p. 19).

Durkheim had other intellectual limitations. His work on the family shows very little development over the years. One could put a review or article from Volume I of *Année sociologique* side by side with one from Volume XII and not notice a great deal of difference. I calculate that Durkheim's work on the family was more or less in place by 1898, almost twenty years before his death.[9]

Durkheim did make a sharp change in his analysis of the relationship of suicide to marital status in his 1906 article on "Divorce by Mutual Consent" (Besnard 1973). He became caught up in "the problem of women." And as new policy issues became salient in public debate, he attended to them. He moved to overt political participation in the Dreyfus case and World War I. But essentially, his theory of the family and his policy perspective were unchanged. There is little change of mind on any point once formulated and set down. This suggests a rigidity, not to say stubbornness of thought! More positively, it could be interpreted as Durkheim's having carved an intellectual niche—the establishment of the discipline of sociology—which he then developed and completed as a life's work.

Durkheim's reluctance to endorse the equality of women illustrates the rigidity that was a weak point in his thinking. For Durkheim, equality and similarity were distinct concepts; the republican value of equality did not imply the similar social status of men and women. This was not an unusual view in his time and is still represented in "difference" feminism. But Durkheim's other political sympathies should have drawn him into a more straightforward egalitarian view of the sexes. Durkheim's theory of structural differentiation appeared to constrain his view of the appropriate role of women to a rather traditional conceptualization, and he opposed such feminists as Marianne Weber who argued for full-scale equality. Durkheim resolved the dilemma posed by the conflict between his liberal values and his theory of differentiation by assigning women an equal status but different sphere of activity and by some vague allusions to the future. Durkheim did not limit women to the home nor exclude them from the life of the mind. But their primary focus would be the family and their public activity would be in the less valued cultural arena, not the political and economic sphere.

Durkheim's approach to women's equality is an instance of a general difficulty in integrating policy making and theoretical reflection. In addressing specific social problems one by one, Durkheim had the compassionate approach of a social liberal. He tended to seek viable solutions to empirical problems in the context of social reality rather than to assert the need to return to a more traditional family form and restore patriarchal authority, as some did in his time. Durkheim was "not a simple status quo conservative" (LaCapra [1972] 1985:19).

Durkheim had to do some fancy dancing to mediate the tension between theory and social reality. Would providing illegitimate children an entitlement to paternal support undercut the distinction between legal marriage and free union? Durkheim struggled to argue that it would not. Durkheim opposed divorce by mutual consent as a threat to conjugal solidarity and the institution of the family. Did that mean there should be no divorce? No, divorce *should* take place in the case of a marriage that was dysfunctional and could no longer accomplish its purpose. But how to accomplish the task of sorting functional from dysfunctional marriage, if not at the initiative of the couple? Durkheim urged judges to take a more active role in investigating the facts of the marriage.

Could the freedom of individuals extend to contracting the details of their marriage? The concept of freedom of contract was highly popular in the late nineteenth and early twentieth centuries (Glendon 1981:42). But for Durkheim, the freedom and individuality of modern marriage was mostly up front: the choice of whether and with whom to enter a marriage. Marriage itself had to be regulated. Durkheim's tendency to define away dilemmas—individual versus society, for example, or the interests of men in conflict with those of women—is very visible and has been duly noted (Lehmann 1990:166, 1994:82). To see in the Roman patriarchal family a marker on the way to female equality is a truly amazing feat!

As a practical policy thinker, Durkheim was responsive to changing social reality. In debates on social policy issues, Durkheim tended to argue a liberal position, at least one that claimed some purchase for individual needs set against formal rules of family constitution. But ultimately, Durkheim's liberal instincts came up against barriers posed by his theory of the family. His pragmatic policy positions did not feed back into theoretical analysis. At the same time, his structural-differentiation model is applied over and over to every social phenomenon.

Moreover, Durkheim ignored the implications of social control for the less advantaged categories of society: "[He] remained throughout his life blind to the authoritarian implications of . . . his . . . system" (Zeitlin 1968:240). Yet Durkheim was very concerned to see himself as "not a reactionary" (Durkheim 1906a:549).

A related criticism is that Durkheim had all the virtues usually attributed to the French: rationality, logic, and moderation. But these could be

intellectual handicaps, as well. Durkheim is always moderate and reasonable in tone, and his views tended to seek the "golden mean."[10] His
moderation permits one to predict his position on almost any issue: it is
"yes, but." Durkheim does not reject divorce, as did many in his time,
but he opposed divorce by mutual consent. Yes, there is much to modify
regarding the juridical status of women, but let us not go too far. We
should encourage sex education and the provision of scientific information about sex, but sexuality should not be treated as a natural
phenomenon, and young males should be convinced of the necessity of
premarital abstinence. In the conjugal family, each has his or her individuality, but solidarity is crucial. These are all arguable positions, of
course. As a pattern, they represent liberal-secular politics yet concern
about regulation and solidarity as the *sine qua non* of society. This tension is intrinsic to the intellectual Durkheim.

Durkheim's massive reading and steady grip on sociological developments at home and abroad gave him an authority and confidence that
may have limited his receptiveness to other points of view. The combat-
ive approach necessary to establish sociology as a discipline in an
unreceptive educational milieu may have made Durkheim reluctant to
give an inch. Durkheim's logic is brilliant but often used as a weapon to
destroy an opponent's position rather than as a tool with which to in-
vestigate and understand the social world. At times, I suspect, his
opponent may have had the truth of it. One has to admire Durkheim's
mental powers, for he could seemingly find a way around any objection
raised to his point of view. But year after year, volume after volume, this
becomes tiresome. Also, while he grounded these views in his theoretical work and his analysis of empirical data, one could argue that they
sometimes expressed subjective values more than scientific reasoning
(Jones 1986:80-81).

Some contradictions in Durkheim's work are simply there, with no
confrontation or resolution. This is notable regarding his basic assertion
that institutions are socially grounded, not biological, while at the same
time, women's behavior is seen as biologically influenced. Durkheim had
women as less inclined to deviance, including suicide, because they are
asocial, not integrated, while men are protected from suicide by greater
involvement in society. Inexplicably, Durkheim threw a biological hand
grenade into his sociological theory, wreaking "theoretical havoc"
(Lehmann 1991:164; and see Besnard 1973:29-30; Danigelis and Pope
1979; Lehmann 1994; and Wityak and Wallace 1981).

Contradictions in Durkheim's work mean not only that Durkheim
can be legitimately criticized but also that there is no right answer regarding interpretation. Varying interpretations of Durkheim's position
are arguable, as there is usually ample material to support a number of

renditions. Both LaCapra ([1972] 1985:293) and Lehmann (1995b:567) see Durkheim's theory as containing elements of conservative, liberal, and radical traditions, which he tried to synthesize, not an easy task.

Still, we must in the end revere Durkheim's genius. It is impressive to go through the years of good work, to see not only innovative concepts but also a whole discipline invented and established. One is amazed by the clarity, logic, and frequent rightness of his complex and sophisticated thinking. The complexity is exemplified by his grasp of the paradoxical elements of the physical sexual relationship: a transgression of autonomy, a building of intimacy. Durkheim's criticism of his antagonists is exceedingly penetrating, and his comments on biological analogies, instinct theories, ethnographic parallels, and survival theories also have merit.

One is also surprised to find the problems we think of as novel being dealt with by Durkheim, who grasps them and offers creative analyses and policies. There is a certain boldness in his unquestionable acceptance of modernization, his willingness to seek solutions to the problems of modernity rather than retreating into nostalgia or fearful efforts at restoration of the traditional past.

One can hardly question the intellectual significance and originality of his thought, which is as evident in his lesser known work on the family as in his major works. Would that his writing on the family had become a major work instead of a casualty of World War I! The contradictions that abound in Durkheim's work are there because of the extensiveness and complexity of his thought: He is indeed large and multitudinous.

DILEMMAS OF EXISTENCE

Some of Durkheim's contradictions may be inevitable as existential dilemmas. The conflict between individualism and solidarity is inherent in real-world dilemmas and family commitment. We are struggling with many of the same issues and contradictions that Durkheim faced in the social world and in theoretical creation. Such dilemmas are intrinsically incapable of easy resolution. These questions remain on our agenda, put here in present-day terms.

What is a family? The family formed by legal marriage and biological parenthood? Or alternatives to that, ranging from formal or informal adoption to heterosexual cohabitation, gay and lesbian families, and postmodern families formed by marriage-divorce-remarriage linkages?

Is it possible to have love, freely chosen, *and* commitment? Is voluntarism unworkable in marriage and the family? Can intentional families be created and successfully maintained on a voluntaristic basis, or is it only the conventional nuclear family and kin that will persist through time?

Is it possible to support autonomy and individuality for family members and still maintain a family? Will the family devolve into isolated individuals?

Is it possible to have a domestic life and a presence in the public world? Durkheim noted that the family served as a refuge, a place of restoration and personal happiness. Will emphasis on achievement in the public world and pressures on family time (for both sexes, now) dramatically change family life?

Are women the same as or different from men? We thought we had the best answer to this in an equality feminism of sameness and formal legal equality. But equal-rights feminism has been challenged by cultural-social feminism as well as by conservatives, who emphasize women's special qualities and contributions. Communitarians' views are less essentialist, but they are equally concerned about the changes in women's roles that draw them away from family and child rearing.

Is it possible to be socially responsible for children born to unmarried parents, while not undercutting marriage? What are the claims and responsibilities of unmarried biological parents? What is the role of the state?

Are children desired? Are they welcome? Will fertility stabilize at replacement level or decline? Does this depend on the economic and social support provided to parents (Hewlett and West 1998; Hunt and Hunt 1986)? Is parenthood becoming a purely voluntary relationship, such that it is spontaneously broken by parents who wish to abandon parental responsibility?

Who *is* a parent? This is not a question Durkheim could have anticipated in terms of reproductive technology. Yet he did address the legal establishment of parenthood in the case of unmarried parents. Sorting out questions of parental responsibility and privilege is complicated today by the complex relations of reproduction, adoption, and fosterage that are possible.

Last, and most general, what is the place of the family in society today? Durkheim believed that intermediate groups, occupational societies in particular, were needed to bind the individual to a society that was no longer encapsulated by the family. Mary Ann Glendon (1981) goes farther down this road to argue that occupational status is now the master social status. Work is replacing the family's role in forging social bonds and providing entitlement to a support system. "The relationships that, unlike marriage and contract, are relatively hard to enter and leave today are the preferred sorts of New Property—good jobs with good fringe benefits" (p. 45). Is the family no longer a passport to social integration and personal caring?

In sum, Durkheim did face the hard questions, no matter how disappointing, even irritating, some of his answers could be. Although his responses to social concerns were sometimes overwhelmed by abstract theory, he saw the central dilemma for the modern family correctly: individuality and spontaneity versus stability. Ideally, this tension is resolved by a bond of commitment that needs no legal regulation or community coercion. In practice, we are less sure about that but cannot find a point at which to draw a line of compulsion, because to do so is to violate modern values of personhood and autonomy. The individual-community tension is a central problem for our age.

Living in an era of change comparable to ours, Durkheim has something to offer contemporary family sociologists, including the comfort of knowing such times are not unique.

Conclusion

Metaphorically speaking, Durkheim still walks among us. The one hundredth anniversaries of the publication of the *Rules* and *Suicide* have been marked by celebratory conferences and publications (Lester 1998; Turner 1995a). Durkheim continues to "command attention" (Alpert 1974:199). I believe this is because he is "large," "contain[ing] multitudes" in scope and ideas. Coming to grips with Durkheim's ideas and contradictions can inspire reflective thought on family and society. Durkheim can be as inspirational to those who are largely critical as well as to enthusiasts:

> The greats (or, if one prefers, the classics) are such precisely because they do not lend themselves to comprehensive, exhaustive readings. Rather, they should be visited and revisited, always with new questions in mind—or even better, with a willingness to let *them* formulate new problems, raise new issues, and suggest new insights. (Poggi 1972:xii)

Notes

1. Neofunctionalists have revived Parsonian theory somewhat (Alexander 1985; and see Turner 1998, chap. 5), but I believe the point is still valid.

2. This is from notes on a presentation made by John H. Scanzoni to the University of Notre Dame Family Seminar in 1973.

3. *Liberal* is used in this chapter in its dominant current sense of a moderately left political perspective that sees a strong role for government in support of its citizens, with attention especially to the disadvantaged. It is used in the sense of "progressive politically or socially; favoring gradual reform, especially political reforms that extend democracy, distribute wealth more evenly, and protect the personal freedom of the individual" (Soukhanov 1999:1039) "Liberal" also describes an almost opposite "free market" economic theory (p. 1039) and political perspective, one that opposed government intervention to regulate the economy or provide for social needs. This is not heard at grassroots levels these days but is used in scholarly contexts.

4. See McIntyre and Sussman (1995) for a sociological overview of law and family. The Areen (1992) family law casebook indicates the reciprocal interest of legal scholars and trial advocates in social science.

5. France has had a very substantial immigration from Islamic nations since after World War II. During the colonial era, French-run colonial schools presented the standard French curriculum, and migrants from the Arab or African colonies were already socialized into French culture. That is not so true now that those nations are independent. Moreover, these economic migrants or political refugees are substantial enough in numbers that they can preserve their culture in ethnic enclaves. France is still committed to assimilation. How long this will be true is uncertain, given the higher birthrates of Islamic populations and resistance to assimilation. There are now distinctively Islamic family practices, for example, underage marriage. Girls are more restricted than boys in Islamic families. In public settings, struggles have occurred between Islamic cultural practices and French secularism. A typical issue is whether or not Islamic girls are permitted to wear their religiously required head scarves to public school.

6. Literally, *orientalism* is the study of East Asia, the orient. But the term is more often used to signal a perspective that makes much of an imputed and highly symbolic dichotomy between East and West. This perspective emphasizes the "otherness" of the East or of any area of the world that is not Western European in culture. It suggests a fascination with what are perceived to be exotic, strange, and usually inferior cultures. Orientalism implies that interest, even admiration, for the particulars of a non-Western culture are accompanied by an attitude of superiority.

7. Durkheim was working on *The Division of Labor* during this time. The first draft was completed in 1886 (Bellah 1973:xiii).

8. Not all agree (e.g., Alexander 1982:214).

9. Posthumously published works, such as "The Conjugal Family" (Durkheim 1921), were often completed considerably earlier; that article is the conclusion to his family course of 1892. Durkheim's writing and speaking on family policy is more visible later, and a great deal was actually written after his arrival in Paris. But seeds of his policy concerns were present quite early—for example, in the article on "Suicide and Natality" (Durkheim 1888b).

Many Durkheim scholars support the notion of consistency in his work: "Durkheim was one of those men who write essentially one book, though in a number of versions. The development is merely the unfolding of what is clearly evident in the germ from the beginning" (Bellah 1973:xiii; also Giddens 1972:12, 41; 1978:82-83; Hynes 1975:101; Munch 1988:25; Simpson 1965:527-28). Cladis (1992), on the other hand, says that "diversity marks Durkheim's work." "His corpus is multifaceted with characteristic themes" but "many paths" (p. 29). Alexander (1982) claims that Durkheim refuted his earlier work, for instance, *The Division of Labor* (Alexander 1982:214; see also Gane 1983:135-36; Jones 1986:16-17). Others too numerous to mention have ventured opinions on this point.

There is some agreement on the notion of a sharp change in one respect around 1895. This was a developing interest in religion that Durkheim himself remarked on (Durkheim 1907a:613; Gane 1992:4; and see Giddens 1972:12-13; Jones 1993:25; and Lukes 1972:180-81). No connection has been made by these scholars to Durkheim's family sociology. Insofar as Durkheim's religious interests shape his family sociology, this was already visible in "The Prohibition of Incest" (Durkheim 1898c).

10. Besnard (1973) offers a detailed discussion of Durkheim's tendency toward the "happy medium" or, alternatively, the resolution of tension between two poles at an equilibrium point (pp. 34-36; 1993a).

References

Works by Durkheim

Buisson, Ferdinand and Emile Durkheim. 1911. "Enfance." Pp. 552-53 in *Nouveau dictionnaire de pédagogie et d'instruction primaire,* edited by Ferdinand Buisson. Paris: Hachette.

Durkheim, Emile. 1885. Review of A. Schaeffle, *Bau und Leben des Sozialem Körpers,* vol. 1. *Revue philosophique* XIX:84-101.

_____. 1886. Review of de Greef, Guillaume, *Introduction à la sociologie,* 1ème Partie, Paris and Brussels. *Revue philosophique* XXII:658-63.

_____. 1888a. "Introduction à la sociologie de la famille." *Annales de la Faculté des Lettres de Bordeaux* 10:257-81.

_____. 1888b. "Suicide et natalité: étude de statistique morale." *Revue philosophique* XXVI:446-63.

_____. 1889. Review of Ferdinand Tönnies, *Gemeinschaft und Gesellschaft: Abhandlung des Communismus und des Socialismus als empirischer Culturformen. Revue philosophique* XXVII:416-422.

_____. [1893] 1978. *De la division du travail social.* Paris: Presses Universitaires de France [Alcan].

_____. [1895a] 1956. *Les Règles de la méthode sociologique.* Paris: Presses Universitaires de France [Alcan].

_____. 1895b. "Revue critique: L'Origine du mariage dans l'espèce humaine, d'après Westermarck." *Revue philosophique* XL:606-23.

———. 1895c. "Lo stato attuale degli studi sociologici in Francia." *La riforma sociale* III: 607-622; 691-707. Pp. 73-108 in *Emile Durkheim: Textes,* vol. 1, edited by Victor Karady. Paris: Les Editions de minuit, 1975.

———. [1897a] 1930. *Le suicide: Étude de sociologie.* Paris: Presses Universitaires de France [Alcan].

———. 1897b. "Il suicidio dal punto di vista sociologico." *Rivista italiana di sociologica* I:17-27. [Italian translation of pp. 1-15 of Emile Durkheim, *Le suicide,* slightly modified.]

———. 1897c. Review of Antonio Labriola, *Essais sur la conception matérialiste de l'histoire,* Paris: Girard et Brière. *Revue philosophique* XLIV:645-51.

———. 1898a. "L'individualisme et les intellectuels." *Revue bleue* (4e série) X:7-13. (Also cited as *Revue politique et littéraire.*)

———. 1898b. "Préface." *Année sociologique* I:i-vii.

———. 1898c. "La Prohibition de l'inceste et ses origines." *Année sociologique* I:1-70.

———. 1898d. Letter to the Editor. *American Journal of Sociology* 3:848-49.

———. 1898e. Review of B. H. Baden-Powell, *The Indian Village Community,* London: Longmans, Green, 1896. *Année sociologique* I:359-63.

———. 1898f. Review of Ernest Grosse, *Die Formen der Familie und die Formen der Wirthschaft,* Fribourg-en-Brisgau: Mohr. *Année sociologique* I:319-32

———. 1898g. Review of Jobbé-Duval, "La Commune annamite," Nouvelle Revue historique de droit français et étranger, Oct., Dec. 1896. *Année sociologique* I: 363-66.

———. 1898h. Review of Joseph Kohler, *Zur Urgeschichte der Ehe. Totemismus, Gruppenehe, Mutterrecht,* vol. 1, Stuttgart: Enke. *Année sociologique* I:306-19.

———. 1898i. Review of Ed. Meynial, "Le Mariage après les invasions," *Nouvelle Revue historique de droit français et étranger* (1896:4, 6; 1897:2). *Année sociologique* I:340-43.

———. 1898j. Review of Ernest Miler, "Die Hauskommunion der Südslaven," 1897, pp. 199-222 in *Jahrbuch der Internationalen Vergleichen de Rechtswissenschaft und Volkswirtschaftelehre, Division I. Année sociologique* I:339.

———. 1899a. "Antisémitisme et crise sociale." Pp. 59-63 in H. Dagan, *Enquête sur l'antisémitisme.* Paris: Stock.

———. 1899b. "Morphologie sociale." *Année sociologique* II:520-21.

———. 1899c. "Préface." *Année sociologique* II:i-vi.

———. 1899d. Review of W. v. Bulow, "Die Ehegesetze der Samoaner," *Globus* 73:185ff. *Année sociologique* II:343.

———. 1899e. Review of Stanislas Ciszewski, *Künstliche Verwandtschaft bei Den Südslaven,* Dissertation, University of Leipzig, 1897. *Année sociologique* II:321-23.

———. 1899f. Review of A. Lefas, "L'Adoption testamentaire à Rome," *Nouvelle Revue historique de droit français et étranger,* No. 6. 1897. *Année sociologique* II:325-27.

———. 1899g. Review of D. Théophil Loebel, *Hochzeitsbräuche in der Türkei,* Amsterdam: J.-H. de Bussy, n.d. *Année sociologique* II:334-36.

———. 1899h. Review of K. Heinrich Schaible, *Die Frau im Altertum,* Karlsruhe: Braun, 1896. *Année sociologique* II:313-14.

———. 1899i. Review of W. I. Thomas, "The Relationship of Sex to Primitive Social Control," *American Journal of Sociology* 3 (1898):754-76. *Année sociologique* II:328-329.

———. 1900a. Review of Franz Boas, *The Social Organization and the Secret Societies of the Kwakiutl Indians. Année sociologique* III:336-40.

———. 1900b. Review of Arsène Dumont, *Natalité et démocratie,* Paris: Schleicher, 1898. *Année sociologique* III:558-61.

_____. 1900c. Review of J. Goldstein, *Die vermeintlichen und die wirklichen Ursachen des Bevoelkerungsstillstandes in Frankreich,* Munich: Piloty & Loehle, 1989. *Année sociologique* III:561-63.

_____. 1900d. Review of N. Klugmann, *Vergleichende Studien zur Stellung Frau im Talmud,* Frankfurt: Kauffmann, 1898. *Année sociologique* III:388-89.

_____. 1900e. Review of Anna Lampérière, *Le rôle social de la femme,* Paris: Alcan, 1898. *Année sociologique* III:390-91.

_____. 1900f. Review of Victor Marx, *Die Stellung der Frauen in Babylonien,* Leipzig: Pries, 1989. *Année sociologique* III:389-90.

_____. 1900g. Review of A. Posada, *Feminismo,* Madrid: Fé, 1899. *Année sociologique* III:391.

_____. 1900h. Review of Prinzing, "Die Sterblichkeit der Ledigen und der Verheirateten," *Allgemeines Statistisches Archiv,* vol. 1, Halband. *Année sociologique* III:563.

_____. 1900i. Review of G. B. Salvioni, "Zur Statistik der Haushaltungen," pp. 191-236 in *Allgemeines Statistiche Archiv,* vol. 1. *Année sociologique* III:571-73.

_____. 1900j. Review of C.-V. Starke, *La famille dans les différentes sociétés,* Paris: Giard et Brière, 1899. *Année sociologique* III:365-70.

_____. 1900k. Review of Thorstein Veblen, *The Beginnings of Ownership. Année sociologique* III:398.

_____. 1900l. Review of Thorstein Veblen, "The Barbarian Status of Women," *American Journal of Sociology* 4 (1899):503-15. *Année sociologique* III:392.

_____. 1901a. "Introduction" [to the section on] "Sociologie criminelle et statistique morale." *Année sociologique* IV:433-36.

_____. 1901b. Review of Albert Cahuzac, *Essai sur les institutions et le droit malgaches,* vol. 1. Paris: Chevalier-Maresq, 1900. *Année sociologique* IV:342-45.

_____. 1901c. Review of Alfred Fouilleé, *La France au point de vue moral,* Paris: Alcan, 1900. *Année sociologique* IV:443-45.

_____. 1901d. Review of J.-G. Fraser, "Suggestions as to the Origin of Gender in Language," *The Fortnightly Review* (Jan. 1900):79-90. *Année sociologique* IV:364-65.

_____. 1901e. Review of Ludwig Fuld, "Die frauen und das Bürgerliche Gesetzbuch," *Zeitschrift für Socialwissenschaft,* 1900, No. 4. *Année sociologique* IV:365.

_____. 1901f. Review of Paul Kollmann, "Die sociale Zusammensetzung der Bevoelkerung im Deutschen Reiche," *Jahrbuch für Gesetzgebung, Verwaltung und Volkswirtschaft* (1900):59-107. *Année sociologique* IV:436-38

_____. 1901g. Review of Friedrich Lindner, *Die unehelichen Geburten als Socialphaenomon,* Leipzig: A Deichert, 1900. *Année sociologique* IV:441-43.

_____. 1901h. Review of Jacques Lourbet, *Le problème des sexes,* Paris: Giard et Briére, 1900. *Année sociologique* IV:364.

_____. 1901i. Review of Prinzing, "Die sociale Lage der Witwe in Deutschland;" *Zeitschrift für Socialwissenschaft,* 1900, No. 2:96-109; No. 3:199-205; "Grundzúge und Kosten eines Gesetzes über die Fürsorge für die Witwen und Waisen der Arbeiter, *Zeitschrift für Socialwissenschaft,* 1900, No. 4:262-77. *Année sociologique* IV:438-40.

_____. 1901j. Review of W. Rein, "Jugendliches Verbrechertum und seine Bekaempfung," *Zeitschrift für Socialwissenschaft,* 1900, No. 1:41-57. *Année sociologique* IV:451-52.

_____. 1901k. Review of Fritz Roeder, *Die Familie bei den Angelsachsen,* Halle: Niemeyer, 1899. *Année sociologique* IV:357-58.

_____. 1902a. "Quelques remarques sur les groupements professionels." "Préface." Pp. i-xxxvi in *De la division du travail social,* 2d ed. Paris: Alcan.

_____. 1902b. "Sur le totémisme." *Année sociologique* V:82-121.

_____. 1902c. Review of J. Bertillon, "Nombre d'enfants par famille," *Journal de la société de statistique de Paris* (1901), No. 4:130-45. *Année sociologique* V:435-36.

_____. 1902d. Review of Ernest Crawley, *The Mystic Rose: A Study of Primitive Marriage,* London: Macmillan, 1902. *Année sociologique* VI:352-58.

_____. 1902e. Review of de J. Du Plessis Grenédan, *Histoire de l'autorité paternelle et de la société familiale en France avant 1789,* Paris: Artur Rousseau, 1900. *Année sociologique* V:376-79.

_____. 1902f. Review of Havelock Ellis, *Studies in the Psychology of Sex,* Philadelphia: Davis, 1901. *Année sociologique* V:392.

_____. 1902g. Review of Freidrich Prinzing, "Die eheliche Fruchtbarkeit in Deutschland," *Zeitschrift für Socialwissenschaft* 1901, Issue 1:336-338; Issue 2:290-311; Issue 3:188-90. *Année sociologique* V:436-37.

_____. 1902h. Review of Félix Dupré la Tour, *De la recherche de la paternité en droit comparé,* Paris: Rousseau, 1900. *Année sociologique* V:379-81.

_____. 1903a. Review of R. Caillemer, *Origines et développement de l'exécution testamentaire,* Lyon: 1901. *Année sociologique* VI:345-50.

_____. 1903b. Review of Maurice Courant, *En Chine: moeurs et institutions,* Paris: 1901. *Année sociologique* VI:367-69.

_____. 1903c. Review of A. Esmein, "Les coutumes primitives dans les écrits mythologiques grecs et romains," *Nouvelle revue historique de droit français et étranger* 5-32; 113-46. *Année sociologique* VI:359-61.

_____. 1903d. Review of Abel Pouzol, *La recherche de la paternité: Etude critique de la sociologie et de législation comparée,* Paris: Giard et Brière, 1902. *Annèe sociologique* VI:415-18.

_____. 1903e. Review of William Rullkoeter, *The Legal Protection of Woman Among the Ancient Germans,* Chicago: 1900. *Année sociologique* VI: 366.

_____. 1903f. Review of C.-A. Stuart Verrijn. "Untersuchungen über die Beziehung zwischen Wohlstand, Natalität und Kindersterblichkeit in den Niederlanden," *Zeitschrift für Socialwissenschaft,* 1901, Issue 10:649-62. *Année sociologique* VI:546-47.

_____. 1904a. "L'Elite intellectuelle et la démocratie. *Revue bleue* 5ème, 1. No. 23 (June 4):705-706.

_____. 1904b. "La Sociologie et les sciences sociales." Resumé d'une conference à l'Ecole des hautes études sociales à Paris (1903). *Revue internationale de sociologie* XII: 83-87.

_____. 1904c. Remarks at oral examination of doctoral candidate Glotz on "Solidarity of the Family in the Criminal Law of Ancient Greece." *Revue de Philosophie* IV (2) (Oct.). Translation (by Lukes) pp. 624-26 in Steven Lukes, *Emile Durkheim.* New York: Harper, 1972.

_____. 1904d. Review of Max Bauer, *Das Geschlechtsleben in der deutschen Vergangenheit,* Leipzig, 1902. *Année sociologique* VII:439-40.

_____. 1904e. Review of E. Glasson. *Histoire du droit et des institutions de la France,* vol. VIII *Epoque Monarchique,* Paris: F. Pichon, 1902. *Année sociologique* VII: 428-33.

_____. 1904f. Review of Charles Letourneau, *La condition de la femme dans les diverses races et civilisations,* Paris: Giard et Brière, n.d. *Année sociologique* VII:433-34.

_____. 1904g. Review of E. Maurel, *Causes de notre dépopulation,* Paris: Doin. *Année sociologique* VII:655.

_____. 1904h. Review of Richard Niese, "Das Personnen—und Familienrecht der Suaheli," *Zeitschrift für vergleichende Rechtswissenschaft* 16:203-48, Stuttgart, 1903. *Année sociologique* VII:420-23.

_____. 1904i. Review of Pierre-André Pidoux, *Histoire du mariage et du droit des gens mariés en Franche-Comté,* Dôle: 1902. *Année sociologique* VII:436-38.

_____. 1904j. Review of Hans Stockar, *Ueber den Entzug der vaeterlichen Gewalt im roemischen Recht,* Zurich: Schulthess, 1903. *Année sociologique* VII:427-28.

_____. 1904k. Review of Max Thal, *Mutterrecht, Frauenfrage und Weltanschauung,* Breslau: Schottlander, 1903. *Année sociologique* VII:418.

_____. 1905a. "Sur l'organisation matrimoniale des sociétés australiennes." *Année sociologique* VIII:118-47.

_____. 1905b. "Le Problème de la solidarité familial et du totémisme chez les Hébreux." Resumé du débat à la soutenance de thèse de L. Germain-Lévy. *Revue de Philosophie* V:486-89. Pp. 130-33 in Emile Durkheim. *Textes,* vol. 2. Edited by Victor Karady. Paris: Les Editions de minuit.

_____. 1905c. Review of Gustave Glotz, *La Solidarité de la famille dans le droit criminel en Grèce,* Paris: Funtemoing,1904. *Année sociologique* VIII:465-72.

_____. 1905d. Review of Clément Juglar, *Tableau des naissances en France, en Angleterre, en Prusse, en Allemagne, et dans leurs capitales,* Orléans: Paul Pigelet, 1903:20 in 8r (Extrait du compte rendu de l'Academie des sciences morales et politiques). *Année sociologique* VIII:616-17.

_____. 1905e. Review of A.-N. Kiaer, *Statistische Beitraege zur Beleuchtung der ehelichen Fruchbarkeit,* Christiana: Jacob Dybwad, 1903. *Année sociologique* VIII:618-19.

_____. 1905f. Review of Fusamaro Tsugaru, *Die Lehre von der Japanischen Adoption,* Berlin: Mayer and Müller. *Année sociologique* VIII:409-13.

_____. 1905g. Review of Kojiro Twasaky, *Das japonische Eherecht,* Leipzig: 1904 and of Saburo Sakamoto, *Das Ehescheidungsrecht Japans,* Berlin: 1903. *Année sociologique* VIII:421-25.

_____. 1906a. "Le Divorce par consentement mutuel." *Revue bleue,* 5e série, V:549-54.

_____. 1906b. Review of George Elliott Howard, *A History of Maltrimonial Institutions,* 3 vols, London: Fisher Unwin; Chicago: Callahan. *Année sociologique* IX:384-92.

_____. 1906c. Review of Othmar Spann, "Die Stiefvaterfamilie unehelichen Ursprungs. Zugleich eine Studie zur Methodologie der Unehelichkeits-Statistik, *Zeitschrift für Socialwissenschaft* (1904):539-74. *Année sociologique* IX:435-38.

_____. 1906d. Review of Alfred Valensi, *L'application de la loi du divorce en France,* Paris: Larose et Tenin, 1905. *Année sociologique* IX:438-43.

_____. 1906e. Review of Edward Westermarck, "The Position of Women in Early Civilization," *American Journal of Sociology* 10 (1904):408-21. *Année sociologique* IX:380.

_____. 1907a. "Deuxième Lettre de M. Durkheim." *Revue néo-scolastique* XIV:612-14.

_____. 1907b. Review of James Bryce, *Marriage and Divorce,* New York: Oxford University Press, 1905. *Année sociologique* X:436-37.

_____. 1907c. Review of Thad. Engert, *Ehe-und-Familienrecht der Hebräer,* München, Lenther'sche Buchhandlung 1905. *Année sociologique* X:427-29.

_____. 1907d. Review of Henri Guigon, *La succession des bâtards dans l'ancienne Bourgogne,* Dijon: 1905. *Année sociologique* X:435-36.

_____. 1907e. Review of Edward Westermarck, *The Origin and Development of the Moral Ideas,* vol. 1, London: Macmillan 1906. *Année sociologique* X:383-95.

_____. 1908. Débat sur l'explication en histoire et en sociologie. *Bulletin de la société française de philosophie* VIII:229-45, 347.

_____. 1909a. "Sociologie et sciences sociales." Pp. 259-85 in *De la Méthode dans les Sciences,* 1ère série, edited by Félix Alcan. Paris: Alcan.

_____. 1909b. Contribution to discussion of "Mariage et divorce." Pp. 258-59, 261-62, 266-68, 270, 273, 277-83, 293 in *Libres entretiens: Questions relatives à la condition Economique et Juridique des Femmes.* Paris: Union pour la vérité.

_____. 1910a. Contribution to discussion of "La Notion d'égalité sociale" (Dec. 30, 1909). *Bulletin de la société française de philosophie* 10:59-63, 65-67, 69-70. Translated as "A Debate on Egalitarian Ideas." Pp. 86-193 in Emile Durkheim, *On Politics and the State,* edited by Anthony Giddens. Translated by W. D. Halls. Cambridge: Polity Press, 1986.

_____. 1910b. Review of Georg Buschan, *Geschlecht und Verbrechen,* Berlin and Leipzig, Hermann Seemann, n.d. *Année sociologique* XI:492-94.

_____. 1910c. Review of Joseph Kohler, "Ueber Totemismus und Urehe." *Zeitschrift für vergleichende Rechtswissenshaft* XIX:177-88; "Eskimo und Gruppenehe," *Z.f.v.R.* XIX:423-32; "Nochmals ueber Gruppenehe und Totemismus," *Z.f.v.R.* XIX:252-67. *Année sociologique* XI:359-61.

_____. 1910d. Review of H. A. Krose, *Die Ursachen der Selbstmordäufhigkeit,* Freiburg: B. Herder, 1906. *Année sociologique* XI:511-15.

_____. 1910e. Review of Alfred Obrist, *Essai sur les origines du testament romain,* Lausanne: 1906. *Année sociologique* XI:352-54.

_____. 1910f. Review of Gaston Richard, *La femme dans l'histoire,* Paris: 1909. *Année sociologique* XI:369-71.

_____. 1910g. Review of Alexa Stanischitsch, *Ueber den Ursprung der Zadruga: Eine Soziologische Untersuchung,* Bern: Buchdruckeri Scheitlin, Spring and Co., 1907. *Année sociologique* XI:343-47.

_____. 1910h. Review of Otto Stoll, *Das Geschlechtsleben in der Voelkerpsychologie,* Leipzig: Viet, 1908. *Année sociologique* XI:375-83.

_____. 1910i. Review of Marianne Weber, *Ehefrau und Mutter in der Rechtsentwicklung.* *Année sociologique* XI:363-69.

_____. 1911. Contribution to discussion of "L' Education sexuelle." *Bulletin de la societé française de philosophie* XI:33-38, 44-47. Pp. 241-51 in Emile Durkheim, *Textes,* vol. 2. Paris: Les Editions de minuit, 1975.

_____. [1912] 1979. *Les Formes élémentaires de la vie religieuse.* Paris: Presses Universitaires de France [Alcan].

_____. 1913a. Review of Gaëtan Aubéry, *La Communauté de biens conjugale,* Paris: Pichon et Durand-Auzias, 1911. *Année sociologique* XII:434-37.

_____. 1913b. Review of Franz Boas, *The Mind of Primitive Man,* New York: Macmillan. *Année sociologique* XII:31-33.

_____. 1913c. Review of Richard Gebhard, *Russisches Familien - und Erb-recht,* Berlin: Guttentag, 1910. *Année sociologique* XII:424-26.

_____. 1913d. Review of Otto Opet, *Brauttradition und Consensgespräch in mittelalterischen Trauungsritualen,* Berlin: Vahlen, 1910. *Année sociologique* XII:433.

_____. 1915a. *L'Allemagne au-dessus de tout: La mentalité allemande et la guerre.* Paris: Colin.

_____. 1915b. "La Sociologie." Pp. 39-49 in *La science française,* vol. 1. Paris: Larousse. For the "Exposition universelle et internationale de San Francisco."

_____. 1917. "Durkheim (André-Armand)." *L'Annuaire de l'association amicale des anciens élèves de l'Ecole Normale Supérieure.* Pp. 446-52 in Emile Durkheim: *Textes,* vol. 1, edited by Victor Karady. Paris: Les Editions de minuit, 1975.

_____. 1921. "La famille conjugale." *Revue philosophique* XC:1-14. Edited with notes by Marcel Mauss.

_____. 1922. *Education et Sociologie.* Paris: Alcan.

_____. [1925] 1974. *L'éducation morale.* Paris: Presses Universitaires de France [Alcan].

_____. [1938] 1969. *L'Evolution Pédagogique en France,* 2ème ed. Paris: Presses Universitaires de France.

———. 1950. *Leçons de sociologie: physique des moeurs et du droit.* Paris: Presses Universitaires de France; Istanbul: Université d'Istanbul. Translated by Cornelia Brookfield as *Professional Ethics and Civic Morals.* London: Routledge, 1957.

———. 1973. "Lettres d'Emile Durkheim à Georges Davy." Pp. 299-313 in *L'homme; le fait social et le fait politique,* edited by Georges Davy. Paris: Mouton.

———. 1986. *Durkheim on Politics and the State,* edited by Anthony Giddens. Translated by W. D. Halls. Cambridge: Polity Press.

Durkheim, Emile and A. Bianconi. 1913. Review of Torday and Joyce, "Notes ethnographiques sur les peuples communément appelés Bakuba, ainsi que sur les peuplades apparentées Les Bushongo," *Annales du Musée du Congo belges,* Bruxelles: Spineux, 1911 and Hilton-Simpson, *Land and Peoples of the Kasai,* London: Constable, 1911. *Année sociologique* XII:384-90.

Durkheim, Emile and E. Denis. 1915. *Qui a voulu la guerre?: L'origines de la guerre d'après les documents diplomatiques.* Paris: Colin.

Durkheim, Emile and Paul Fauconnet. 1903. "Sociologie et sciences sociales." *Revue philosophique* LV:465-97.

Durkheim, Emile and Marcel Mauss. 1903. "De quelques formes primitives de classification: contribution à l'étude des representations collectives." *Année sociologique* VI:1-72.

Works by Other Authors

Abercrombie, Nicholas, Stephen Hill, and Bryan S. Turner. 1994. *The Penguin Dictionary of Sociology,* 3d ed. London: Penguin.

Abrams, Philip. 1982. *Historical Sociology.* Ithaca, NY: Cornell University Press.

Acock, Alan C. and David H. Demo. 1994. *Family Diversity and Well-Being.* Thousand Oaks, CA: Sage.

Adams, Bert N. 1968. *Kinship in an Urban Setting.* Chicago: Markham.

———. 1971. *The American Family: A Sociological Interpretation.* Chicago: Markham.

———. 1995. *The Family: A Sociological Interpretation,* 5th ed. New York: Harcourt Brace.

Adams, Bert N. and Suzanne Steinmetz. 1993. "Family Theory and Methods in the Classics." Pp. 71-94 in *Sourcebook of Family Theories and Methods,* edited by Pauline G. Boss, William J. Doherty, Ralph LaRossa, Walter R. Schumm, and Suzanne K. Steinmetz. New York: Plenum.

Adams, Bert N. and R.A. Sydie. 2001. *Sociological Theory.* Thousand Oaks, CA: Pine Forge.

Ahrons, Constance. 1994. *The Good Divorce: Keeping Your Family Together When Your Marriage Comes Apart,* rev. ed. New York: Harper.

Aldous, Joan. 1972. "An Exchange between Durkheim and Tönnies on the Nature of Social Relations, with an Introduction by Joan Aldous." *American Journal of Sociology* 77:1191-200.

———. 1991. "In the Families' Ways." *Contemporary Sociology* 20:660-62.

Alexander, Jeffrey C. 1982. *The Antonomies of Classical Thought,* vol. 2. *Marx and Durkheim.* Berkeley: University of California Press.

———. 1985. *Neofunctionalism.* Beverly Hills, CA: Sage.

Alexander, Jeffrey C., ed. 1988. *Durkheimian Sociology: Cultural Studies.* Cambridge, England: Cambridge University Press.

Allen, Katherine R., Rosemary Blieszner, and Karen A. Roberto. 2000. "Families in the Middle and Later Years: A Review and Critique of Research in the 1990s." *Journal of Marriage and the Family* 62:911-926.

Alpert, Harry. [1939] 1961. *Emile Durkheim and His Sociology.* New York: Russell and Russell.

———. 1974. Review of *Emile Durkheim: His Life and Work,* by Steven Lukes. Harper and Row, 1972. *Contemporary Sociology* 3:198-200.

A. M. P. 1997. "The Ups and Downs of Testosterone." *Psychology Today,* November/ December, p. 18.

Andrews, Howard F. 1993. "Durkheim and Social Morphology." Pp. 111-35 in *Emile Durkheim: Sociologist and Moralist,* edited by Stephen P. Turner. London: Routledge.

Areen, Judith. 1992. *Cases and Materials on Family Law,* 3d ed. Westbury, NY: Foundation Press.

Ariès, Phillipe. 1962. *Centuries of Childhood: A Social History of Family Life.* New York: Knopf.

Bachofen, J. J. [1861] 1948. *Das Mutterrecht.* Basel: Benno Schwabe.

———. [1880] 1966. *Antiquarische Briefe.* Basel: Schwabe.

Bainville, Jacques. 1924. *Histoire de France.* Paris: Arthème Fayard.

Bamberger, Joan. 1974. "The Myth of Matriarchy: Why Men Rule in Primitive Society." Pp. 263-280 in *Women, Culture, and Society,* edited by Michelle Z. Rosaldo and Louise Lamphere. Stanford, CA: Stanford University Press.

Bane, Mary Jo. 1976. *Here to Stay: American Families in the Twentieth Century.* New York: Basic.

Bartholet, Elizabeth. 1993. *Adoption and the Politics of Parenting* Boston: Houghton-Mifflin.

Bartlett, Katharine T. 1988. "Re-Expressing Parenthood." *Yale Law Journal* 98:293-430.

———. 1999. "Improving the Law Relating to Postdivorce Arrangements for Children." Pp. 71-102 in *The Postdivorce Family: Children, Parenting, and Society,* edited by Ross A. Thompson and Paul R. Amato. Thousand Oaks, CA: Sage.

Bartos, O. J. 1996. "Postmodernism, Postindustrialism, and the Future." *The Sociological Quarterly* 37:307-25.

Baumrind, Diana. 1971. "Current Patterns of Parental Authority." *Developmental Psychology Monograph* 4:1-102.

Beauvoir, Simone de. [1949] 1978. *The Second Sex.* New York: Knopf.

Becker, Gary. 1960. "An Economic Analysis of Fertility." Pp. 209-40 in *Demographic and Economic Change in Developed Countries* for National Bureau of Economic Research. Princeton, NJ: Princeton University Press.

———. 1981. *A Treatise on the Family.* Cambridge, MA: Harvard University Press.

Bedford, Victoria Hilkevitch. 1995. "Sibling Relationships in Middle and Old Age." Pp. 201-22 in *Handbook of Aging and the Social Sciences,* edited by Rosemary Blieszner and Victoria H. Bedford. Westport, CN: Greenwood.

Bell, Norman W. and Ezra F. Vogel, eds. 1960. *A Modern Introduction to the Family.* Glencoe, IL: Free Press.

Bellah, Robert N. 1959. "Durkheim and History." *American Sociological Review* 24:447-61.

———. 1973. "Introduction." Pp. ix-lv in *Emile Durkheim on Morality and Society: Selected Writings.* Chicago: University of Chicago Press.

Bellah, Robert N., Richard Madsen, William M. Sullivan, Ann Swidler, and Steven M. Tipton. 1985. *Habits of the Heart: Individualism and Commitment in American Life.* Berkeley: University of California Press.

Bendix, Reinhard. 1968. "Max Weber." Pp. 493-502 in *International Encyclopedia of the Social Sciences,* vol. 16, edited by David L. Sills. New York: Macmillan.

Berger, Peter I. and Hansfried Kellner. 1970. "Marriage and the Construction of Reality." Pp. 49-73 in *Recent Sociology No. 2,* edited by Hans-Peter Dreitzel. New York: Macmillan.

Bernard, Jessie. 1986. "The Good-Provider Role: Its Rise and Fall." Pp. 125-44 in *Family in Transition,* 5th ed., edited by Arlene S. and Jerome H. Skolnick. Boston: Little, Brown.

Bernstein, Richard. 1990. *Fragile Glory: A Portrait of France and the French.* New York: Knopf.

Bertillon, Jacques. 1880. *La statistique humaine de la France: Naissance, mariage, mort.* Paris: Baillère.

Besnard, Philippe. 1973. "Durkheim et les femmes ou le *Suicide* inachevé." *Revue française de sociologie* XIV:27-61.

———. 1982. "A New Revised Durkheim." *Contemporary Sociology* 11:509-11.

———, ed. 1983. *The Sociological Domain: The Durkheimians and the Founding of French Sociology.* Cambridge, UK: Cambridge University Press.

———. 1993a. "Anomie and Fatalism in Durkheim's Theory of Regulation." Pp. 169-90 in *Emile Durkheim: Sociologist and Moralist,* edited by Stephen P. Turner. London: Routledge.

———. 1993b. "When Was L'Education Morale Written?/De quand date l'Education morale?" *Durkheim Studies/Etudes durkheimiennes* 5:8-10.

———. 1996. Review of Jennifer M. Lehmann, *Durkheim and Women. European Sociological Review* 12:106-107.

———. 1997. "Mariage et suicide: la théorie durkheimienne de la régulation conjugale à l'épreuve d'un siècle." *Revue française de sociologie* XXXVIII:735-58.

Besnard, Philippe and Marcel Fournier. 1998. "Introduction." Pp. 1-19 in *Emile Durkheim,* Lettres à Marcel Mauss, presentées par Philippe Besnard et Marcel Fournier. Paris: Presses Universitaires de France.

Binford, Lewis and Sally Binford. 1966. "A Preliminary Analysis of Functional Variability in the Mousterian of Levallois Facies." *American Anthropologist* 68:238-95.

Black, Naomi. 1989. *Social Feminism.* Ithaca, NY: Cornell University Press.

Blau, Peter M. 1964. *Exchange and Power in Social Life.* New York: John Wiley.

Blumberg, Rae L. and Robert F. Winch. 1972. "Societal Complexity: Evidence for the Curvilinear Hypothesis." *American Journal of Sociology* 77:898- 920.

Bohl, Joan C. 1997. "Family Autonomy vs. Grandparent Visitation: How Precedent Fell Prey to Sentiment in *Herndon v. Tuhey.*" *Missouri Law Review* 62:755ff.

Booth, Alan, ed. 1991. *Contemporary Families: Looking Forward, Looking Back.* Minneapolis, MN: National Council on Family Relations.

Booth, Alan and Paul R. Amato. 1997. *A Generation at Risk: Growing Up in an Era of Family Upheaval.* Cambridge, MA: Harvard University Press.

Booth, Alan, Karen Carver, and Douglas A. Granger. 2000. "Biosocial Perspectives on the Family." *Journal of Marriage and the Family* 62:1018-1034.

Boss, Pauline, William J. Doherty, Ralph L. LaRossa, Walter R. Schumm, and Suzanne K. Steinmetz. 1993. *Sourcebook of Family Theories and Methods: A Contextual Approach.* New York: Plenum.

Bottoms v. Bottoms. S.C. of Virginia. 1995. 249 Va 410, 457 S.E.2d 102.

Boulding, Elise. 1977. *Women in the Twentieth Century World.* New York: Halsted (Sage).

Bourgin, Hubert. 1913a. Review of Edith Abbott, *Women in Industry: A Study In American Economic History,* New York: Appleton. *Année sociologique* XII: 760.

———. 1913b. Review of Elizabeth Beardsley Butler, *Saleswomen in the Mercantile Store, 1909,* New York: Charities Publishing Co., 1911. *Année sociologique* XII:762.

_____. 1913c. Review of Elizabeth Beardsley Butler, *Women and the Trades, Pittsburgh 1907-08*, New York: Charities Publishing Co., 1911. *Année sociologique* XII: 761-62.

Boxer, Marilyn. 1981. "When Radical and Socialist Feminism Were Joined: The Extraordinary Failure of Madeleine Pelletier." Pp. 51-73 in *European Women on the Left*, edited by Jane Slaughter and Robert Kern. Westport, CN: Greenwood.

Bridenthal, Renate. 1982. "The Family: The View from a Room of Her Own." Pp. 225-39 in *Rethinking the Family: Some Feminist Issues*, edited by Barrie Thorne. New York: Longmans.

Brines, Julie and Kara Joyner. 1999. "The Ties That Bind: Principles of Cohesion in Cohabitation and Marriage." *American Sociological Review* 64:333-55.

Broderick, Carlfred. 1971. "Beyond the Five Conceptual Frameworks: A Decade of Development in Family Theory." *Journal of Marriage and the Family* 33:139-59.

_____. 1993. *Understanding Family Process: Basics of Family Systems Theory*. Newbury Park, CA: Sage.

Brody, Jane E. 1998. "Genetic Ties May be Factor in Violence in Stepfamilies." *New York Times*, February 10, pp. B9, B12.

Brogan, D. W. 1966. *The Development of Modern France, Vol.1. From the Fall of Empire to the Dreyfus Affair*. New York: Harper.

Brooks v. Parkerson. Ga. S.C. 1995. 265 Ga. 189, 454 S.E.2d 769.

Brown, Clair Vickery. 1982. "Home Production for Use in a Market Economy." Pp. 151-67 in *Rethinking the Family: Some Feminist Issues*, edited by Barrie Thorne. New York: Longmans.

Buehler, Cheryl. 1995. "Divorce Law in the United States." Pp. 99-120 in *Families and Law*, edited by Lisa J. McIntyre and Marvin B. Sussman. New York: Haworth.

Burgess, Ernest W. and Harvey J. Locke. [1945] 1960. *The Family: From Institution to Companionship*, 2d ed. New York: American Book.

Burgess, Ernest W. and Paul Wallin. 1953. *Engagement and Marriage*. Philadelphia: Lippincott.

Burns, Michael. 1991. *Dreyfus: A Family Affair, From the French Revolution to the Holocaust*. New York: HarperCollins.

Burr, Wesley R. 1973. *Theory Construction and the Sociology of the Family*. New York: John Wiley.

Burr, Wesley R., Reuben Hill, F. Ivan Nye, and Ira L. Reiss, eds. 1979a. *Contemporary Theories About the Family*, 2 vols. New York: Free Press.

_____. 1979b. "Introduction." Pp. 3-16 in *Contemporary Theories About the Family*, vol. 1, edited by Wesley Burr et al. New York: Free Press.

Bynder, Herbert. 1969. "Emile Durkheim and the Sociology of the Family." *Journal of Marriage and the Family* 31:527-33.

Caldwell, John C. 1999. "The Delayed Western Fertility Decline: An Examination of English-Speaking Countries." *Population and Development Review* 25:479-513.

Campbell, Donald T. and Julian C. Stanley. 1966. *Experimental and Quasi-Experimental Designs for Research*. Chicago: Rand McNally.

Carlson, Allen C. 1988. *Family Questions: Reflections on the American Social Crisis*. New Brunswick, NJ: Transaction.

_____. 1993. *From Cottage to Work Station: The Family's Search for Social Harmony in the Industrial Age*. San Francisco: Ignatius.

_____. 1998. "The State's Assault on the Family." Pp. 39-49 in *The Family in Civil Society*, edited by Christopher Wolfe. Lanham, MD: Rowman and Littlefield.

Challenger, Douglas. 1996. Review of Jennifer M. Lehman, *Durkheim and Women. Social Forces* 75:350-51.

Charle, Christophe. 1984. "Le Beau Mariage d'Emile Durkheim." *Actes de la recherche en sciences sociales* 55:45-49.

Chateaubriand, François R., Vicomte de. [1827] 1905. *Atala.* Boston: Heath.

Cheal, David. 1988. "Theories of Serial Flow in Intergenerational Transfers." *International Journal of Aging and Human Development* 26:261-74.

Cherlin, Andrew J. 1998. *Public and Private Families.* Boston: McGraw-Hill.

———. 2000. "Generation Ex-." *The Nation.* December 11. Retrieved April 30, 2001(www.thenation.com).

Christensen, Bryce. 1993. "Caring for America's Elderly: Washington's Way vs. Clinton's Way." *The Family in America* 8(11):1-8.

Christensen, Harold T. 1964a. "Development of the Family Field of Study." Pp. 3-32 in *Handbook of Marriage and the Family,* edited by Harold T. Christensen. Chicago: Rand McNally.

———, ed. 1964b. *Handbook of Marriage and the Family.* Chicago: Rand McNally.

Cladis, Mark S. 1992. *A Communitarian Defense of Liberalism: Emile Durkheim and Contemporary Theory.* Stanford, CA: Stanford University Press.

———. 1995. Review of Jennifer Lehmann, *Durkheim and Women,* Lincoln: University of Nebraska Press, 1994. *Philosophy of the Social Sciences* 25:535-39.

Clark, Terry N. 1968a. "Bertillon, Jacques." Pp. 69-71 in *International Encyclopedia of the Social Sciences,* vol. 2, edited by David L. Sills. New York: Macmillan.

———. 1968b. "Tarde, Gabriel." Pp. 509-14 in *International Encyclopedia of the Social Sciences,* vol. 15, edited by David L. Sills. New York: Macmillan.

———. 1973. *Prophets and Patrons: The French University and the Emergence of the Social Sciences.* Cambridge, MA: Harvard University Press.

Clignet, Remi. 1995. "Efficiency, Reciprocity, and Ascriptive Equality: The Major Strategies Governing the Selection of Heirs in America." *Social Science Quarterly* 76:274-93.

Collier, Jane, Michelle Z. Rosaldo, and Sylvia Yanigisako. 1982. "Is There a Family? New Anthropological Views." Pp. 25-39 in *Rethinking the Family,* edited by Barrie Thorne. New York: Longmans.

Concise Columbia Encyclopedia. 1994. New York: Columbia University Press.

Connel-Thouez, Katherine. 1987. "Succession and the Family: Reflections on the Evolution of Social Structures, Fundamental Values, and Civil Law." *Canadian Journal of Family Law/Revue canadienne de droit familiale* 6:103-108.

Connell, R.W. 1997. "Why Is Classical Theory Classical?" *American Journal of Sociology* 102:1511-57.

Cooley, Charles H. 1909. *Human Organization.* New York: Scribners.

Coontz, Stephanie. 1992. *The Way We Never Were: American Families and the Nostalgia Trap.* New York: Basic.

———. 1997. *The Way We Really Are: Coming to Terms with America's Changing Families.* New York: Basic.

———. 1999. "Divorcing Reality: New State Laws That Slow Down Divorce." Pp. 377-79 in *Sociology of Families: Readings,* edited by Cheryl Albers. Thousand Oaks, CA: Pine Forge.

———. 2000. "Historical Perspectives on Family Studies." *Journal of Marriage and the Family* 62:283-97.

Cooper, David Graham. 1971. *The Death of the Family.* New York: Pantheon.

Copley, Antony. 1988. *Sexual Moralities in France, 1790-1980: New Ideas on Family, Divorce, and Homosexuality; An Essay on Moral Change.* London: Routledge.

Coser, Lewis A. 1960. "Durkheim's Conservatism and Its Implications for Sociological Theory." Pp. 211-32 in *Emile Durkheim, 1858-1917; A Collection of Essays.* Columbus: Ohio State University Press.

Cott, Nancy F. 1986. "Feminist Theory and Feminist Movements: The Past Before Us."
    Pp. 49-62 in *What Is Feminism?* edited by Juliet Mitchell and Ann Oakley. New
    York: Pantheon.
Cotterrell, Roger. 1991. "The Durkheimian Tradition in the Sociology of Law." *Law and
    Society Review* 25:923-45.
Cova, Anne. 1991. "French Feminism and Maternity: Theories and Policies 1890-1918."
    Pp. 119-37 in *Maternity and Gender Policies: Women and the Rise of the European
    Welfare States, 1880s-1950s.* London: Routledge.
Cowan, Philip. 1993. "The Sky *Is* Falling, but Popenoe's Analysis Won't Help Us Do
    Anything About It." *Journal of Marriage and the Family* 55:548-52.
Craib, Ian. 1997. *Classical Social Theory: An Introduction to the Thought of Marx, Weber,
    Durkheim, and Simmel.* New York: Oxford University Press.
Crittenden, Danielle C. 1999. *What Our Mothers Didn't Tell Us: Why Happiness Eludes
    the Modern Woman.* New York: Simon and Schuster.
Danigelis, Nick and Whitney Pope. 1979. "Durkheim's Theory of Suicide as Applied to
    the Family: An Empirical Test." *Social Forces* 57:1081-106.
Darwin, Charles. [1859] 1964. *On the Origin of Species.* Cambridge, MA: Harvard
    University Press.
Daudet, Alphonse. 1927. "La dernière classe." Pp. 4-12 in *Contes de lundi,* nouvelle ed.
    Paris: Charpentier.
Davis, Kingsley and Judith Blake. 1956. "Social Structure and Fertility: An Analytical
    Framework." *Economic Development and Cultural Change* 4:211- 235.
Davy, Georges. 1919. "Emile Durkheim: L'homme." *Revue de métaphysique et de morale*
    26:181-98.
———. 1925. "Vues sociologiques sur la famille et la parenté d'après Emile Durkheim."
    Revue philosophique 100:79-117.
———. [1931] 1950. "La famille et la parenté d'après Durkheim." Pp. 6-122 in *Sociologues
    d'Hier et d'Aujourd'hui,* 2d ed., edited by Georges Davy. Paris: Presses Universitaires
    de France. Reprint of Davy 1925.
Degler, Carl N. 1980. *At Odds: Women and the Family in America From the Revolution
    to the Present.* New York: Oxford.
———. 1991. *In Search of Human Nature: The Decline and Revival of Darwinian Social
    Thought.* New York: Oxford.
"Divorce, American Style." 2000. Letters from David Blankenhorn and Judith S.
    Wallerstein. Reply from Katha Pollitt. *The Nation.* December 4, pp. 43-44.
Dixon, Suzanne. 1992. *The Roman Family.* Baltimore: Johns Hopkins Press.
Dolgin, Janet L. 1993. "Just a Gene: Judicial Assumptions About Parenthood." *UCLA
    Law Review* 40:637-94.
Donzelot, Jacques. 1979. *The Policing of Families.* New York: Pantheon.
Dorsey, James Owen. 1884. "Omaha Sociology." Pp. 205-370, 595-606 in *3d Annual
    Report of the U.S. Bureau of Ethnography, 1891-92.* Washington, DC: Bureau of
    Ethnography.
Dörmann, Johannes. 1968. "Johann Jacob Bachofen." Pp. 493-94 in *International
    Encyclopedia of the Social Sciences,* vol. 1, edited by David L. Sills. New York:
    Macmillan.
"Elian Decision Is Protested in Miami." 2000. *New York Times.* January 6, p. A16.
Eller, Cynthia. 2000. *The Myth of Matriarchal Prehistory: Why an Invented Past Won't
    Give Women a Future.* Boston: Beacon.
Emigh, Rebecca Jean. 1994. "Cultural Anthropology and Formal Demography: A
    Sociological Treatment of Inheritance Strategies." Paper presented at the annual
    meeting of the American Sociological Society, August 8-9, San Francisco.

Engels, Friedrich. [1884] 1972. *The Origin of the Family, Private Property, and the State.* Edited with an introduction by Eleanor Burke Leacock. New York: International Publishers.

Erickson, Victoria Lee. 1992. "Back to the Basics: Feminist Social Theory, Durkheim, and Religion." *Journal of Feminist Studies in Religion* 8: 35-46.

———. 1993. *When Silence Speaks: Feminism, Social Theory, and Religion.* Minneapolis, MN: Fortress.

Erlanger, Steven. 2000. "Birthrate Dips in Ex-Communist Countries." *New York Times,* May 4, p. A8.

Etzioni, Amitai. 1993. *The Spirit of Community: Rights, Responsibilities and the Communitarian Agenda.* New York: Crown.

Evans, Sara M. 1979. *Personal Politics: The Roots of Women's Liberation in the Civil Rights Movement and the New Left.* New York: Knopf.

Farber, Bernard. 1964. *Family Organization and Interaction.* San Francisco: Chandler.

———. 1973. *Family and Kinship in Modern Society.* Glenview, IL: Scott, Foresman.

———. 1981. *Conceptions of Kinship.* New York: Elsevier.

Farrington, Keith and Ely Chertock. 1993. "Social Conflict Theories of the Family." Pp. 357-81 in *Sourcebook of Family Theories and Methods,* edited by Pauline Boss et al. New York: Plenum.

Fenton, Steve. 1984. *Durkheim and Modern Sociology.* Cambridge, UK: Cambridge University Press.

Ferrante, Joan. 2000. *Sociology: The United States in a Global Community.* Belmont, CA: Wadsworth.

Filloux, Jean-Claude. 1970. "Introduction." Pp. 5-71 in Emile Durkheim, *La science sociale et l'action,* edited by Jean-Claude Filloux. Paris: Presses Universitaires de France.

———. 1976. "Il ne faut pas oublier que je suis fils de rabbin. *Revue française de sociologie* 17:259-66.

———. 1977. *Durkheim et le socialisme.* Paris: Droz.

———. 1993. "Inequalities and Social Stratification in Durkheim's Sociology." Pp. 211-28 in *Emile Durkheim: Sociologist and Moralist,* edited by Stephen P. Turner. London: Routledge.

Fineman, Martha Albertson. 1991. *The Illusion of Equality: The Rhetoric and Reality of Divorce Reform.* Chicago: University of Chicago Press.

———. 1995. *The Neutered Mother, the Sexual Family, and Other Twentieth Century Tragedies.* New York: Routledge.

Fletcher, Alice C. and Francis LaFlesche. 1911. "The Omaha Tribe." Pp. 15-672 in the *27th Annual Report of the Bureau of Ethnography.* Washington, DC: Bureau of Ethnography.

Fletcher, Yaël Simpson. 1991. "'La solution équitable, juste, humaine, moderne, démo-cratique': The Advocacy of Legal Divorce in France, 1858-1884." M.A. thesis, University of Maryland.

Fouillée, Alfred. 1893. "La Psychologie des sexes et les fondements physiologiques." *Revue des deux mondes,* série 9 (Sept. 15):397-429.

———. 1897. "Les jeunes criminels: l'école et la presse." *Revue des deux mondes,* série 10, v. 139:417-49.

Frazer, James Q. [1887] 1910. *Totemism and Exogamy,* 4 vols. London: Macmillan.

Freeman, Jo. 1995. "From Suffrage to Women's Liberation: Feminism in Twentieth Century America." Pp. 509-28 in *Women: A Feminist Perspective,* 5th ed., edited by Jo Freeman. Mountain View, CA: Mayfield.

Friedan, Betty. 1963. *The Feminine Mystique.* New York: Norton.

Friedl, Ernestine. [1975] 1984. *Women and Men: An Anthropological View.* Prospect Heights, IL: Itasca.

Fustel de Coulanges, Numa Denis. [1864] 1912. *La Cité Antique*. Paris: Hachette.

Gallagher, Maggie. 1989. *Enemies of Eros: How the Sexual Revolution Is Killing Family, Marriage, and Sex, and What We Can Do About It*. Chicago: Bonus.

———. 1996. *The Abolition of Marriage: How We Destroy Lasting Love*. Washington, DC: Regnery.

Gane, Mike. 1983. "Durkheim: Woman as Outsider." *Economy and Society* 12: 227-70.

———. 1992. *The Radical Sociology of Durkheim and Mauss*. London and New York: Routledge.

———. 1993. *Harmless Lovers: Gender Theory and Personal Relationships*. New York: Routledge.

———. 1995. "Jennifer Lehmann's Durkheim." *Durkheimian Studies* 1:63-69.

Giddens, Anthony. 1964. "The Suicide Problem in French Sociology." *British Journal of Sociology* 16:3-18.

———. 1971. *Capitalism and Modern Social Theory: An Analysis of the Writings of Marx, Durkheim, and Max Weber*. Cambridge, UK: Cambridge University Press.

———. 1972. "Introduction." Pp. 1-50 in *Emile Durkheim: Selected Writings*, edited by Anthony Giddens. Cambridge, UK: Cambridge University Press.

———. 1976. "Classical Social Theory and the Origins of Modern Sociology." *American Journal of Sociology* 81:703-29.

———. 1978. *Durkheim*. London: Fontana.

———. 1986. "Introduction." Pp. 1-31 in Emile Durkheim, *Durkheim on Politics and the State*, edited by Anthony Giddens. Cambridge, MA: Polity Press.

Giele, Janet S. 1988. "Gender and Sex Roles." Pp. 291-323 in *Handbook of Sociology*, edited by Neil J. Smelser. Newbury Park, CA: Sage.

———. 1996. "Decline of the Family: Conservative, Liberal, and Feminist Views." Pp. 89-115 in *Promises to Keep: The Decline and Renewal of Marriage in America*, edited by David Popenoe, Jean Bethke Elshtain, and David Blankenhorn. Lanham, MD: Rowman and Littlefield.

Gilder, George. 1973. *Sexual Suicide*. New York: Triangle.

———. 1974. *Naked Nomads: Unmarried Men in America*. New York: Quadrangle.

———. 1986. *Men and Marriage*. Gretna, IA: Pelican/Quadrangle.

Gilligan, Carol. 1982. *In a Different Voice: Psychological Theory and Women's Development*. Cambridge, MA: Harvard University Press.

Giraud-Teulon, Alexis. 1874. *Les origines de la famille: questions sur les antécédents des sociétés patriarchales*. Geneva: Cherbuliéz.

———. 1884. *Les origines du mariage et de la famille*. Geneva: Cherbuliéz.

Glendon, Mary Ann. 1977. *State, Law and Family: Family Law in Transition in the United States and Western Europe*. Amsterdam: North Holland.

———. 1981. *The New Family and the New Property*. Toronto: Butterworths.

———. 1987. *Abortion and Divorce in Western Law*. Cambridge, MA: Harvard University Press.

———. 1989. *The Transformation of Family Law: State, Law, and Family in the United States and Western Europe*. Chicago: University of Chicago Press.

———. 1991. *Rights Talk: The Impoverishment of Political Discourse*. New York: Free Press.

Glenn, Norval D. 1993. "A Plea for Objective Assessment of the Notion of Family Decline." *Journal of Marriage and the Family* 55:542-44.

———. 1996. "Values, Attitudes, and the State of American Marriage." Pp. 15-33 in *Promises to Keep: The Decline and Renewal of Marriage in America*, edited by David Popenoe, Jean Bethke Ehlstain, and David Blankenhorn. Lanham, MD: Rowman and Littlefield.

———. 1997a. *Closed Hearts, Closed Minds: The Textbook Story of Marriage*. New York: Institute for American Values.

_____. 1997b. "A Critique of Twenty Family and Marriage and Family Textbooks." *Family Relations* 46:197-208.

Goetting, Ann. 1986a. "The Developmental Tasks of Siblingship Over the Life Cycle." *Journal of Marriage and the Family* 48:703-14.

_____. 1986b. "Parental Satisfaction: A Review of Research." *Journal of Family Issues* 7:83-109.

Goffman, Erving. 1959. *The Presentation of Self in Everyday Life*. New York: Anchor.

Goldscheider, Frances K. and Linda J. Waite. 1991. *New Family, No Family?* Berkeley: University of California Press.

Goode, Erica. 2000a. "Back to the Stone Age." *New York Times*, December 31, p. F1.

_____. 2000b. "Human Nature: Born or Made?" *New York Times*, March 14, pp. D1, 9.

Goode, William. 1959. "Horizons in Family Theory." Pp. 178-96 in *Sociology Today*, edited by Robert K. Merton, Leonard, Broom, and Leonard S. Cottrell, Jr. New York: Basic Books.

_____. 1963. *World Revolution and Family Patterns*. New York: Free Press.

_____. [1964] 1982. *The Family*, 2d ed. Englewood Cliffs, NJ: Prentice Hall.

_____. 1982. "Why Men Resist." Pp. 31-50 in *Rethinking the Family: Some Feminist Questions*, edited by Barrie Thorne. New York: Longmans.

Gouldner, Alvin W. 1970. *The Coming Crisis of Western Sociology*. New York: Basic.

Graglia, F. Carolyn. 1998. *Domestic Tranquility: A Brief Against Feminism*. Dallas, TX: Spence.

Gramont, Sanche de. 1969. *The French: Portrait of a People*. New York: Putnam.

Granquist, Hilma. 1968. "Edward Westermarck." Pp. 529-31 in *International Encyclopedia of the Social Sciences*, vol. 16, edited by David L. Sills. New York: Macmillan.

Green, Martin. 1974. *The Von Richtofen Sisters: The Triumphant and the Tragic Modes of Love*. New York: Basic.

Greenberg, Louis M. 1976. "Bergson and Durkheim as Sons and Assimilators: The Early Years." *French Historical Studies* 9:619-34.

Greenhouse, Linda. 2000. "Case on Visitation Rights Hinges on Defining the Family." *New York Times*, January 4, p. A14.

Gruber, Jacob W. 1968. "John Lubbock." Pp. 487-88 in *International Encyclopedia of the Social Sciences*, vol. 9, edited by David L. Sills. New York: Macmillan.

Habakkuk, H. D. 1955. "Family Structure and Economic Change in Nineteenth-Century Europe." *Journal of Economic History* 15:1-12.

Hadden, Jeffrey K. and Marie L. Borgatta, eds. 1969. Introduction to "Origins of the Family: Some Early Works." Pp. 19-20 in *Marriage and the Family: A Comprehensive Reader*. Itasca IL: Peacock.

Hafen, Bruce C. 1990. "Individualism in Family Law." Pp. 161-77 in *Rebuilding the Nest: A New Committment to the American Family*, edited by David Blankenhorn, Steven Bayme, and Jean Bethke Ehistain. Milwaukee, WI: Family Service of America.

Halbwachs, Maurice. 1918. "La doctrine d'Emile Durkheim." *Revue philosophique* 85:353-411.

Hall, Robert T. 1988. *Ethics and the Sociology of Morals*. New York: Greenwood.

Hause, Steven. 1987. *Hubertine Aubert: The French Suffragette*. New Haven: Yale.

Hause, Steven and Anne Kenney. 1984. *Women's Suffrage and Social Politics in the French Third Republic*. Princeton, NJ: Princeton University Press.

Hayden, Doloros, ed. 1981a. "Introduction." Pp. 3-29 in *The Grand Domestic Revolution*, edited by Doloros Hayden. Boston: MIT Press.

_____. 1981b. *The Grand Domestic Revolution: A History of Feminist Designs for American Homes and Neighborhoods*. Boston: MIT Press.

Heilbron, Johan. 1995. *The Rise of Social Theory*. Minneapolis: University of Minnesota Press.

Henry, Jules. 1971. *Pathways to Madness.* New York: Random House.

Hewlett, Sylvia Ann and Cornel West. 1998. *The War Against Parents: What We Can Do to Help Beleaguered Moms and Dads.* New York: Houghton Mifflin.

Hill, Gretchen. 1995. "Inheritance Law in an Aging Society." *Journal of Aging and Social Policy* 7:57-83.

Hill, J. L. 1991. "What Does It Mean to be a 'Parent'?: The Claims of Biology as the Basis for Parental Rights." *NYU Law Review* 66:353-420.

Hill, Reuben and D. Hansen. 1960. "The Identification of Conceptual Frameworks Utilized in Family Study." *Marriage and Family Living* 22:299-311.

Hinkle, Roscoe E., Jr. 1960. "Durkheim in American Sociology." Pp. 267-95 in *Emile Durkheim, 1857-1917,* edited by Kurt H. Wolff. Columbus: Ohio State University Press.

Hochschild, Arlie. 1989. *The Second Shift: Working Parents and the Revolution at Home.* New York: Viking.

Hoffman, Lois W. and Martin Hoffman. 1973. "The Value of Children to Parents." Pp. 19-76 in *Psychological Perspectives on Population,* edited by James T. Fawcett. New York: Basic Books.

Hoffman, Lois W. and Jean D. Manis. 1979. "The Value of Children in the United States: A New Approach to the Study of Fertility." *Journal of Marriage and the Family* 41:583-96.

Homans, George C. 1961. *Social Behavior: Its Elementary Forms.* New York: Harcourt Brace.

Huber, Joan. 1973. "Symbolic Interaction as a Pragmatic Perspective." *American Sociological Review* 38:274-84.

Huber, Joan and Glenna Spitze. 1988. "Trends in Family Sociology." Pp. 425-48 in *Handbook of Sociology,* edited by Neil J. Smelser. Newbury Park, CA: Sage.

Hughes, John A., Peter J. Martin, and W. W. Sharrock. 1995. *Understanding Classical Sociology: Marx, Weber, and Durkheim.* Thousand Oaks, CA: Sage.

Hunt, Janet G. and Larry L. Hunt. 1986. "The Dualities of Careers and Families: New Integration or New Polarization?" Pp. 275-86 in *Family in Transition,* 5th ed., edited by Arlene S. Skolnick and Jerome H. Skolnick. Boston: Little, Brown.

Hunt, Lynn. 1992. *The Family Romance of the French Revolution.* Berkeley: University of California Press.

Hutter, Mark. 1981. *The Changing Family: Comparative Perspectives.* New York: John Wiley.

Hynes, Eugene. 1975. "Suicide and *Homo Duplex*: An Interpretation of Durkheim's Typology of Suicide." *Sociological Quarterly* 16:87-104.

Johnson, Barclay D. 1994. "Suicide and the Birth Rate, a Study in Moral Statistics: A Translation and Commentary." Pp. 115-204 in *Emile Durkheim: Le Suicide One Hundred Years Later,* edited by David Lester. Philadelphia: Charles.

Johnson, Kathryn K. 1979. "Durkheim Revisited: Why Do Women Kill Themselves?" *Suicide and Life-Threatening Behavior* 9:145-53.

Jones, Robert Alun. 1974. "Durkheim's Response to Spencer: An Essay Toward Historicism in the Historiography of Sociology." *Sociological Quarterly* 15:341-58.

————. 1986. *Emile Durkheim: An Introduction to Four Major Works.* Beverly Hills, CA: Sage.

————. 1993. "Durkheim and *La Cité Antique.*" Pp. 25-51 in *Emile Durkheim: Sociologist and Moralist,* edited by Stephen P. Turner. London: Routledge.

"Josef Kohler." *Encyclopedia Britannica.* Retrieved January 26, 2001 (www.britannica.com).

Kandal, Terry R. 1988. *The Woman Question in Classical Sociological Theory.* Miami: Florida International University Press.

Kando, Thomas M. 1976. "L'Annee Sociologique: From Durkheim to Today." *Pacific Sociological Review* 19:147-74.

Kantor, David and William Lehr. 1975. *Inside the Family*. New York: Harper.

Kao, Emily, Gong-Soog Hong, and Richard Widdows. 1997. "Bequest Expectations: Evidence From the 1989 Survey of Consumer Finances." *Journal of Family and Economic Issues* 18:357-77

Karady, Victor. 1981. "The Prehistory of Present-Day French Sociology (1917-1957)." Pp. 33-47 in *French Sociology: Rupture and Renewal Since 1968*, edited by Charles C. Lemert. New York: Columbia University Press.

Kerber, Linda K. 1980. *Women of the Republic: Intellect and Ideology in Revolutionary America*. Chapel Hill: University of North Carolina Press.

Kerckhoff, Alan. 1965. "Nuclear and Extended Family Relationships: A Normative and Behavioral Analysis." Pp. 93-112 in *Social Structure and the Family: Generational Relations*, edited by Ethel Shanas and Gordon Streib. Englewood Cliffs, NJ: Prentice Hall.

Kimmel, Michael S. 1987. "Men's Responses to Feminism at the Turn of the Century." *Gender and Society* 1:261-83.

Kingsbury, Nancy and John Scanzoni. 1993. "Structure-Functionalism." Pp. 195-217 in *Sourcebook of Family Theories and Methods*, edited by Pauline Boss et al. New York: Plenum.

Kirkpatrick, Clifford. 1968. "Family: Disorganization and Dissolution." Pp. 313-322 in *International Encyclopedia of the Social Sciences*, vol. 5, edited by David L. Sills. New York: Macmillan.

Klein, David M. and Joan Jurich. 1993. "Metatheory and Family Studies." Pp. 31-67 in *Sourcebook of Family Theories and Methods*, edited by Pauline Boss et al. New York: Plenum.

Klein, David M. and James M. White. 1996. *Family Theories: An Introduction*. Thousand Oaks, CA: Sage.

Kohler, Josef. 1889a. *Johann Jakob Bachofen und das Natursymbol*. Basel: Schwabe.

_____. 1889b. "Johann Jakob Bachofen." *Zeitschrift für Vergleichende Rechtwissenschaft* 8:148-55.

_____. [1897] 1975. *On the Prehistory of Marriage: Totemism, Group Marriage, and Mother Right*. [*Zur Urgeschichte der Ehe*]. Chicago: University of Chicago Press.

Konner, Melvin. 1988. "The Aggressors." *New York Times Magazine*, August 14, p. 33.

Krause, Harry D. 1986. *Family Law in a Nutshell*, 2d ed. St. Paul, MN: West.

Kubali, Hüssein Nail. 1950. "Avant-propos." Pp. i-iv in *Leçons de sociologie* by Emile Durkheim. Paris: Presses Universitaires de France.

Labriola, Joseph. [1896] 1966. *A Materialist Conception of History*. New York: Monthly Review Press.

LaCapra, Dominick. [1972] 1985. *Emile Durkheim: Sociologist and Philosopher*. Chicago: University of Chicago Press.

Ladd, Everett Carll. 1999. *The Ladd Report*. New York: Free Press.

Laing, Ronald D. 1972. "The Family and the 'Family.'" Pp. 3-19 in R. D. Laing, *The Politics of the Family and Other Essays*. New York: Random House.

Laing, Ronald D. and A. Esterson. 1970. *Sanity, Madness, and the Family*. Harmondsworth, Middlesex, UK: Penguin.

Lamanna, Mary Ann. 1990. "Durkheim on Women and the Family: Theoretical Models and Social Reality." Paper presented to the University of Notre Dame Sociology Department, April 6, Notre Dame, IN.

Lampérière, Anna. 1898. *Le rôle social de la femme*. Paris: Alcan.

Lasch, Christopher. 1977. *Haven in a Heartless World: The Family Beseiged*. New York. Basic Books.

Laslett, Peter. 1965. *The World We Have Lost: England Before the Industrial Age*. New York: Scribner.

Lawler, Edward J. and Shane R. Thye. 1999. "Bringing Emotions Into Exchange Theory." *Annual Review of Sociology* 25:217-44.

Lawler, Edward J. and Jeongkoo Yoon. 1993. "Power and the Emergence of Commitment Behavior in Negotiated Exchange." *American Sociological Review* 58:465-81.

Leacock, Eleanor Burke. 1972. "Introduction." Pp. 7-67 in Friedrich Engels, *The Origin of the Family, Private Property, and the State.* New York: International.

Lee, Gary R., and Linda Haas. 1993. "Comparative Methods in Family Research." Pp. 117-31 in *Sourcebook of Family Theories and Methods,* edited by Pauline Boss et al. New York: Plenum.

Lee, John Allen. 1973. *The Colours of Love.* Toronto: New Press.

Leeuwen, Louis Th. van. 1981. "Early Family Sociology in Europe: Parallels to the United States." Pp. 95-139 in *A Social History of American Family Sociology, 1865-1940,* by Ronald L. Howard, edited by John Mogey. Westport, CN: Greenwood.

LeGates, Marlene. 1995. "Feminists Before Feminism: Origins and Varieties of Women's Protest in Europe and North American Before the Twentieth Century." Pp. 494-508 in *Women: A Feminist Perspective,* edited by Jo Freeman. Mountain View, CA: Mayfield.

Lehmann, Jennifer M. 1990. "Durkheim's Response to Feminism: Prescriptions for Women." *Sociological Theory* 8:163-87.

———. 1991. "Durkheim's Women: His Theory of the Structures and Functions of Sexuality." *Current Perspectives in Social Theory* 11:141-67.

———. 1993. *Deconstructing Durkheim: A Post-Post-Structuralist Critique.* London: Routledge.

———. 1994. *Durkheim and Women.* Lincoln: University of Nebraska Press.

———. 1995a. "Durkheim's Theories of Deviance and Suicide: A Feminist Reconsideration." *American Journal of Sociology* 100:904-30.

———. 1995b. "The Question of Caste in Modern Society: Durkheim's Contradictory Theories of Race, Class, and Sex." *American Sociological Review* 60:566-85.

Le Play, Frédéric. [1855] 1877-79. *Les ouvriers européenes,* 2d ed. Tours, France: Mame.

Lester, David, ed. 1998. *Emile Durkheim: Suicide 100 Years Later.* Philadelphia: Charles.

L'Huillier, Fernand. 1955. *Histoire de L'Alsace.* Paris: Presses Universitaires de France.

LeTourneau, Charles. [1888] 1894. *L'Evolution du mariage et de la famille.* Paris: Vigot.

Levenger, George. 1974. "A 3-level Approach to Attraction: Toward an Understanding of Pair Relatedness." In *Foundations of Interpersonal Attraction,* edited by T. L. Huston. Orlando, Florida: Academic.

Levi-Strauss, Claude. 1945. "French Sociology." Pp. 503-37 in *Twentieth Century Sociology,* edited by Georges Gurvitch and Wilbert E. Moore. New York: Philosophical Library.

Lewin, Tamar. 2000. "Grandparents Play a Big Part in Grandchildren's Lives, Survey Finds." *New York Times,* January 6, p. A16.

Levy, Marion J., Jr. 1968. "Marcel Granet." Pp. 241-43 in *International Encyclopedia of the Social Sciences,* vol. 6, edited by David L. Sills. New York: Macmillan.

Libres entretiens, 5e série. 1909. *Questions relatives à la condition économique et juridique des femmes.* Paris: l'Union pour la Vérité.

Libres entretiens, 8e série. 1912. *Sur la culture générale et la réforme de l'enseignement.* Paris: l'Union pour la Vérité. P. 322 presented as "Remarque sur l'évolution récente de la famille," pp. 104-105 in Emile Durkheim, *Textes,* vol. 3, edited by Victor Karady. Paris: Les Editions de minuit.

Lienhart, R. B. 1968. "James George Frazer." Pp. 550-53 in *International Encylopedia of the Social Sciences,* vol. 5, edited by David L. Sills. New York: Macmillan.

Litwak, Eugene. 1960a. "Geographical Mobility and Extended Family Cohesion. *American Sociological Review* 25:385-94.

———. 1960b. "Occupational Mobility and Extended Family Cohesion." *American Sociological Review* 25:9-21.

———. 1965. "Extended Kin Relations in an Industrial Democratic Society." Pp. 290-323 in *Social Structure and the Family: Generational Relations,* edited by Ethel Shanas and Gordon Streib. Englewood Cliffs, NJ: Prentice Hall.

Llobera, Josep R. 1981. "Durkheim, the Durkheimians, and their Collective Misrepresentation of Marx." Pp. 214-40 in *The Anthropology of Pre-capitalist Societies,* edited by Joel S. Kahn and Josep R. Llobera. London: Macmillan.

Lourbet, Jacques. 1896. *La femme devant la science contemporaine.* Paris: Alcan.

———. 1900. *Le problème des sexes.* Paris: Giard et Brière.

Lubbock, John. [1870] 1912. *The Origin of Civilization and the Primitive Condition of Man: Mental and Social Conditions of Savages,* 7th ed. New York: Longmans.

Lukes, Steven. 1972. *Emile Durkheim: His Life and Work.* New York: Harper and Row.

———. 1985. *Emile Durkheim: His Life and Work,* 2d ed. Stanford, CA: Stanford University Press.

Lyotard, Jean-François. 1984. *The Postmodern Condition: A Report on Knowledge.* Minneapolis: University of Minnesota Press.

The Mabinogion. 1976. Translation and introduction by Jeffrey Gantz. New York: Dorset.

Macionis, John J. 2000. *Society: The Basics,* 5th ed. Upper Saddle River, NJ: Prentice Hall.

Maine, Henry Sumner. [1861] 1888. *Ancient Law.* New York: Holt.

Mannheim, Karl. 1936. *Ideology and Utopia: An Introduction to the Sociology of Knowledge.* New York: Harcourt Brace.

Marciano, Teresa Donati. 1987. "Families and Religions." Pp. 285-315 in *Handbook of Marriage and the Family,* edited by Marvin B. Sussmann and Suzanne K. Steinmetz. New York: Plenum.

Marx, Karl. [1848] 1988. *The Communist Manifesto.* New York: Norton.

Masters, William H. and Virginia Johnson. 1974. *The Pleasure Bond: A New Look at Sexuality and Commitment.* Boston: Little, Brown.

Mauss, Marcel. 1920. Untitled introduction to Emile Durkheim. "Introduction à la morale." *Revue philosophique* 89:79-80.

———. 1925. "In memoriam: l'oeuvre inedité de Durkheim et de ses collaborateurs." *Année sociologique,* n.s. 1:7-29.

———. 1927. "Notice biographique: Madame Louise Emile DURKHEIM." *Année sociologique,* n.s. 2:8-9.

———. 1969. "André DURKHEIM." P. 498 in *Oeuvres,* vol. 3, edited by Victor Karady. Paris: Les Editions de minuit.

Mazeaud, Henri, Léon Mazeaud, and Jean Mazeaud. 1967. *Leçons de droit civil,* vol. 1, 4th ed., edited by Michel de Juglart. Paris: Montchrestien.

Mayntz, Renate. 1968. "Georg Simmel." Pp. 251-58 in *International Encyclopedia of the Social Sciences,* vol. 14, edited by David L. Sills. New York: Macmillan.

McGuire v. McGuire. 1953. 157 Neb. 226, N.W. 2d 336 (S. Ct. of Neb.).

McIntyre, Lisa J. 1995. "Law and the Family in Historical Perspective: Issues and Antecedents." Pp. 5-30 in *Families and Law,* edited by Lisa J. McIntyre and Marvin B. Sussman. New York: Haworth.

McIntyre, Lisa J. and Marvin B. Sussman, eds. 1995. *Families and Law.* New York: Haworth.

McLain, Raymond and Andrew Weigert. 1979. "Toward a Phenomenological Sociology of the Family: A Programmatic Essay." Pp. 160-205 in *Contemporary Theories About the Family,* vol. 2, edited by Wesley Burr, Reuben Hill, F. Ivan Nye, and Ira Reiss. New York: Free Press.

McLennan, John Ferguson. [1865] 1970. *Primitive Marriage: An Inquiry Into the Origin of the Form of Capture in Marriage Ceremonies.* Chicago: University of Chicago Press.

McNamee, Stephen J. and Robert K. Miller. 1989. "Estate Inheritance: A Sociological Lacuna." *Sociological Inquiry* 59:7-29.

_____. 1998. "Inheritance and Stratification." Pp. 193-213 in *Inheritance and Wealth in America,* edited by Robert K. Miller and Stephen J. McNamee. New York: Plenum.

Mead, George Herbert. 1934. *Mind, Self, and Society.* Chicago: University of Chicago Press.

Mellman, Mark, Edward Lazarus, and Allan Rivlin. 1990. "Family Time, Family Values." Pp. 73-92 in *Rebuilding the Nest,* edited by David Blankenhorn, Steven Baynes, and Jean Bethke Ehlstain. Milwaukee, WI: Family Services of America.

Merton, Robert K. [1957] 1968. "On the History and Systematics of Sociological Theory." Pp. 1-38 in *Social Theory and Social Structure,* 2nd ed. New York: Free Press.

Meštrović, Stjepan G. 1988. *Emile Durkheim and the Reformation of Sociology.* Totowa, NJ: Rowman and Littlefield.

_____. 1991. *The Coming Fin de Siècle: An Application of Durkheim's Sociology to Modernity and Postmodernism.* New York: Routledge, Chapman.

_____. 1992. *Durkheim and Postmodern Culture.* New York: Aldine.

_____. 1996. Review of Jennifer Lehmann, *Durkheim and Women. Humanity and Society* 20: 84-85.

Meyer v. Nebraska. 1923. 262 U.S. 390, 43 S.Ct. 625, 67 L.Ed. 1042.

Michael M. v. Superior Court of Sonoma County, 450 U.S. 464 (1981).

Miller, Robert K. and Stephen J. McNamee, eds. 1998. *Inheritance and Wealth in America.* New York: Plenum.

Mitterauer, Michael and Reinhard Sieder. 1982. *The European Family.* Chicago: University of Chicago Press.

Moen, Phyllis and Kay B. Forest. 1999. "Strengthening Families; Policy Issues for the Twenty-First Century." Pp. 633-63 in *Handbook of Marriage and the Family,* 2d ed., edited by Marvin Sussman, Suzanne K. Steinmetz, and Gary W. Peterson. New York: Plenum.

Moore, Barrington. 1958. "Thoughts on the Future of the Family." Pp. 160-78 in Barrington Moore, *Political Power and Social Theory.* Cambridge, MA: Harvard.

Morgan, D. H. J. 1975. *Social Theory and the Family.* London: Routledge and Kegan Paul.

_____. 1985. *The Family: Politics and Social Theory.* London: Routledge.

Morgan, Lewis Henry. 1871. *Systems of Consanguinity and Affinity of the Human Family,* Smithsonian Contributions to Knowledge, vol. 17, Publication No. 218. Washington, DC: Smithsonian Institution.

_____. [1877] 1964. *Ancient Society.* Cambridge, MA: Belknap Press of Harvard University.

Morrison, Ken. 1995. *Marx, Durkheim, Weber: Formation of Modern Social Thought.* Thousand Oaks, CA: Sage.

Morselli, Enrico. [1879] 1882. *Suicide: An Essay on Comparative Moral Statistics [Il Suicido].* New York: Appleton.

Moses, Claire. 1984. *French Feminism in the Nineteenth Century.* Albany: SUNY.

Münch, Richard. 1988. *Understanding Modernity: Toward a New Perspective Going Beyond Durkheim and Weber.* London: Routledge.

Murdoch, George P. 1949. *Social Structure.* New York: Free Press.

Nandan, Yash, ed. 1980a. *Contributions to L'Année sociologique.* New York: Free Press.

_____. 1980b. "Editor's Introduction." Pp. 1-44 in *Emile Durkheim: Contributions to L'Année sociologique,* edited by Yosh Nandan. New York: Free Press.

Naughton, Kevin. 2001. "Billionaire Backlash." *Newsweek,* February 26, p. 48.

"Nécrologie: Emile Durkheim." 1918. *Revue philosophique* 85:95-96.

Nichols, Julie E. 1997. "Grandpa Take Me Home: The Constitutionality of Michigan's Grandparent Visitation Statue Under the Due Process Clause." *Wayne Law Review* 43:1887ff.

Nielsen, François. 1994. "Sociobiology and Sociology." *Annual Review of Sociology* 20:267-303.

Nisbet, Robert. 1966. *The Sociological Tradition.* New York: Basic Books.

Nock, Steven L. 1998. *Marriage in Men's Lives.* New York: Oxford University Press.

Nye, F. Ivan and Felix M. Berardo, eds. [1966] 1981. *Emerging Conceptual Frameworks in Family Analysis,* 2d ed. New York: Praeger.

Oates, Joyce Carol. 1973. "The Myth of the Isolated Artist." *Psychology Today* 6:74-75.

Offen, Karen. 1984. "Depopulation, Nationalism, and Feminism in Fin-de-Siécle France." *American Historical Review* 89:648-76.

———. 1987. "Feminism, antifeminism, and National Family Politics in Early Third Republic France." Pp. 177-86 in *Connecting Spheres: Women in the Western World, 1500 to the Present,* edited by Marilyn J. Boxer and Jean H. Quataert. New York: Oxford University Press.

———. 1988. "Defining Feminism: A Comparative Historical Approach." *Signs* 14:115-57.

Ogburn, William F. 1933. "The Family and Its Functions." Pp. 661-708 in *Recent Social Trends in the United States.* Report of the President's Research Committee on Social Trends. New York: McGraw Hill.

Ogburn, William F. and Meyer F. Nimkoff. 1955. *Technology and Changing Family.* Boston: Houghton Mifflin.

Oppenheimer, Valerie Kincade. 1997. "Women's Employment and the Gain to Marriage: The Specialization and Trading Model." *Annual Review of Sociology* 23:431-53.

Orrù, Marco. 1995. Review of Jennifer Lehmann, *Durkheim and Women. Contemporary Sociology* 24:283.

Ortner, Sherry B. 1996. "Is Female to Male as Nature Is to Culture?" Pp. 21-42 in *Making Gender: The Politics and Erotics of Culture.* Boston: Beacon.

Papanek, Hanna. 1973. "Men, Women, and Work: Reflections on the Two- Person Career." Pp. 90-110 in *Changing Women in a Changing Society,* edited by Joan Huber. Chicago: University of Chicago Press.

Parsons, Talcott. [1937] 1949. *The Structure of Social Action,* vol. 1. New York: Free Press.

———. 1951. *The Social System.* Glencoe, IL: Free Press.

———. 1954. "The Kinship System of the Contemporary United States." Pp. 177-196 in *Essays in Sociological Theory,* rev. ed. Glencoe, IL: Free Press.

———. 1955a. "The American Family: Its Relations to Personality and Social Structure." Pp. 3-33 in *Family Socialization and Interaction Process,* edited by Talcott Parsons and Robert F. Bales. Glencoe, IL: Free Press.

———. 1955b. "Family Structure and the Socialization of the Child." Pp. 35-131 in *Family Socialization and Interaction Process,* edited by Talcott Parsons and Robert F. Bales. Glencoe, IL: Free Press.

———. 1960. "Durkheim's Contribution to the Theory of Integration of Social Systems." Pp. 118-53 in *Emile Durkheim, 1858-1917,* edited by Kurt H. Wolff. Columbus: Ohio State University.

———. 1961. "An Outline of the Social System." Pp. 30-79 in *Theories of Society: Foundations of Modern Social Theory,* vol. 1, edited by Talcott Parsons, Edward Shils, Kaspar Naegele, and Jesse Pitts. New York: Free Press.

———. 1965. "The Normal American Family." Pp. 31-50 in *Man and Civilization: The Family's Search for Survival,* edited by Seymour Farber, Piero Mustacchi, and Roger H. L. Wilson. New York: McGraw-Hill..

———. 1968a. "Durkheim, Emile." Pp. 311-20 in *International Encyclopedia of the Social Sciences,* vol. 4, edited by David L. Sills. New York: Macmillan.

Parsons, Talcott and Robert F. Bales. 1955. *Family Socialization and Interaction Process.* Glencoe, IL: Free Press.

Parsons, Talcott and Renee Fox. 1952. "Illness, Therapy, and the Modern American Family." *Journal of Social Issues* 8:31-44.

Pearce, Frank. 1989. *The Radical Durkheim.* London: Unwin Hyman.

Peters, E. L. 1968. "William Robertson Smith." Pp. 329-35 in *International Encyclopedia of the Social Sciences,* vol. 14, edited by David L. Sills. New York: Macmillan.

Pickering, W. S. F. 1994. "The Enigma of Durkheim's Jewishness." Pp. 10-39 in *Debating Durkheim,* edited by W. S. F. Pickering and H. Martins. New York: Routledge.

Pierce v. Society of Sisters. 1925. 268 U.S. 510, 45 S.Ct. 571, 43 /S.Ct. 625.

Pitts, Jesse R. 1964. "The Structure-Functional Approach." Pp. 51-124 in *Handbook of Marriage and the Family,* edited by Harold T. Christensen. Chicago: Rand McNally.

———. 1968. "Le Play, Frédéric." Pp. 84-91 in *The International Encyclopedia of the Social Sciences,* vol. 9, edited by David L. Sills. New York: Macmillan.

Platt, Jennifer. 1995. "The United States Reception of Durkheim's *The Rules of the Sociological Method.*" *Sociological Perspectives* 38:77-105.

Pollitt, Katha. 2000. "Social Pseudoscience." *The Nation,* October 23. Retrieved February 26, 2001 (www.thenation.com).

Poggi, Gianfranco. 1972. *Images of Society: Essays on the Sociological Theories of Tocqueville, Marx, and Durkheim.* Stanford, CA: Stanford University Press.

"The Poorest Adult Sibling Gets Most from Parents." 1994. *Population Today* (June): 4.

Popenoe, David. 1988. *Disturbing the Nest: Family Change and Decline in Modern Society.* New York: Aldine de Gruyter.

———. 1990. "Family Decline in America." Pp. 39-51 in *Rebuilding the Nest: A New Commitment to the American Family,* edited by David Blankenhorn, Steven Bayme, and Jean Bethke Ehlstain. Milwaukee, WI: Family Service America.

———. 1993. "American Family Decline, 1960-1990: A Review and Appraisal." *Journal of Marriage and the Family* 55:527-42.

Popenoe, David, and Barbara Dafoe Whitehead. 1998-99. *The State of Our Unions: The Social Health of Marriage in America.* Report of the National Marriage Project. New Brunswick, NJ: Rutgers University.

———. 2000. *The State of Our Unions 2000: The Social Health of Marriage.* New Brunswick, NJ: Rutgers University, National Marriage Project.

Porter, Theodore M. 1995. "Statistical and Social Facts from Quételet to Durkheim." *Sociological Perspectives* 38:15-26.

Postema v. Postema. 1991. 189 Mich.App. 89, 471, N.W.2d 912.

Putnam, Robert. 1995. "Bowling Alone." *Journal of Democracy* 6: 65-78.

———. 2000. *Bowling Alone: The Collapse and Revival of American Community.* New York: Simon and Schuster.

Putnam, Ruth. 1915. *Alsace and Lorraine: From Caesar to Kaiser, 58 B.C.-1871 A.D.* New York: Putnam.

Quale, G. Robina. 1988. *A History of Marriage Systems.* Westport, CN: Greenwood.

Queen, Stuart A., Robert W. Habenstein, and Jill S. Quadagno. 1988. "The Family of the Ancient Romans." Pp. 2-16 in *Family Relations: A Reader,* edited by Norval D. Glenn and Marion Tolbert Coleman. Chicago: Dorsey.

Rawls, Anne Warfield. 1997. "Durkheim's Epistemology: The Initial Critique, 1915-1924." *Sociological Quarterly* 38:111-45.

Ray, J. 1913. Review of Sophonisba Breckinridge and Edith Abbott. *The Delinquent Child and His Home.* Charities Publication Committee, 1912. *Année sociologique* XII: 574-78.

Reher, David Sven. 1998. "Family Ties in Western Europe: Persistent Contrasts." *Population and Development Review* 24:203-34.

Reiss, Ira J. 1965. "The Universality of the Family: A Conceptual Analysis." *Journal of Marriage and the Family* 27:443-53.

———. 1971. *The Family System in America.* New York: Holt, Rinehart, Winston.

Reskin, Barbara and Patricia Roos. 1990. *Job Queues, Gender Queues: Explaining Women's*

Inroads Into Male Occupations. Philadelphia: Temple.

Rheinstein, Max. 1972. *Marriage Stability, Divorce, and the Law*. Chicago: University of Chicago Press.

Richard, Gaston. 1900. Review of Prinzing (Fred.), "Der Einfluss der Ehe auf die Kriminalitaet des Mannes" and "Die Erhoehung der Kriminalitaet des Weibes durch die Ehe," Berlin, *Zeitschrift für Socialwissenschaft*, Nos. 1, 2, and 6, 1899. *Année sociologique* III:466-69.

Rockett, Ian R. H. 1998. *Injury and Violence: A Public Health Perspective. Population Bulletin* 53, No. 4 (December).

Rosaldo, Michelle Zimbalist. 1974. *Women, Culture, and Society*. Stanford, CA: Stanford University Press.

Rossi, Alice S. 1984. "Gender and Parenthood." *American Sociological Review* 49:1-19.

Roth, Guenther. 1989-90. "Durkheim and the Principles of 1789: The Issue of Gender Equality." *Telos* 14:71-88.

Rowe, D. C. 1994. *The Limits of Family Influences: Genes, Experience, and Behavior*. New York: Guilford.

Rude-Antoine, Edwige. 1986. "Les Familles maghrebines en France et l'heritage." *Sociologia del Diritto* 13:95-104, abstracted (English) in Sociological Abstracts, #87R2690.

Russett, Cynthia Eagle. 1989. *Sexual Science: The Victorian Construction of Womanhood*. Cambridge, MA: Harvard University Press.

Ryun, Jim and Anne Ryun. 1995. "Courtship Makes a Comeback." *Focus on the Family* (November):10-12.

Sabatelli, Ronald M. and Constance L. Shehan. 1993. "Exchange and Resource Theories." Pp. 385-417 in *Sourcebook of Family Theories and Methods*, edited by Pauline Boss et al. New York: Plenum.

Sapiro, Virginia. 1994. *Women in American Society: An Introduction To Women's Studies*, 3d ed. Mountain View, CA: Mayfield.

Scanzoni, John H. 1970. *Opportunity and the Family*. New York: Free Press.

Scheppele, Kim Lane. 1994. "Legal Theory and Social Theory." *Annual Review of Sociology* 20:383-406.

Schmergel, Greg, ed. 1990. *Let's Go: France*. New York: St. Martin's.

Schneider, David. 1968. *American Kinship: A Cultural Account*. Englewood Cliffs, NJ: Prentice Hall.

Schoenfeld, Eugene and Stjepan G. Meštrović. 1989. "Durkheim's Concept of Justice and Its Relationship to Social Solidarity." *Sociological Analysis* 50:111-27.

Schutz, Alfred. 1970. *On Phenomenology and Social Relations*. Chicago: University of Chicago Press.

Schwartz, T. R. 1996. "Durkheim's Prediction about the Declining Importance of Family and Inheritance: Evidence from the Wills of Providence, 1775-1985. *Sociological Quarterly* 36:503-19.

Scott, Joan Wallach. 1996. "The Rights of 'the Social': Hubertine Aubert and the Politics of the Third Republic." Pp. 90-124 in *Only Paradoxes to Offer: French Feminists and the Rights of Man*, edited by Joan W. Scott. Cambridge, MA: Harvard University Press.

Seligman, B. Z. 1950. "The Problem of Incest and Exogamy: A Restatement." *American Anthropologist* 52:305-16.

Sennett, Richard. 1970. *Families Against the City: Middle Class Homes of Industrial Chicago, 1872-1890*. Cambridge, MA: Harvard University Press.

Shope, Janet Hinson. 1994. "Separate but Equal: Durkheim's Response to the Woman Question." *Sociological Inquiry* 64:23-36.

Shorter, Edward. 1975. *The Making of the Modern Family*. New York: Basic Books.

Simmel, Georg. [1890-1911] 1985. *Schriften zur Philosophie und Soziologie der Geslecter*.

Frankfurt: Suhrkamp.

Simpson, George. 1965. "A Durkheim Fragment." *American Journal of Sociology* 70: 527-36.

Sirjamaki, John. 1964. "The Institutional Approach." Pp. 33-50 in *Handbook of Marriage and the Family,* edited by Harold T. Christensen. Chicago: Rand McNally.

Skolnick, Arlene S. 1991. *Embattled Paradise: The American Family in an Age of Uncertainty.* New York: Basic Books.

————. 1996. *The Intimate Environment: Exploring Marriage and the Family,* 6th ed. New York: HarperCollins.

Skolnick, Arlene and Jerome Skolnick. 1999. "Introduction." Pp. 1-15 in *Families in Transition,* 10th ed., edited by A. and J. Skolnick. New York; Longmans.

Slaughter, Jane and Robert Kern. 1981. "Introduction." Pp. 3-12 in *European Women on the Left.* Westport, CN: Greenwood.

Smelser, Neil J. 1988. "Introduction." Pp. 9-19 in *Handbook of Sociology,* edited by Neil J. Smelser. Newbury Park, CA: Sage.

Smith, Raymond T. 1968. "Family: Comparative Structure." Pp. 301-13 in *International Encyclopedia of the Social Sciences,* vol. 5, edited by David L. Sills. New York: Macmillan.

Somerville, John. 1982. *The Rise and Fall of Childhood.* Beverly Hills: Sage.

Soukhanov, Anna, ed. 1999. *Encarta: World English Dictionary.* New York: St. Martin's.

Spencer, Baldwin and F. J. Gillen. 1899. *The Native Tribes of Central Australia.* London: Macmillan.

————. 1904. *The Northern Tribes of Central Australia.* London: Macmillan.

Spencer, Herbert. [1873] 1961. *The Study of Sociology.* Ann Arbor, MI: University of Michigan Press.

————. [1876-96] 1898-99. *Principles of Sociology.* New York: Appleton.

Spiro, Melford E. [1958] 1965. *Children of the Kibbutz: A Study in Child Training and Personality.* Cambridge, MA: Harvard University Press.

————. 1960. "Is the Family Universal?—The Israeli Case." Pp. 64-75 in *A Modern Introduction to the Family,* edited by Norman W. Bell and Ezra F. Vogel. Glencoe, IL: Free Press.

Sprey, Jetse. 1990. *Fashioning Family Theory: New Approaches.* Newbury Park, CA: Sage.

Stacey, Judith. 1990. *Brave New Families: Stories of Domestic Upheaval in Late Twentieth-Century America.* New York: Basic Books.

————. 1993. "Good Riddance to 'The Family'": A Response to David Popenoe. *Journal of Marriage and the Family* 55:545-47.

Stack, Carol B. 1974. *All Our Kin: Strategies for Survival.* New York: Harper and Row.

Stetson, Dorothy McBride. 1987. *Women's Rights in France.* New York: Greenwood.

Stocking, George W., Jr. 1968. "Edward Burnett Tylor." Pp. 170-77 in *International Encyclopedia of the Social Sciences,* vol. 16, edited by David L. Sills. New York: Macmillan.

————. 1987. *Victorian Anthropology.* New York: Free Press.

Stone, Lawrence. 1979. *The Family, Sex, and Marriage in England, 1500-1800.* New York: Harper and Row.

Strathern, Marilyn. 1985. "Kinship and Economy: Constitutive Orders of a Provisional Kind." *American Ethnologist* 12:191-209.

Straus, Murray A. 1964. "Power and Support Structures of the Family in Relation to Socialization." *Journal of Marriage and the Family* 26:318-26.

————. 1994. *Beating the Devil Out of Them: Corporal Punishment in American Families.* New York: Lexington.

Strenski, Ivan. 1997. *Durkheim and the Jews of France.* Chicago: University of Chicago Press.

Sussman, Marvin B. 1965. "Relationships of Adult Children with Their Parents. Pp. 62-92 in *Social Structure and the Family: Generational Relations,* edited by Ethel Shanas and Gordon Streib. Englewood Cliffs, NJ: Prentice Hall.

Sussman, Marvin B. and Lee Burchinal. 1969. "Kin Family Network: Unheralded Structure in Current Conceptualizations of Family Functions." Pp. 133-52 in *The Family and Change,* edited by John M. Edwards. New York: Knopf.

Sussman, Marvin B. and Suzanne K. Steinmetz, eds. 1987. *Handbook of Marriage and the Family.* New York: Plenum.

Sydie, Rosalind A. 1987. *Natural Women, Cultured Men: A Feminist Perspective on Sociological Theory.* New York: New York University Press.

Talbot, Margaret. 2000. "Who Wants to Be a Legionnaire?" *New York Times Book Review,* June 25, pp. 11-12.

Thibaut, John W. and Harold S. Kelley. 1959. *The Social Psychology of Groups.* New York: Wiley.

Thomas, Darwin and H. B. Roghaar. 1990. "Postpositivist Theorizing: The Case of Religion and Family." Pp. 136-70 in *Fashioning Family Theory,* edited by Jetse Sprey. Newbury Park, CA: Sage.

Thompson, Ross A. and Jennifer M. Wyatt. 1999. "Values, Policy, and Research on Divorce; Seeking Fairness for Children." Pp. 191-232 in *The Postdivorce Family: Children, Parenting, and Society,* edited by Ross A. Thompson and Paul R. Amato. Thousand Oaks, CA: Sage.

Thorne, Barrie, ed. 1982. *Rethinking the Family: Some Feminist Issues.* New York: Longmans.

Tiger, Lionel. 1978. "Omnigamy: The New Kinship System" *Psychology Today* 12: 14ff.

Tilly, Louise A. 1981. "Women's Collective Action and Feminism in France 1870-1914." Pp. 207-31 in *Class Conflict and Collective Action,* edited by Louise A. Tilly and Charles Tilly. Beverly Hills, CA: Sage.

Tiryakian, Edward A. 1995. Review of Jennifer Lehmann, *Durkheim and Women. American Journal of Sociology* 100:1375-77.

Tönnies, Ferdinand. 1887. *Gemienschaft und Gesellschaft.* Leipzig, Germany: Reisland.

_____. 1896. "Review of Emile Durkheim, *De la division du travail social." Archiv fur systematische Philosophie* 2:497-99.

Tosti, Gustavo. 1898. "Suicide in the Light of Recent Studies." *American Journal of Sociology* 3:464-478.

Traugott, Mark, ed. 1978. *Durkheim on Institutional Analysis.* Chicago: University of Chicago Press.

Trevino, Alberto Javier (organizer). 1999. Session on "Systems-Functionalist Theory After Talcott Parsons: From 1979 and Beyond." Annual meeting of the American Sociological Association, August 6, Chicago, IL.

Troxel v. Granville. 1999. S.C. No. 99-138, 137 Wash. 2d 1, 969 P. 2d 2l, affirmed.

Turner, Bryan S. 1999. *Classical Sociology.* London: Sage.

Turner, Jonathan. 1998. *The Structure of Sociological Theory,* 6th ed. Belmont, CA: Wadsworth.

Turner, Jonathan, Leonard Beeghley, and Charles H. Powers. 1998. *The Emergence of Sociological Theory,* 4th ed. Belmont, CA: Wadsworth.

Turner, Stephen P. 1986. *The Search for a Methodology of Social Science: Durkheim, Weber, and the Nineteenth-Century Problem of Cause, Probability, and Action.* Dordrecht: Reidel.

_____. 1993. "Introduction." Pp. 1-22 in *Emile Durkheim: Sociologist and Moralist,* edited by Stephen P. Turner. London: Routledge..

_____, ed. 1995a. "Celebrating the 100th Anniversary of Emile Durkheim's *The Rules of the Sociological Method." Sociological Perspecitves* 38(1) [Special Issue].

———. 1995b. "Durkheim's *The Rules of the Sociological Method*: Is It a Classic?" *Sociological Perspectives* 38:1-13.

———. 1996. "Durkheim Among the Statisticians." *Journal of the History of the Behavioral Sciences* 32: 354-78.

Tylor, Edward B. [1871] 1958. *Primitive Culture*, 2 vols. Gloucester, MA: Smith.

Udry, J. Richard. 2000. "Biological Limits of Gender Construction." *American Sociological Review* 65:443-57.

United Nations, Department of Economic and Social Affairs. 2000. *The World's Women: Trends and Statistics*. New York: United Nations.

Vargus, Brian S. 1999. "Classical Social Theory and Family Studies: The Triumph of Reactionary Thought in Contemporary Family Studies." Pp. 179-204 in *Handbook of Marriage and the Family*, 2d ed, edited by Marvin B. Sussman, Suzanne K. Steinmetz, and Gary W. Peterson. New York: Plenum.

Ventura, Stephanie, Joyce A. Martin, Sally C. Curtin, T. J. Mathews, and Melissa M. Park. 2000. *Births: Final Data for 1998*. *National Vital Statistics Reports* 48 (3). Hyattsville, MD: U.S. National Center for Health Statistics.

Vogt, W. Paul. 1976a. "The Politics of Academic Sociology in France, 1890-1914." Unpublished Ph.D. dissertation, Indiana University, Bloomington, IN.

———. 1976b. "The Uses of Studying Primitives: A Note on the Durkheimians." *History and Theory* 15:33-44.

———. 1993. "Durkheim's Sociology of Law: Morality and the Cult of the Individual." Pp. 71-94 in *Emile Durkheim: Sociologist and Moralist*, edited by Stephen P. Turner. London: Routledge.

Von Bertalanffy, L. 1975. *Perspectives on General System Theory: Scientific-Philosophic Studies*. New York: Braziller.

Vucht Tijssen, Lieteke van. 1991. "Women and Objective Culture: Georg Simmel and Marianne Weber." *Theory, Culture, and Society* 8:203-18.

Wadlington, Walter. 1995. *Cases and Materials on Domestic Relations*, 3d ed. Westbury, NY: Foundation Press.

Waite, Linda J. 1995. "Does Marriage Matter?" *Demography* 32:483-507.

———. 2001. "The Family as a Social Organization: Key Ideas for the Twenty-First Century." *Contemporary Sociology* 29:463-69.

Waite, Linda J. and Maggie Gallagher. 2000. *The Case for Marriage: Why Married People Are Happier, Healthier, and Better Off Financially*. New York: Doubleday.

Waline, Marcel. 1945. *L'individualisme et le droit*. Paris: Domat Montchrestien.

Walker, Samuel E. 1998. *The Rights Revolution: Rights and Community in Modern America*. New York: Oxford.

Wallerstein, Judith and Sandra Blakeslee. 1989. *Second Chances: Men, Women and Children a Decade After Divorce*. New York: Ticknor and Fields.

Wallerstein, Judith, Julia M. Lewis, and Sandra Blakeslee. 2000. *The Unexpected Legacy of Divorce: A 25-Year Landmark Study*. New York: Hyperion.

Wallwork, Ernest. 1972. *Durkheim: Morality and Milieu*. Cambridge, MA: Harvard University Press.

Wattenberg, Benjamin J. 1987. *The Birth Dearth*. New York: Pharos.

Weber, Eugen. 1986. *France: Fin de Siècle*. Cambridge, MA: Belknap.

Weber, Marianne. 1907. *Ehefrau und Mutter in der Rechtsentwicklung*. Tübingen: Mohr.

———. 1919. "Die Fraue und die objektive Kultur." In Marianne Weber, *Frauenfrage und Frauengedanke*. Tübingen: Mohr.

———. 1927. *Max Weber, ein Lebensbild*. Heidelberg.

Webster's Third New International Dictionary of the English Language, Unabridged. 1976. Editor-in-Chief, Philip Babcock Gove. Springfield, MA: Merriam.

References

Weeks, John R. 1999. *Population: An Introduction to Concepts and Iss* CA: Wadsworth.

Weigert, Andrew J. and Darwin L. Thomas. 1971. "Family as a Cor *Journal of Marriage and the Family* 33:188-94.

Weisberg, D. Kelly. 1993. "The Equality Debate: Equal Treatment v. Pp. 121-27 in *Feminist Legal Theory*, edited by D. Kelly We Temple University Press.

Weitzman, Lenore. 1981. *The Marriage Contract: Spouses, Lovers* York: Free Press.

———. 1985. *The Divorce Revolution: The Unexpected Social and Ecc for Women and Children in America*. New York: Free Press.

Westermarck, Edward. [1891] 1921. *The History of Human Marri* Macmillan.

Whitchurch, Gail G. and Larry L. Constantine. 1993. "Systems Th *Sourcebook of Family Theories and Methods*, edited by Pau York: Plenum.

White, Edmund. 1999. *Marcel Proust*. New York: Viking Penguin.

White, Leslie. 1968. "Lewis Henry Morgan." Pp. 496-98 in *Intern of the Social Sciences*, vol. 10, edited by David L. Sills. New Y

White, Lynn K. and Agnes Riedmann. 1992. "When the Brady Bu Half- and Full-Sibling Relationships in Adulthood." *Journal Family* 54:197-208.

Whitehead, Barbara Dafoe. 1996. *The Divorce Culture*. New York

Whyte, Martin King, ed. 2000. *Marriage in America: A Commu* Lanham, MD: Rowan and Littlefield.

Williams, Wendy. 1991. "The Equality Crisis: Some Reflections or and Feminism." Pp. 15-34 in *Feminist Legal Theory: Reading* edited by Katharine T. Bartlett and Rosanne Kennedy. Boulde

Winch, Robert F. and Rae L. Blumberg. 1974. "Societal Com Organization: Evidence for the Curvilinear Hypothesis." Pp. 94 in *Marriage and the Family*, 4th ed., edited by Robert F. Winch Rinehart, Winston.

Winton, Chester A. 1995. *Frameworks for Studying Families*. Guil

Wisconsin v. Yoder. 1972. 406 U.S. 205, 92 S.Ct. 1526, 32 L.Ed. 2

Wityak, Nancy and Ruth Wallace. 1981. "Durkheim's Non-Social and Women." *Sociological Inquiry* 51:61-67.

Wolfe, Alan. 1998. *One Nation, After All: What Middle-Class A About God, Country, Family Racism, Welfare, Immigration, the Right, the Left, and Each Other*. New York: Viking.

———. 1999. "Bowling with Others." *New York Times Book Revi*

Wolff, Kurt H. 1960. *Emile Durkheim, 1858-1917: A Collection* Ohio University Press.

Young, Frank W. 1994. "Durkheim and Development Theory." *Soci* 82.

Zeitlin, Irving M. 1968. *Ideology and the Development of Social Th* NJ: Prentice-Hall.

Zeldin, Theodore. 1984. *The French*. London: Fontana.

Zelditch, Morris, Jr. 1964. "Family, Marriage, and Kinship." Pp. of Modern Sociology, edited by Robert E. L. Faris. Chicago:

Zelizer, Viviana. 1985. *Pricing the Priceless Child: The Changing S* New York: Basic Books.

Index

About the Author

Mary Ann Lamanna is Professor of Sociology and Anthropology at the University of Nebraska at Omaha, where she has been on the faculty since 1977. She spent a postbaccalaureate year at the University of Strasbourg, France, on a Fulbright Scholarship. She earned an MA in sociology is from the University of North Carolina at Chapel Hill and a PhD in sociology from the University of Notre Dame (1977).

She is the author (with Agnes Riedmann) of *Marriages and Families: Making Choices in a Diverse Society,* now in its seventh edition. She has published articles on nineteenth-century women, adolescent women's discourse on sexuality and reproduction, images of mothers in legal opinions, gender issues in the teaching of criminal law, the gift exchange in organ and tissue donation, and the sociological framing of the abortion issue. She plans a future book on sociological themes in the writings of Marcel Proust.